The Maya and Climate Change

INTERDISCIPLINARY APPROACHES TO PREMODERN SOCIETIES AND ENVIRONMENTS

Series Editors John Haldon, Adam Izdebski, Lee Mordechai, Timothy Newfield, Arlene Rosen, and Erika Weiberg.

The Maya and Climate Change
*Human-Environmental Relationships in
the Classic Period Lowlands*
Kenneth E. Seligson

The Maya and Climate Change

Human-Environmental Relationships in the Classic Period Lowlands

KENNETH E. SELIGSON

OXFORD
UNIVERSITY PRESS

OXFORD
UNIVERSITY PRESS

Oxford University Press is a department of the University of Oxford. It furthers
the University's objective of excellence in research, scholarship, and education
by publishing worldwide. Oxford is a registered trade mark of Oxford University
Press in the UK and certain other countries.

Published in the United States of America by Oxford University Press
198 Madison Avenue, New York, NY 10016, United States of America.

Library of Congress Cataloging-in-Publication Data
Names: Seligson, Kenneth E., author.
Title: The Maya and climate change : human-environmental relationships in
the classic period lowlands / Kenneth E. Seligson, Ph.D.
Description: New York, NY, United States of America : Oxford University Press, [2023] |
Series: Interdisciplinary approaches to premodern societies
and environments | Includes bibliographical references and index.
Identifiers: LCCN 2022029905 (print) | LCCN 2022029906 (ebook) |
ISBN 9780197652923 (hardback) | ISBN 9780197652947 (epub) |
ISBN 9780197652930 | ISBN 9780197652954
Subjects: LCSH: Human ecology—Mexico—History. | Mayas—Civilization. |
Climatic changes—Mexico—History. | Mayas—History. | Human
beings—Effect of climate on—Mexico.
Classification: LCC GF516 .S45 2023 (print) | LCC GF516 (ebook) |
DDC 304.20972—dc23/eng/20220805
LC record available at https://lccn.loc.gov/2022029905
LC ebook record available at https://lccn.loc.gov/2022029906

DOI: 10.1093/oso/9780197652923.001.0001

1 3 5 7 9 8 6 4 2

Printed by Sheridan Books, Inc., United States of America

To my parents, Terry and José,
whose love and support have meant everything.

Contents

Figures

Acknowledgments

I am extremely grateful to the many friends and colleagues who generously shared their insights, encouragement, data, images, and candid critiques to help me complete this project. I would not be where I am today without the support and sage advice of my mentors and friends, George Bey, Tomás Gallereta Negrón, and Bill Ringle, who have guided me through a decade of research and growth in the northern Maya lowlands. I would especially like to thank Tom Garrison, who got me started down the path of Maya archaeology and provided excellent feedback during the writing process. I am also indebted to my great friends Evan Parker, Betsy Kohut, Melissa Galván Bernal, and Lauren Santini, all of whom provided helpful comments and suggestions on specific chapters. Many thanks to Jerry Moore and Sarah Taylor, who shared valuable guidance regarding the writing and publication process, and to Sarah Clayton and Nam Kim for being excellent mentors, colleagues, and friends.

I want to thank everyone who contributed helpful information, drawings, and photographs to this book: Omar Alcover Firpi, Ed Barnhart, Tim Beach, Antonio Benavides Castillo, Mark Brenner, Adrian Chase, Mary Clarke, Ryan Collins, Jason Curtis, Alyce de Carteret, Maia Dedrick, Nick Dunning, Alan Farahani, Scott Fedick, Tomás Gallareta Negrón, Melissa Galván Bernal, Tom Garrison, David Hodell, Takeshi Inomata, Rachel Horowitz, Nam Kim, Bruce Love, Sheryl Luzzadder-Beach, Rossana May Ciau, Patricia McAnany, Heather McKillop, Sol Ortiz, Lauren Santini, Vern Scarborough, Stephanie Simms, Sarah Taylor, Rogelio Valencia, Brent Woodfill, Jason Yaeger, and Marc Zender. I had the privilege of first being introduced to Maya studies as a wide-eyed undergraduate by Steve Houston, and I cannot thank him enough. I am very appreciative to Stefan Vranka at Oxford University Press for believing in this project, for his patience, and for guiding me through the production process.

The book is dedicated to my parents, Terry Scheiner and José Seligson, for providing me with the opportunity to pursue this dream of a life in archaeology, but an especially warm gratitude is reserved for my wife, Jeanelle Uy, who continues to support and encourage me through everything, especially when I doubt myself.

1

Shifting the Focus

Suffice it to say that it is as intriguing to ask how and why the Maya sustained a state-level society for 1,500 years as to focus on the collapse.

—Vernon Scarborough, 2000

The Classic Maya civilization was not exceptional. Other cultures thrived for longer, developed larger cities, and experienced faster declines. So why do the ancient Maya remain endlessly fascinating to scholars and the public alike? Part of the answer surely lies in the fact that after over a century of continuous archaeological research in the Maya lowlands, we are still frequently reminded of how much more we have to learn. As recently as 2017, archaeologists identified massive platforms and extensive settlement sprawls that are now leading us to rethink the origins and scale of social complexity in the Maya area.[1] A second level of intrigue surrounding the ancient Maya stems from an outsized focus on the demise of the Classic Period socio-political system, an era colloquially known as the "Maya Collapse." The images of colossal stone temple pyramids swallowed by tropical forests invite people to ask, "Who built these monuments and what happened to them?"

The Classic Maya civilization thrived from approximately 200 to 1000 CE (Common Era) in eastern Mesoamerica. Throughout that time, Maya communities faced numerous environmental challenges, including those wrought by climate change. Their abilities to adapt their resource-management and food-production practices over time played crucial roles in allowing them to survive as long as they did. The true extent of Maya resilience becomes clearer when we view Classic Period developments as part of the longer Pre-Colonial Maya cultural trajectory. Cultural and socio-ecological resilience should be among the first things that come to mind when we think of the Classic Maya. Fascination with the societal transformations at the end of the Classic Period is understandable, but it should not overshadow the centuries of adaptations and growth that came before it. The main arguments of the book are (1) that it is more amazing that the Classic Maya civilization endured for over 700 years than that it eventually broke down, and (2) that the most significant lessons we can learn from the Pre-Colonial Maya are to diversify our resource-management practices to reflect

The Maya and Climate Change. Kenneth E. Seligson, Oxford University Press. © Oxford University Press 2023.
DOI: 10.1093/oso/9780197652923.003.0001

the broad variety of natural settings we inhabit and to be willing to adapt our socio-ecological practices before it is too late.

A Long-Standing Fascination with Collapse

A popular line of questioning put to Mayanists—that is, researchers who study the ancient Maya—concerns the breakdown of the Classic Period civilization. Inquiries generally take the form of "What happened to the Maya? What caused their collapse?" There is obviously a lot to unpack there, but the gist of the inquiry is unsurprising, given society's long-standing fascination with the breakdown of ancient civilizations. Sure, images of depopulated cities engulfed by vegetation, dystopian depictions like those in the movie *Apocalypto*, the dire themes surrounding the misunderstood 2012 "Maya Apocalypse," and a focus on the provocative term "ecocide"[2] are partly to blame, but the obsession with societal collapse goes beyond this (Figures 1.1, 1.2). It is also a result of the ways that Mayanists have approached investigating the decline of Classic Period communities, as well as how we have—or have not—communicated our understandings to broader audiences.[3]

Figure 1.1 Calakmul Structure 1 poking through the dense forest canopy of southeastern Campeche, Mexico (photo courtesy of Rachel Horowitz).

Figure 1.2 An intact 1,200-year-old structure within the Kuche Group at the site of Kiuic in the Puuc region of the northern Maya lowlands (photo by author).

Before delving into more of the underpinnings of this fascination, it is important to recognize that many scholars prefer to use terms like decline, transformation, or reorganization to describe the end of the Classic Period instead of "collapse." Although large-scale political changes occurred and many communities were depopulated, ancient Maya civilization did not necessarily *collapse* and the Maya people most definitely did not *disappear*. Seven million Maya living in eastern Mesoamerica and around the world today are most certainly alive and well. Many even trace their heritage back to the Classic Period culture. It is true that the Classic Maya communities responsible for constructing huge garden cities centered on divine monarchies and temple pyramid complexes are no longer flourishing. It is also true that, in the end, many centers did experience relatively rapid population declines due to a combination of several long-term trends and, possibly, an immediate political crisis.[4] However, different areas experienced breakdowns at different times over a period of *more than two centuries*, while others flourished during that span.[5]

The term "collapse," with its connotation of suddenness, oversimplifies the long lead up to the final depopulation episodes as well as the range of responses during those 200-plus years.[6] Although it can justifiably be applied to certain aspects of Maya cultural and socio-political systems toward the end of the Classic Period, the allure of the word "collapse" overshadows the resilience that characterized Maya communities for generations. Recognition of Pre-Colonial resilience is necessary not just for the sake of accurately representing bygone communities but, again, also for the sake of their 7-million-plus descendants living in the region and abroad today who continue cultural practices passed down over millennia.[7]

Our contemporary fascination with societal breakdown stems from several, often overlapping, lines of curiosity. One relates to our innate interest in things going wrong—schadenfreude writ large. Another embraces the uncomfortable feeling that future historians and archaeologists will look back on our present-day as a period of decline—or even a societal "collapse!" One does not need hindsight to recognize that we are living amidst a series of global crises, perhaps even societal breakdown and reorganization. Given the appalling news coming from nearly every corner of the planet in the early twenty-first century, it is hard to disagree with this portrait of the present. It raises hypothetical questions about kindred spirits in the ninth-century Maya lowlands looking around at the decline of the Classic political order and wondering how future generations might try to unravel the myriad processes at play.

Thinking about the demise of complex ancient civilizations like the Classic Maya, we cannot help but think about the impermanence of our own society. Especially concerning for us is the potentially outsized role that climate change played in triggering the breakdown of Classic Maya society. We are currently experiencing the terrible effects of relatively rapid, human-induced climatic changes. Looking outside my window in Los Angeles, the sky is a mix of dark gray and orange due to the forest fires burning in the mountains around the city. A fascination with societal breakdown leads people to see ancient civilizations like the Maya as providing a model for how our own complex society may succumb to similar forces.[8]

Another, more hopeful, line of thinking looks to these ancient civilizations as models from which we can gain insights to avoid a similar fate. We have more nuanced understandings of the world and our place in it, and therefore we have the potential to effect more immediate and impactful changes. However, having the capacity to adapt does not always translate to the willingness to adapt. Additionally, although people may draw hope from thinking that the demise of ancient civilizations like the Classic Maya could have been prevented by our modern technology and scientific information, they simultaneously run the risk of falling into a mindset that categorizes these ancient civilizations as "primitive" or "backward." Such a perspective becomes especially insidious when those stigmatizing descriptors are extended to their cultural heirs.

A Brief Introduction to Maya History and Culture

Mayanists divide the Pre-Colonial Era broadly into the Paleo-Indian, Archaic, Preclassic, Classic, and Postclassic Periods (Figure 1.3). These divisions represent

Postclassic Period 1000-1542 CE		Gradual demographic growth and an increased focus on coastal trading. The development of relatively decentralized administrative units.	1453 CE: Sultan Mehmed II conquers Constantinople.
Late Postclassic	1200-1542 CE	Gradual population growth with an increased focus on inter-regional, maritime trade networks. Mayapan, the last great Pre-Colonial Maya center reaches its peak.	1438 CE: Inca Empire begins expansion in the Andes. Early 1400s: Aztec Empire begins expansion in Mexico.
Early Postclassic	1000-1200 CE	A period of social reorganization. A few larger population centers persist in well-watered areas, but in general smaller settlements become the norm throughout the lowlands.	1300s CE: Decline of Angkor. 1206 CE: Genghis Khan forges Mongol Empire.
Classic Period 200-1000 CE		The most well-studied era of Pre-Colonial Maya civilization, characterized by large city-states with temple-pyramids, palace complexes, elaborate pottery, and an intricate hieroglyphic script.	1000-1100s CE: Peak era of Cahokia. Mid-1000s CE: Great Zimbabwe founded.
Terminal Classic	800-1000 CE	The "Classic Maya Collapse." A period of breakdown and transformation in which most large Classic sites are depopulated due to an array of factors that includes climate change.	900s-1100s CE: Major Chaco Canyon complexes built. 802 CE: Angkor founded. c. 800s CE: Peak era of Tiwanaku in Bolivia.
Late Classic	600-800 CE	The culmination of centuries of cultural developments in architecture, art, writing, socio-politics, and socio-ecological practices. A network of hundreds of city-states and the era of peak Pre-Colonial population.	Late 700s-1000s CE: Viking Age in Northern Europe. Early 300s CE: Earliest settlers reach Hawaii.
Early Classic	250-600 CE	The beginning of a new period of demographic growth and agricultural intensification. Development of a new socio-political landscape that includes dozens of independent city-states ruled by divine monarchies.	27 BCE: Caesar Augustus becomes 1st Roman Emperor. 221 BCE: Qin Shi Huang becomes 1st Emperor of China.
Proto-Classic	150-250 CE	The "Preclassic Collapse." A transformational time of socio-political breakdown in which many larger sites are depopulated.	322-184 BCE: Maurya Empire in South Asia. 338-323 BCE: Conquests of Alexander the Great.
Preclassic Period 2000 BCE – 200 CE		Major developments in socio-political complexity, material culture, and agriculture that became emblematic of Pre-Colonial Maya civilization.	431-404 BCE: Peloponnesian War.
Late Preclassic	300 BCE – 200 CE	The peak of Preclassic population growth and architectural expansion, exemplified by large conurbations like El Mirador in northern Guatemala.	509 BCE: Traditional founding of Roman Republic. 660 BCE: Imperial House of Japan founded.
Middle Preclassic	1000-300 BCE	Increasing socio-political complexity and centralization of authority. Agricultural extensification and intensification, including the construction of terraces and raised fields.	900-200 BCE: Chavin culture thrives in the Andes.
Early Preclassic	2000-1000 BCE	Large farming villages develop throughout the Maya lowlands. Monumental architecture is constructed by the end this period.	2334 – 2154 BCE: Akkadian Empire in Mesopotamia. c. 2600-1900 BCE: Peak of Indus Valley Civilization.
Archaic Period 3500-2000 BCE		The transition from foraging to sedentary agricultural communities. Groups begin to make significant changes to the natural environment.	2500s BCE: Great pyramids built at Giza. c. 9500-8000 CE – Gobekli Tepe thrives in Turkey.
Paleoindian Period >11,000-3500 BCE		Earliest foragers enter and spread throughout the area that would become known as the Maya lowlands.	

Figure 1.3 Chronology of the Maya lowlands including approximate dates, significant developments for each period of Maya history, and a rough timeline of significant world events for comparison.

approximate markers for changes in material culture, and it is important to recognize that transitions between periods were not uniformly experienced across the lowlands. It was not as though word went out from Tikal to remind their neighbors of the upcoming transition to the Late Classic and to prepare their material cultural innovations accordingly. Material culture evolves organically over time as styles come in and out of fashion and new technologies are developed. Although archaeologists draw on as much data as possible to try to categorize societal shifts as accurately as we can, there is necessarily going to be a measure of imprecision. Researchers continue to debate the starting and ending points for different periods, with some suggesting that we eschew such categorizations in favor of simply referring to Gregorian centuries or the Classic Maya Long Count's twenty-year *katun* cycles.

Researchers began to apply the "Classic Period" label in the 1950s to the era that they saw as the pinnacle of Pre-Colonial Maya architectural and sculptural achievements. Investigations since then have proven that many of the trappings of the Classic Period culture had antecedents in an earlier period to which was given the apt designation of "Preclassic." The Postclassic Period, as you may have surmised, comes after the Classic Period. Each of these three broad time periods (Preclassic, Classic, and Postclassic) is then subdivided into shorter spans such as the Early, Middle, and Late subperiods, as well as even more specific subdivisions like Terminal Classic in some cases.[9]

There is no universal consensus regarding the proper temporal divisions for these archaeological periods. The only thing that most archaeologists can agree upon is that the boundaries of each are approximate. However, it is still useful to have common reference points to compare developments across the Maya area and Mesoamerica more broadly. For the purposes of tracing broader cultural and socio-ecological trends, I will use the following designations: the Preclassic Period spans 2000 BCE–200 CE, subdivided into the Early Preclassic (2000–1000 BCE), Middle Preclassic (1000–300 BCE), and Late Preclassic (300 BCE–200 CE). The Classic Period spans 200–1000 CE, subdivided into the Early Classic (200–600 CE), Late Classic (600–800 CE), and Terminal Classic (800–1000 CE). It should be noted that the timing and designation of the Terminal Classic Period is especially contentious.

Archaeologists trace the antecedents of Maya culture back thousands of years to the Archaic Period (c. 3500–2000 BCE in eastern Mesoamerica). More of a phase than a timeframe bracketed by hard dates, the Archaic Period refers to the era when small groups of nomadic or semi-nomadic people in Mesoamerica became increasingly familiar with their natural surroundings and began to settle down. Over many generations, this familiarity with the landscape led to active interference by humans in the life cycles of plants and animals. Domestication is the process of changing the morphology (and sometimes the genetic composition) of plant and animal species through this type of selection. We currently have evidence for maize agriculture in northern Belize at least as early as the fourth millennium BCE (over 5,000 years ago). However, the transition from a semi-nomadic to purely sedentary lifeway remains unclear due to lack of data.[10] The Archaic began at least as far back as 8000 BCE in other sub-regions of Mesoamerica, and future finds may very well lead us to shift the Maya Archaic Period to an earlier start date as well.

This gradual shift from a mainly hunting, gathering, and fishing diet to one increasingly reliant on agricultural production fostered tremendous population growth as groups began to settle in one place and produce a surplus of food. This in turn contributed to the development of increasingly complex social institutions that were needed to organize and manage the needs of the growing population centers. By the start of the Middle Preclassic Period (c. 1000 BCE), small farming communities in several areas had grown into large centers with monumental civic architecture. On the western edge of the Maya area in the modern Mexican state of Tabasco, communities built massive platforms up to 0.85 miles long at sites like Aguada Fénix that were likely used as plazas for large civic-ceremonial gatherings.[11] These early Maya communities did not develop in a vacuum. They were influenced by (and influenced in turn) their neighbors immediately to the west in the Olmec lowlands, to the southwest in the Soconusco region along the Pacific Coast, and farther to the west in the highland regions of Oaxaca and Central Mexico.

Over the course of the Middle (1000–300 BCE) and Late (300 BCE–200 CE) Preclassic Periods, communities continued to grow across the Maya lowlands. Many cultural aspects that would come to characterize the later Classic Period civilization began to crystallize during the Preclassic. Pottery became widespread with local variations in paste, form, and decoration. Large stucco masks depicting supernatural beings were affixed to the facades of civic structures and beautiful murals adorned the interiors of stone-vaulted rooms. A writing system—the precursor to the Classic Maya hieroglyphic system—was already in use by at least as early as 300 BCE.[12] Some of the largest ever Maya sites developed during the Preclassic Period, including El Mirador in northern Guatemala, which may have reached a population of over 100,000 individuals. The Danta and Tigre pyramid complexes at El Mirador are two of the largest Pre-Colonial constructions in the Americas and likely reflected the institutionalization of political power. We see similar architectural expressions of political centralization early on in places like Egypt, where the pharaohs constructed the iconic pyramids over a relatively short time span near the very beginning of their 3,000-plus year rule.

The Late Preclassic to Early Classic Period transition (c. 100–300 CE) was characterized by the abandonment of several of the largest Preclassic centers including El Mirador. This "Preclassic Collapse" presaged the Classic Period breakdown approximately 700 years later and was likely a result of similar factors, including climate change, environmental degradation, and socio-political instability. Like the later Classic Period breakdown, not all subregions or communities were affected in the same ways. Some sites, like Tikal, survived the transition and grew to become powerful Classic Period centers.

The Classic Period is seen by many as the peak of Pre-Colonial Maya civilization. It was a period of steady demographic growth, and the socio-political landscape was characterized by hundreds of independent city-states ruled by divine dynasts. Although Mayanists are wary of applying the term "empire" to any individual dynasty, it is clear that there were hierarchies of authority in which some monarchs recognized other monarchs as their overlords. Since the 1990s, epigraphers (experts in ancient scripts) have deciphered over 90% of the tremendously complex Classic Maya hieroglyphic system. As a result, we can now read primary sources on Classic Maya history in a similar fashion to how we read Classical Greek or Roman texts. To be sure, the corpus of Maya inscriptions is much smaller and covers a restricted set of topics, but we can use the actual names of rulers previously known only by nicknames and refer to sites using the place-names that would have been recognizable to the people who inhabited them. We can read about political alliances sealed by inter-dynastic marriages, about battles waged between rival dynasties, and about the life achievements of individual monarchs. For instance, we know that Classic Period politics were greatly influenced by the rivalry between Tikal's Mutul Dynasty and the Kaanu'l (Snake) Dynasty of Dzibanche then Calakmul. Their shifting systems of alliances spread across much of the southern lowlands and involved dozens of other monarchies.

The Classic Period also saw the development of beautiful new ceramic styles, including painted codex-style vessels from northern Guatemala, and intricate sculptural traditions. Dynasties across the lowlands oversaw the construction of monumental temple pyramids and royal palaces. Rulers commissioned thousands of monoliths called stelae (singular = stela), many of which were carved with their likenesses and extolled their accomplishments. Over the course of the Classic Period, there were large elite or noble classes at many sites, but the vast majority of the population belonged to non-elite households involved in agrarian pursuits. Recent estimates put the population of the southern and central lowlands as high as 7 to 11 million during the Late Classic Period.[13] The elaborate and multivariate environmental-management strategies developed by Classic communities to support such large populations will be the main focus of the book.

The Terminal Classic Period (c. 800–1000 CE) was characterized by the breakdown and reorganization of the Classic Period socio-political system. I will discuss the multiple factors and processes involved in this momentous transition in greater depth in Chapter 7. Most of the large Classic capitals were abandoned during this time and populations reorganized into smaller communities. The subsequent Postclassic Period (c. 1000–1500 CE) saw an increased focus on seaborne trade with other regions of Mesoamerica, and new commercial centers like the well-trafficked tourist site of Tulum popped up along the coasts of the Yucatan Peninsula. Despite the breakdown of many socio-political and cultural traits that had characterized the Classic Period, many others survived and continued to evolve throughout the Postclassic Period and into the Spanish Colonial Era.

I will reference dozens of Pre-Colonial sites ranging from smaller peripheral towns to the largest monumental centers (Figure 1.4). Since the 1970s, research projects across the lowlands have contributed growing data sets from a range of smaller population centers to add to the massive data sets from prominent sites like Tikal and Chichen Itza. The few areas of the lowlands that have remained relatively remote even from modern Maya communities are now becoming accessible to archaeological investigations via airborne laser scanning technology. However, even if the laser scans allow archaeologists to document architectural features not visited for centuries, it would be more accurate to say that we are *uncovering* or *identifying* them for research purposes rather than *discovering* them. The latter term would strip the ancient residents of the site and their descendant communities of their agency and direct connections to the built landscape.

Shifting the Focus

One of the main goals of the book is to present an updated overview of the current academic understandings of ancient Maya human-environment relationships for a broader audience. In so doing, I hope to shift the focus away from the decline of the Classic Period city-states and toward the amazing array of socio-ecological adaptations that sustained growing populations for seven centuries. I will also attempt to walk a fine line by extolling the remarkable achievements of Classic Maya communities while avoiding the advancement of Maya exceptionalism. The divine rulers of ancient Egypt and Mesopotamia oversaw the construction of massive pyramids and buildings on par with and even larger than those of the Classic Maya rulers.[14] The engineers of ancient Angkor developed complex water-management systems to help sustain massive populations in the tropical landscapes of Southeast Asia.[15] The modern British monarchy traces its roots back over 900 years—longer than any known Classic Maya dynasty.

Such parallels with other civilizations past and present should pique our interest in understanding the particular ways in which Classic Maya societies

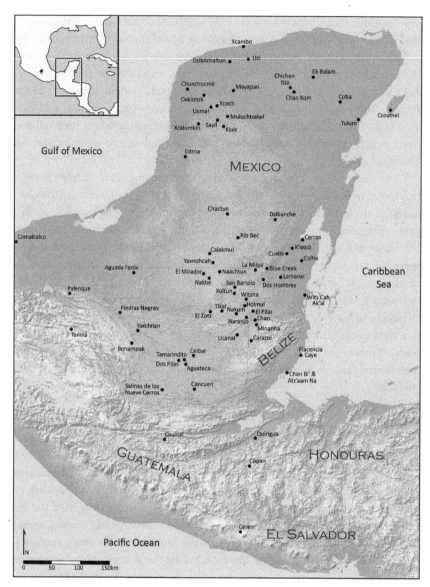

Figure 1.4 Topographic map of the Maya lowlands highlighting the locations of archaeological sites mentioned in the book (map adapted by author using base map by NASA/JPL).

addressed common social and environmental challenges. We can (and should) certainly marvel at all that the Classic Maya accomplished, but we must also recognize that the mechanisms underlying Maya resilience are familiar. Exceptionalism is a small step away from exoticism, and continuing to think of the Classic Maya in that way can be detrimental not only to their legacy but also to millions of Maya people today.[16]

The fact that it would be a mischaracterization to say that Classic Maya civilization was exceptional in the long span of human developments does not lessen the importance of their long list of remarkable achievements. The list begins with the fact that they were able to develop such a productive array of resource-management systems in a challenging tropical forest environment. Like ancient civilizations in other tropical regions of the world, Classic Maya communities developed a series of environmental-management systems tailored to the specific assets and deficits of various ecological zones across the lowlands. They wove themselves into these ecosystems that they heavily modified to meet their needs. The quickness with which the forests reclaimed cities after they were depopulated is a testament to the degree of active management that was required to maintain a human-environmental balance during the Classic Period.

Another challenge of living in the Maya lowlands was the stark contrast between the dry and rainy seasons. We tend to think of all tropical environments as perpetually wet and verdant, but many, including even the monsoon belt of South Asia, experience a significant dry spell in the early months of the year. Many Classic Maya communities had to survive through a four-to-six-month dry season in which almost no rain fell at all. Even the life-giving rains of the wet season could occasionally turn deadly in the form of hurricanes and floods. Thinking about the destructive power of hurricanes today, in an age when we have days or even weeks of advance notice of their arrival, you can only imagine how devastating they would have been to Classic populations. An average of at least one hurricane or major tropical storm crosses the Maya lowlands every year.[17] Maya communities may have had at most a day or two's anticipation of a large storm's arrival, but the majority of the population would have been living in structures that could not withstand hurricane force winds. Tremendous physical- and social-rebuilding efforts would have been frequent due to powerful storms and other natural disasters.

Finally, one of the most impressive things about Classic Maya socio-ecological systems is that they supported continuous growth for so long. Frequent re-evaluation and adaptation of practices were necessary to produce enough food for the populations that we now know existed across the lowlands by the Late Classic Period. Tikal in Guatemala and Caracol in Belize supported growing populations for over 700 years. To put this in perspective, Angkor, the capital of the Khmer (or Angkorian) Empire, existed for just over 600 years as a dominant capital city. The metropolis of Teotihuacan in Central Mexico existed as a large, powerful center for likely under 600 years. Yinxu, the last capital of China's Shang Dynasty, was constructed and then largely abandoned all within a 300-year period.

The modern iterations of cities like New York and Los Angeles can trace their origins back roughly 400 and 200 years, respectively. Yes, New Yorkers deal with unpleasant winters and Los Angeles continues to sprawl across what is essentially a desert coastal environment, but both are located in temperate climates and neither depends on food-production systems within their own borders to feed their populations. They also both have access to modern technologies, while residents of Tikal and Caracol did not even have access to metal, let alone electric, tools. The fact that Classic Maya communities were not only able to survive these ecological challenges but also thrive in their tropical forest environment should be more prominent in the popular understanding of the Maya.

The Maya Environmental Mosaic

The discipline of archaeology incorporates methods and theoretical frameworks from the natural sciences, social sciences, and humanities to piece together the puzzle of what happened in the past. It is a puzzle that we must try to solve without having access to all the pieces and without ever seeing the full picture on the front of the box. It is thus crucial to pursue interdisciplinary approaches and integrate as many lines of evidence as possible. Over the past several decades, archaeologists, epigraphers, geographers, environmental scientists, and other specialists have developed increasingly detailed insights into the origins, daily lives, and declines of hundreds of Classic Maya communities. The continuous accumulation of data, combined with advances in paleoenvironmental reconstructions and survey technology, now provide an in-depth understanding of the many ways that Classic Maya communities experienced and modified their natural environments.

The Maya lowlands are characterized by numerous microenvironments that spawned an array of localized human-environmental adaptations (Figure 1.5).[18] The "Maya area" refers to the entirety of the Mexican states of Quintana Roo, Yucatan, and Campeche, as well as much of the states of Chiapas and Tabasco. It includes all of Guatemala and Belize, as well as parts of western Honduras and El Salvador. Despite a shared culture, each subregion of communities existed and interacted with the natural world in their own specific ways. The high-canopy forests of central Guatemala are very different from the marshy lagoons of coastal Belize or the drier scrub forests of the northern Yucatan. Topography, precipitation patterns, surface water, vegetation matrices, and soil compositions vary

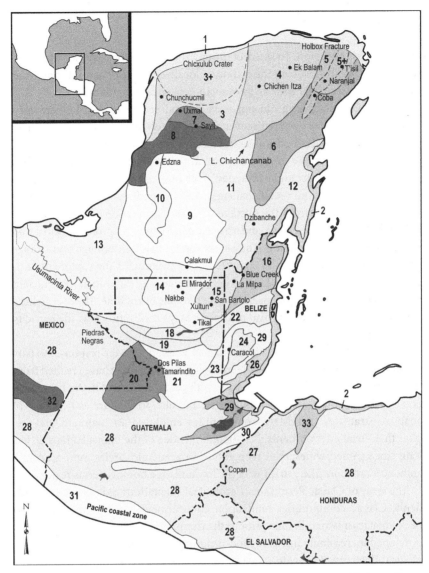

Figure 1.5 Map of the Maya lowlands divided into microenvironmental "adaptive" regions based on factors including geology, vegetation, hydrology, and precipitation patterns (map by Nick Dunning and colleagues; color added by author, included with the permission of). Number designations as listed in Dunning and Beach 2010, p. 370: "1. North Coast; 2. Caribbean Reef and Eastern Coastal Margin; 3. Northwest Karst Plain; 3+. Chicxulub impact feature; 4. Northeast Karst Plain; 5. Yalahau; 5+. Holbox fracture; 6. Coba-Okop; 7. Puuc-Santa Elena; 8. Puuc-Bolonchen Hills; 9. Central Hills; 10. Edzna-Silvituk Trough; 11. Quintana Roo Depression; 12. Uaymil; 13. Río Candelaria-Río San Pedro; 14. Peten Karst Plateau and Mirador Basin; 15. Three Rivers Horst and Graben; 16. Rio Hondo; 17. Lacandon Fold; 18. Peten Itza Fracture; 19. Libertad Anticline; 20. Río de la Pasión; 21. Dolors; 22. Belize River Valley; 23. Vaca Plateau; 24. Maya Mountains; 25. Hummingbird Karst; 26. Karstic Piedmont;" 27. Copan Valley Area; 28. Highlands; 29. Lago de Izabal Coastal Zone; 30. Motagua River Valley; 31. Pacific Coastal Zone; 32. Central Chiapas Depression; 33. Río Ulua Valley

greatly across the region. To speak of the environment of the Maya lowlands as a whole would be to gloss over the extremely localized range of natural conditions that spawned an equally wide array of socio-ecological adaptations.

The Pre-Colonial Maya did not leave behind secret or long-lost environmental knowledge for us to rediscover. Unfortunately, that is rarely how archaeology works. However, a critical lesson that we can learn from studying Classic Maya civilization is the importance of diversification and socio-ecological adaptability—the ability and willingness to change cultural practices to address both long-term environmental challenges and impending crises. Classic Maya communities learned from the mistakes of earlier generations. They developed increasingly elaborate terrace and irrigation networks to protect against soil runoff and nutrient depletion. They engineered intricate drainage and storage systems that mimicked natural ecosystems and maximized the capture of rainwater. They carefully managed their forest resources and developed fuel-efficient technologies to manufacture essential materials like burnt lime. The overarching key to the 700-plus-year survival of Classic Maya civilization was the capacity and willingness to adapt.

In some cases, distinctive socio-ecological adaptations were responses to particular environmental stimuli, while in others, strategies may have resulted from the whims of powerful decision-makers with their own agendas. Archaeologist Scott Fedick coined the term "managed mosaic" to capture the variety of adaptive strategies that Maya communities employed to maintain and exploit their local environments.[19] Although the idea of the managed mosaic has long since gained widespread recognition in academic circles, non-academic audiences are more likely to think of the lowlands as a homogeneous region.

The array of Classic Period socio-ecological adaptations did not develop suddenly. Classic communities built upon cultural developments that extended back for at least two millennia prior to the Common Era. Successive generations developed increasingly intricate food-production systems while preserving ecological diversity. The wide range of agroforestry systems supported steadily growing populations for centuries, reflecting the adaptability of the communities that created them. Classic Period communities learned from the mistakes made by their Preclassic forebears and employed new socio-ecological strategies. Thus, although the Classic Period will be the main temporal focus of the book, it will also make use of newly available Preclassic data sets. The focus will occasionally extend into the Early Postclassic Period as well, to demonstrate the continuity of cultural practices through the end of the Classic Period. This will provide a more comprehensive overview of the various ways in which Classic communities adapted their socio-ecological practices to overcome climatic, demographic, and environmental challenges. Subsequent chapters will explore the myriad ingenious ways in which communities developed localized environmental-management and food-production programs that preserved natural diversity while sustaining growing populations.[20]

Book Overview

Chapter 2 provides an overview of the advances in archaeological technology, methods, and theoretical frameworks that have changed our understanding of human-environmental relationships in the Pre-Colonial Maya lowlands. It sets the foundation for Chapters 3 through 6 that delve into specific areas of human-environment interactions, progressing from those that generally required the least intensive alteration of the natural environment to those that required the most. Chapter 3 focuses on the management of forests. As communities grew and altered socio-ecological balances, they needed to create new mechanisms to sustainably exploit forest resources. Chapter 4 explores the agricultural adaptations that sustained gradual population growth up through the demographic explosion of the Late Classic Period. Traditional *milpa* systems were supplemented by a wide range of land-modification strategies that included extensive terrace networks and wetland raised-field systems. Chapter 5 highlights the changing water capture, management, and distribution systems that characterized Maya lowland communities over the course of the Classic Period. Researchers have identified various systems tailored to local microenvironments that include individual household cisterns, large communal reservoirs, dams and flow channels, irrigation systems, and wetland agricultural fields.

Chapter 6 focuses on stone processing and utilization by the Classic Maya, including the production of burnt lime from limestone and the production of salt from brine. Both processes required the combustion of wood fuel, and the development of fuel-efficient production techniques represents yet another example of Classic Maya ingenuity and adaptation. Chapter 7 discusses the period of breakdown and reorganization referred to colloquially as the Classic Maya Collapse. Viewing this period through the lens of resilience theory highlights how the Classic to Postclassic transformation was part of a much longer cyclical trajectory that can be used to characterize all civilizations in human history. The final chapter summarizes the main points discussed in the earlier chapters and brings them together to paint a comprehensive picture of Classic Maya civilization as an environmentally conscious and socio-ecologically adaptive society. The book concludes by re-emphasizing the fundamental lessons that we can learn from Classic Maya resilience: the importance of accruing knowledge about human-environmental relationships, developing plans that reflect the nuances of local natural environments, and maintaining the capacity and willingness to adapt socio-ecological strategies to meet long-term goals.

2

From *Camera Lucida* to Lidar

A Brief History of Maya Archaeology

Assigning identities to individuals who lived over a millennium ago through an examination of their material culture is a challenging exercise. The deeper into the past we look, the more difficult it is to argue that a given community should definitively be considered Maya. The earliest securely dated archaeological evidence yet uncovered for what we label Maya culture dates to over 4,000 years ago, though it is almost certain that no one living in the region at that time would have referred to themselves as Maya. In fact, the ethnonym "Maya" really began to be used during the early Spanish Colonial Period in the mid-1500s.[1]

Tracing a common Maya identity deep into the past requires recognizing similarities in material markers like architecture, ceramic vessels, and stone artifacts. The peoples of eastern Mesoamerica only began to espouse a pan-regional Maya identity that spanned from the highlands of Guatemala to the north coast of Yucatan in the latter half of the twentieth century. Prior to that, individuals were much more likely to self-identify based on localized ethnic identities (such as Yucatec or Tzeltal) or even based on their hometowns (Ticuleña/o from Ticul). The adoption of a pan-Maya identity was in part a response to the horrors experienced by highland Maya communities who were the target of genocidal campaigns during the Guatemalan Civil War of the 1960s to 1990s. As a pragmatic response to the injustices perpetrated against Indigenous peoples across the region, many began to embrace the broader communal solidarity of a Maya identity. As such, the embracing of a pan-Maya identity is itself an example of resilience and adaptability to changing circumstances. This relatively recent espousal of a common identity is rooted in a shared cultural ancestry and ability to adapt that can be traced back for millennia.[2]

Mayanists refer to the complex agricultural societies that have inhabited eastern Mesoamerica for more than four millennia as Maya in recognition of this long cultural trajectory. However, at the same time that we identify the past and present cultures of the region broadly as Maya, we are careful to recognize the local subregional idiosyncrasies, including localized socio-ecological adaptations to a range of microenvironments.[3] For over 130 years, we have constantly updated our understandings of Pre-Colonial Maya culture through the accumulation of new data, the development of new technologies, and the

The Maya and Climate Change. Kenneth E. Seligson, Oxford University Press. © Oxford University Press 2023.
DOI: 10.1093/oso/9780197652923.003.0002

application of new approaches. Despite how far we have come in piecing together the past, many questions remain unanswered and within those unanswered questions lies the potential for a skewed representation of the Classic Maya as "mysterious."

The Maya Enigma

Ever since the earliest reports of depopulated cities in the jungle began to circulate widely, there has been a general public interest in learning more about ancient Maya civilization. Well-regarded newspapers cultivated the intrigue by couching their scientific reporting in the language of mystery. An 1890 article in the *New York Times* Sunday edition described the site of Uxmal in the Mexican state of Yucatan as a remnant of a "dead civilization."[4] This not only enticed readers to think about *why* and *how* this civilization died but also contributed to the popular notion that the Maya people disappeared. A few decades later, another *New York Times* article stated, "Many archaeologists have . . . sought to clear up the mystery of the Mayan civilization."[5] It does not clarify a specific mystery, implying either that everything about the civilization remained mysterious or that by the 1930s it was a well-ingrained public trope that no one knew why the ancient Maya civilization declined. A 1954 review of eminent Maya scholar J. Eric S. Thompson's *The Rise and Fall of Maya Civilization*, in which he summarized over half a century's accumulation of data, was simply titled "The Maya Enigma."[6]

Newspapers continued to use extravagant terminology through most of the twentieth century. In some cases, journalists deliberately endeavored to promote greater socioeconomic investments in Yucatan by U.S. stakeholders through their portrayals of Maya culture.[7] Even as archaeologists and epigraphers uncovered more and more details about the Classic Maya, popular dissemination of the information almost necessarily included phrases like "vanished" or "mysteriously, it died."[8] Although outlets like the *New York Times* have updated their reporting in recent decades to incorporate direct contributions from archaeologists and other researchers, sensationalist terminology now abounds on the internet. There is no shortage of digital publications and blog posts ensuring that anyone who prefers to focus on the "mysteries" of the ancient Maya will have plenty of fodder.

The continued aura of mystery partly results from the framework of the scientific method itself. Scientific knowledge is based on the systematic testing, refuting, and refining of ideas. Responsible science requires acknowledging and stating the limits of our understandings. As a result, many scholarly publications finish with some version of the phrase, "More research will be necessary to clarify our understanding." These necessary caveats leave the door open for popular publications to finesse "there is still much more learn" into "remains a mystery." The use of exaggerated language to focus on what we do not know overshadows the wealth of information that we do have about the ancient Maya.

Confusingly, it almost seems as though the more information we accumulate about the Classic to Postclassic Period transition (c. 800–1000 CE), the stronger the aura of mystery becomes.[9] Since at least the 1970s, Mayanists have recognized the breakdown of the Classic socio-political system to be the result of a complex interplay of many factors, some longer term, some proximate. The identification of so many contributing factors has in turn resulted in the acknowledgment that Maya societies "transformed to varying degrees, in different places, at different times."[10] The fact that there is unlikely to ever be a scholarly consensus around a single *most important* factor necessitates the usage of technically correct phrases like "scholars continue to debate the reasons," which can be tweaked and misinterpreted as "the reasons for the decline remain enigmatic." Fascination with the unknown continues to outshine any promising, though technically uncertain, understanding of the past. Hence, a 1980 article titled "Knowledge of Mayas Greatly Extended" included the statement: "Around A.D. 900, Maya culture collapsed. Nobody knows why."[11]

To be fair, it is a very similar sentiment that drives Mayanists to continue to study the same topics that have garnered scientific attention for well over a century. We can always apply updated methodologies and technologies to uncover new evidence that helps us refine our understandings of age-old questions. The fascination with the unknown is what drives scholarly and public interest alike. The public's disproportionate emphasis on the unknown is partly the result of popular outlets needing to entice readers and viewers.[12] However, it is also the result of an academic publication system that obliges scholars to circulate their research in increasingly inaccessible journals using increasingly esoteric language.

Thinking About Maya Human-Environment Relationships

The Early Explorers

Scholarly interest in Pre-Colonial Maya civilization began almost immediately after the Spanish invasion when explorers learned of depopulated cities in the jungle. Few Classic Period centers were actually "lost," as local populations were quite familiar with the ancient cities. Ceramic incense holders dating to the Postclassic and Colonial Periods indicate that pilgrimages to these ancient sites had been common practice since they were originally depopulated.[13] Just because an archaeologist has not yet visited a site does not mean that it is lost.

The point is exemplified (unfortunately) by the fact that when archaeologists first visit a site, no matter how remote, they are inevitably confronted by a plethora of looter trenches.

By the late 1700s, a growing nationalist interest in the history of Indigenous America among Guatemalan and Mexican scholars led to the organization of multiple survey expeditions to ancient cities. Reports of the Maya sites reached King Carlos III of Spain (the sixth great-grandfather of the current Spanish King Felipe VI), who was told that they represented the remnants of the most impressive of all civilizations in the Spanish American Empire. In the 1780s, the king instructed Don José Estachería, president of the Captaincy General of Guatemala, to organize a series of reconnaissance missions specifically focusing on Palenque, which is located in present-day Chiapas, Mexico. After initial explorations by José Antonio Calderón, then Antonio Bernasconi (the royal architect of Guatemala), the task fell to Artillery Captain Antonio del Río to complete the survey. With the help of seventy-nine local workers and a human-made "great conflagration," del Río's team felled trees throughout the Palenque site center to better map the layout.[14]

Ricardo Almendáriz was a Guatemalan artist who accompanied del Río and made several drawings of the site's monuments that were later enhanced by Jean-Frederic Waldeck for the English translation of del Río's report (Figure 2.1). In both del Río's report and Waldeck's modification of Almendáriz's drawings, we see an attempt to link Indigenous American social complexity to Old World civilizations like the Greco-Romans or Pharaonic Egypt or even the Lost Tribes of Israel.[15] The refusal to believe Indigenous cultures could produce such impressive material culture was widespread during the Colonial Era. It continues today a little more insidiously through such television programs as *Ancient Aliens*. Though audiences may not consciously think about it in such terms, frameworks that include ancient extraterrestrials or Old World origins are in fact perpetuating racist ideas that diminish or eliminate the accomplishments of Indigenous American civilizations.[16]

The early explorers disseminated their findings among high society crowds in North America and Europe, stoking interest in the ancient Maya. Fascination really intensified after the publication of two travelogues by American diplomat John Lloyd Stephens titled *Incidents of Travel in Central America, Chiapas, and Yucatan* (1841) and *Incidents of Travel in Yucatan* (1843). Stephens's evocative descriptions of the ancient sites went a long way toward piquing readers' interests but were truly brought to life by the incredibly detailed drawings of British artist Frederick Catherwood (Figure 2.2). Catherwood used the *camera lucida* technique to produce by far the most meticulous renderings yet. The *camera lucida* used a slanted circular glass pane or mirror to "project" an image from in front of the artist down onto the paper directly below the device. This effectively allowed

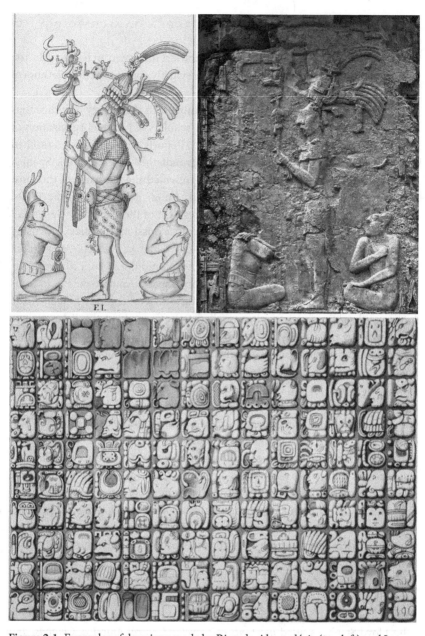

Figure 2.1 Examples of drawings made by Ricardo Almendáriz (top left) and Jean-Frederic Waldeck (bottom) of monuments from Palenque demonstrating a limited grasp of Maya iconography and lack of attention to detail. The top right image is a photograph of the monument that Almendáriz attempted to draw. Unfaithful representations like these contributed to misunderstandings of the origins of Maya civilization by promoting possible connections to Old World cultures. For instance, Waldeck included an elephant head in the second row of glyphs from the top in the fifth block from the right (top left and bottom images accessed through the public domain; bottom right image by Wolfgang Sauber—Own work, CC BY-SA 3.0, accessed through Wikimedia Commons).

Figure 2.2 Examples of drawings made by Frederick Catherwood using the *camera lucida* technique. Stela D at Copan (left) and the north building of the Nunnery Quadrangle at Uxmal (right) (both images originally included in the 1844 publication *Views of Ancient Monuments in Central America, Chiapas, and Yucatan* and were accessed through the public domain).

the artist to "trace" the image. Some of Catherwood's prints are so comprehensive that they continue to aid epigraphic and archaeological study today. To their credit, Stephens and Catherwood did not believe there to be any connection between the ancient Maya and any Old World civilizations.[17] Their volumes inspired growing interest in the "lost" jungle civilization, and by the end of the nineteenth century, several early scientific investigations were underway across the lowlands.

Teobert Maler, an Austrian soldier who helped install Maximilian of Habsburg-Lorraine as Maximilian I, emperor of Mexico in 1862, introduced photography as a tool for studying ancient Maya sites in the 1870s. Drawing conventions that he developed to document collapsed buildings and site layouts are still used today.[18] He was followed by the British diplomat Alfred Maudslay, who photographed hieroglyphic monuments at several prominent sites across the lowlands. By the early 1900s, academic institutions including Harvard's Peabody Museum, the University of Pennsylvania Museum, Tulane University, and the Carnegie Institution of Washington were sponsoring larger research expeditions throughout the lowlands.[19]

Early Frameworks for the Decline of Classic Maya Civilization

As new information trickled back to the United States and Europe, it fed the flames of curiosity about the ancient Maya. Despite the limits imposed by the technologies of the time, the early explorers recovered a wide range of useful data and developed insightful theoretical frameworks for their era. Some hypotheses regarding the breakdown of Classic Maya civilization proposed in the 1910s remain viable today. For instance, at a conference in Washington, DC in 1915, Ellsworth Huntington proposed that an increasingly unstable climate was the main culprit spurring the demise of Classic Maya civilization.[20] Modern paleo-environmental reconstructions generally support the idea that climatic changes played a central role in the breakdown of Classic Period communities in many sub-regions of the lowlands. Where Huntington went wrong was the *type* of climate change—he proposed a period of *increasing* rainfall was to blame whereas we now know that droughts were a much more significant problem.

By the 1930s, many scholars laid the blame on the ancient Maya's presumed reliance on slash-and-burn (swidden) agriculture. This method involved cutting down large swaths of forest, using controlled burns to clear any remaining vegetation, and then farming the cleared area for two or three years before moving on to a new plot (Figure 2.3). If used exclusively by steadily growing populations, over time it would have degraded the environment and made it more susceptible to climatic drying.[21] The idea that the Maya were constantly doing battle with their natural environments and may have overexploited their resources in some areas has continued in academic circles in different iterations up through the present.[22]

Sylvanus Morley oversaw expeditions for the Carnegie Institution to sites across the northern and southern lowlands between the 1910s and 1930s and was a strong proponent of the swidden hypothesis for much of his career. However, by the time he wrote the first major synthesis of Pre-Colonial Maya civilization in 1946, he was leaning more toward a sociological explanation for the decline of the major Classic Period communities. He stated that it would be difficult to explain the widespread breakdown via environmental factors alone and instead favored a revolt of the lower classes as the main cause.[23] Other scholars like J. Eric S. Thompson, who dominated Maya studies for the middle part of the twentieth century, also highlighted the role of internal socio-political factors as the main drivers of decline. In fact, he pointed to "moral degeneration" playing a key role.[24] It may not be surprising that such internal rebellion models became particularly popular during the era of the Red Scare in the United States.

Early twentieth-century scholars were already disagreeing over the time scale and proper terminology for what happened at the end of the Classic Period. Charles Wythe Cooke favored "decline" and saw the silting in of the low-lying

Figure 2.3 Modern swidden agriculture in the northern Maya lowlands. Farmers recently cleared the milpa of trees and dried maize stalks and are now using controlled fires to clear the remaining vegetation and add nutrients back to the soil (photograph courtesy of Sarah Taylor).

seasonal swamps (called *bajos*) as a gradual process that negatively affected Classic communities.[25] Morley entertained the possibility of either a sudden demise or a gradual exodus from the southern lowlands.[26] Huntington referred to a collapse at 600 CE, likely resulting from communities struggling against an increasingly unfavorable climate until they finally gave out.[27]

A fixation on the swidden hypothesis remained an obstacle preventing more nuanced understandings of Classic Maya human-environment relationships. Early twentieth-century scholars ignored the mounting evidence for more intensive forms of agriculture, including the identification of terrace systems. The swidden hypothesis included a conception of Classic Maya sites as vacant ceremonial centers only visited by larger congregations occasionally throughout the year. Research biases were partly to blame, as excavations and mapping in the early 1900s focused almost exclusively on site cores with monumental architecture. The result was that scholars preferred to view Classic Maya civilization as an anomaly among ancient civilizations rather than entertain the possibility that the swidden framework was wrong.[28] Researchers today are still reckoning with the idea of Maya exceptionalism, which became ingrained in the popular imagination.

Settlement Patterns and Human-Environment Relationships

The advent of settlement pattern studies in the Maya lowlands in the 1950s and 1960s finally changed the prevailing models of Classic Maya urbanism and agriculture. The empty center model was abandoned in favor of thinking about Classic Maya centers as densely populated "garden cities." By the late 1980s, the pendulum had swung so much that archaeologist T. Patrick Culbert exclaimed, "The Maya lowlands seem to have been one of the most densely populated areas in the preindustrial world."[29] Recent lidar imagery seems to support this statement. The documentation of more and more terracing and raised-field systems finally reached a critical mass, helping dispel the swidden hypothesis once and for all by the mid-1970s.[30]

The new wave of settlement pattern data brought ecological and climatic explanations for the decline of Classic Maya civilization back to the fore in the 1970s and 1980s. Overshoot hypotheses had been around since the earliest days of Maya archaeology, originally focusing on the vagaries of swidden agriculture. Newer iterations focused on massive populations eventually exceeding the capacity of their agricultural systems to provide sustainable returns. Systems stretched to the brink of being able to support themselves for long enough would eventually pass a threshold and snap back. Such conceptualizations were useful for explaining what many researchers were coming to understand as a rapid and massive collapse. A 1970 symposium specifically devoted to updating models regarding the demise of the Classic Period city-states held the straightforward title "The Classic Maya Collapse."[31] Participants in the meeting generally agreed that the breakdown of the Classic socio-political order was a result of many combined factors, but their data sets focused mainly on larger sites in the south and west.[32]

The focus on the dire consequences of environmental overexploitation reflected contemporary concerns for the destruction of natural environments, particularly tropical forests. However, a disconnect developed between academic and certain public perceptions of ancient Maya human-environmental relationships. At the same time that archaeologists and environmental scientists were recognizing the significant degree to which the Maya modified their environments, New Age enthusiasts were searching for ancient models of a harmonious existence with "nature." Aided by evocative reconstructions in the pages of *National Geographic*, the notion of ancient Maya communities living in tune with a pristine rainforest took hold within some sectors of the broader public. Popular outlets argued that humans of the late twentieth century should act more like the ancient Maya, who lived in harmony with their idyllic forest environment.[33] This false perception continues in some circles today, demonstrating that once skewed perceptions of the past become ingrained in the popular imagination, they can be quite difficult to dislodge.

The Managed Mosaic

At the same time that many scholars were arguing for a rapid collapse in some regions, they were also beginning to recognize the heterogeneity of processes that affected sites across the lowlands. Archaeologists and environmental scientists uncovered evidence of the diversity of socio-ecological relationships not only between different subregions and settlements but also *within* settlements where a variety of subsistence practices were employed.[34] They also began to form more nuanced understandings of the range of environmental, demographic, and climatic challenges that Classic communities were able to overcome. Now, for many scholars, the most incredible characteristic of Classic Maya civilization is not that the system eventually underwent drastic transformations, but that it thrived for as long as it did.[35]

Since the 1990s, the "managed mosaic" has become the prevailing paradigm in academic conceptualizations of ancient Maya human-environment relationships.[36] This model recognizes that the ancient Maya were both integral components and shapers of their natural environments. It posits that the Classic Period landscape was a patchwork of milpas, tended forests, sophisticated agricultural infrastructure, and garden cities (Figure 2.4). Today's forests are not the remains of primordial jungles, but rather the results of selection and manipulation by generations of Maya agroforesters—they are, in the words of Scott Fedick, "gardens gone to seed."[37] Instead of viewing Classic Maya farmers as doing battle with their natural environments, we should instead view them as careful cultivators, turning the natural relationships and growth cycles of the forest to their advantage. Knowing what we now do about the extent to which the Maya intensified agricultural production and modified their environments, the level of biodiversity they were able to preserve is remarkable.[38]

At the heart of the managed mosaic were Classic Maya garden cities and smaller communities that molded their local environments to fit their food-production needs. Although some of the larger urban areas had populations approaching or exceeding 100,000 residents, the populations were more dispersed than modern cities. If a plane were somehow to fly over Late Classic Tikal or Caracol, the pilot would see the bright whites and reds of the plastered and painted civic-ceremonial zone, surrounded by and intertwined with a patchwork of trees, stone and thatch roofs, milpas, dirt paths, and paved roadways (*sakbeob*

Figure 2.4 A reconstruction of Palenque in the Mexican state of Chiapas, highlighting the mosaic of buildings, forests, and agricultural infrastructure that characterized Classic Period garden cities (image courtesy of Trasancos 3D: Anxo Miján, Alejandro Soriano, Andrés Armesto, Carlos Paz and Diego Blanco).

in Mayan). The tracts of seemingly "wild" forest around the garden cities would in fact be carefully managed patches of productive species. The pilot would be able to recognize that this was an extensive human settlement, but it might look more like a mix of a modern suburbs and rural farm towns than a modern city. It would certainly look quite different from early *National Geographic* images of nearly invisible thatch huts wedged between 1,000-year-old trees.[39] This Late Classic mosaic landscape would have been the product of thousands of years of ecological knowledge put to the purpose of supporting larger populations than would ever inhabit the interior lowlands again.

Resilience Theory

To account for the decline of this carefully managed system, recent theoretical frameworks have reincorporated many older hypotheses and tested them against new data. Sunk cost hypotheses point to the inability or unwillingness of communities to abandon practices and infrastructure that they had already invested much time and effort. Ecological overshoot hypotheses posit that growing populations eventually degraded local food-producing environments to the point where communities could no longer feed themselves. Both ideas factor into contemporary academic perceptions of the Terminal Classic breakdown. Another factor now recognized as playing a critical role was diminished socio-ecological resilience.

C.S. Holling introduced the concept of ecological resilience in 1973 to refer to the capacity of an ecosystem to survive and recover from major disturbances.[40] This framework recognizes that it is unlikely that a system will return to the exact same starting point from which it was disturbed and instead sees resilience as the ability of the system to maintain functionality amidst necessary change.[41] The framework centers on an adaptive cycle, usually visualized as an ellipsis that includes four successive phases—exploitation, conservation, release, and re-organization (Figure 2.5). The resilience of a given ecosystem depends on the system's inherent capacity to change, the flexibility of its interconnected component parts, and its vulnerability to unforeseen challenges.[42] The concept of panarchy was adopted into the system to account for the nesting of adaptive cycles of multiple scales within one another. Each nested cycle is linked with and potentially affects the others.

Since the early 2000s, archaeologists have adapted ecological resilience theory to the study of the long arcs of human civilizations.[43] Human socio-political systems, like ecological systems, are constantly fluctuating and evolving, with several networks nesting within one another at any point in time. In social science applications of the theory, the adaptive cycle phases are perhaps best perceived as

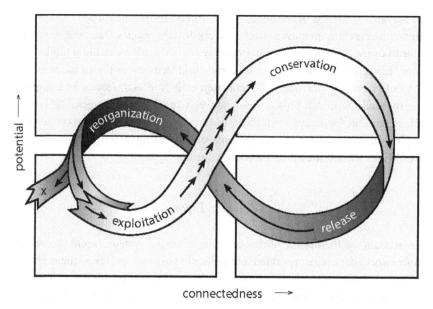

Figure 2.5 Diagram of the adaptive cycle used in resilience theory (originally published in Holling and Gunderson 2002, image courtesy of Island Press).

growth, conservation, breakdown, and reorganization. The focus on social and socio-ecological systems as opposed to purely natural ecosystems introduces human agency, creativity, and innovation into the mix.[44] These factors can speed up or slow down the transition from one phase to the next compared with natural ecosystems. In some cases, human social and demographic factors can lead to the skipping of certain phases, such as an extenuated growth phase leading directly into a breakdown or collapse phase. In others, you can have a blending of two, such as when breakdowns and reorganizations happen simultaneously as "transformations."

One of the key benefits of the resilience theory model is the framing of societal growth and decline as part of much larger, continuous cycles. Thus, the Maya Classic Period should not be approached as its own standalone phenomenon, but rather part of a longer cultural trajectory dating back to the earliest vestiges of social complexity in eastern Mesoamerica. The lengthy Preclassic growth phase was followed either by a brief conservation phase or led directly into a breakdown known as the "Late Preclassic Collapse." This was followed by the Protoclassic (c. 150–250 CE) reorganization phase that was in turn followed by the Classic growth and conservation phases, which eventually gave way to the Terminal Classic breakdown, and so on.[45]

Another key insight from resilience theory is the role that increasing complexity and interconnectedness can play in diminishing a society's ability to adapt to new environmental challenges. This combines aspects of both sunk costs and overshoot frameworks. Each subregion or polity had its own local adaptive cycles nested within the broader adaptive cycles of lowland civilization. Within each community, nested adaptive cycle hierarchies included individual families, larger household groups, social factions, and the overarching state, each of which employed differing but interconnected socioecological adaptive strategies. As Classic Period communities grew, so too did their intensive water-management and agricultural infrastructures. Larger and more intricate organizational systems developed to ensure effective cultivation and distribution of foodstuffs, linking more and more components of Classic society.[46]

With so many moving parts, it is perhaps best to view the Classic Period not as an era of stability bracketed by periods of turmoil, but rather as a dynamic system that required constant adaptation and adjustment to maintain some semblance of constancy.[47] The fact that Classic communities maintained this dynamic equilibrium for over seven centuries is remarkable. By the Terminal Classic, however, the complex interconnectedness of the system may have limited its capacity to adapt and continue to make the adjustments necessary to overcome a series of crises that included drastic climate change. The development of a range of new methodological and technological approaches now allows researchers to understand the intricacies and diversity of human-environment relationships across the lowlands like never before.

Recent Developments in Technology and Methodology

As researchers have reviewed and updated theoretical frameworks over the past hundred years, technological and methodological approaches have advanced relentlessly forward. The wealth of new data accumulated over the past several decades is the result of both the proliferation of larger projects and the application of new methods that allow us to address questions and data sets that were erstwhile impossible. The integration of approaches from various fields in the natural and social sciences, as well as the humanities, is crucial for developing as accurate and well-rounded an understanding of the ancient Maya as possible. "Archaeometry" refers to a range of natural science techniques that archaeologists and other scientists now apply to the study of the past, including multi-elemental, radioisotopic, stable isotope, and remote sensing analyses, among others.

Reconstructing the Precipitation Record

Lake Cores

Lake core analysis is one of the main ways that paleoenvironmental scientists reconstruct the ancient precipitation record of the Maya lowlands. Lake cores are records of the sediments deposited at the bottom of perennial water sources. Researchers use long, cylindrical tools called corers to retrieve the samples of the lakebed stratigraphy. Layers often represent hundreds (or even thousands) of years of sediment buildup that can be used to identify dryer or wetter periods in the past.

Embedded in many sediment layers are tiny freshwater snail shells composed of calcium carbonate (similar to the makeup of limestone). Calcium carbonate molecules are composed of one calcium atom, one carbon atom, and three oxygen atoms. The vast majority of the oxygen isotopes on earth are ^{16}O isotopes, but a small percentage are the heavier ^{18}O isotopes. Both isotopes are stable; ^{18}O atoms simply have two extra neutrons. During periods of decreased rainfall, there will be a higher relative ratio of evaporation to precipitation than during periods of increased precipitation. The lighter ^{16}O isotopes are more likely to evaporate first, leaving behind a higher than average concentration of the heavier ^{18}O in the lake water during periods of decreased rainfall. The shells of snails that were growing in the lake during periods of decreased rainfall will thus absorb higher than average $^{18}O/^{16}O$ ratios. When the shell stops growing, the oxygen isotope ratios are fixed in the calcium carbonate molecules forever. When the snails die, their shells are often preserved on the lake floor and can be used as proxies for identifying periods of decreased rainfall.

Researchers can also use concentrations of salt and gypsum in sediment layers as indicators of drought. A severe decrease in rainfall can lead to the complete, or near complete, drying up of lakes in the Maya lowlands. During extended droughts, salt or gypsum particles that would normally be relatively dispersed in a freshwater lake will coalesce and sit on the dry lakebed in clumps. The same thing will happen if you have a glass of salt water and set it out on a counter for the water to evaporate. After a couple of days, the water will have completely evaporated, leaving behind aggregated clumps of salt particles. The presence of salt bands in lake sediment cores can thus be used to identify periods of severe drought that caused all the freshwater of the lake to evaporate (Figure 2.6).[48]

It is important that the stratigraphy is well preserved in the lake core because the scientists also need to recover datable materials from the same exact layers as the snail shells or salt clumps. The most useful material for establishing absolute dates is charred wood. Radiocarbon dating, a method that uses the known half-life of the Carbon-14 isotope, can return fairly precise date ranges (c. 15–30 years in certain cases) for when an organism died. The origins of radiocarbon dating can be traced back to the U.S. military's Manhattan Project during the 1940s. Today, advanced forms of radiocarbon dating that use accelerator mass spectrometry (AMS) can produce more precise date ranges using smaller carbon samples. Charred bits of organic matter have the best chance of preservation for long periods of time, and wood charcoal is the most common organic material used for radiocarbon dating.[49]

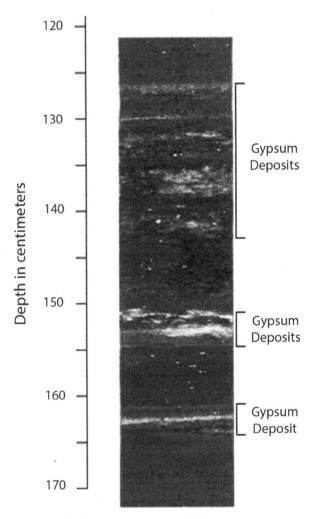

Figure 2.6 A lake core sediment profile from Lake Chichancanab in the northern Maya lowlands. The lighter bands are gypsum deposits that represent episodes when the lake water evaporated, leaving behind layers of sediment (image adapted from Hodell et al. 2005 with the permission of David Hodell, Jason Curtis, and Mark Brenner).

If small bits of wood charcoal are recovered from the same sediment layer as salt clumps or snail shells with high $^{18}O/^{16}O$ ratios, researchers can use them to identify a narrow range of dates for past episodes of decreased rainfall. So far, prominent examples of lake cores used for reconstructing paleoclimatic records in the Maya lowlands have come from Lake Chichancanab in the north-central Yucatan and from the Peten Lakes region in north-central Guatemala, as well as a few other subregions. They all indicate that a period of frequent and intense droughts affected several subregions of the Maya lowlands in the ninth and tenth centuries CE.[50]

Speleothems

Speleothems are cave formations created by the deposition of minerals over time. The most commonly known forms are stalactites (which hang from the cave ceiling) and stalagmites (which protrude from the cave floor). Stalagmites form when water seeps through the limestone cave ceiling and deposits tiny calcium carbonate sediments at the spot where the water droplets make contact with the floor of the cave. In some cases, researchers can use speleothems to clarify the chronology of past precipitation trends. At a basic level, researchers can measure ratios of the heavier oxygen ^{18}O isotope to the lighter ^{16}O isotope in a given section of a stalagmite. The main factor influencing variations in this ratio in the Maya lowlands is fluctuating amounts of precipitation during a given period. In years with especially wet rainy seasons, there would be a lower ^{18}O to ^{16}O ratio.[51]

Uranium-thorium dating follows the same isotopic half-life principles as radiocarbon dating but can be used to date calcium carbonate materials like limestone instead of organic matter. Scientists can thus analyze a speleothem sample using a combination of uranium-thorium radio-isotopic dating and $^{18}O/^{16}O$ analyses to develop accurate records of relative annual rainfall intensities in the past. So far, researchers have completed three prominent speleothem studies in the Maya lowlands: one in the northwestern Yucatan and two in southern Belize. All indicate a period of increased drought frequency toward the end of the Classic Period and beginning of the Postclassic Period.[52] Of course, due to the fact that rainfall patterns can be highly variable from subregion to subregion, more studies will be needed in the future to further refine localized reconstructions.

Reconstructing Forest Management and Agricultural Practices

Paleoethnobotanical and isotopic techniques allow researchers to reconstruct many of the ways that the ancient Maya altered their landscapes.[53] Combining archaeometric lines of inquiry with ethnohistoric and ethnographic accounts, researchers can understand how patterns that we see in the archaeological record relate to different types of land-use strategies. The following subsections outline the more prominent methods for studying ancient forest management and agricultural practices available to archaeologists and environmental scientists today.

Microbotanical Analyses

Paleoethnobotanists (scientists specializing in the use of plants in the past) can identify such environmental changes as the introduction of nonnative species, forest clearance, and changing species compositions by examining changes in microbotanical frequencies in sediment records. Three of the most common microbotanicals used are fossil pollen, phytoliths, and starch granules. Fossil pollen, as the name suggests, refers to fossilized specimens of individual pollen grains. Phytoliths are tiny silicate structures assembled by plant cells that survive long after the rest of the plant decomposes. Starch granules are reserve glucose chains formed and stored in the roots, seeds, and fruits of plants. They preserve in tiny cracks in archaeological materials like pottery and stone tools, from which paleoethnobotanists can recover them to help reconstruct ancient foodways.[54] All three types of microbotanicals—fossil pollen, phytoliths, and starch granules—possess morphological traits that are often distinctive to different genera or even species of plants. They thus serve as unique markers of the plants that produced them.

Fossil pollen grains can preserve fairly well in oxygen-poor and acidic environments and are thus most commonly recovered from lake sediment cores. They are also occasionally recovered from non-lake sediment samples but in far lower quantities with variable preservation rates. Pollen grains preserved in lake core strata with datable bits of charcoal can serve as proxies for understanding broad changes in forest compositions. Comparing frequencies of the pollen from a specific species or genus from different layers can help trace fluctuations in floral populations that may be indicative of human activities.

For instance, the recovery of maize and squash pollen in the New River Lagoon of northern Belize after 2000 BCE from the same sediment layers as pollen from "disturbance taxa" (e.g., weeds and grasses) and large quantities of charcoal indicates a period of forest clearance for the planting of agricultural crops near the site of Lamanai.[55] Likewise, researchers used pollen ratios in a core extracted from Laguna Tamarindito in the Petexbatun region of the southwestern lowlands to argue for two distinct periods of forest clearance: one during the Preclassic Period and another during the Late Classic Period. Pollen levels from fruit-producing and other valuable trees remained consistent at Tamarindito throughout the Pre-Colonial Maya occupation, suggesting active management by residents.[56] However, pollen levels in the site's reservoirs indicate that overall Late Classic forest cover may have been as much as 60% lower than it is today.[57]

This is not terribly surprising, considering population levels were much greater in the Petexbatun during the Late Classic than they are currently.

It is also important to recognize the limitations of using pollen as a proxy for overall forest cover and composition. Pollen from only a few tropical species is easily dispersed by wind; most are dispersed by animal species like bats, birds, and bees.[58] This restricts the overall utility of comparing relative frequencies of *different* species from the *same* layer. For instance, the pollen of many tree species may not have been carried far enough to reach the New River Lagoon. Thus, proximity to the lagoon would have been a key factor influencing which species' pollen are well represented. The higher levels of maize pollen recovered from the lagoon compared with those recovered at other sites in northern Belize may be simply due to the proximity of cropped fields, not necessarily a higher proportion of land cleared for maize production.[59] Pollen frequencies are likewise not considered reliable indicators of the *absence* of floral species but can be useful positive indicators of a species' presence.

Phytoliths are more likely to preserve in sediment samples recovered from excavation units and dry soil core samples than fossil pollen. Also, unlike pollen particles, they tend to be deposited locally wherever the plant breaks down.[60] They can thus be especially useful for identifying species cultivated in homegardens or infields when recovered from sediment cores extracted across ancient sites. Analysis of phytoliths from sites like El Pilar, Belize, indicate that residents of the ancient community consumed products from twenty of the tree species that dominate the forests around the site today. This in turn suggests that the composition of the modern El Pilar forest is likely the result of ancient cultivation strategies.[61]

Like phytoliths, starch granules can be recovered from sediment samples or the surfaces of artifacts.[62] Improvements in starch granule analysis over the past two decades have been instrumental in broadening our understanding of Pre-Colonial Maya diets. Archaeologists always suspected that the ancient Maya ate a wide range of plant foods, but most remained virtually invisible in the archaeological record until recently. A particularly significant find has been the prominence of starchy tubers like manioc, arrowroot, and malanga in Classic diets.[63]

Macrobotanical Analyses

Archaeologists and environmental scientists also occasionally recover macrobotanical samples (larger bits of organic materials that are visible with the naked eye) representing a range of plant species. The most common macrobotanical ecofacts include charcoal and charred rinds or seeds. If the samples are well-enough preserved, they can be identified at the species level. Depending on the context from where charred wood samples are recovered, they could indicate which species were preferred for domestic cooking fuel, and which may have been used for construction.[64] Wood ash can also be used as an indicator of continued access to fuel, but it is not as useful for species-level identifications. Macrobotanicals recovered from several contexts around the small community of Chan, Belize, indicate that residents maintained steady access to mature tree resources throughout the ancient site's 2,000-year occupation.[65]

A unique macrobotanical data set from the site of Ceren, El Salvador, provides an extraordinary window into what farming strategies looked like at the beginning of the Late Classic Period. Around 600 CE, a volcanic eruption buried Ceren in a thick layer of ash that hardened, preserving many macrobotanical samples and creating three-dimensional "molds" of others. The amazing circumstances have allowed Payson Sheets and colleagues to map the locations of individual plants in homegardens and milpas, providing direct evidence for Pre-Colonial food production systems.[66]

Landscape Analyses

Landscape modifications provide another line of evidence of past agroforestry practices. Researchers draw on ethnohistoric and ethnographic accounts of how modern communities use certain landscape features to interpret how similar features in the archaeological record may have been used by ancient communities. For instance, modern communities in the northwest Yucatan construct mounds and circles of small limestone boulders to preserve soil moisture and serve as anchors for valuable fruit trees. Similar "stone mulch" formations identified in the archaeological record at the northwestern site of Chunchucmil, Mexico, likely served similar functions. Stone mulch has also been identified at the site of Dos Hombres, Belize, as part of a flood-prevention and water-retention system.[67]

Stone terraces are the most visible indicators of past agricultural practices. Although the presence of Classic Period agricultural terraces in the Maya lowlands has been known for nearly a century, the true scale of even well-known terrace systems such as those at Caracol, Belize, only became apparent in the 2010s with the introduction of lidar laser-scanning technology to archaeological studies. Lidar imagery provides a detailed map of local topographies, including human-made stone alignments, now buried beneath jungle vegetation. However, even lidar cannot penetrate the ground, and any terraces that collapsed or were buried by sediment remain hidden.

Analysis of site layouts can help identify open spaces that likely served as growing areas within the Classic Maya "garden cities." We now know that extensive homegardens, orchards, and even milpa infields separated residential patio groups throughout Classic communities. Thus, certain areas within site boundaries that lack architectural features are good candidates for cultivation zones. In some cases, relatively high proportions of Classic community lands were dedicated to agricultural production or forest management. For instance, even the most densely settled sectors of El Pilar still included 40% "unsettled" land.[68]

Other archaeological features related to Pre-Colonial agricultural practices include stone alignments in wetlands that may have served to direct water flow or manage soil buildup.[69] Stone enclosures in and around communities like Mayapan may represent "pens" for limited animal husbandry.[70] Although turkeys may be the only animals fully domesticated by Mesoamericans, it is possible that some specialists in the lowlands may have raised such species as rabbits, turtles, and iguanas. Researchers can also draw on indirect lines of evidence such as soil erosion to infer ancient landscape-modification practices. In addition to yielding microbotanical and precipitation record samples, lake sediment layers can be used to track erosion from the surrounding catchment area. An increase in erosion can be correlated with periods of increased tree removal.[71]

Isotopic Analyses

Stable carbon isotope analyses provide another method for identifying general patterns in past agroforestry practices. They are specifically useful in the Maya lowlands for identifying local shifts to maize cultivation. Photosynthesis in plants includes a step called carbon fixation, which can be accomplished through one of three metabolic pathways. Approximately 95% of plants on the planet use the C_3 pathway, including the majority of plants native to the Maya lowlands. C_3 plants, as they are known, have lower percentages of C^{13} isotopes than C_4 plants. Maize, which is not native the Maya lowlands, just so happens to be a C_4 plant, meaning that its isotopic signature generally includes higher percentages of C^{13} isotopes. Over time, the organic matter from the plants erodes into the soil, transferring their relative isotopic signatures to the sediment record. Thus, researchers can use C^{13} isotopic ratios to help identify localized shifts from predominantly C_3 (non-maize) to C_4 (maize) plants in sediment cores.[72] Isotopic signatures can also potentially be used to identify which areas of a site were dedicated to maize cultivation. For instance, measurements at Tikal indicate lower C^{13} levels in the reservoirs closer to the site center than in the peripheral ones, suggesting that maize was grown outside the site center.[73]

Isotopic analyses of a person's bones can indicate the prevalence of animal protein in their diet. Higher levels of protein can be used as an indirect indicator of healthy forests that supported sufficient wildlife for hunting. These can also be combined with archaeofaunal analyses of midden (ancient trash heap) assemblages. However, we know that reliable access to animal protein in Classic Maya communities was highly correlated with socioeconomic status. Thus, isotopic levels also varied based on social status, not just the presence or absence of potential quarry.[74]

Ethnohistoric and Ethnographic Evidence

A final key method for deducing ancient forest-management practices involves drawing on ethnohistoric accounts from soon after the Spanish invasion and ethnographic research conducted in Maya communities in the twentieth and twenty-first centuries. These resources provide useful starting points for developing ideas about what Pre-Colonial agricultural practices may have looked like. It is important to remember, however, they do not represent perfect analogues for Classic Period practices, as much has changed since then.

Ethnographic research of Itza and Lakandon Maya agroforestry practices, for instance, provides a baseline for understanding the level of detailed knowledge that Maya agriculturalists may have had about their environments in the past. However, such research is limited in its utility by the fact that modern farmers mainly practice rotating-field swidden forms of agriculture. They do not engineer their landscapes in the same ways that the Classic Maya communities did with their massive terracing and raised-field projects. Also, many modern farmers use chemical fertilizers and pesticides and clear their fields using metal machetes.[75]

The fact that twentieth-century ethnographic accounts are 1,000 years removed from the Classic Period and that several large-scale transformations have occurred in that span means that many agricultural practices may have changed since the Classic communities were depopulated. Even early ethnohistoric accounts by Spanish colonizers are at least 500 years removed from the Classic Period, and these accounts were also distorted by language barriers and a Spanish preoccupation with maize over the variety of other native cultigens.[76] Despite the limits of ethnohistoric and ethnographic data, they do provide a basis for understanding how native crops grow well together in milpa fields, and the crucial role that homegardens have played in Maya agricultural systems. They also provide possible models to be tested against archaeological and archaeometric lines of evidence.[77]

Reconstructing Ancient Stone-Processing Techniques

Burnt lime has been a critical material for so many aspects of daily Maya life, including architecture and nutrition, since at least the Preclassic Period. It is made by heating small pieces of limestone to around 800°C for over twenty hours, which would have required significant amounts of wood fuel. Over the past two decades, archaeologists have re-evaluated the role that lime production may have played in Pre-Colonial deforestation. Thanks to the influx of more detailed data and methodological approaches, we now know that just like almost every other facet of Classic Maya society, lime production and its potential consequences were heterogeneous across the lowlands. Although excessive production of burnt lime may have contributed to environmental degradation in a few areas, evidence from other regions points to the development of resource-conservation strategies like fuel-efficient pit-kilns and the planting of fast-growing tree crops specifically to use as fuel.[78]

A range of new approaches allows for a more detailed analysis of the variety of Pre-Colonial lime production methods. Stable carbon and oxygen isotope analyses of materials recovered from within pit-kilns helped prove that these features were indeed used to produce burnt lime. Fourier transform infrared spectroscopy (FTIR) can be used to identify the temperature range to which stone samples within the ancient pit-kilns were heated. This method measures the vibration of molecular bonds within the pit-kiln samples, allowing researchers to compare the results with reference samples that had been heated to known temperatures. Archaeomagnetic studies can now be used to complement accelerator mass spectrometry (AMS) and ceramic analyses to refine the chronologies of lime-production events within the pit-kilns.[79] Advances in scanning electron microscopy (SEM) allows researchers to identify the species of wood fuel used to produce the lime.

Chronology of production and consumption trends are of key interest to researchers studying lime in the Pre-Colonial Maya lowlands. When did large-scale production begin in different regions? What effects did it have on local resource-management strategies? Although ceramic chronologies can be useful for tracking such changes, researchers have also developed methods for dating the lime plaster or mortar itself. These include the recovery of small bits of carbonized organic materials from within the plasters, as well as using archaeomagnetic techniques. Other methods for dating lime plaster include applying radiocarbon dating to the carbon atoms trapped in the reconstituted calcium carbonate. As burnt lime dries, it absorbs carbon dioxide molecules from the air, which are then fixed in the resulting calcium carbonate. With the radioisotopes then decaying at steady rate, the carbon dioxide molecules provide a reference point for when the plaster or mortar matrix originally dried.[80] Combining these lines of evidence, researchers can model the resource-conservation strategies that Classic communities employed to adapt to environmental and climatic challenges.[81]

The Lidar Revolution

Unlike the incremental advances in other technological and methodological approaches that have gradually refined our understanding of Classic Maya lifeways for the past century, the application of airborne lidar scanning technology has been transformative. It was already apparent by the 1980s that many areas of the Maya lowlands were much more densely populated than they are today, but lidar imagery provides a much clearer picture of just how densely settled these areas really were. The new spatial data sets have implications for agricultural-intensification practices, forest-management practices, and resource-conservation strategies, as well as a range of other settlement pattern issues.[82]

Lidar (light detection and ranging) is used as a blanket term for a series of airborne laser-scanning technologies and applications that allow for the creation of detailed topographical models. The most common approach used in the Maya lowlands to date involves attaching a lidar instrument to the bottom of a low-flying aircraft that flies back and forth over a designated research area. The lidar instrument emits upwards of 150,000 laser pulses per second, which bounce off the landscape and back to the instrument's sensor. The instrument measures the amount of time it takes for the pulse to hit something and return, thereby generating a read-out of the vertical distance between the instrument and the first thing to block the laser's path below. Horizontal coordinates are triangulated using nearby GPS reference points.[83]

In the heavily forested regions of the Maya lowlands, more than 99.9% of the lidar pulses bounce off the dense vegetation. However, with upwards of 150,000 pulses emitted per second, even if only 0.01% reach through the small holes in the canopy, the instrument's sensor will still receive a handful of points per square meter that made it all the way to the ground. Stitching together these handfuls of points, researchers are able to create detailed digital models of the sub-canopy terrain, some of which have better than 50 cm resolution. Separating the canopy laser points from the underlying terrain points effectively allows researchers to "peel back" the forest cover to reveal the array of ancient buildings and landscape features below (Figure 2.7).

Archaeologists recognized the potential benefits of lidar technology for addressing archaeological research questions after a flyover to analyze flood-prone areas in Honduras in 2001 happened to include the archaeological site of Copan in the survey zone.[84] In 2007, Arlen and Diane Chase and colleagues commissioned the first lidar flyover for specifically archaeological purposes at Caracol, and Mayanists have not looked back. Over a decade has passed since this first archaeological lidar flyover wowed Mayanists and the broader public alike with the amazing three-dimensional visualizations of the Classic Maya–built landscape.[85] That first flyover ushered in a new phase of archaeological survey in the Maya area, referred to as a "revolution" by many researchers. Today dozens of projects in eastern Mesoamerica use lidar to address a wide range of research questions relating to polity boundaries and inter-community relationships, intra-community organization, water control and management,

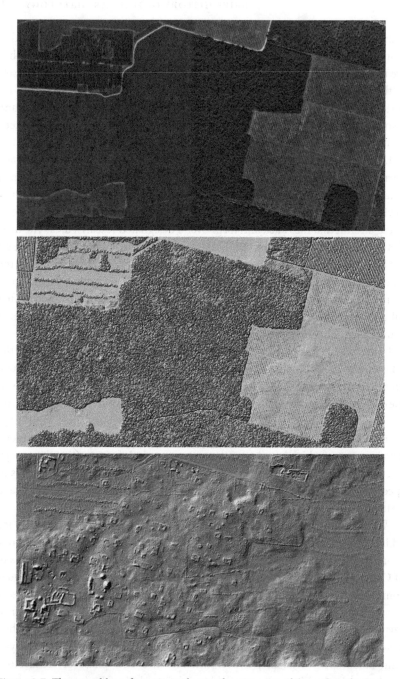

Figure 2.7 The same bloc of terrain in the northeast sector of the archaeological site of Muluchtzekel in the northern Yucatan as seen in Google Earth satellite image (top); lidar-derived digital terrain model of the forest canopy (middle); and, lidar-derived digital terrain model of the ground terrain (bottom) (lidar images courtesy of Bill Ringle).

agricultural land and soil management, ritual spaces and cave distributions, and defensive landscape modifications.[86]

The relative ease with which lidar bare earth models allow for spatial and contextual analyses of Maya communities and landscapes has fostered a new wave of macro-scale research foci. Large-scale flyovers organized by the Patrimonio Cultural y Natural Maya (PACUNAM) initiative have gathered over 2,000 km^2 of digital geographic data in northern Guatemala, allowing researchers to address political, social, and environmental issues on a broader regional scale.[87] Beyond its utility for facilitating a bird's-eye view of archaeological sites previously hidden by dense forest canopies, researchers have used terrestrial lidar technology to map archaeological excavation tunnels and ancient cisterns, as well as to scan monuments.[88]

As with all archaeological methods, there are limits to the application of lidar technology. Despite the incredible clarity of most lidar-generated digital terrain models (DTMs) and their ability to render the forest overlay "invisible," pedestrian surveys and stratigraphic excavations remain integral to the archaeological research process. Bare earth images provide a static snapshot of the final occupation of a given site, but most Maya sites are palimpsests representing hundreds or thousands of years of material cultural accumulation. Occasionally, inferences about site chronology can be made from the lidar imagery alone. Archaeologists have noted that Preclassic architectural features exhibit a "melted" appearance compared with later Classic and Postclassic Period features.[89] This "melting" effect is likely due to both the increased time depth and the use of disparate wall fill materials between the different periods. Incorporating cursory chronological analyses based on the melting effect into lidar image analysis can better inform follow-up pedestrian survey and excavation programs.

Another important point to remember is that the lidar bare earth models are not perfect representations of reality.[90] Future algorithms may hone the fidelity of the models, but even then, there are certain classes of structures that are very difficult to identify using even the most high-resolution lidar technology. For instance, the vast majority of Classic Maya households most likely lived in residences constructed predominantly of perishable materials. Rudimentary stone foundation braces would be the only surviving remnants of such houses. Foundation outlines are occasionally visible in lidar imagery, but the vast majority are not. Researchers in some areas face problems posed by low and highly variable vegetation.[91] Thus, pedestrian surveys will continue to play integral roles in any archaeological survey projects.

Archaeologists are also still confronting several ethical issues surrounding the use of lidar. Permission to conduct lidar flyovers in the Maya region is usually granted by government institutions at the state or federal level. In some subregions of the lowlands, especially in the northern Yucatan, survey areas

often include lands administered by modern communities or even private properties. It is still rare that archaeologists seek permission from these potential local
stakeholders, and, depending on the size of the flyover area, soliciting permission would be impractical. Although the specifications applied to the lidar point
cloud processing do a great job of weeding out any modern structures from the
digital elevation models, the system is not perfect, and it is possible that some
contemporary structures might make their way into lidar DTMs. Guidelines are
currently being developed to protect against inadvertent invasion of privacy, but
a set of universal standards have yet to be adopted.

There are also issues surrounding the publication of archaeological site
locations, even in academic journals. Looting of archaeological sites remains an
issue in several parts of the Maya lowlands. The contemporary socioeconomic
factors influencing the proliferation of looting are beyond the scope of this book,
but the fact remains that publishing the locations of newly identified sites (some
of which may have been previously unknown to looters) would open them up to
potential vandalism and destruction. Guidelines have already been developed to
protect against these potential risks, including prohibitions on publishing geo-
coordinates, yet the possibility remains for triangulation based on the locations
of previously known sites. Archaeologists will continue to refine protective
guidelines to safeguard the privacy and well-being of both the archaeological
sites and the contemporary populations that live near them.

Keeping in mind the need to fine-tune ethical guidelines, it cannot be denied
that this technology has already contributed to amazing advances in our understanding of Classic Maya settlement patterns and landscape use. For example, the
landscape around Caracol, Belize, had been intensively studied for decades, and
pedestrian surveys had already uncovered massive agricultural terrace networks.
The initial lidar flyover of Caracol in 2007 demonstrated that terraces were even
more widespread across the landscape than previously known, extending to
nearly every surface in the region.[92]

Lidar-based investigations are also transforming our understanding of the
origins of lowland Maya socio-political complexity. One of the most dramatic
lidar-related developments began to unfold in 2019 in the Mexican state of Tabasco,
where Takeshi Inomata and colleagues identified more than twenty massive human-
modified platforms that had been hiding in plain sight. Detailed lidar-derived
digital terrain models revealed that what had previously looked to be natural hill
formations are actually monumental platforms complete with extensive causeway
systems and supporting dozens of smaller platform mounds around their edges.[93]

Stratigraphic excavations at Aguada Fénix, one of the largest of these monumental centers, demonstrate that construction of the central platform dates to
approximately 1100–800 BCE (Figure 2.8). This pushes the earliest monumental
architecture in the Maya lowlands back several centuries prior to the previous

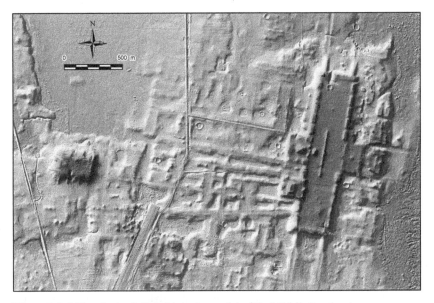

Figure 2.8 Lidar-derived digital terrain model of the Middle Preclassic archaeological site of Aguada Fénix in the state of Tabasco, Mexico, highlighting the immense scale of the site's central rectangular platform (image courtesy of Takeshi Inomata and colleagues).

earliest examples from the Mirador region of northern Guatemala. These findings, along with Inomata and colleagues' reanalysis of chronological sequences in the Olmec lowlands to the west provide further evidence of consistent communication and interaction between the two cultural regions. Ongoing research across the lowlands is demonstrating the massive potential that lidar digital elevation models yet hold to transform our ideas of ancient Maya lifeways.

After over one hundred years of continuous research in the Maya lowlands, archaeologists, environmental scientists, and other researchers are still refining our understandings of Pre-Colonial Maya lifeways. The amount of knowledge that we have accumulated about Classic Period human-environment relationships is truly astounding, and yet so much still remains unknown. The consistent incorporation of new methodologies and technologies to the study of the past ensures that our understandings will become even more nuanced as research continues. Drawing on the theoretical frameworks and recent methodological advances discussed above, the following chapters detail just how much we have learned about Pre-Colonial Maya human-environment relationships. Classic Period communities not only developed intricate food-production and resource-management systems, but they also demonstrated a remarkable capacity to adapt their socio-ecological practices over time.

3

Forests

Introduction

A common misconception of tropical forests today is that they are, and always
have been, relatively devoid of substantial human populations—that they are
pristine natural refuges, unsullied by our touch. Popular movies conjure images
of adventurers traveling deep into "virgin" forests where no humans stepped before. The reality, however, is that most tropical forests around the world reflect
thousands of years of human modification and management. The Maya lowland
forests are no exception. From the high canopy jungle of the southern lowlands
to the drier scrub forests of the north, modern distributions of arboreal species
reflect the choices made by many generations who have called the region home.
They are the remnants of the Maya forest gardens that surrounded relatively low-
density garden cities for hundreds of years.[1]

Deforestation technically refers to the removal of trees beyond the rate of
replacement.[2] It is one of the more visible forms of natural ecosystem destruction today and is thus a potent symbol of general environmental mismanagement. It also remains a prominent issue in discussions about the breakdown of
Classic Maya civilization. If the Classic Maya denuded landscapes across the
lowlands, then they were obviously mismanaging their natural resources—that
is how the thinking goes. Archaeologists and environmental scientists do not
refute the idea that communities during the Late and Terminal Classic Periods
harvested substantial amounts of timber and fuel to satisfy the needs of rapidly
growing populations. However, we also recognize that the felling of large quantities of trees does not equal deforestation, nor does it indicate that the managing
populations did not understand their local environments.

Classic Period communities learned from the mistakes of their Preclassic
forebears. They developed sustainable forest-management strategies that preserved biodiversity and supported growing populations for centuries. This
chapter provides an overview of Classic Maya forest conservation and utilization, as well as agroforestry—that is, the integration of trees into agricultural-
production systems.[3] Increasingly nuanced understandings of the degrees to
which Pre-Colonial Maya communities shaped their tropical forest homes are
leading to a greater appreciation for the productivity and ecological balance that
they were able to maintain. Paleoenvironmental reconstructions demonstrate

The Maya and Climate Change. Kenneth E. Seligson, Oxford University Press. © Oxford University Press 2023.
DOI: 10.1093/oso/9780197652923.003.0003

that from the time of the earliest settled villages in the lowlands, agroforesters began to modify natural environments into carefully managed mosaics of farms, orchards, homegardens, and semi-domesticated forests from which they harvested a wide range of resources.[4] The higher concentrations of fruit-bearing and medicinal tree species that surround ancient sites are remnants of Maya home- and forest gardens that have "gone feral."[5]

By the end of the Classic Period some of the largest communities had begun to stress their local forest resources, which left them more vulnerable to climatic and socio-political changes. However, instead of viewing the Classic Maya as steadily building toward socio-ecological disaster or deforestation, we should appreciate their ecosystem management practices for the 700-plus-year sustainability they supported in many subregions of the lowlands. Forests provided firewood for cooking and warmth, fuel for ceramic, burnt lime, and salt production; and timber for tools, furniture, and construction; as well as medicine, fruit, and other purposes.[6] Careful monitoring of tree extraction would have been necessary to be able to support continuous population growth over such a long time while maintaining biodiversity.

Before delving into specific examples of Classic Maya forest-management practices, it is important to clarify the related terms that I will be using. I will use "silviculture" to refer to the tending or management of a whole forest using sustainable principles that mimic natural, ecological patterns. "Arboriculture" differs slightly in that it refers to the tending or management of individual trees. "Agroforestry" is a system that incorporates trees into a broader spectrum of agricultural practices that includes non-tree crops and even animals.[7] These terms, of course, are all based on modern American cultural understandings of human-environment relationships. One of the keys to understanding how Maya communities were able to accomplish what they did is to try to understand how the ancient Maya likely conceived of their forests on their own terms. Thus, at various points throughout the chapter I incorporate the Mayan nomenclature for agroforestry practices, several of which continue to the present.

Maya Conceptions of "Forest"

Mischaracterizations of Pre-Colonial Maya resource management practices date to as early as the first encounters between Spanish conquistadors and Maya communities. At the heart of the false impressions are cultural discrepancies regarding conceptions of "forest" and "agricultural land." Spanish conquistadors interpreted the environments of the Maya lowlands and Maya resource-exploitation practices from their own Western European perspectives. To the Spaniards, the forest was something to be feared—hence all the European fairytales where children encounter dangers in the woods. Cultivation looked like monocrop fields with neat rows of wheat or barley, or neatly trimmed hedges, lawns, and flower beds. They saw the interwoven agroforestry systems of the Maya as generally untamed or mismanaged lands. This provided the conquistadors with a handy justification for appropriating said lands. In reality, the "mismanaged" or "wild" lands surrounding Maya communities represented complex systems that mimicked the natural growing circumstances of a wide range of productive plant species.[8]

It is not surprising that sixteenth-century Spanish ethnohistoric documents concerning Maya land management were filtered through a sixteenth-century Spanish cultural perspective. However, colonialist or colonialist-influenced frameworks continued to dominate the study of Maya human-environment relationships through much of the nineteenth and twentieth centuries. Unfortunately, we have little in the way of firsthand Classic Maya textual or iconographic evidence concerning forest-management issues. We are thus missing direct evidence of the emic, or internal cultural perspective, of how Classic communities truly conceived of their natural environments.

More recently, scholars have turned to ethnographic research on contemporary Maya human-environment relationships to better understand Indigenous perspectives. Traditional ecological knowledge concerning the most effective management strategies for various microenvironments across the lowlands has been passed down for generations.[9] Thus, although contemporary communities are more than a millennium removed from the Classic Period, their understandings provide much more appropriate analogues than any non-Maya perspectives. Additionally, although we have still not identified any Classic Era manuscripts dealing with forest-management practices, advances in iconographic and epigraphic analyses now allow for as close to a basic Classic cultural perspective as we have ever had. This general emic perspective can help us interpret patterns uncovered through archaeological and paleoenvironmental research.

Whereas the Spanish conceived of a strict division between cultivated and uncultivated lands, Maya communities understood this dichotomy to be more indefinite and changeable. Their perspective can best be understood through a comparison of the Yucatec Mayan terms k'ax and kol. K'ax (or k'aax) is often translated as "forest" but can refer to many different types of wooded terrain, including land that was only relatively recently left to fallow.[10] Even though they exist as places populated by wild trees and animals, forests are still, at various times, places for resistance, for interpolity battles, and for resource extraction.[11] Maya agroforesters interwove forests and fields and even tended valuable trees beyond the boundaries of their communities. Thus, k'ax could still be part of the broader Maya agroforestry landscape even if it was not under active cultivation.

Kʾax can, however, also carry a similar connotation to "wilderness" when juxtaposed with *kol,* which generally refers to an agricultural field or sanctified space.[12] *Kʾax* in this case is more precisely understood to mean a *"lugar poblado por arboles silvestres"* [place populated by wild trees],[13] which may serve as the abode for numerous spirits and entities beyond the scope of daily human lives. An example of the broader Mesoamerican emphasis on duality, some forests are understood to be dark, precarious places full of tangible and intangible dangers like evil spirits, fierce animals, and hidden sinkholes. Clear similarities exist with European fairytales in which forests are depicted as the foreboding lairs of wolves and witches. In the general European tradition, places populated by wild trees are natural wildernesses to be conquered by humans. They are contrasted with the safety, light, and relative openness of fields and community.[14]

For the Maya, although places populated by wild trees may temporarily exist outside the cultivated *kol,* they are still integral parts of their broader home environment and a space from which they regularly harvest valuable resources (Figure 3.1).[15] Even the wilder forest elements were integrated into Classic Maya communities through artistic depictions of trees with animals like pumas and snakes on monuments and architecture within site centers.[16] The fact that *kʾax*

Figure 3.1 Forests often weave in and out of milpas in the Maya lowlands. Here, a recently planted milpa is surrounded by forest near the village of Ek Balam in northern Yucatan (photo courtesy of Sarah Taylor).

encompasses a much broader meaning than just "forest" was either lost on the Spaniards or ignored by them. They did not recognize that k'ax land can be sanctified and ordered into kol for a certain stretch of time before returning to k'ax once again. The rapid regrowth of tropical vegetation may have made the forested areas of the Maya lowlands seem that much farther outside the bounds of the cultivated world than their own fallowed fields in Spain. Nor could they fathom that the high frequencies of productive species in the forests surrounding communities were the result of careful cultivation by generations of Maya agroforesters. The Spaniards instead saw "unused" stretches of forest wilderness. Even today, many people raised in urbanized cultures see an "inverse relationship between human actions and the well-being of the natural environment"[17]—a mindset that hinders appreciating how large-scale, complex societies may simultaneously conserve and exploit their forest homes.

Maya Forests

Maya communities have played such a crucial role in shaping the forests that it is difficult to piece together what they may have looked like prior to the onset of silvicultural practices during the Paleo-Indian or Archaic Periods. Researchers have recognized the tremendous impact of ancient Maya forest management on contemporary forest compositions since at least as far back as the 1930s.[18] Maya communities have been actively interfering in forest growth cycles and compositions for over 4,000 years. Except for a few remaining isolated patches, the vast majority of the lowland forests today are technically secondary growth.[19] We must recognize and acknowledge the limits of paleoenvironmental reconstructions to deduce intricate details of pre-Maya forest compositions. However, paleoethnobotanical analyses can provide information about general species distribution patterns and how millennia of Maya agroforesters have shaped them.

Cores from Laguna Tamarindito and the Peten Lakes region in the southern lowlands indicate that a tropical moist forest started to develop in the region near the beginning of the Holocene Epoch, around 9000 BCE. This means that the earliest people to traverse the lowlands encountered a colder, drier, more savannah-like environment. Laguna Tamarindito itself was a dry depression during the last Ice Age, but as temperatures and humidity levels gradually rose, the small basin became a perennial water source. Savannahs and grasslands transformed into forests across the lowlands. Frequent fluctuations in rainfall likely resulted in significant changes in forest compositions throughout the Archaic Period before the vegetation arrived at the general subregional characteristics that we still see today.[20]

The northern Yucatan receives the least amount of annual rainfall in the Maya lowlands, and, as a result, forests in this area range from tropical deciduous varieties to drier thorn-woodland savannahs. The canopy is generally two tiered and lower than the semi-evergreen and evergreen seasonal forests farther to the south. In the north, the upper canopy may lose up to two-thirds of its foliage at the height of the dry season. Sections of the north-central Peten are characterized by stretches of savannah zones. Tropical moist forests cover the southernmost parts of the lowlands, the only subregion that can technically be described as a "rainforest," though it too experiences a stark dry season for half of the year.[21] Throughout the central and southern lowlands, raised areas referred to as "uplands" generally support tropical deciduous forests while the lower areas, or *bajos*, support seasonal swamp forests that include such useful species as logwood (*Haematoxylum campechianum* L.). Some areas of the interior have perennial wetlands called *civales* (Figure 3.2). The few riverine regions of the lowlands, such as those in northern Belize, include riverbed eco-zones with perennial vegetation. However, in general, upland forests tend to exhibit more biological diversity than the riverine zones or coastal plain areas.[22]

Figure 3.2 A *cival*, or year-round wetland, in the Buenavista Valley to the west of Tikal as viewed from the hilltop fortress of La Cuernavilla (photo courtesy of Thomas Garrison, Proyecto Arqueológico El Zotz).

Ramonales are stretches of upland Peten forest where the *ramón*, or breadnut, tree (*Brosimum alicastrum* Sw.) is the most common species (Figure 3.3). Their counterparts are *zapotales*, upland forests characterized by the prevalence of *sapote* (or *sapodilla*) trees (*Manilkara zapota* L.). The usefulness of these species for food and lumber suggests that their prevalence may result from ancient Maya selection practices.[23] Other common trees in the central lowlands that may also owe their distributions at least in part to Maya intervention are those in the palm (*Arecaceae*), mulberry (*Moraceae*), mahogany (*Melicaceae*), and laurel (*Lauraceae*) families.[24] Pine (*Pinus caribaea* Morelet) was prized particularly for ritual purposes.

Although pine trees might not immediately come to mind when thinking of the tropical Maya lowland, large stretches of pine forests do exist, mainly in Belize and northeastern Guatemala, but also in patches scattered across the region.[25] The persistence and circumscription of a cluster of pine trees in the northeastern part of Tikal's Classic Period catchment area suggests careful management and perhaps even propagation by the city's ancient residents.[26] Paleoethnobotanical studies periodically indicate that certain species were more prevalent around Classic communities than they are today, which suggests that

Figure 3.3 A stretch of upland forest in the Buenavista Valley of northern Guatemala known as a "ramonal" because it is dominated by the *ramón*, or breadnut, tree (photo by Omar Alcover Firpi, courtesy of the Proyecto Arqueológico El Zotz).

these species benefited from the active support of ancient foresters when the sites were inhabited.[27]

Pre-Colonial Maya agroforesters took advantage of microenvironments like *rejolladas* (sinkholes with deep soils and higher humidity levels) and *dzadzob* (*rejolladas* in which at least part of the floor reached the water table) to cultivate special, but fickle, tree crops like cacao (*Theobroma cacao* L.).[28] Despite being one of the cultivars most widely associated with Maya culture today, cacao trees are not native to northern Central America. They, like the cashew tree (*Anacardium occidentale* L.) that was also cultivated by Classic Maya agroforesters, were likely imported via trade from their original homeland in northern South America. Some lines of evidence suggest that cacao subsequently underwent more intensive domestication and cultivation by the Maya than they had in the forests of South America, though the exact process and timeline remain unclear. Cashew trees provided not only edible fruits but construction materials as well.[29]

The Bounty of the Forest

Maya communities had access to such a diverse range of forest products that I unfortunately cannot discuss them all. Forests were sources of food, as well as materials used for fuel, construction, medicine, spices, soap, utensils, ornaments, fish poisons, dyes, natural beehives, thatch, wine, and rituals. They were places where people could forage for fungi, both edible and psychedelic. Forest vines were used as cordage for construction purposes; hanging vessels and tools from roof beams; lowering water-collecting vessels into cisterns; and an array of other carrying purposes. Many trees that we may think of as mainly providing fruit also supplied a variety of other useful products, as well as ecosystem services, such as shade, wind protection, and watershed maintenance.[30]

At least as far back as the Archaic Period (though likely even earlier), semi-sedentary groups began to tend the forests, promoting the growth of especially useful species. Researchers have noted particularly high concentrations of fruiting trees in the vicinity of ancient sites that were likely remnants not only of homegardens "gone feral," but also selective propagation and cultivation by Maya arboriculturists.[31] Among the wide range of fruit remains recovered by archaeologists and paleoethnobotanists at Classic Maya sites are avocados (*Persea americana* Mill.), sapote, guanabana (*Annona muricata* L.), nance (*Byrsonima crassifolia* L.), guava (*Psidium guajava* L.), papaya (*Carica papaya* L.), and mamey (*Pouteria sapota* Jacq.).[32] Many other species, including allspice (*Pimenta dioica* L.) and achiote (annatto, *Bixa orellana* L.), were cultivated in forests and homegardens as flavoring agents.[33]

Firewood was one of the main resources gathered from the forest. Charcoal remains from Classic Period sites across the lowlands indicate that the ancient Maya used a wide range of tree species as fuel. Domestic cooking needs were likely responsible for the bulk of fuel consumption, but regular firing episodes would have also been necessary for ceramic and lime production, as well as for ritual purposes such as in braziers. Dry, seasoned wood is preferable for cooking fuel, as it catches and burns more quickly, and thus the Maya could have presumably collected such fuel from forest floors in a relatively sustainable manner. Greenwood, or freshly cut fuel, would have been preferable for ceramic and lime production fires that needed to burn hotter and more slowly. Species with high water contents like *chacah* (*Bursera simaruba* L., or gumbo-limbo) were especially useful in this regard.[34]

Classic Maya communities also exploited a wide range of tree species for construction purposes. Paleoethnobotanical and archaeological evidence suggests that especially choice timber, like the extremely dense and durable *sapodilla*, may have been restricted to elite consumption at some sites. *Sapodilla* takes at least fifty-two years (and sometimes up to 260 years) to fully mature. Thus, selective harvesting of this species would have been crucial for maintaining population numbers.[35] Among other uses, logwood trees, avocado, nance, and wild fig trees (*Ficus spp.*) were also sources of natural dyes.[36] In addition to their utility in construction, members of the *Sapotaceae* family and ramón trees provided edible and medicinal products,[37] and the sap of several *Sapotaceae* species, known as "chicle," formed a natural latex used for chewing gum and other purposes.[38] Ethnographic evidence indicates that the nutritious ramón nut (breadnut) is used as a fallback or famine food, sometimes even substituting for maize in bad harvest years (Figure 3.4).[39] Copal (*Protium copal* Schltdl. & Cham.) trees were cultivated, or at least protected, so that their hardened sap could be burned as an incense in rituals to summon rainclouds or to dislodge unpleasant odors from homes.[40]

Despite having a restricted natural range in the Maya area today, pine is one of the most common tree species recovered from ancient Maya sites, indicating that its natural range used to be a lot broader, that it was actively traded across the lowlands, and/or that it was carefully propagated and tended by agroforesters.[41] In addition to its use for construction and fuel, ethnographic and archaeological evidence indicate it was favored for ritual fires. Pinewood produces a relatively large amount of smoke and noise, which symbolizes the breath or essence of a ceremony, and fragrant pine resin functioned as incense. Ethnographic accounts also liken pine torches to candles, which are commonly offered as sacrifices during ethnographically documented rituals. A passage from the *Popol Vuh* (Maya creation stories collected soon after the Spanish invasion but originating millennia earlier) mentions specifically that the Hero Twins carried a pine torch

Figure 3.4 An assortment of useful forest flora: *ramón*, or breadnut, tree (Brosimum alicastrum Sw.) (top left); wild papaya tree (Carica papaya L.) (middle left); wild papaya fruits (bottom left); and, chacah, or gumbo limbo (Bursera simaruba) (right) (photos courtesy of Lauren Santini).

on their journey to the Underworld. Pine tea is used as a treatment for loose teeth and spider bites.[42]

At Lamanai in northern Belize there is evidence from pollen concentrations in the archaeological record that the ancient Maya cultivated coyol (*Acrocomia aculeate* Jacq.) and cohune (*Attalea cohune* Mart.) palms. The products of both trees served many useful purposes. Coyol palm fruits are edible and along with the sap can be used to make palm wine. Coyol palm flowers were used as offerings in rituals and for adorning the interiors of temples. Oil extracted from cohune palm kernels can be used for cooking, while the leaves are useful as thatch for structure roofs. Maya arboriculturists actively cultivated them while never fully reaching the level of domestication. Even though these palms were native to the Maya lowlands, there is evidence that the Maya extended their natural growth range by bringing coyol to places like the Copan Valley in the southeast highlands.[43]

Agroforesters harvested a variety of products from nondomesticated species in the forests that surrounded their communities. The sap of the matapalo strangler tree (*Clusia spp.*) was used for medicinal purposes, while the bark was peeled for basketry, and wood could be used for fuel and construction.[44] Salmwood (*Cordia alliodara* Ruiz & Pav.) was used for construction while its flowers were admired for their beauty and its leaves were used for medicinal purposes, such as treating insomnia and diarrhea.[45] Wild tamarind (*Leucaena spp.*) wood was used in construction, but the seeds of the fruit could be used as medicine or poison depending on the concentration.[46] The coloradillo (*Hamelia patens*) produced beautiful flowers and was used for medicinal purposes. Even avocado trees were not only used to produce food, but also their "seeds can be used as a pesticide, the bark is a source of dye, the rind serves [to deter vermin], and oil from the fruits can be used for cosmetic purposes."[47] Spanish cedar (*Cedrela odorata* L.), also a native of the New World tropics, has been used to carve idols for ceremonies, in addition to being used as a construction material and for its fragrance.[48]

In addition to the trees and other floral species, forests were home to a variety of fauna exploited by Maya communities. Hunting was the main source of animal protein, as domesticated or semi-domesticated sources were limited to turkeys, dogs, and possibly turtles and iguanas. Maya communities preserved healthy ecosystems from which mammals, such as deer, tapirs, peccaries, and agouti; reptiles, such as turtles, snakes, and lizards; snails; insects; and avian species could all be harvested as food sources. Some forest animals were likely attracted to the food growing in agricultural fields, as well as the food remains included in the organic trash produced by Maya communities. Beyond meat, forest animals provided valuable skins, such as the jaguar pelts that adorned royal bodies and furniture, and brilliant bird feathers for rituals.[49]

The forest environments also met social needs such as providing seclusion for secret romantic rendezvouses or hatching political resistance plots. Forests could provide dark, sheltered areas for the performance of ceremonies, as well as more accessible areas for hunting grounds and locations for battles (Figure 3.5).[50] Despite a lack of specific iconographic or epigraphic evidence, one can imagine the forests being used for family outings or for adolescent gatherings away from the watchful eyes of overbearing parents. Forests would also have been the classrooms where mentors passed on traditional ecological knowledge to the next generations through hands-on learning experiences.

Figure 3.5 A rollout image of a successful deer hunt depicted on a Classic Period cylindrical vessel. Six members of the hunting party announce their triumphant return using conch shells while two carry the captured deer using tumplines (image courtesy of Dumbarton Oaks Research Collection and Library, Justin Kerr, and the Maya Vase Database, Kerr Number 808).

Archaic and Preclassic Period Agroforestry

In 2021, researchers securely dated a set of footprints to 19,000–21,000 BCE in White Sands National Park, New Mexico, proving that humans were already spreading across the western hemisphere well before the end of the last Ice Age.[51] Future investigations will undoubtedly tell us more about these earliest peoples. What we already know now is that by 13,000 BCE, large groups of migrants with ancestral ties to northeast Asia had reached almost every part of the Americas. Unfortunately, Ice Age coastal settlements around the world are now lost at sea as ocean levels have risen more than 220 ft. in some areas since the end of the last Ice Age, around 12,000 years ago.[52] We may never know if the earliest explorers of the Yucatan peninsula stayed close to the coastline and how early they actually arrived in the region. What we do know is that people were already familiar with the cave systems of northeastern Yucatan by the start of the Holocene Epoch. A teenage girl nicknamed Naia by researchers was laid to rest in the Hoyo Negro cave near Tulum around 11,000 BCE. The cave system at that time would have been mainly dry, but sea levels have risen so much since then that Naia was found at a depth of over 130 ft. below the modern sea level.[53]

The earliest groups in the lowlands hunted megafauna like mammoths, bison, and camels that once dominated the open plains and savannahs of Ice Age Yucatan. Over the succeeding millennia, a combination of hunting and climate change led to the extinction of most of those large mammals.[54] The hunter-gatherer-fishers who had relied heavily on those species for sustenance increasingly familiarized themselves with the other fauna and flora of their home territories. The open plains and savannahs gave way to tropical forests as the

climate became warmer and wetter. Ancestors of the Maya may have begun interfering in the growth cycles of the forests that soon spread across the lowlands as
early as 6000 BCE. The limited paleoethnobotanical and archaeological evidence
available from this time suggests early exploitation of fruit-bearing trees and the
likely cultivation of certain species that would be domesticated well before the
Classic Period.[55] It is possible that the erratic climate of the Archaic Period promoted active management of plant food resources. Fluctuations in Archaic forest
compositions appear to have been at least partly a result of two intense drying
periods around 4500 BCE and 2900 BCE.[56]

Pollen, charcoal, and sediment evidence recovered from lake and *bajo* cores
in the central Peten Lakes zone indicate that significant forest clearance began
around 2000 BCE. The core strata dating to this period show increased levels of
charcoal from large-scale forest burns. They also show increases in pollen from
disturbance taxa that colonized the recently cleared areas, as well as the introduction of maize (*Zea mays* L.) pollen, a nonnative grass species. Maize and cotton
pollen appear in Late Archaic levels (c. 2400–1800 BCE) from Actun Halal cave
in the Belize River Valley. It is unclear whether the earliest maize agriculturalists
migrated into the region with their suite of domesticates already intact or the
local hunter-gatherers themselves transitioned to an agricultural lifestyle and
obtained maize through trade. It is possible that the transition reflected a combination of both and that it varied by subregion.[57]

The Maya lowlands were one of the last areas of Mesoamerica to see the transition to full-scale swidden agriculture. Part of this delay was undoubtedly due
to the effort required to clear the dense forests for milpa planting. The earliest
agricultural settlements were proximal to seasonally inundated terrain such as
riverbeds and *bajo* margins. For example, the earliest villages in the Petexbatun
region circled Lake Petexbatun. The pollen record from the smaller Laguna
Tamarindito, located 2–3 km to the west, suggests intermittent periods of clearance and regrowth beginning around 1200 BCE. This may represent the gradual
expansion of agricultural clearing away from the initial settlements around Lake
Petexbatun.[58]

The widespread clearance of upland forests during the Middle Preclassic
suggests that many communities had developed intensive agricultural cycles
with reduced fallow periods and extensive forest clearance by the end of the Late
Preclassic.[59] However, the timelines and intensities of forest clearance activities
varied across the lowlands. The Mirador area that straddles Guatemala's northern
border with Mexico may have retained a higher proportion of savannah lands
and grassy marshes than other parts of the interior lowlands for longer. Pollen
evidence for limited human alteration of the environment appears as early as
2650 BCE in this region, but large-scale clearance for agriculture does not occur
until the Middle and Late Preclassic Periods (after c. 600 BCE) when the sites of

Nakbe and El Mirador were growing rapidly.[60] Soil erosion due to forest clearance began even earlier around Lake Salpeten in northern Guatemala. There, lake cores indicate intensive erosion began at the start of the Early Preclassic Period (c. 2000 BCE) and increased up through the Late Preclassic.[61] Soil erosion at Tikal began to accelerate during the Late Preclassic Period. Unlike the Archaic Period instabilities in forest cover and compositions, Preclassic fluctuations do appear to have been anthropogenic in nature.[62]

Mature forests were still present throughout the Middle Preclassic Period in the vicinity of K'axob in northern Belize but may have been largely cleared from the uplands soon afterward. By the Late Preclassic, we see K'axob residents switch to collecting the majority of their wood fuel from swampy lowlands as well as burning economically valuable species. This suggests that by the Late Preclassic, the primary upland forests no longer existed or that remaining climax forests were so reduced that there was a prohibition placed on their further exploitation.[63]

Sedimentation rates doubled in the Petexbatun region from the end of the Archaic Period up through the Classic Period, while it increased forty times over in the Peten Lakes region. Erosion levels suggest that Preclassic populations deforested the lowlands at higher rates than their Classic Period successors. This perhaps resulted from communities viewing the sparsely inhabited forests as an endlessly renewable resource. However, we cannot discount the possibility that one of the reasons for lower Classic Period erosion rates was that less soil remained to erode after the Preclassic mismanagement. Although deforestation reached critical levels in several areas of the lowlands during the Late Preclassic, there is also evidence from core samples that many valuable species were spared, including fruiting, lumber-producing, and ritually important trees. The pollen record suggests that valuable tree species were even more common in the region around Laguna Tamarindito than they were prior to the Preclassic Period.[64]

Preclassic deforestation likely played a significant role in the socio -political breakdown and transformation known as the "Late Preclassic Collapse." Between roughly 100–300 CE, many prominent Late Preclassic centers, including El Mirador, San Bartolo and Ceibal in Guatemala, and Cerros in Belize, were depopulated. Most would never see significant levels of habitation again. Archaeologists point to the fact that Preclassic communities denuded their landscapes of soil-anchoring forests and suffered when fertile soils washed into basins. Paleoenvironmental data also suggest that there may have been a downturn in precipitation in some subregions around this time, which could have been exacerbated by the drop in forest cover.[65] These two factors were among those that would play crucial roles in the transformations at the end of the Classic Period. In the immediate aftermath of the Preclassic breakdown, however, communities learned from the consequences of rampant deforestation to develop conservation strategies that allowed for centuries of Classic Period sustainable growth.

Classic Maya Forest Management

Ethnographic Insights

Recent lidar-based surveys suggest that by the end of the Classic Period, few (if any) corners of the lowlands remained completely untouched by humans. Late Classic populations in most areas rose to higher levels than they had ever seen before (and would ever see again). Even in the most densely settled areas, Classic communities developed more sustainable forest exploitation practices than their Preclassic forebears.[66] Pollen records from the large site of Coba in northeast Yucatan indicate widespread forest clearance beginning as early as the 800s BCE and continuing through the 700s CE. However, no significant increase in disturbance taxa pollen during the Classic Period suggests that environmental degradation may have dropped off after lessons were learned from the consequences of Preclassic deforestation.[67] Diversity and flexibility were at the heart of the Classic Maya forest-management system, both with regard to the range of species cultivated and the range of methods employed.

The results of these sustainable methods are visible in the paleoenvironmental record in the form of continued use of a variety of tree species and existence of mature forests into the Late Classic Period. For insight into the specific methods and forest-nurturing practices, however, we must turn to the twentieth-century ethnographic record. There, we find detailed accounts of traditional ecological strategies that were likely passed down since at least the Classic Period and provide the closest thing to a firsthand account to which we have access. It must be reiterated, however, that certain aspects of traditional cultivation systems have necessarily changed with the introduction of metal implements and electric machinery. Additionally, most ethnohistoric and ethnographic accounts refer to swidden agroforestry, but we know that Classic communities developed more intensive forms of food production like terracing and raised-field agriculture.[68]

Numerous agroforestry and silvicultural systems are or were until recently in use around the lowlands, including the *pet kot* system and *kannan k'aax* ("well-cared-for forest") in the northern Yucatan, the *kab'al k'aax* ("young forest") of the Itza in northern Guatemala, and the *te'lom* ("place of trees") of the offshoot Huastec Maya to the west.[69] The main objectives of each of these management programs are to encourage the success of valuable species and limit the spread of less useful vegetation. *Pet kot* means "round or circular wall" in Yucatec Mayan and refers to particularly productive patches of high-canopy trees surrounded by low stone walls. Modern communities in the Yucatan know that the *pet koto'ob* (plural of *pet kot*) were created by earlier communities and are the result of generations of selective cultivation. Such cultivated groves would have provided wind protection and sources of volunteer seeds for neighboring milpas.[70] They provide a likely analogue for Classic Maya forest-management practices, as evidenced by the clusters of valuable species found in and around ancient sites throughout the lowlands, including Tikal's pine cluster. Re-evaluation of the pollen record from Late Classic Copan indicates that pine and other forest species were carefully managed all the way up to the site's rapid depopulation in the 800s CE.[71]

Tending the Forests

Maya cultivators closely monitored growth cycles in fallow plots as forest species recolonized the land. Milpas are always surrounded by forest, and thus when a field reaches the end of its active cultivation cycle, seeds from the surrounding forests quickly disperse to recolonize the territory. Studies of regeneration cycles indicate fairly rapid regrowth of secondary forest in milpas and that their compositions are significantly influenced by the compositions of the forests that surrounded them. When agroforesters first clear a tract to plant milpa crops, they leave several valuable tree species standing in the milpa field. This not only provides a shady place to rest but also ensures that useful species will be represented in the forests that regenerate when the field is left to fallow.[72]

During the regrowth process, Maya arboriculturists selected for useful species and weeded out less desirable varieties. By knowing which species should be given priority early on in the regrowth cycle, Maya cultivators influenced the composition of new forests while allowing for natural relationships to play out.[73] A key tenet of the *pet kot* and other management systems is to limit intervention in the growth cycles of useful species as much as possible to take advantage of interspecies feedback systems. Maya cultivators recognize the symbiotic relationships of certain species and support the growth of trees that do not directly provide valuable resources but help protect those that do.[74] For instance, some species help to recycle nutrients for others, and some might depend on animals that nest in other species to disperse their seeds. The Lakandon Maya specifically promote the growth of balsa trees (*Ochroma pyramidale* Cav. ex Lam.), which grow quickly and provide the shade that is necessary for many other useful species to grow to maturity. Balsa trees also play a key role in the regeneration of soil fertility by regularly shedding leaves that enrich the soil's organic matter, and its flowers attract vectors that disperse the seeds of other valuable species.[75] Although the Classic Maya would not have understood what was happening at a molecular level, they would have witnessed the productivity of such interspecies relationships through generations of forest management.[76]

In addition to promoting the growth of certain species, silvicultural practices in newly fallowed fields included attentive weeding, pruning, increasing soil fertility, and even the purposeful planting of some young sprouts. The term "artificial" is thus applicable to several lowland forests in the sense that saplings cultivated in homegardens were occasionally transported to new fallows to help direct forest regrowth.[77] Through their transport of minerals, like salt, into the interior of the Yucatan, Maya cultivators have changed soil compositions and affected forest nutrient cycles.[78] Controlled fires are also a common tool for clearing underbrush and regenerating soil fertility, but it is unfortunately a very difficult practice to identify in the archaeological record. Modern communities in the eastern Peten take steps to protect especially useful stretches of forest from periodic wildfires by clearing "breaks" and building stone walls.[79]

In terms of managing and promoting the continued usefulness of long fallow or mature forests, Maya silviculturalists selectively cut down trees at a sustainable rate. They also coppice particularly useful species, which involves cutting the trees down close to the roots to promote healthy regrowth and helps protect them from the controlled burns that they use to clear out unwanted vegetation.[80] In some cases, fallowed forests may be cleared again for new milpas as frequently as every eight or ten years in what are called "monocyclic systems." In other cases, fallowed fields may be allowed to develop into long, fallow forest stretches from which timber and medicinal resources can be extracted for longer periods of time. Some are even left to fully mature for around seventy years.[81]

By managing certain wild tree species and making the forest more navigable for humans, Maya foresters also promoted the survival of forest animals. Faunal and human osteological analyses from sites like Aguateca suggest that higher status residents maintained access to forest-based proteins throughout the Late Classic Period. Isotopic analyses of the faunal materials indicate that these forest animals continued to have access to forest plants through the Late Classic and did not rely on poaching agricultural crops.[82]

Ramón is used for livestock feed today, and Classic Maya management of ramón in forests around their communities may well have been intentionally aimed toward attracting game species like white-tailed deer. Maintaining stands of ramón in close proximity to milpas not only encourages visits by game animals but also provides a standby source of nutrition for communities during poor harvest years.[83] Dietary flexibility and the incorporation of fallback plans into food strategies depending on annual crop yields bolstered the resilience of Maya communities for generations.[84] Dietary adaptation continued during the Colonial Era with the adoption of nonnative plants into local agroforestry systems. Nonnative trees that are now grown throughout the Maya area include mango varieties (native to South Asia), citrus species (native to East and Southeast Asia), bananas (native to Southeast Asia), and coffee (native to Ethiopia).

Although we must recognize the crucial role that environmental factors played in influencing present forest compositions, especially in the areas largely abandoned after the Classic Period, ancient agroforesters also played a critical role. From the time of the earliest settled villages in the lowlands, agroforesters continuously fostered the growth of the most useful species while culling or limiting the dispersal of less desirable ones. In some cases, the latter were inhibited to the point where they never recovered their earlier natural ranges.[85]

Compared with other tropical forests like the Amazon, the relative homogeneity across subregions of the Maya lowlands provides another line of evidence for long-term management on the part of generations of Maya cultivators.[86] Studies of species pair clustering in and around the ancient site of El Pilar in western Belize indicate that the diversity of useful trees within the ancient site's vicinity cannot be due to random chance. The persistent biodiversity of forests across the lowlands indicates that the ancient Maya did not completely exhaust the bounty of the forests, no matter how dire population and climatic pressures may have become by the end of the Classic Period.[87]

Land Ownership

Ethnohistoric and ethnographic analogies suggest that elites, or even central authorities, controlled access to forest resources at several of the larger Late Classic Period sites. They indicate that at least some forest tracts were controlled by prominent families as "ancestral estates" during the Colonial Period and even recently. It is possible that similar systems existed as far back as the Classic Period.[88]

Patricia McAnany has suggested that there was an increasing trend toward the privatization of forested lands (whether mature growth or fallow) beginning by the Early Classic Period. Stricter centralized management systems may have developed by the Late Classic when forests resources began to be strained by tremendous population expansion. Archaeological, ethnohistoric, and ethnographic evidence all point to the significant connection between ancestors and place, and ancestral ties to managed forest tracts can also be understood under this framework.[89] It is also possible that in addition to lands privately owned by kin groups there were communal forest lands from which all or certain members of the broader community could at least collect fuelwood.

Unfortunately, we will likely never know the specific mechanisms through which top-down or kin-based resource-management schemes were organized or enforced. What we *can* see through analyses of charcoal residues, however, is that at sites like Naachtun and Tikal elite households maintained special access to preferred species of wood through the Late Classic. The harvesting of status-enhancing products, such as jaguar pelts and quetzal feathers, from forest environments provided additional reasons for elites to want to conserve these natural habitats.[90] Other reasons for protecting specific species concerned their ritual significance. The ceiba (*Ceiba pentandra* L.), for instance, is still revered as an *axis mundi*, or world tree, across the Yucatan, where it can be found growing in central town plazas as well as throughout the forests (Figure 3.6).[91]

Figure 3.6 Ceibas are revered as world trees, connecting the underworld, the surface world, and the heavens. A close-up view highlights the distinctive thick thorns of the ceiba trunk (photos courtesy of Lauren Santini).

Agroforestry at Tikal

Tikal provides an excellent case study in the successes and limits of resource management. It was one of the sites that survived the turmoil of the Preclassic to Classic transition and grew to be one of the largest, most densely populated communities of the Classic Period. Pollen and soil erosion evidence suggest that like elsewhere in lowlands, early swidden farmers cleared wide swaths of upland forests around Tikal. It is possible that the memory of the environmental degradation of the Late Preclassic contributed directly to the establishment of more sustainable forest-management programs during the Classic Period.[92] The fact that several particularly valuable forest species were still available for a massive construction program and population surge in the Late Classic Period indicates that an impressive forest-management system existed within the polity.

The forested lands around Tikal included a mix of *ramonal* uplands, seasonally swampy *bajos*, year-round swamps, and transitional areas between these ecozones.[93] The Tikal community harvested trees from each of these zones for a variety of purposes. As with other Classic communities, the predominant use of wood fuel was for domestic cooking and warming needs. The staples that made up the bulk of the Maya diet—foods like maize, beans, squashes, and root crops—were cooked prior to consumption. However, it is also important to recognize that large centers like Tikal were composed of a variety of subcultures based on socioeconomic, occupation-related, and possibly even "ethnic" identities.[94] Differences in socioeconomic status would likely have accounted for the greatest discrepancies in the consumption of forest resources.

Ceramic and burnt lime production also required consistent fuel sources, while construction projects would have required a significant amount of wood relatively infrequently. Elliot Abrams and David Rue estimated that the wood of five moderate-sized trees would have been needed to construct a typical Maya pole-and-thatch house. Such structures were likely rebuilt approximately every twenty to twenty-five years. The larger vaulted-stone residences of the elites required that much more hardwood for scaffolding and other construction activities as well as the fuel necessary to make the lime for plastering and replastering episodes. Sustaining wood resources as the population steadily grew over the course of the Classic Period would have required careful management practices to avoid exhausting local forests.[95]

Despite deforesting large stretches of the landscape, Preclassic and Classic agriculturalists managed to preserve enough old growth forests that massive hardwoods were able to be incorporated into Late Classic construction programs. Paleoenvironmental studies by David Lentz and colleagues indicate that the Tikal community sustained significant areas of mature forests at least up through the 700s CE. Charcoal analyses indicate that Late Classic Tikal residents

continued to have access to the same preferred fuelwood species that still dominate the forests around the site today. Most of the charcoal samples exhibited
parallel ray cells when viewed through a scanning electron microscope. Parallel
rays, as opposed to convergent rays, indicate that the charcoal came from trees
with broad, mature trunks. This indicates that Late Classic residents still had access to mature growth forests for their firewood. Despite the value of pine for
fuel and ritual burns, a 180-hectare patch of pine trees located in a *bajo* about
18 km northeast of the site center was managed carefully enough to remain a resource up through the Late Classic Period. Limited evidence for soil erosion in
any of the reservoirs ringing the relatively steep slopes of the site center suggest
that plenty of trees remained in the area to anchor the soil. Large, old growth
trees were likely felled using a combination of stone axes, fire, and/or girdling,
and were only harvested if other members of its species remained nearby to seed
replacements.[96]

By the Late Classic Period, the civic-ceremonial core was surrounded
by a garden city of residential compounds interspersed with homegardens,
orchards, agricultural plots, young fallowed tracts, and stands of mature, old
growth forests.[97] Using remote sensing and pedestrian survey data, Lentz and
colleagues estimated that over 14.3 million tons of wood would have been
available in the 425 sq. mi. catchment area around the site and that 43,000 tons
(86 million pounds) could have been harvested sustainably per year. Their
calculations of all the wood needs from fuel to construction and everything in
between would have been over 46,000 tons per year based on a population of
45,000 people. This population estimate now appears to be very conservative
after lidar digital elevation models have revealed the full extent of the community. Taken together, it appears that by the time of its population peak during
the 700s CE, Tikal would no longer have been able to continue its earlier sustainable forest-management practices without importing materials from other
regions.[98]

Even when sustainable-management practices began to bend during the population peak of the Late Classic period, it is clear that the community never completely exhausted its local forest resources. In 695 CE, Jasaw Chan K'awiil, the
twentieth-sixth ruler of the Tikal Dynasty won a decisive battle against the arch-
rival Kaanu'l (Snake) Dynasty and restored Tikal to a position of power after a
130-year hiatus in monumental construction. He and his immediate successors
subsequently made up for lost time, overseeing one of the largest construction
programs in the site's history, which included the erection of many of the site's
now iconic temple pyramids. A careful analysis of the species used for the lintels
and roofbeams of these vaunted temples by Lentz and Hockaday shows that sufficient mature sapodilla trees existed for construction purposes into the 700s
CE. Although it is possible that the long break in major construction activities

contributed to the availability of the mature sapodillas, their size indicates that they were already being cultivated and protected prior to the hiatus.[99]

The sapodilla lumber used to construct the first three major temples of this building campaign (Temples II, I, and IV, in chronological order) was from mature trees estimated to be well over 200 years old. Builders may have exhausted the available mature sapodilla supply during these building projects, as they switched to using logwood lumber for construction of Temples V and VI. However, the fact that any sapodilla remained in Tikal's forests at this time suggests that administrators took care to preserve enough of their numbers to allow for the regeneration of the species.[100] Although we do not know the exact mechanisms used to restrict over-exploitation of forest resources, it is likely that certain tracts were privately held as kin-based, heritable lands. It is also possible that the ruling dynasty of Tikal, which was founded near the end of the first century CE, may have directly controlled a portion of Tikal's catchment area in a similar fashion to the private forests of the Aztec *tlatoani* (emperor).[101]

Apiculture

An additional important reason for maintaining healthy tracts of forest around population centers was to support meliponiculture—the tending of *Melipona* bee species (Figure 3.7). This genus of stingless bees is native to the New World tropics, and several species were tended in the Maya lowlands during the Classic Period. Although it is unclear whether the level of interference by humans rose to the level of full domestication, it is clear that communities actively maintained bee colonies for the purpose of enjoying bee products like honey and wax. Unfortunately, most of what we know about Pre-Colonial beekeeping practices derives from Colonial Era ethnohistoric texts. That said, archaeological correlates provide evidence for meliponiculture at least far back as the Early Postclassic, so it is not unlikely that similar beekeeping traditions were thriving during the Classic Period.[102]

In addition to its importance as a food or beverage sweetener, a source of vitamins, and an antibacterial, honey is one of two key ingredients in *balche'*— a fermented mead-like beverage. The other key ingredient is bark from the *Lonchocarpus longistylus* (pittier) tree, which confers hallucinogenic properties. Intoxicating, hallucinogenic balche' was (and still is) an important component of rituals and ceremonies that require participants to enter altered states. The word in Yucatec is related to ba'alche'—which means "wild animal"—an indicator of the transformation that one undergoes after consuming the beverage. It is possible that Maya communities were incorporating balche' into ceremonies at least as far back as the Preclassic Period, if for no other reason than it was also

Figure 3.7 Images of modern-day meliponiculture (the tending of the Melipona bee species) from the town of Ek Balam in northern Yucatan: a hollowed-out log partly sealed on both ends and used as a hive (top left); a wooden box serving as a hive (top right); and, a close-up view of the Melipona bees within the box hive (bottom) (photos courtesy of Sarah Taylor).

used as a purgative and in several ceremonies that called for ritual purging of participants. Honey and fermented honey were also used for medicinal purposes and as offerings to deities.[103] Beehives were so important during the Postclassic Period that destruction of a rival communities' beehives was consistently used as a metaphor for total socioeconomic destruction.[104]

Pre-Colonial meliponiculture was likely but one component of a multi-crafting economic system in which households supplemented other forms of income, such as farming, ceramic production, or tool manufacture, with the relatively low-impact practice of beekeeping. Limestone disks used to cover beehives cultivated in hollow logs have been found throughout the Postclassic urban center of Mayapan, providing evidence for a Pre-Colonial beekeeping practice that may have been used earlier on during the Classic Period. The Mayapan model suggests that households tended apiaries throughout even densely populated urban neighborhoods. The stingless nature of the bees limited the risks of maintaining hives within cities, and their proximity to homegardens would have aided the pollination of useful trees and other plants.[105]

Bee colonies cultivated in Classic Maya communities also provided a necessary source of vectors for pollination of agricultural fields and the surrounding forests. Most of the vegetation in the Maya lowlands is pollinated by animal vectors, and Melipona bees are specifically adapted to pollinate the variety of plant species that comprise the native Maya forests. Healthy forests and fields are as crucial to the survival of bee colonies as the bees are to the survival of the vegetation, and thus it would have been crucial to maintain as many tracts of secondary and older growth forests in proximity to communities as possible. Ethnographic studies have demonstrated that one of the biggest challenges to maintaining healthy colonies today is rampant deforestation, suggesting that concerns for bee colonies may have factored into Pre-Colonial forest-management strategies.[106]

In addition to keeping colonies within communities, there were likely colonies that were maintained in older growth forests where they would be more protected from natural disasters like hurricanes. Healthy forests were also important sources of products used in traditional beekeeping practices, such as the hollowed logs that served as beehives. Trees like gumbo-limbo were also important for beekeeping as their leaves were rubbed on the beehive logs to deter other insects from invading the colonies.[107]

Summary

Most of what we know about Classic Maya forest-management practices is drawn from paleoenvironmental analyses, including pollen, charcoal, and erosion analyses, as well as ethnohistoric and ethnographic analogies. High concentrations of valuable tree species in and around ancient Maya sites are remnants of propagation and cultivation strategies that we now know date back to the Archaic Period. The modern forest compositions of the Maya lowlands have been heavily shaped by generations of knowledgeable agroforesters who promoted the growth of the most useful plants for food, lumber, fuel, medicine, and many other purposes.

The extensive forest clearance that resulted from Preclassic Period swidden farming systems contributed to a series of environmental crises in several subregions of the lowlands during the Preclassic to Classic Period transition. Classic Period communities likely learned from these mistakes and developed forest-management practices that sustained growing populations for over seven centuries. Such practices included shaping and tending the young forests that sprung up from fallowed fields as well as conserving valuable sapodilla and other trees in old growth forests. They protected stands of particularly useful species like pine using systems like the *pet koto'ob* of the modern Yucatec Maya. Elite lineages may have limited the harvesting of certain forest products through their control over ancestral lands. The bee-vegetation feedback loop was likely an integral component of the complex system of natural eco-biological arrangements tended and influenced by Classic communities to get what they needed from their environment while maintaining a socio-ecological balance.

Tree cover in communities like Tikal was carefully managed for much of the Early and Late Classic Periods, but due to political and demographic circumstances, there were episodes of increased consumption over the course of the 700s CE.[108] Fallow periods likely grew increasingly truncated in communities across the lowlands by the Late Classic to sustain the continuous population growth. The socio-ecological symbiosis established among city, forest, and field over the course of the Early and Middle Classic gave way to an increasing proportion of land being used for agriculture. The difficulty of maintaining the forest-conservation strategies that had worked so well for centuries was compounded in the eighth and ninth centuries by climatic and socio-political crises. The role that environmental stress played in the breakdown and reorganization of Maya civilization at the end of the Classic Period will be discussed in further detail in Chapter 7. Paleoenvironmental data indicate that many communities addressed the challenges of that turbulent era by adapting their forest exploitation practices. This socio-ecological resilience is evidenced today by the continued transmission of traditional ecological knowledge and forest-management strategies from generation to generation that date back to the Archaic Period.

4

Fields

Introduction

For much of the twentieth century, researchers believed that the Classic Maya were swidden farmers who used rotating field systems similar to those of the Colonial Era northern lowlands. Swidden, or slash-and-burn, farming involves clearing stretches of forest using handheld tools and controlled fires, growing crops there for two or three years, and then moving to the next plot while the previous is left to regenerate. Practiced around the world, it is considered one of the earliest and most rudimentary forms of agricultural production. The settlement studies of the 1950s to 1960s, however, forced researchers to grapple with the fact that Classic Period population levels were likely too highly elevated to have been supported exclusively by a slash-and-burn agricultural system. Settlement studies also identified ancient landscape modifications, including terraces and raised-field beds, that pointed to more intensive agricultural strategies. Lidar-based studies have allowed for an even more nuanced understanding of just how much the Maya engineered their environments for maximal sustainable food production.[1]

Another big change to our understanding of Classic Maya food production concerns the range of species that they cultivated. Advances in phytolith and pollen analyses, along with a larger data set in general, indicate that beyond maize, squash, and beans, Maya farmers also cultivated a wide variety of chile peppers, root crops, weedy grasses, and fruit trees. Our current picture of Pre-Colonial Maya agricultural systems is very different from the one painted fifty years ago and includes a finer understanding of how they changed over time. If we view Classic agricultural systems as part of the longer arc of Pre-Colonial food-production developments, we see that they represent millennia of traditional ecological knowledge put to work. Through trial and error, Maya communities learned to create sustainable, intensive production programs tailored to specific environmental niches.[2]

By the Late Classic Period, farms across the lowlands were producing massive amounts of a wide range of crops to support burgeoning populations.[3] It is remarkable how Classic Maya communities were able to create immense terrace, canal, and raised-field systems without the help of beasts of burden or wheeled carts. Aside from limited waterborne transport in certain areas, all engineering

The Maya and Climate Change. Kenneth E. Seligson, Oxford University Press. © Oxford University Press 2023.
DOI: 10.1093/oso/9780197652923.003.0004

projects were completed using solely human labor.[4] Updated carrying capacity estimates based on lidar-derived digital elevation models suggest that most centers in the Peten would have had access to sufficient cultivable land to support even the large populations of the Late Classic. Some centers may have even been able to produce agricultural surpluses for export or maintained larger tracts of forests than previously thought.[5]

Diversity was one of the defining characteristics of Classic Period agricultural systems. They were tailored to local environments and socio-political conditions across the lowlands and included mixtures of homegardens, infields, outfields, and managed forests. Farmers used polycultural and multi-cropping strategies that maximized efficiency and sustainability by mimicking natural growing conditions.[6] In general, Classic Maya communities epitomized the idea of the "garden city" with residential compounds interspersed with green areas dedicated to food production. The diversity of strategies employed across the lowlands, as well as within individual communities, provided them with options that allowed residents to adapt to changing social, political, and climatic circumstances. This chapter explores the diversity of local adaptive capacities that allowed Classic Maya agricultural systems and the communities they supported to thrive for over seven centuries.

Crops

By the height of the Classic Period, farmers across the lowlands had adapted species from across Mesoamerica, and even from as faraway as the Amazon, into an ecologically balanced agroforestry suite. They developed cultivation methods that exploited the natural cycles and feedback loops of their crops. Their capacity to adopt new plants into their intricate homegarden and milpa systems presaged the adoption of the numerous species introduced from Asia and Africa after the Spanish invasion. Learning from the natural world around them as well as the experience of dozens of prior generations, Classic Maya farmers created a sustainable agricultural mosaic that met the challenges of steadily growing populations and periodic climatic downturns. Scott Fedick recently compiled an exhaustive list in which he identified 497 food plants that were cultivated by the Pre-Colonial Maya, 451 of which had natural ranges that included the Maya lowlands. It is also important to remember that food plants would not only have been important as sustenance for Maya communities but also as media to communicate with deities through offerings, to convey messages of respect as tribute, or to reinforce social relationships as gifts.[7] What follows is a quick overview of the origins and nutritional contributions of the most prominent crops grown in the Classic lowlands.[8]

The Three Sisters

Maize (*Zea mays* L.), squash (*Cucurbita spp.*), and beans (*Phaseolus spp.*)—the three sisters—were among the most prominent crops of the Classic Maya diet, though we now know they were complemented by a wide range of other cultigens (Figure 4.1). The importance of maize in particular during the Classic Period is supported by palynological, isotopic, and iconographic evidence. Isotopic data from eastern lowlands suggests that maize likely accounted for more than 70% of protein in the average diet during the Classic Period.[9] The Maize God was one of the most important deities of the Classic pantheon, and divine rulers often impersonated him during important ritual events. Maize was central to Maya creation stories in which the gods created humans out of maize.[10] However, we must also recognize that our conception of maize as *the* dominant Maya crop results at least in part from preservation biases and an outsized focus on maize in early ethnohistoric accounts.[11]

Despite its prominence in the Classic Maya diet, maize was not native to the Maya lowlands. The ancestor of maize was a tiny grass called *teosinte* that grew in the highlands of central and western Mexico. Advances in phytolith and starch grain analyses have detected the presence of maize at the Xihuatoxtla rock shelter in the west-central Mexican state of Guerrero dating to as early as 6700 BCE.[12] The Xihuatoxtla dates are in accordance with genetic studies of maize and

Figure 4.1 The three sisters (maize, beans, and squash) growing together in a Mesoamerican milpa (photo by Paul Rogé, accessed and used under the Creative Commons Attribution 4.0 International license).

teosinte that suggest the upper limits of their divergence should be around 9000 BCE. Genetic studies also suggest that there was a single domestication center in the Balsas River drainage area of south-central Mexico, with subsequent diversification in the nearby highlands.[13] Over several millennia, early cultivators selected plants with larger-sized kernels and eventually transported the crop to the lowlands where new varieties were developed. By the Classic Period, Maya communities were consuming maize that looked much more like a modern corncob than like the ancestral *teosinte*.

Full of starch, maize was one of the key sources of carbohydrates for Pre-Colonial Maya populations. The development of *nixtmalization* (the process by which maize kernels are boiled or soaked in burnt lime-infused water) was a critical step paving the way for the grass to become a staple Mesoamerican crop. In addition to facilitating the grinding of kernels into dough, the alkalinity of lime unleashed the large stores of vitamins, like niacin, locked within the maize kernels and increased their calcium content. Alkaline treatment remains a critical step in the preparation of maize, and you may even see the word "nixtamalized" on boxes of corn flour at the supermarket. For the Pre-Colonial populations of Mesoamerica, lime treatment prevented pellagra, a niacin-deficiency condition.[14] Although the process increases the overall nutritional benefits of the kernels, it does not remedy maize's deficiencies in lysine, tryptophan, vitamin A, vitamin C, B vitamins, and iron.[15] These and other nutrients were provided by the variety of cultigens grown and consumed alongside maize.

Beans do not survive long in the archaeological record, and thus it is more difficult to trace the process of bean domestication. The common bean is also an extremely diverse crop today, in terms of both its morphology and the range of environments in which it grows.[16] Although the earliest macrobotanical evidence for domesticated common beans in the archaeological record of Mesoamerica dates to only 300 BCE in the central highlands,[17] genetic evidence suggests a lengthy domestication process on par with maize. Two major gene pools of domesticated beans exist today in the genus *Phaseolus*—one originating in Mesoamerica and the other in Andean South America. Recent research indicates that the main Mesoamerican variety (*Phaseolus vulgaris* L.) stems from one Pre-Colonial Era domestication event in the Lerma-Santiago Basin of west-central Mexico.[18] However, recent research has confirmed that a variety of lima bean (*Phaseolus lunatus* L.) was native to—and domesticated in—the Maya lowlands.[19]

Among other nutritional benefits, beans are a key source of the amino acid lysine, which is absent in both maize and squash. Rounding out its impressive nutritional profile are proteins, iron, phosphorus, magnesium, manganese, and, in lesser amounts, zinc, copper and calcium. The complementary dietary relationship between beans and maize goes beyond the basic nutritional components as both benefit nutritionally from being soaked and cooked. Cooking inactivates heat-labile anti-nutritional compounds in beans and facilitates the digestion and absorption of its starches and proteins.[20]

Squash is likely the earliest domesticated of the three sisters and may be one of the earliest plants of any kind domesticated in Mesoamerica. At least four different species of the *Cucurbita* genus were domesticated in Mesoamerica, one of which—bitter pumpkin, or *Cucurbita lundelliana* L.H. Bailey—may have been domesticated in the Maya lowlands.[21] The oldest current dates for domesticated squash seeds anywhere in Mesoamerica come from Guila Naquitz cave in the southern Mexican state of Oaxaca and date to around 8000 BCE.[22]

All the squash species were likely first cultivated to improve seed production, and it was only later on, over the course of their cultivation histories, that farmers began to select for more edible flesh. The flesh, once it became less bitter and more abundant, proved to be a good source of carbohydrates and some vitamins, but squash's main nutritional contribution came from its seeds. Cucurbita seeds are a rich source of unsaturated fatty acids as well as protein, which accounts for about 24% of the seeds' dry weight. In addition, cucurbita seeds are a good source of antioxidants and vitamin E.[23] Together, the three sisters provided almost every facet of a well-balanced diet for Maya consumers: carbohydrates, lipids, proteins, vitamins, and minerals. They were, however, far from the only dietary options available to Classic Maya communities.

Tree Crops

Among the diverse components of the Classic agricultural system, cultivators tended a variety of reliable fruit trees in their homegardens and nearby orchards.[24] Prominent fruit trees domesticated in the Maya lowlands included guava (*Psidium guajava* L.), hog plum (*Spondias purpurea* L.), nance (*Byrsonima crassifolia* L.), black sapote (*Diospyros nigra* J.F. Gmel.), mamey (*Pouteria sapota* Jacq.), papaya (*Carica papaya* L.), calabash (*Crescenti a cujete* L.), and cacao (*Theobroma cacao* L.). Other fruit trees cultivated by the Classic Maya that were either domesticated elsewhere or never fully domesticated included avocado (*Persea americana* Mill.), fig (*Ficus cotinifolia* Kunth), chico sapote (*Manilkara zapota* L.), cashew (*Anacardium occidentale* L.), and *capulín*/Jamaican cherry (*Muntingia calabura* L.). In addition to providing delicious edible fruits, the leaves, branches, and bark of many of these trees provided medicinal extracts, dyes, kindling, and shade. Maya agroforesters also tended coyol (*Acrocomia aculeata* Jacq.) and cohune (*Attalea cohune* Mart.) palms for food, beverages, and other resources.[25]

Cacao was a special cultivar that only grew in hot, humid environments with deep, moist soil, and plenty of shade.[26] Although it likely originated in Amazonia, cacao was traded northward prior to the start of the Preclassic Period and was eventually domesticated in the Maya lowlands.[27] It was likely originally cultivated for its edible fruit pulp and only later did cultivators discover the enticing properties of its seeds, or "beans." The toasted and ground beans are, of course, the foundational ingredient in chocolate. There is little evidence, however, that the Classic Maya enjoyed chocolate in the same way that people around the world do today: as a sweetened candy bar. For the Maya, cacao (or cocoa) powder was mixed with water, chiles, and other savory flavors and imbibed as a (possibly fermented) liquid. Poured back and forth between special vessels until it was light and foamy, cacao beverages were largely restricted to elite consumption. Classic Period vessels depict the enjoyment of these special beverages in palace scenes and suggest a close connection between the all-important Maize God and cacao.[28]

Classic Period farmers across the lowlands took advantage of any possible microenvironments, no matter how small, to cultivate this difficult, alluring crop. Even in the dry north, farmers reserved the special microenvironments of some *rejolladas* for cacao cultivation. Cave entrances in the hills west of Tikal likewise could have been engineered to serve as circumscribed cacao orchards. Cacao may have even been cultivated in special growing areas at Tikal as well. The singular value of cacao beans eventually led to their use as currency in parts of Mesoamerica by the Postclassic Period, a time when money really did grow on trees. Cacao's uniqueness continues into the present as it is possibly the only word to make its way into modern English from Classic Mayan (*kakaw*) (Figure 4.2).[29]

Additional Crops

Researchers had long suspected that root crops played a larger role in Pre-Colonial Maya agricultural systems than could be identified using early twentieth-century analytical techniques.[30] Advances in phytolith and pollen analyses, as well as the spectacular preservation of the farming village of Ceren in El Salvador has now confirmed that Classic Period communities did indeed cultivate a range of tubers. Most prominent among them was manioc (*Manihot esculenta* Crantz), also known as cassava, likely native to and domesticated in Amazonia but imported into the Mesoamerican lowlands by at least 3000 BCE. Though not as flavorful as maize, the more drought-tolerant manioc would have been a more reliable source of starchy calories if growing conditions declined.[31] Recent residue analyses of ceramic vessels from the site of Copan in Honduras

Figure 4.2 A cacao tree (*Theobroma cacao*) with ripe cacao pods growing from the trunk (photo by Nasser Halaweh, accessed and used under the Creative Commons Attribution 4.0 International license).

suggest that residents of elite households consumed fermented manioc and maize beverages, probably flavored with chiles and cacao.[32]

At Ceren, and most likely many other Classic communities, manioc was grown on sloping terrain to avoid waterlogged soil. The thick soils deposited on the margins of seasonally inundated low-lying areas called *bajos* throughout the central lowlands would have provided prime areas for manioc and other tuber cultivation.[33] Many root crops produce pollen with especially poor preservation rates, and thus even though we now have secure evidence they were grown across the lowlands, their relative contributions to local diets are likely still underreported.[34] Other root crops now identified as part of the Classic Maya diet through phytolith, pollen, and microscopic carbonized evidence include malanga (*Xanthosoma spp.*), sweet potato (*Ipomoea batatas* L.), jicama (*Pachyrhizus erosus* L.), and arrowroot (*Maranta arundinacea* L.). Jicama, sweet potato, and a species of malanga were likely domesticated in the Maya lowlands.[35]

Classic Period cultivators rounded out their diets by tending a variety of chile peppers (*Capsicum annum* L.), herbs like amaranth (*Amaranthus spp.*), epazote (*Chenopodium berlandieri* Moq.), tomatoes (*Lycopersicon esculentum* Mill.), tomatillos (*Physalis philadelphica* Lam.), and sunflowers (*Helianthus annuus* L.), gourds including chayote (*Sechium edule* Jacq.), legumes, and cacti. Vanilla (*Vanilla planifolia* Andrews) is a species of orchid that was domesticated in the Maya lowlands.[36] Among the cactus species cultivated and at least semi-domesticated by Maya communities was pitahaya (*Hylocereus undatus* Haw.), also known as pitaya or dragon fruit. Although today the plant is perhaps most closely associated with Southeast Asia (the world's largest exporter), it is indigenous to the tropical Americas. Evidence suggests that lowland cultivators were already selecting for specific traits of the fruit as far back as 3400 BCE, and it was undoubtedly grown in homegardens across the lowlands during the Classic Period.[37] Nopal cactus (*Opuntia spp.*) may have been more common in the dryer northern lowlands, cultivated for its edible pads and sweet fruit known in English as prickly pear and in Spanish as *tuna*. Not only would the prickly pears have provided a source of sugar, B vitamins, and vitamin C, but the seeds could also be ground into an edible paste.[38]

Other xerophytic cultivars especially useful at northern sites like Chunchucmil were acacia (*Propsopis spp.*), several agave species (*Agave spp.*) like henequen, and bottle gourd (*Leucaena* spp.). In addition to providing food and alcohol like *pulque*, agave was also used to create fibers for cordage and textiles. Rope would have been necessary to fasten roof beams together, to hang food and implements, and to fish, among other miscellaneous uses.[39] Another important cultivar that would have served both dietary and utilitarian purposes was cotton (*Gossypium hirsutum* L.), which was cultivated at least as early as the Middle Preclassic Period.[40] Cottonseed oil was used for cooking purposes, and cotton fibers were one of the most widely used materials for making textiles for clothing, curtains, and blankets, as well as the tapestries that lined the walls of elite buildings.[41]

In addition to the preferred food species, Maya cultivators also knew which plants might sustain them through periods of food stress when other crops were failing. As discussed in the previous chapter, ramón, or breadnut, trees (*Brosimum alicastrum* Sw.) were prevalent in and around Classic Period settlements. Ethnohistoric and ethnographic accounts relate the consumption of ramón nuts by communities during years of poor maize harvests. Although the nuts themselves were not very tasty, the tree is hardier than many other food-bearing plants and thus could have continued to produce edible materials in times of drought. Tending, or at least not felling, ramón trees around settlements would have provided a buffer for communities when preferred food sources failed. There is also some evidence that the weedy spinach-like plant chaya (*Cnidoscolus aconitifolius* Mill. and *Cnidoscolus chayamansa*), which was likely domesticated in the northern lowlands and tended in homegardens, could have been regarded as a famine food in the past. It would also likely have served as a rich source of protein, calcium, and vitamin C even under normal conditions, though it would have required special management to avoid harm from the tiny prickles that cover the leaves of several varieties.[42] During extreme, multiyear droughts, communities could have turned first to root crops like manioc and yucca (*Yucca guatemalensis*) for a few years, and then to hearts of palm, cactus pads, and even tree bark in extremely dire circumstances.[43] The switch to consuming mainly ramón nuts, cacti, and other semi-cultivated plants when necessary demonstrates the adaptive flexibility of Maya communities. Willingness to adapt dietary patterns in times of stress is a key component of socio-ecological resilience.[44]

A brief summary of the plant foods grown or tended by Classic Maya cultivators includes (but is not limited to) maize, beans, squash, agave, amaranth, arrowroot, avocado, black sapote, bottle gourd, cacao, calabash, chaya, chayote, chico sapote, chiles, coyol palm, epazote, figs, guava, hog plum, jicama, malanga, mamey, manioc, nance, figs, nopal, papaya, pitahaya, ramón, sunflower, sweet potato, tomatoes, tomatillos, and vanilla. Keep in mind that this is just a tiny snippet of the extensive list of edible plants cultivated by Classic Period Maya farmers. Analyses of residues scraped from the insides of ancient pottery can provide insights into what types of foods were contained therein and even which ones may have been mixed together. However, aside from a few hieroglyphic vessels that list the specific types of cacao- or maize-based beverages that could be found inside (Figure 4.3), no written recipes survive from the Classic Period.[45] One can only imagine the wide range of delicious recipes that Classic Maya cooks developed with such a long list of ingredients.

The Earliest Maya Farmers

As far back as the Paleo-Indian Period, humans were altering the Mesoamerican landscape and becoming more familiar with local plants and animals. Domestication was already underway for certain squash varieties by 8000 BCE, indicating that the process began even earlier. Domesticated maize was transported from its homeland in southwestern Mesoamerica to South America

Figure 4.3 A roll-out image from a cylindrical Classic Period ceramic vessel. The inscription along the top rim of the vessel reads "*ti yuta[l] kakaw*" or "for fruity cacao" (image courtesy of Dumbarton Oaks Research Collection and Library, Justin Kerr, and the Maya Vase Database, Kerr Number 1941; translation courtesy of Marc Zender).

as early as 5500 BCE, where it underwent continued selection for larger kernels.[46] The development of the suite of crops that would eventually compose the Classic Period Maya cornucopia was a gradual process. Even during the Classic Period, continued selection for certain characteristics in different parts of the lowlands led to the development of even more varieties of each of the domesticated and semi-domesticated species.

Pollen, charcoal, and erosion evidence suggest that early agriculturalists were clearing forest tracts to plant crops like maize as early as 3400 BCE in northern Belize. It is unclear whether these early agriculturalists were new migrants to the region or a suite of domesticates and the knowledge of how to grow them diffused to foraging groups already living there. Recent genetic evidence suggests a south to north migration of small populations into the region between 5300 and 3600 BCE that mixed with existing local populations. These migrants may have brought with them a suite of domesticates that included new strains of maize.[47] The transportation and adoption of new food plants meant that some cultural practices and aspects of ancestral landscapes may have been transplanted and recreated in the Maya lowlands.[48] The early agriculturalists took advantage of the moist conditions of the river systems on the edges of the region to combat the challenges of the stark dry season. Either groups of these early farmers or their agricultural knowledge and botanicals followed the river floodplains farther and farther inland, eventually branching out around seasonal and perennial wetlands or isolated freshwater springs.[49]

Maize-based agriculture took hold at different rates in different parts of the Maya lowlands, but by the start of the Middle Preclassic Period (c. 1000 BCE) small sedentary communities existed in most subregions.[50] The peripheral river system regions exhibit the most precocious developments in architecture and population size, likely resulting from their earlier transition to sedentary life. The massive scale of the recently identified Middle Formative Usumacinta (MFU) sites like Aguada Fénix on the western edge of the Maya lowlands suggests that relatively large populations were already established in the region by 1000 BCE. We do not yet have many details about early agriculture in this region, but local farmers undoubtedly took advantage of the Usumacinta floodplain to support food production. Large agricultural communities also developed by around 1000 BCE in northern Belize. Though we do not yet have evidence for sites quite as massive in scale as the MFU sites, centers like Cuello represented the culmination of centuries of increasing social complexity resulting from the transition to agricultural production.[51]

The earliest farmers in the interior of the Maya lowlands were swidden (slash-and-burn) cultivators. They would cut down most of the trees and vegetation in a chosen tract and then use controlled burns to clear remaining vegetation and re-introduce organic nutrients back into the soil. If done correctly, slash-and-burn is one of the lowest intensity forms of agriculture, requiring much less labor and time than the construction of the advanced terrace or raised-field systems that came later. Land availability was not an issue during the Preclassic Period, at least not at the beginning, and it appears ever larger portions of forest were cleared for agriculture. As groups became increasingly sedentary and the populations of the Preclassic centers continued to grow, one of the main paths to greater food production was extensification—that is, doing the same thing over a more extensive area. This led to the erosion of soils from hillsides and the filling in of some bajos at Preclassic sites like El Mirador, San Bartolo, and Tikal.[52]

The consequences of the extensive swidden agriculture that characterized the latest stages of the Preclassic Period would have informed later Classic Period agricultural practices as populations began to rise once more. However, the disasters of extensification were not the only lessons passed on to Classic Period communities by their Preclassic forebears. The earliest levels of some raised wetland fields in northern Belize date to the Late Preclassic, indicating that Maya farmers were already engineering non-arable lands into food-producing tracts very early on.[53] Likewise, Late Preclassic communities like San Bartolo and Minanha, in Belize attempted to stem the tide of soil erosion by constructing terraces.[54] Terrace construction at the small farming village of Chan in Belize may have begun as early as the Middle Preclassic.[55] In some areas, Preclassic terraces and wetland fields were continuously farmed all the way through the Classic Period.

Classic Period Agriculture

The benefits of agricultural intensification were passed on from generation to generation and from community to community. As populations trended upward again during the Classic Period, communities developed numerous ways to produce as much food as necessary from their local environments while avoiding the environmental degradation that stressed many of the large Late Preclassic centers. In some regions, Classic farmers were even able to take advantage of the soils that accumulated at bajo margins because of earlier erosion. Generations of socio-ecological knowledge fed the development of a series of sustainable agricultural systems that powered the great cultural fluorescence of the Classic Period.

Social Organization

Ethnohistoric and ethnographic insights in combination with settlement-pattern analyses provide general models for the social organization of Classic Period agricultural production. The first families to settle in a given area would claim ownership of the best arable lands, in turn influencing where the earliest population centers developed. Tracing family lineages would have included a significant spatial component. Burying ancestors under household residences is a long-standing practice in Mesoamerica, which serves to both spiritually and literally tie families to their lands. Over time, households staked claims to new territories that had either never previously been farmed or had been abandoned by earlier tenants. Agricultural wealth was undoubtedly a key source of social status during the Classic Period, differentiating elite from non-elite households on a broad spectrum. The investment in such landscape modifications as agricultural terraces reflected the significance of owning and controlling agricultural land for promoting socioeconomic status.[56]

Settlement-pattern studies and landscape analyses indicate that there was likely a range of management practices across the lowlands, including highly centralized landscape-modification projects, completely autonomous household production, and every possible combination in between. For the most part, day-to-day agricultural production was likely organized at the household or cooperating household level.[57] Lineage-based agricultural plots allowed successive generations to take advantage of and build upon the agricultural infrastructure of their forebears. The spatial correlates of such household plots are now being identified thanks to lidar digital elevation models in some areas, like north-western Belize.[58]

Within small-scale communities like Chan, households likely joined together to occasionally add new terraces, slowly expanding their networks over time. At least within such smaller communities, households were largely self-sufficient in terms of food production, though they might also be obliged to donate a portion of their annual yields to authorities at the nearest large center.[59] In some cases, smaller farming villages may have decided on and organized labor for agricultural landscape modifications at the community level. This does not mean there was a central authority overseeing the project, but relations between households were direct enough that they could make joint decisions about community planning.[60] Spatial analyses of sparsely settled areas with ample farmland like southern Belize highlight the importance of intra- and inter-household social dynamics for determining houselot locations and the development of inequality.[61]

Household-level agricultural self-sufficiency occasionally benefited from centralized agricultural projects instituted within larger communities like Caracol in western Belize. The relative rapidity and uniformity with which a massive Classic Period terracing program was implemented at Caracol suggests that authorities at the site center oversaw the project. Relatively even spacing of farmsteads across the Caracol landscape indicates some form of standardized land-management code in which each residential group had approximately 2.2 hectares to farm. Arlen and Diane Chase propose that each household would have been agriculturally self-sufficient and even produced surpluses for sale at local markets.[62] In other communities, like Tikal and El Zotz in northern Guatemala, some degree of centralized planning would likely have been necessary to engineer the large-scale bajo and bajo margin cultivation zones that have now been uncovered using lidar.[63] The larger and denser the population of a community, the more likely that some form of centralized decision-making would have been necessary to ensure sustainable production.

Elite households were directly involved in agricultural production in some communities, although it is unclear how many members would have been involved in day-to-day field operations.[64] As is the case around the world, it is more likely that individuals from lower status households engaged in the more grueling aspects of food production. Isotopic and archaeo-faunal analyses indicate that elite households enjoyed access to a wider range of foodstuffs than non-elite households. This meant that their diets were more liable to fluctuate based on socio-political and ecological conditions. For example, non-elites consumed higher proportions of maize or manioc than their elite counterparts. On the one hand, they enjoyed much less frequent access to animal protein and may have more frequently eaten less desirable sources of calories like ramón or chaya, a leafy plant that has a surprisingly high protein content.[65] The foods that made up the vast bulk of their diet were thus the most reliable products of the agricultural system. Elite diets, on the other hand, included rarer products such as wild game, the most economically valuable fruits, and plant foods imported from other communities. Should ecological downturns diminish harvests of specialty crops or trade routes be disrupted, the normally diverse elite diet might be restricted to something more in line with that of their non-elite neighbors.[66]

A Mosaic of Agricultural Practices

Homegardens, Infields, and Orchards

There were much higher proportions of green space interspersed between residences of Classic Maya communities than in the major population centers of today. Maya households tended gardens adjacent to and scattered among their homes. These gardens contained cultivars used for food, medicine, and other utilitarian functions. Why waste space on a handsome grass lawn when you could grow guava and avocado trees to provide fresh fruits for snacking, chile peppers to spice up your midday meal, and arrowroot to add a starch to your supper? Not to mention the fact that the larger trees provided shaded locations to prepare meals and some measure of protection from powerful storms. Variously called homegardens, housegardens, household gardens, houselot gardens, and door-yard gardens in the scholarly literature, these residence-adjacent areas of culti-vation incorporated a wide array of economically important plants in multiple interlocking strata. They were an efficient and practical use of space that provided not only a measure of food security and autonomy for individual households but also a protected area to tend saplings and seedlings before transporting them to the more distant milpas.[67]

Homegardens would have served as testaments to generations' worth of ec-ological knowledge as well as conveniently located "classrooms" for passing knowledge onto the next generations. Residents could enrich the garden soils by adding organic waste produced by the household and watered by pot irriga-tion (pouring water from ceramic vessels).[68] Homegardens were undoubtedly used for growing medicinal plants to have handy for emergencies or to sell at the marketplace,[69] as well as special fruits that families might gift to neighbors and friends to maintain social ties.[70] They could also serve as laboratories for selecting new traits and crossbreeding certain varieties. In addition to growing a wide variety of plants, homegardens were also the locations for raising turkeys, dogs, rabbits, and other domesticated or semi-domesticated animals. Melipona apiculturalists likely had at least some of their colonies in homegardens as well.[71]

There is a distinction to be made between homegardens (which are located within houselots) and agricultural infields (which are larger plots where food plants are tended within settlement clusters). In addition to cultivating economically valuable trees and smaller plants in their own homegardens, Maya families relied on larger, extra-household networks to tend agricultural infields, likely at the neighborhood level. Infields mirrored the distant, more extensive outfields in terms of the milpa crops they grew—maize, beans, squash, herbs, and assorted tubers to name a few.

The large spaces that archaeologists find between residential architectural clusters within Classic Period settlements are most likely remnants of infields or orchards. Recent lidar-based studies have identified large houselots demarcated by stone walls in northwestern Belize that could have included a mix of homegardens, orchards, and infields within their boundaries.[72] Growing staple crops in such proximity to residences would have facilitated the meticulous management of crop growth cycles and avoided any complications that might have arisen from having to travel longer distances to produce food.[73] It also would have enabled the enhancement of soil productivity through the frequent addition of organic and human wastes. By contrast, the soilscapes of most modern urban centers are paved over and unused.[74] Diversity of growing locations, plot sizes, and cultigen combinations fostered resilience by providing alternative options should changes in environmental or socio-political circumstances lead to the failure of one component of the broader system.

Ethnographic and ethnohistoric evidence suggests that orchards of fruit-bearing trees were also woven into settlements. Archaeologists have uncovered mounds of rough boulders at northern sites like Chunchucmil that bear striking resemblance to the features modern farmers use to aggregate soil and provide anchors for fruit trees. Areas with shallow soils could still be used to grow many of the fruit-bearing trees discussed above. Surrounding infields and homegardens with larger stands of productive trees provided an added measure of protection from the elements—both the hot sun of the dry season and the powerful rains of the wet season.

Filled with homegardens, infields, and orchards, the garden cities of the Classic Period were thus largely self-sustaining places of sustenance. The urban farming boom of recent decades in the United States makes these agricultural cities a little less difficult to imagine. It would be like walking through a residential area today and instead of just seeing carefully curated flowerbeds, every home would have impressive vegetable gardens. Instead of vast suburban grass lawns, houselots would have ridged milpas of maize, squash, and manioc, interspersed with fruit-bearing trees. The small patches of trees that border houselots in some neighborhoods would all be utilitarian varieties—bearers of food, medicine, cordage, or dyes.

The agricultural systems that Maya communities developed over the course of the Preclassic and Classic Periods took advantage of every possible opportunity to contribute to subsistence security and sustainability. Many local systems successfully supported near continuous growth for the 700-plus years of the Classic Period. The knowledge and methods associated with the variety of Classic Period agricultural strategies survived both the Classic to Postclassic transition and the Spanish invasion and are still in use today.

Milpa Fields

In all likelihood, the archetypal Maya milpa written about in the earliest Spanish ethnohistoric accounts was quite similar to the majority of Classic Period agricultural outfields in many sub-regions of the lowlands.[75] Despite the effort required to clear forest tracts for planting, slash-and-burn is actually one of the most cost-effective agricultural strategies in terms of overall labor input.[76] Unfortunately, it is very difficult to identify low-intensity milpa production in the archaeological record. Ethnohistoric and ethnographic observations provide the most useful method for inferring how Classic Period farmers would have managed their milpa fields (Figure 4.4).

Figure 4.4 A modern Maya milpa in the early stages of the growing season outside the village of Ek Balam in northern Yucatan (photo courtesy of Sarah Taylor).

The milpa cycle begins toward the end of the dry season (the exact month varies based on annual conditions and local traditions). Farmers select and measure a forest tract to clear and sow. Wood cleared from the milpa is used for a variety of purposes including construction and fuel. After cutting down the most substantial vegetation in the plot, farmers use controlled fires to clear the remaining low-lying vegetation. This not only clears the land for crops but also reintroduces organic nutrients to the soil. Cultivators made sure to leave a number of particularly valuable trees untouched to provide shade, anchor the soil, and help seed the new forest that would spring up when the field was eventually left to fallow.

At the start of the rainy season, farmers plant their first round of crops. First, they plant fast-growing vine crops, such as chayote, to help fix nutrients in the soil and prevent erosion. Next up are maize, squashes, beans, and root crops interspersed with one another. The low-growing squash and root crop species help limit the growth of unwanted weeds.[77] Tomatoes, chile peppers, and other supplementary plants may be grown in patches throughout the milpa, though they are more likely to be found in homegardens. Intensive maintenance of the milpa during the growing season means protecting the crops from predatory insects and animals, removing harmful weeds, and encouraging the growth of useful "weeds" like silkleaf (*Lagascea mollis*) that stifle the growth of more toxic weeds.[78] The harvest usually begins toward the end of the rainy season. The edible parts are removed, and the rest of the plant is left in the field to dry and wither once the rains stop, reintroducing nutrients back to the soil.[79]

The next year, farmers restart the cycle by clearing the remaining vegetation from the previous year's crops. The secondary growth forest that develops when a milpa plot is left to fallow is carefully tended by farmers who prioritize the growth of the most useful species. It is never really abandoned, as agriculturalists continue to manage growth cycles and harvest edible and other useful products.[80] The regrowth of the forest species captures and reintroduces nutrients to the soil, which then allow the cycle to start anew. In some cases, the milpa cycle may be restarted after only seven to ten years of regrowth.[81]

It is possible that this system of relatively short fallow periods is a remnant of strategies developed during periods of population growth in the past. The original swidden milpa cycle may have included much longer fallow periods that would have allowed for the reintroduction of more nutrients to the soil and thus provided greater long-term sustainability. However, over the course of the Late Classic as landscapes became saturated and populations continued booming, farmers needed to experiment with methods for intensifying production that likely included shortening their fallow periods. Studies suggest that a short fallow system of one year of cropping followed by three years of rest or three years of cropping followed by five years of rest would have sustained high-level food production for many decades, albeit with gradually diminishing returns.[82] This may have been the scenario that characterized the final decades of the Classic Period.

Polyculture and Multi-Cropping

Classic Maya farmers employed a range of alternative methods to maximize efficiency and sustainability beyond shortening fallow periods. Polyculture—growing multiple crops at the same time on the same land—is a defining characteristic of the milpa system.[83] Grown together in a milpa plot, maize, gourds, and legumes enhance one another's growth and productivity. Increasing plant diversity enhances the microbial biomass content of the soil, in turn increasing the nutrients made available by carbon cycling. The three sisters provide an especially productive example of this system.[84]

Beans are the linchpin in this group, again hinting at an earlier adoption into the system than suggested by the archaeological record. The roots of leguminous plants mix with bacteria to produce specialized nitrogen-fixing nodules that help regulate nitrogen levels in the soil.[85] The nitrogen-regulating capacity of the bean thus increases the nitrogen available for the other sisters through both direct transfer of fixed nitrogen and the lack of competition that results from the legume's use of atmospheric instead of terrestrial nitrogen. On a non-molecular level, the sizes and shapes of the three plants complement each other. Maize grows tall, and its rigid stalks provide a structure for the bean vines to climb. Squash is a low grower whose broad leaves shade the ground in between the maize stalks, preventing the growth of weeds and maintaining soil humidity.[86]

Interspersing different species on the same plot helps sustain nutrient levels and moisture in the soil and allows species of different heights to enjoy varying amounts of sunlight.[87] Polyculture maximizes both vertical and horizontal space beyond the basic model of the three sisters. Subterranean tubers like manioc, arrowroot, or sweet potato would only require small patches aboveground for their stems and leaves. They can be interspersed with medicinal and culinary herbs that require even less space.[88]

It is also likely that many communities across the lowlands developed multi-cropping strategies by the Late Classic Period—that is, they planted sequential crops on the same land during the same growing season. The Itza farmers of the northwest Peten were still using this strategy in the 1990s to take advantage of existing soil viability and protect against potentially devastating species-specific pests.[89] Different crops are planted at different times throughout the growing season to maximize the productivity of each. The early planting of fast-growing gourds is followed by maize, beans, and root crops. Faster growing strains of maize might be harvested as soon as halfway through the rainy season, allowing for a third round of crops to be planted in their place. Maximizing diversity and space during the rainy season protects farming communities against the potential vagaries of crop failure due to irregular precipitation or climatic patterns, or an unfortunate infestation of crop-killing insects.

Agricultural Terracing

In several areas of the lowlands, polyculture and multi-cropping strategies were not enough to support the continuously growing Classic populations forever. Many communities developed intensification strategies that involved modifying their natural landscapes, to (1) produce more food within the same amount of cultivated territory; (2) produce food more often in the same amount of cultivated territory while minimizing environmental degradation; and/or (3) cultivate lands within their territory that were formerly unsuitable for milpa agriculture.

Stone terraces are one of the most archaeologically visible forms of intensified agricultural production in the Maya lowlands. Some communities built only a few terraces, while others—most prominently Caracol—converted almost every inch of sloping land into interlocking terrace systems. Lidar-derived digital elevation models have revealed that terracing practices were even more widespread than previously thought. The hundreds of terrace systems visible in the lidar imagery do not even account for the full range that were originally constructed as many were destroyed over time or remain buried by sediment.[90]

Terraces are found throughout the lowlands, though the greatest concentrations yet identified exist around the sprawling site of Caracol in west-central Belize, the site of La Milpa in northwestern Belize, in the Mopan River Valley of west-central Belize, in the Petexbatun region of the southwest Peten, Guatemala, and in the Río Bec region of Campeche State, Mexico. Although terrace construction in some places began as early as the Middle Preclassic, most larger terrace systems date to the Middle and Late Classic eras when population pressure motivated communities to intensify food production.[91] They helped farmers maximize agricultural land use while minimizing soil erosion and nutrition depletion.

Terraces are not found everywhere in the lowlands, however, and even communities with booming Late Classic populations and suitably sloping terrain such as Tikal did not appear to invest in much terrace construction. Somewhat surprisingly, hardly any terraces have been identified in the hilly Puuc region of northern Yucatan. The heterogeneity of land-management practices throughout the lowlands points to the importance of local socio-political and cultural preferences. Similarities in microenvironments and topographies did not necessarily translate to similarities in agricultural production schemes.[92]

Maya farmers and engineers shaped their agricultural landscapes with four general types of terraces: contour, cross-channel, box, and foot-slope.[93] Contour terraces, as their name suggests, follow the contours of hillslopes. They serve as retaining walls to prevent soil from eroding down the slope. By transforming a portion of previously forested hillsides into agricultural terraces, farmers maximized local food production while minimizing environmental degradation.[94] In addition to promoting soil and nutrient retention, contour terraces directed the flow of water down hillslopes and served to retain soil moisture.[95] In places like Chan, Belize, farmers excavated reservoirs uphill from their terrace systems with irrigation ditches running between individual terraces. This downhill irrigation allowed farmers to extend their crop cycles beyond the end of the rainy season. Some terraces were even constructed with their own small rainfall catchment areas for more localized irrigation. The over 1,200 terraces at Chan averaged 0.9 m high and ranged between 53 and 85 m in length, a construction effort that would have been spread out over many generations.[96]

The terrace systems of northern Belize, the Petexbatun, Río Bec, and other regions were likewise built up over time as farming households (or groups of households) occasionally extended existing terraces or constructed new ones. Although mainly built on noticeably sloping terrain, retention walls were also built at angles or even perpendicular to the gentler slopes of valley floors. These low, broad terraces trapped excess rainwater cascading off the slopes and allowed it to seep down into the deep valley soils for long-term retention.[97] In some areas, such as around Tamarindito in the Petexbatun, terraces were also likely watered by pot irrigation as suggested by the recovery of ceramic water vessels from within terrace plots.[98] The complexity of contour terrace systems across the lowlands demonstrates an intricate knowledge of landscape and dedicated foresight that spanned generations. The resulting networks so successfully took advantage of localized soil compositions, hydrology, and topographical nuances that they almost appear to have all been constructed from a master plan.[99]

Cross-channel terraces transect ravines or slope channels. They are also sometimes referred to as weirs or check dams and are discussed in more detail in the following chapter on water-management strategies. This type of terrace may have been more important for controlling water flow and soil erosion than providing a locale for agricultural production. By diverting water and soil flow horizontally instead of vertically, cross-channel retention walls fed the agricultural beds of the adjacent contour terraces.

Box terraces were built on either very gentle slopes or flat terrain and served as raised beds of deeper soils. Usually found near household structures, farmers likely used them as nurseries to manage the early stages of growth before special cultivars were transplanted to their final growing areas. Finally, foot- or toe-slope terraces were built at the foot of hillslopes to catch and retain soils eroding from above. Heavy rains would wash soil down the slopes into the toe-slope beds, frequently resupplying them with nutrients. The soil beds would also catch precipitation runoff to maintain soil moisture in the large, flat, growing areas.[100] Such deep soils would have provided desirable locations for not only growing the three sisters and their companion crops but also root crops like manioc.[101]

Even though terraces limited soil erosion, continuous cropping in one place would have led to the extraction of nutrients from the soils. Even if the right balance of milpa species were planted within the terraces, nutrients like phosphorus would not be replenished by any of the plants themselves. The lack of beasts of burden for transport or plowing also meant the lack of manure produced by those animals. Instead, Maya farmers likely recycled organic refuse from their households, such as wood ash and composted foodstuffs, as well as night soil (human fecal matter).[102] The recovery of snail shells from terrace plots may provide evidence of these household garbage-dumping episodes. The practice would have served the dual purpose of fertilizing the soil and drawing animal or insect scavengers away from the home. Elemental analyses of soil samples are one of the most important methods for uncovering such ancient fertilization strategies.[103] Broken bits of pottery in agricultural terraces are also evidence of recycling methods at places like Caracol.[104]

Scholars have completed in-depth studies of the local terrace system in the Río Bec region where ancient farmsteads spread across the hilly, terraced countryside. Most terraces in this region are of a narrow contour variety, averaging about 2 m wide with retaining walls that average only 30 cm high. They prevent hillslope soil erosion and create growing beds with soils that are 30–50 cm deep.[105] Dating of the terrace systems has mainly been based on ceramic chronologies, and it appears that they were a late development in the region, built sometime after 600 CE. Their late development marks them as an adaptive response to the demands of growing populations.[106] Similar to the terrace systems of La Milpa, Tamarinditio, Chan, and the Upper Belize River Valley, the Río Bec terraces were likely built in stages by groups of farming households. By expanding their terraces bit by bit, farmers limited the amount of labor and resources they needed to muster at any given point. Thus, in the end, the terrace systems may have been even more cost-effective for food production than slash-and-burn methods.[107]

Only Caracol and the Vaca Plateau's extensive terrace system in south-central Belize appears to have been the result of a relatively rapid, centrally directed construction program. Caracol was one of the largest metropolitan areas of the Classic Maya world, with a grand civic-ceremonial complex centered on the Kaana palace. The site center was surrounded by a contiguous sprawl of households and hamlets that covered as much as 68 sq. mi. across the plateau. The extensive terrace system of Caracol has been studied for decades, but its truly remarkable scale did not become apparent until a lidar flyover was completed in 2009. The residents of Caracol built terraces across nearly every bit of terrace-able land, covering at least 66 sq. mi. Studies of the wild vegetation that has grown over them since the site was depopulated demonstrate that the environmental benefits continue through the present.[108]

It also appears that the majority of the terraces at Caracol were constructed in quick succession during the Late Classic population peak. Excavations indicate that workers did not just build retention walls to naturally capture eroding soil—rather, they deconstructed the hillsides down to the bedrock, built the terrace wall systems, and then filled in the terrace beds with especially nutrient-rich soils harvested from elsewhere.[109] The massive scale and rapidity of the undertaking suggests a centrally directed agricultural plan, a unique situation in the lowlands (at least as far as we know at this point). It appears that central authorities at Caracol instituted a massive renovation to local agricultural practices and mobilized their resources to reshape the local landscape to maximize sustainable food production in a remarkable example of top-down socio-ecological flexibility.[110]

Wetland Agriculture

Another way that Maya cultivators modified their natural landscapes to intensify food production was to excavate drainage canals and build raised fields in wetland areas. A significant portion of the southern lowlands are covered by wetlands. Coastal areas and riverine floodplains are dotted with perennial freshwater marshes and as much as 60% of the southern interior land cover consists of bajos.[111] Periodic fluctuations in precipitation throughout the Preclassic Period may have encouraged farmers in some areas to experiment with irrigation canal construction to provide water for their crops. In other areas, they began to dig drainage canals and build raised crop beds to combat a steadily rising water table. Although wetland modification began during the Preclassic, communities expanded them greatly during the Classic Period to feed rapidly growing populations. Until recently, researchers believed wetland fields were purely a coastal region adaptation. Now, lidar flyovers demonstrate that canaled and/or raised wetland fields existed across the bajos of the interior as well (Figure 4.5). Wetland cultivation was undoubtedly an integral feature of Classic Maya civilization, practiced across the lowlands in slightly different ways to adjust for localized wetland conditions.[112]

Some of the earliest research on ancient Maya wetland agriculture was conducted by Billie Lee Turner and Peter Harrison at Pulltrouser Swamp in northern Belize in the 1980s.[113] They identified two landscape modifications indicative of wetland field cultivation: drainage channels and raised fields. Drainage channels freed sections of potentially arable land from waterlogging on either a seasonal or year-round basis, thereby creating more land for food production. Raised fields, such as those identified at Pulltrouser Swamp, were constructed by farmers using soil dredged from the channels. By raising the

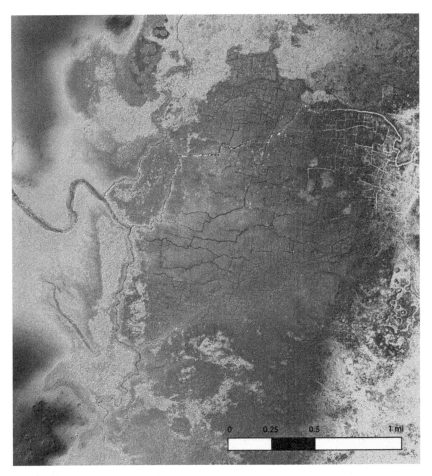

Figure 4.5 A lidar-based digital terrain model of a network of ancient raised fields in northern Belize highlighting the ease with which some ancient landscape modifications are visible in images generated from airborne laser scanning (image courtesy of Tim Beach, Sheryl Luzzadder-Beach, and colleagues).

growing beds above the water level, they ensured that the root systems would not become waterlogged. In many cases, the two strategies of drainage channels and raised fields were pursued simultaneously.[114] The result was similar to the "floating garden" *chinampas* of the Aztecs, in which rows of raised growing areas were surrounded by perennial canals.

The canal and raised-bed system allowed for multi-cropping and perhaps even aquaculture. Farmers could direct water flow through the channels in accordance with the requirements of different seasons and crops. Multi-cropping in rainfall-dependent milpa fields was much riskier than multi-cropping on raised wetland beds.[115] However, to maintain the productivity of the raised fields, farmers had to develop methods for aerating the topsoils and reintroducing nutrients through a range of organic fertilization methods.[116] The transformation of wetlands previously hostile to milpa farming into particularly productive raised and irrigated fields was a major agricultural adaptation made by Preclassic and Classic Maya communities.

The modification of perennial wetlands in the Three Rivers Region of northwestern Belize began at least as early as the Late Preclassic Period, an era characterized by growing populations and climatic instability. Extensive wetland canals may have even been under construction by the Middle Preclassic when groundwater levels were already rising. The wetland channel and field systems identified in Cobweb Swamp adjacent to the site of Colha in northern Belize likely date back to the Preclassic Period as well. Stratigraphic excavations indicate that in some cases, the agricultural fields began as dryland milpas. They were necessarily converted to wetland field systems over the course of the Late Preclassic as the water table rose.[117]

In other areas, like the Río Bravo watershed of northwest Belize, the engineering of wetland fields began during the Late Classic when farmers were looking to intensify food production in an increasingly inundated landscape. Farming households in the small community of Chan Cahal, which was part of the Classic Period polity of Blue Creek, used a complex wetland field system to meet local food demands. Construction of some of the raised fields in this system may date as far back as the Late Preclassic Period, but the system was expanded during the Terminal Classic Period, perhaps in response to increasingly dire drought conditions. Engineers constructed at least 14 km^2 of raised fields in this area, crisscrossed by drainage canals. Through these modifications, Maya cultivators in northwest Belize overcame the challenges of changing environmental conditions and continued to support thriving communities into the Early Postclassic Period.[118]

Recent lidar flyovers of the interior southern lowlands have conclusively demonstrated what has long been suspected—that the seasonally inundated bajos were exploited for agricultural production. Lidar imagery clearly shows grids of drainage canals carved into sections of bajos closest to the settled areas on their margins. Drainage channels in much of the wetland field areas thus far surveyed average 3 to 6 ft. in width, approximately 0.5 to 1.5 ft. in depth, and individual channels can extend for over half a mile. Some channelized field networks grew to cover at least 12 sq. mi. Such landscape-modification projects required significant amounts of time and labor, organized either by centralized authorities or groups of farming households. Whichever the case, these communities demonstrated flexibility and ingenuity by modifying the landscape and adapting their dryland milpa agricultural system to a wetland environment. The fact that bajos were under intensive cultivation during the Classic Period changes earlier carrying-capacity estimates and helps solve the problem of how the larger communities were able to feed themselves.[119]

The Yalahau region of the northeastern Yucatan provides another example of a distinct wetland cultivation strategy. Here, the water table actually pokes through to the surface, forming a series of wetlands that extend 50 km south from the north coast. Settlement in the Yalahau wetlands dates mainly to the Late Preclassic and Early Classic Periods (c. 100 BCE–450 CE). During this time, residents built systems of rock alignments to control surface water and sediment flows. Agriculturalists had to combat shifting sea and water table levels, and the stone barriers could have been used to block runoff from invading cultivated areas. Although researchers have not identified raised beds in the Yalahau region, high local population levels in the Early Classic indicate that local communities were indeed intensifying their agricultural production by using the wetlands. By the middle of the Classic Period, however, it appears communities in the northeastern Yucatan were already dealing with significant climatic changes that included decreases in precipitation and rising sea levels. These changes were severe enough to limit any large-scale repopulation of the region through the rest of the Pre-Colonial Era.[120]

Rejolladas

The northern lowlands have been saddled with an unfair reputation as an agriculturally inhospitable region ever since the earliest Spanish accounts marveled at the ability of Maya farmers to grow seemingly any crop from the thin, rocky soils. People like Diego de Landa were awestruck by the amount of luscious fruit trees and maize fields the Maya appeared to coax forth from stone (Figure 4.6).[121] More recently, false impressions of agricultural potential have been based on USDA soil assessments, which are calibrated for modern forms of mechanized monocultures.[122] It is true that few areas of the northern lowlands were suitable for intensified forms of agriculture like terracing or raised wetland cultivation. Instead, northern communities developed alternative methods to maximize food production that included growing special crops in microenvironments provided by the karst landscape of the northern plains. Integral to this niche-cropping scheme were the *rejolladas*, or partly filled in sinkholes, that dotted the landscape.

Rejolladas are sinkholes that formed when limestone caprock collapsed into underlying caverns (Figure 4.7). However, unlike cenotes, many rejollada floors are not completely submerged beneath the water table and are thus suitable for sowing crops. A specific type of rejollada, the *dzadz* (plural = *dzadzob*), has a floor that reaches the water table at least in some areas. I will use the term "rejollada" to refer to the broader category of features that includes both rejolladas and

Figure 4.6 Milpa crops growing from the thin soils directly on top of and out of the bedrock in the northern Yucatan. Sights like this astonished Spanish missionaries like Diego de Landa who wrote that it appeared farmers were coaxing crops from stone (photo courtesy of Sarah Taylor).

Figure 4.7 Farmers and agroforesters use the deep soils and relatively humid microclimates of rejolladas, or partially filled-in sinkholes, to cultivate high-value tree crops, just as agriculturalists likely did during the Classic Period (photos courtesy of Maia Dedrick and Patricia McAnany).

dzadzob. Rejolladas range from 2 m to 20 m deep and can be more than 100 m in diameter. They are more suitable for growing crops than the average terrain of the northern plains because they are filled with deep, rich soils—some layers are more than 6 ft. deep. The proximity of rejollada floors to the water table also helps keep the soil moist, and, in some cases, plant roots may even be fed via capillary action by the underlying water table. A final advantage of the rejollada microenvironment is the slightly cooler temperatures provided by the semi-subterranean, moister conditions compared with the surrounding surface.[123]

Classic Period farmers took advantage of the unique microenvironments to grow a wider array of crops than the normal surface conditions would allow and thereby intensified food production. In some cases, the rejolladas provided the only locations in the northern lowlands where cultivators could grow crops that grew more easily in other regions of the lowlands. For instance, the sinkholes provided the only microenvironment in the north capable of sustaining ec-onomically valuable species like cacao that would have difficulty growing on the surface. It is likely that rejolladas were controlled by elite families in an-tiquity, as they have been in more recent eras. Their importance is also indi-cated by the clustering of Pre-Colonial residential structures around their rims, which suggests that the crops grown within required frequent oversight and maintenance.[124]

Ethnographic evidence suggests that some farmers may have used rejolladas to grow standard milpa crops alongside the more valuable tree species. The special microenvironment and deep soils provide ideal conditions for multi-cropping with the three sisters planted during the start of the rainy season and root crops planted toward the end. Ethnographic observations of ritual cereme-nies performed within rejolladas reinforce the special role that these sinkholes continue to play in the agriculture of the northern lowlands.[125] The persistence of feral stands of cacao, avocado, guanabana, sapote, and other especially valu-able fruit tree species in rejolladas indicate that the ancient Maya were indeed taking advantage of the special growing conditions to cultivate particularly prized trees.[126]

Rejolladas were not the only topographic quirks of the northern landscape that facilitated niche agriculture. Much of the limestone bedrock exposed to the surface in the north has very small surface pockets where the caprock has eroded. These pockets, many of which are only a foot or two wide, have filled with soils sometimes several feet deep. Ethnographic analogues suggest that Classic farmers would not have missed the opportunity to sow individual plants in these tiny container gardens (Figure 4.8).[127] Hence, the early Spanish chroniclers' amazement at crops growing directly from the bedrock. The aggregation of these tiny plots, which were most likely watered using pot irrigation, represented yet another adaptation to local conditions that maximized agricultural output.

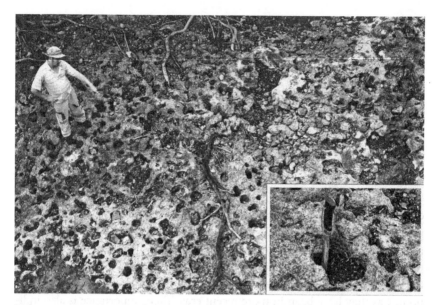

Figure 4.8 A patchwork of tiny container garden beds used by Classic Period agriculturalists in the Yalahau region of northeastern Yucatan (image courtesy of Scott Fedick, © 2012 Society of Ethnobiology).

Bajo Margins

In the southern lowlands, communities took advantage of the deep soils along the edges of bajos (Figure 4.9). Through both lidar-generated digital elevation models and pedestrian surveys archaeologists have identified areas where Classic Period cultivators modified bajo margins for agricultural purposes. Many low-lying areas that would become seasonal swamps by the Classic Period were likely year-round wetlands during the Preclassic. Their margins may have been some of the earliest environments of the interior southern lowlands to be cultivated. The wetland margins were similar in many ways to the riverine floodplains of northern Belize cultivated by the earliest Maya agriculturalists.[128]

The origins of bajo margin farming may date to very early in the Preclassic Period, but the practice intensified during the Classic Period. Soils washed down slopes denuded by Preclassic communities and settled at the edges of the low areas, providing wide fans of deep, fertile soil. Classic Period farmers took advantage of the byproducts of Preclassic forest clearance to intensify their yields. It appears that while Tikal farmers may not have terraced the many upland ridges and slopes within their polity, they certainly modified the deep soils of the bajo margins for agricultural production. They constructed terraces and retaining walls along the bajo margins to maintain the deep soils. In some cases, they built

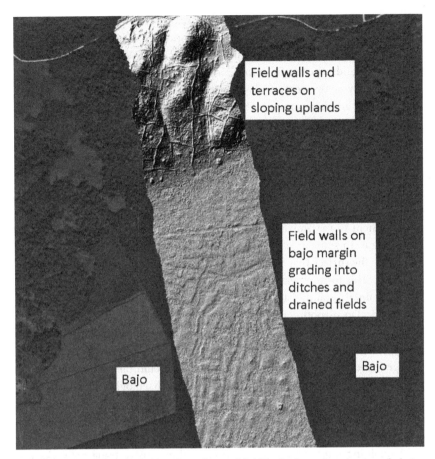

Figure 4.9 A network of field walls and raised field beds along the margins of a bajo in southern Quintana Roo, Mexico (image courtesy of Nick Dunning, Tim Beach, and colleagues).

reservoirs right above the bajo edge with gates that could be opened to irrigate the bajo margin growing fields below.

The combination of deep moisture-retentive soils and reservoir-irrigation systems would have allowed for a multi-cropping intensification strategy at places like Tikal and Yaxnohcah into the dry season. In this way, farmers could have grown many different crops over the course of the year, including maize-centered aboveground cultivars and root crops that required deep soils. Farmers may have also mined fertile soils from the bajos and bajo margins to fill terrace beds at places like La Milpa in Belize.[129]

To the west of Tikal, Classic Period agriculturalists cut a large drainage canal through a Preclassic causeway to feed water from one wetland area into cultivated fields at the edge of another. Bajo margin landscape modifications may have even facilitated year-round wetland cultivation on raised fields or "islands" deeper within the bajos. Lidar flyovers are proving especially useful at identifying such agricultural landscape modifications, demonstrating that bajo margin exploitation was a key component of Classic Period agricultural systems. Bajo margin farming is yet another example of how Classic farmers adapted their milpa cultivation practices to new environments, some of which formed as a result of earlier anthropogenic activities.[130]

Additional Intensification Practices

Beyond landscape modification and niche environment exploitation, Classic Maya farmers developed multiple recycling and fertilization practices that allowed them to maximize food production while minimizing environmental degradation. In some areas of the northern Yucatan, the water table was close enough to the surface that farmers could excavate wells to provide water for pot irrigation. This form of watering crops from a ceramic water vessel could have helped maintain soil moisture in small bedrock "container beds" and artificial raised beds. Deep-rooting fruit trees reached the relatively moist *sascab* (slightly softer, unconsolidated limestone) levels below the caprock, allowing for a more energy-efficient method of food production.[131] Elaborate water capture and storage strategies were also key components of agricultural sustainability in the dry north.[132] Low stone walls identified in the archaeological record of places like Chunchucmil represent the remains of raised beds of fertile soils transported from nearby regions. Residents also employed mounds of small pieces of limestone as lithic mulches to anchor tree crops and maintain soil moisture.

Maintaining inter-community relations and expansive trade networks was another component of socio-ecological resilience that would have been especially important given extremely localized discrepancies in rainfall and growing conditions.[133] The very thin soils and relatively little annual rainfall in the Northern Plains region could have been mitigated by focusing more efforts on xerophytic plants like henequen and cotton, which could be traded for foodstuffs grown elsewhere.[134] Farming families could have minimized the risk of subpar harvests by diversifying their intensification strategies and planting a wide array of different cultivars over a range of local microenvironments. This would have provided them with several different options to mitigate challenges posed by inconsistencies in precipitation or the arrival of a natural disaster.[135]

Another way Maya farmers addressed the challenges of thin or nutrient-deficient soils was to apply fertilizers that reintroduced nutrients like phosphorus and nitrogen into the growing layers. Abnormally high phosphorus levels recorded in some soil plots at Chunchucmil represent the remnants of ancient intensive fertilization. Strategies likely involved a combination of the following: recycling organic household and human wastes, using burnt *sascab*, and transporting nutrient-rich soils from the nearest coastal areas or other locales with deep, fertile sediments. Burnt lime was used for decreasing soil acidity and possibly for deterring animal pests from disturbing crops.[136]

The use of human waste to fertilize fields is a risky strategy, as fecal matter in agricultural produce can spread disease. The fact that Maya farmers appear to have successfully incorporated night soil into their fertilization toolkit is a testament to the level of knowledge and skills transmitted over generations. Accomplishing this feat would have solved two problems for high-population centers like Caracol—the need to reintroduce necessary nutrients to plant beds and to dispose of hazardous waste.[137] Farmers may also have used the *tapado* method of mulching, in which legume and weed clippings are reintroduced to plant beds to improve soil nitrogen and phosphorus levels.[138] There is also tantalizing evidence at a few northern sites that cultivators imported nutritious algae from coastal regions to enhance their local soil.[139] Although it is difficult to identify specific combinations of agricultural strategies, the fact that cities like Chunchucmil thrived in areas of low natural soil productivity is a testament to the resourcefulness of Classic Period farmers.[140]

Another method for sustaining agricultural production that is unfortunately even less visible in the archaeological record involves maintaining individual trees in hillside milpas to prevent soil erosion. Classic Period farmers likely learned lessons from the negative consequences of Preclassic forest clearance. The fact that soil erosion during the Classic Period was not nearly as severe provides indirect evidence of the implementation of such tree-preservation strategies.[141] However, it is also possible that there just was not as much soil left on the hillsides to erode after so much had worn away during the Preclassic.[142]

Ceren

Around 660 CE, the Loma Caldera volcano in western El Salvador erupted and covered the nearby farming village of Ceren in over 13 ft. of volcanic ash. Early warnings of an eruption gave villagers enough time to flee to safety, but all the components of their livelihoods were left behind. The volcanic ash cooled and hardened, preserving not only residences and artifacts but also the outlines of an array of plants in homegardens, infields, and outfields as well. Although most of the organic materials decomposed over time, archaeologists adopted a similar liquid-plaster technique to the one used for making casts of empty spaces at Pompeii. When excavations arrive at an open space in the ash layer, they inject dental plaster that molds to the shape of the empty cavity and hardens. Then, archaeologists excavate the plaster casts to reveal the shapes of plants that grew in situ over 1,300 years ago. Careful excavations at Ceren have provided an unparalleled look into the perishable, organic world of Classic Period plant cultivation. This "New World Pompeii" is located on the southeastern border of the Maya cultural sphere, but available evidence suggests Ceren's agricultural systems serve as an instructive analogue for contemporaneous agricultural practices throughout the Maya lowlands.

Payson Sheets and colleagues excavated several household compounds, infields, and outfields at Ceren. The evidence they have uncovered provides a model of what Classic Period food-production systems looked like. A range of species, including economically valuable trees, were grown in homegardens (Figure 4.10). Sheets and his team have recovered evidence of guava, avocado, achiote, coyol palm, nance, calabash, and hog plum trees in homegardens alongside chile peppers and common beans, as well as root crops like manioc and malanga.[143] Ceren homegardeners even cultivated cacao, despite the high altitude.[144] Carefully watered, fertilized, and tended, homegardens provided a steady source of supplemental calories and flavors throughout the year.[145]

Farmers grew maize, beans, squash, and manioc in the infields alongside fruit tree orchards that were distributed between household compounds. They

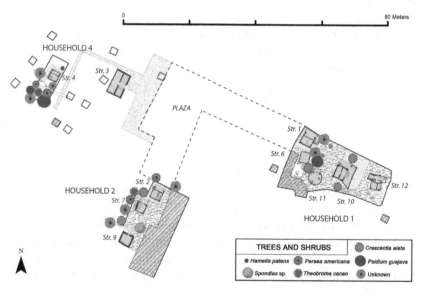

Figure 4.10 A diagram of housegarden plant cultivation at Ceren, El Salvador, including coloradillo (*Hamelia patens*), hogplum (*Spondias sp.*), avocados (*Persea americana*), cacao (*Theobroma cacao*), calabash (*Crescentia alata*), and guava (*Psidium guajava*) (image courtesy of Alan Farahani and colleagues).

also grew maize, manioc, and another root crop called malanga in the outfields on the southern edge of the village. One of the bigger surprises for researchers was the massive quantity of manioc plants cultivated in ridged fields along the gentle slopes of the southern milpa where the soils could drain and avoid excessive moisture levels. Although maize was by far the most ubiquitous plant found throughout the Ceren excavations, manioc probably rivaled maize in terms of calories. The evidence from Ceren suggests that manioc cultivation was likely a much larger component of Classic Period diets across the lowlands than previously recognized. It is even possible that while maize was preferred taste-wise, manioc was the more important staple calorie-wise in many drier parts of the lowlands.[146] Although we do not know for certain how widespread the ridged field practice was across the lowlands, the proliferation of other shared agricultural strategies suggests it would have been quite common. By alternating raised rows with ditched rows, farmers could concentrate nutrients, facilitate weeding and mulching, and control for the differential moisture needs of different cultivars in the same plot.[147]

Plant materials including a wide array of charcoal specimens recovered from the patio areas of Ceren's households indicate what species were stored and prepared for consumption at the time of the eruption. Households tended a number of fruiting trees in their gardens, including guava, calabash, avocado, cacao, and capulin.[148] Chile peppers, common beans, calabash, and cacao were found close to one another, suggesting their combination in dishes. The beans recovered from patio groups in the midst of preparation were a mix of both domesticated and wild varieties, indicating that Classic farmers continued to harvest wild species perhaps for variety and as a risk-management strategy. The distribution of chile peppers across domestic floor spaces suggests they had originally been hung to dry from roof beams.[149] The charcoal samples also reveal the extent to which villagers harvested both food and construction materials from the mosaic of environments that surrounded the community.[150]

Agave, cotton, and calabash likely served both edible and utilitarian purposes at Ceren. Agave pulp is indeed edible, if not desirable, and cottonseeds were ground to produce cooking oil. Agave twine, cotton fibers, and calabash bowls were recovered from several areas of the village. Mirasol (*Tithonia rotundifolia*) and a species of grass used for thatch were also found within the household compounds. These and other wild species were likely gathered from nearby forests and fallowed fields. Inter-cropping maize with manioc and other assorted plants in smaller pockets throughout the infields and outfields facilitated annual multi-cropping that ensured the resilience of the local community.[151] Taken altogether, the unique data sets from Ceren provide corroborating support for the variegated agricultural production systems identified via microbotanical, archaeological, and ethnographic evidence at other Classic Period sites.

Summary

Hundreds of Classic Maya communities grew steadily from the second century into the ninth century CE, overcoming numerous social and environmental challenges. Despite a relatively stable climate in many subregions, Classic Maya farmers still faced occasional years of diminished precipitation, destructive hurricanes, and influxes of pests. Perhaps the biggest challenge centered on the rapidly growing populations that required ever greater amounts of food. Drawing on knowledge passed down for generations and from harsh lessons learned at the end of the Preclassic, Classic farmers transformed their landscapes and developed sustainable food-production strategies.

At the heart of all these intensification strategies was an in-depth knowledge of all aspects of the natural environment and how they could best sustain growing human populations. Farmers developed intimate understandings of precipitation and growth cycles, plant and animal roles, and soil compositions.[152] They knew which species grew well together at which points of the rainy season, in which types of soils, and with which types of fertilization. The question of how Classic Maya communities sustained such high populations for so many centuries in such a challenging tropical environment no longer perplexes researchers. We now know of a multitude of techniques that farmers used to sustainably and efficiently manage food production across the mosaic of lowland microenvironments for over seven centuries.[153]

The success of the Classic agricultural intensification strategies, attested by the Late Classic population boom, may have contributed to the eventual breakdown of the prevailing socio-political order in the 800s and 900s. Communities needed to develop increasingly intricate systems to meet the demands of the growing populations, thereby inherently limiting their flexibility and capacity for large-scale adaptations. In Chapter 7, I will discuss how a cascade of simultaneous stressors may have caused agricultural systems to falter in several subregions, and, how even amidst societal transformation, we still see evidence of Classic Maya resilience.

5

Water

Introduction

Access to water is *the* most important underlying factor allowing for the growth of complex societies. Water scarcity, whether caused by droughts or underdeveloped infrastructure, is becoming an increasingly dire problem in many areas of the world today. The United Nations projects that 1.8 billion people around the world will be living under conditions of absolute water scarcity by 2025.[1] Droughts and desertification are already forcing people to flee their homes as climate refugees at rates never before seen in recorded history.

Popular depictions of Classic Maya communities thriving in a water-rich jungle environment distort the reality of annual shortages to which the Maya had to adapt. Terms like "tropical forest" tend to conjure pictures of steamy jungles with raindrops cascading off thatched roofs. This picture is not too far from reality for much of the Maya lowlands—at least during the afternoons of the rainy season. However, for approximately half of the year, almost *no rain at all* falls in the Maya lowlands, transforming them into a "green desert" (Figure 5.1).[2]

To survive these conditions, Classic Period polities developed intricate water-management systems. The fact that they were able to do so without advantages available to Old World communities such as metal implements or beasts of burden is all the more impressive. In the Maya lowlands, all excavation, construction, and transportation activities were completed by human labor alone. Archaeologists have uncovered intricate hydrologic technologies and infrastructure networks across the lowlands that may very well represent *the* most significant examples of Classic Maya resilience and resourcefulness.

Imagine Tikal's gigantic human-made reservoirs brimming with water-cleaning plants and animals, cascading one into the next as they filled up over the course of the rainy season. Close your eyes and picture smooth-stoned channels and lime-plastered aqueducts funneling water under and around hillside plazas at Palenque. Try to zoom out and visualize thousands of water capture platforms in the high and dry northern hill country funneling the first deluges of the rainy season into watertight subterranean storage tanks. The Classic Maya developed these and other ingenious systems to survive the challenges of an annual dry season that lasted for at least four months.

The Maya and Climate Change. Kenneth E. Seligson, Oxford University Press. © Oxford University Press 2023.
DOI: 10.1093/oso/9780197652923.003.0005

Figure 5.1 The density of the forest vegetation changes dramatically between the end of the dry season in early May (top) and the middle of the rainy season in August (bottom) across much of the Maya lowlands (photos by author).

Residents of Early Classic Period communities drew on knowledge passed down from generations that had lived through climatic downturns and the challenges of water scarcity. Collective memories recounted in families from one generation to the next informed the construction of new storage and distribution infrastructure. Trial and error likely played a central role in the development of ever more productive management schemes as well. Communities recognized the importance of developing management systems that would stand the test of time while also retaining a capacity for modification and expansion.[3]

Classic Period communities adapted their flexible water storage and distribution structures to support exploding populations and changing precipitation patterns. The ubiquitous human-made reservoirs, canals, terraces, aqueducts, and cisterns in use throughout the lowlands during the Classic Period are testaments to Maya adaptability and engineering skills. The fact that early twentieth-century archaeologists at Tikal were able to rely on water from a reservoir constructed over 1,500 years earlier demonstrates the lasting impact that Maya landscape modifications have had for supporting life in the tropical forest.[4]

Maya communities benefited from relatively stable climatic conditions for much of the Classic Period, though there were still annual fluctuations in precipitation patterns. Even if the general climate did not pose too dire a challenge throughout much of the Classic Period, water managers still needed to adapt their practices to sustain booming populations and the environmental changes they wrought. As smaller communities blossomed into larger urban centers, some constructed massive reservoirs, others built canals or dams, and still others excavated household wells and cisterns. Only in the face of increasingly erratic precipitation and a host of other destabilizing factors in the 700–900s CE did local management systems begin to fray.

The range of Classic Period hydrologic systems reflects local environmental, topographic, and historical conditions, exemplifying the variability of Maya adaptability. It is easy to lose sight in the archaeological record of the individuals and families that built and used the hydrologic infrastructure. We must try to imagine these masterful water-management systems as they once were—working, churning systems populated by farmers, artisans, housemakers, and children.[5] Water administrators likely oversaw large crews of water-system workers at some of the bigger reservoir and canal sites. They were at the heart of the vibrant complexities of Classic Maya life. It is easy to overlook the hydrologic infrastructure in favor of massive pyramids, elaborate monuments, and complex hieroglyphic scripts, but none of these other cultural facets would have been possible without the underlying water-management systems.

The Natural Hydrologic Setting

The environmental heterogeneity that characterizes the Maya lowlands includes a wide range of annual precipitation rates, a diversity in access to surface water, and varied depths to the freshwater table. All these factors contributed to the development of many different water-management infrastructures across the lowlands.[6] Paleoenvironmental data suggest that the Classic Period climatic and environmental patterns across the Maya lowlands were relatively similar to what they are today, albeit perhaps with slightly cooler average temperatures than our current twenty-first-century trend.

With regard to rainfall, there is a general decrease in annual precipitation the farther north you go. In a given year, the southernmost lowlands may receive 700% more rain than the northwest (approximately 155 in. compared to 20). To put this in perspective, Los Angeles may receive up to 20 in. of rain over the course of what would be considered a particularly wet year, and New York City receives an average of 50 in. per year. Surprisingly, London receives only 24 in. annually on average, but it is relatively evenly spread out throughout the year. You might be thinking, then, that even the northwest Yucatan must have received plenty of rain to support large populations and that the southern lowlands received more than enough. In terms of annual averages, that would be a fair assumption. The situation, however, is a bit more complicated.

Three factors complicate what would otherwise have been a rosy precipitation outlook for the lowland forests. First, year-to-year rainfall totals can vary by up to 40% in any given subregion, which could have significant consequences for agricultural production.[7] Farmers had to adapt on an annual basis, not knowing if they might receive much more or less rain than the previous year. The second variable was the start of the rainy season. Today, the start of the rainy season can vary by up to five months![8] Although the annual arrival of rain was likely not quite as erratic during the Classic Period, any delay in an expected arrival would have put a tremendous strain on farmers waiting to figure out when to plant crops or hoping to refill storage tanks.

Not only does the start of the rainy season vary annually, but also in most years they are broken up by a short dry period called the *canícula* (from the Latin *dies caniculares*—the "dog days" of summer) or *veranillo* (small summer). The *canícula* usually begins one month after the start of the rainy season and lasts for three or four weeks, bringing a brief return to dry season conditions. The variability of this interruption would have likewise led farmers to fret about when to plant the main crops. An extensive *canícula* could also cut into the expectations for refilling reservoirs and cisterns.[9]

The third factor was perhaps the most significant for general water consumption—the stark seasonality of rainfall. Almost all rain fell between the end of May and beginning of December throughout most of the lowlands. For the other five to six months of the year, almost no rain fell at all. Around Mayapan in the Northern Plains region, rainfall averages 40 in. per year, but only about eight of those inches fall between November and April. The karst, limestone bedrock of the Maya lowlands, is prone to either rapid runoff in inclined areas or rapid vertical drainage in flatter areas, both of which limited natural water storage potential.[10]

A few areas of the lowlands benefited from year-round terrestrial water resources. Several large Classic centers developed close to the Peten Lakes zone of north-central Guatemala, along river systems at the eastern and western edges of the lowlands, or near clusters of *cenotes*, or sinkholes, in the northern Yucatan. Approximately 40–60% of the southern lowlands are covered by low areas called *bajos*, many of which filled with water during the rainy season. Some may have even held standing water year-round. Although they are often lumped under the general category of low-lying, water catchment areas, there is much variability in bajo geology and hydrology, let alone size and shape. Each type of bajo required its own form of exploitation and management.[11] Freshwater springs also dot the edges of the Peten Plateau where fault lines push water from the relatively low-lying table up to the surface.[12]

Even perennial water sources were affected by precipitation seasonality. During the dry season, rivers became muddy and dropping water levels in bajos left behind concentrations of salts, gypsum, and other natural pollutants.[13] Standing water also leads to the proliferation of parasites and water-borne diseases.[14] Communities located close to the coast, or even 50 mi. inland in parts of northern Belize, faced occasional saltwater pollution of the water table as sea levels steadily rose.[15] Communities without any surface water at all would have found it very difficult to dig wells deeper than 20 ft. without metal tools.

A final seasonal challenge was a destructive natural phenomenon that is nearly invisible in the archaeological record: hurricanes. In Yucatec Mayan, violent storms like hurricanes are called *chan ik'*—serpent wind. They are often conceptualized as violent, snake-like spirits terrorizing communities with their unpredictability and tremendous power. Other times, they are understood as byproducts of battles between benevolent and malevolent manifestations of the rain god Chahk.[16] At least one hurricane crosses the Maya lowlands every 2.5 years.[17] If tropical storms are included in this calculation, the frequency goes up to at least one per year. Communities unlucky enough to be close to the center of the storm would suffer the greatest devastation, but Category 5 storms like Hurricane Gilbert in 1988 managed to destroy 90% of the year's maize crop across most of the northern Yucatan.[18] Even the concrete and brick houses of today are often no match for 200-plus mile-per-hour winds—wood and thatch huts never stood a chance. Thus, in addition to dealing with seasonal droughts, the lowland Maya dealt with frequent dreadful storms that had the power to flatten entire regions.

All these challenges added up to a relatively inhospitable region, water-wise. Archaeologist Vernon Scarborough posits that a good deal of planning went into the initial colonization projects in the interior lowlands. He imagines advance parties making the initial incursions for the explicit purposes of setting up water-management systems.[19] The fact that Maya families were able to establish a foothold in the interior, let alone support populations that likely rose to over 10 million by the Late Classic Period,[20] is a testament to the success of their planning and adaptability.

The Importance of Water

Physical Water Necessities

At the most basic level, water is a requirement for sustaining human life. Doctors advise drinking at least 2 L. of water per day in temperate climates. In the tropics, however, a person may lose as many as *10 L.* of fluid per day via sweat alone, necessitating consistent access to a water-replenishment source.[21]

Maya communities also required water for their crops. The booming Late Classic Period city-states with populations upward of 40,000 people relied on an agricultural base. The farmers (who composed the bulk of the population) needed consistent access to agricultural water resources. Maize needs a relatively large amount of water compared with such Old World grains as millet, sorghum, or rice. Not only were many of the strains of maize grown by the Classic Maya less productive with limited water, but they also became more susceptible to fungal plagues that could sicken the humans who consumed them.[22]

Beyond agriculture, water was also important for bathing, cleaning clothes, and sustaining domesticated dogs and turkeys. Some communities needed freshwater pools for cultivating snails, crabs, and turtles for consumption.[23] Water was also necessary for a range of artisanal activities and construction projects, including the production of burnt lime and ceramic vessels.[24] Most construction events likely took place during the dry season to avoid the interference of precipitation episodes. Thus, water necessary for plaster and mortar, as well as to rehydrate the thousands of sweating workers, would have had to come from local water storage systems that would not be replenished until the rains returned. Potters used water to soften and shape the clay needed to constantly create new vessels to replace worn and broken ones.

Water was also important for the distribution of goods in certain areas as large trading centers developed along the Usumacinta River in the west and the Belize and Hondo Rivers in the east. There is also some evidence that residents of the central interior created semi-artificial lakes around Calakmul and other sites by damming natural drainage channels. If these bajo-rich landscapes experienced enough flooding, people and their commodities could travel by canoe over vast stretches of inland travel corridors during parts of the rainy season.[25]

Ideological Significance

By the start of the Classic Period, royals and elites at many sites co-opted the basic need for water, and through the elaboration of water-related rituals, imbued centralized water-management systems with ideological significance. The iconographic record clearly reflects the importance of maintaining access to clean water sources, especially for drinking and cooking purposes. Elites blended aquatic imagery such as water lilies (*Nymphaea spp.*), reeds, and crocodilian creatures with other emblems of power. Some Maya elites even referred to themselves as water lily lords to highlight their role as water managers in larger population centers. The narcotic properties of a few water lily species may have made them useful in elaborate water-related ceremonies.[26]

Lisa Lucero and colleagues have argued that rulers may have even counted the purveyance of clean water as one of their main responsibilities to their constituents and thus one of the main justifications for their elevated status, at least early in the Classic Period. Elaborate ceremonies and other ritual practices reinforced the connection between water and power even as households relied increasingly on their own smaller reservoirs and wells for daily consumption. The presence of large reservoirs as some of the most visible sources of water during the dry season served the purpose of physically tethering populations to the larger site centers controlled by political elites.[27]

There are ongoing debates regarding the degree to which central authorities continued to manage water resources at many of the larger sites into the Late Classic Period. Lidar-based settlement pattern studies have indicated the prevalence of smaller household reservoirs even at those sites with massive central reservoirs like Tikal. As cities expanded and residential clusters developed far from the ceremonial site core, it would make sense for far-flung households to rely increasingly on their more local water sources instead of trekking to the site center.[28] The central reservoirs may have come to serve mainly as important buffers during the dry season or years with especially low-precipitation levels. It is thus possible that the development of increasingly intricate water-related ceremonies by site center elites over the course of the Classic Period was a direct response to a decrease in the importance of their physical control over water access.[29]

Water and wetlands are explicitly connected with origin stories and the life-death cycle. Classic iconography highlights how *itz*, the force that imbues and gives life to everything in our world, is connected with rainwater and semen—all three contribute to the fertility of the earth and society. The placement of reservoirs in and around the temple pyramids of Classic site centers may have deliberately linked the human-made mountains to the symbolically important cosmic boundaries represented by water.[30] The Classic Maya perceived of water as a veil between our own world and a more explicitly supernatural one.

To "enter the water" was a metaphor that the Classic Maya used for the act of dying, and depictions of an underworld often include watery imagery.[31] One of the most famous such scenes, carved on a bone recovered from the tomb of the great Tikal King Jasaw Chan K'awiil, shows two Paddler Gods transporting the king via canoe to the watery afterlife.[32] The ritual ballgame played throughout the Maya lowlands during the Classic Period is also connected with themes of death and a watery underworld. At sites like Ucanal in northern Guatemala, archaeologists have uncovered mechanisms by which the ballcourt floor could be purposely flooded for ceremonial events throughout the year.[33]

In the mid-2000s, archaeologist Arthur Demarest and colleagues uncovered a gruesome scene at the Classic Period site of Cancuen, Guatemala, that connected royal authority, water-related ceremonies, and the underworld. As a trade capital located on a river, residents of Cancuen would not have been wanting for fresh water. The small reservoir near the central palace was thus likely a focal point for water-related rituals and not necessarily a key source of sustenance. It was quite a surprise when archaeologists uncovered the skeletal remains of at least thirty individuals—most likely the royal household—who had unceremoniously been deposited into the pool. Most of them exhibit skeletal markers of having died by violent means. The event was both a recognition of the connections between watery boundaries and death and a forceful rejection of the royal family's power.[34]

Societies throughout Mesoamerica understood that water emerged from caves or wells (subsumed under the category of *ch'een*) either as springs, streams, or mist that became rainclouds. Often paired with sacred mountains that connected our own world with the celestial realms, caves were thus a significant element in the Maya understanding of the cosmos.[35] Places of natural water storage or emergence are ideologically important to cultures around the world and ancient shrines often mark their locations.[36] It has even recently been suggested that the *moai* sculptures of Rapa Nui (Easter Island) were located specifically to mark areas where freshwater springs emerge around the edges of the island.[37]

Many early Maya sites were founded near or on top of caves not only to take advantage of the water within but also because of the ideological significance they commanded. Scarborough argues that the quatrefoil (four-lobed) images that we know represent caves in Maya iconography may also represent reservoirs.[38] In the northern lowlands, the *ch'een* most frequently encountered were cenotes—sinkholes that accessed subterranean river systems or a near surface water table. One of the largest sites of them all, Chichen Itza, was unsurprisingly located in a region with many cenotes. Recent research has even suggested that the city planners used the natural arrangement of cenotes to guide their construction of the central pyramid as a true *axis mundi*, or center point of the world, and thereby shape their city as a cosmogram.[39]

The Preclassic to Early Classic Period Transition

A critical factor contributing to the longevity of Classic Maya civilization was the capacity and willingness of communities to modify existing practices, incorporate new ideas, and learn from prior failures. The water-management systems were intricate, but they were not static. Many of the lessons that informed the increasingly intricate water storage networks of the Classic Period stemmed from the chaotic transition from the Late Preclassic to the Early Classic. In terms of the broader Maya adaptive cycle, this was an era of release and reorganization. Some of the largest Preclassic sites like El Mirador, Cerros, and San Bartolo declined and were depopulated. Other sites like Tikal and Xultun in northern Guatemala and La Milpa in Belize survived the turmoil and grew to become prominent Classic Period centers. The paleo-climatic record suggests that intense, multiyear droughts played a critical role in provoking the socio-political transition, but human modifications of the landscape and Preclassic water-management strategies also played a role in some areas.[40]

Vernon Scarborough and colleagues have identified the "concave microwatershed" as the standard reservoir model for many of the largest Preclassic centers in the northern Peten region, as well as Edzna in Campeche and Cerros in Belize. Communities used gravity and fortuitous natural topography to limit energy costs associated with maintenance. Site centers were located in generally low-lying areas that were modified to catch runoff from the surrounding uplands. This catchment system was also used by El Mirador, whose ceremonial center was flanked by a mix of seasonal bajos and, possibly, year-round lakes. El Mirador residents modified depressions along hillslopes and at the edges of bajos into semi-artificial reservoirs to better capture rainwater around the site center.[41] The site center of Cerros in northern Belize was surrounded by a 0.8 mi. long, 32 ft. wide, and 6.5 ft. deep canal that filled with water during the rainy season. Late Preclassic residents of both Cerros and La Milpa altered low-lying areas and transformed quarries into reservoirs to take advantage of passive filling processes.[42]

The Preclassic concave systems supported the construction of huge civic-ceremonial architecture and maintained large populations for over three centuries during a period of increasing climatic unpredictability. Between roughly 100 and 250 CE, however, increasingly frequent droughts would began to strain water resources at the larger population centers not only for daily consumption but for agricultural production as well.[43] Problems related to diminishing precipitation levels were compounded by the silting in of water sources at some of the larger sites due to extensive forest clearance. Occasional storms swept clay-rich sediments freed from hillsides into the bajos. Not only did this reduce the water storage capacities of bajos and reservoirs, but it also tampered with the ability of seasonal wetlands to regenerate at the start of each rainy season. Archaeologists and paleoenvironmentalists uncover thick layers of this dense clayey sediment dubbed "Maya Clay" dating to the Preclassic in lake and bajo cores across the southern lowlands.[44]

Significant population centers were already developing in the Puuc region of the northern Yucatan as early as the Middle Preclassic Period (c. 700 BCE). Puuc settlements were even more at the mercy of the rains than elsewhere in the lowlands due to the lack of surface water and a relatively deep water table. Sites like Muluchtzekel were likely depopulated for a time during the Preclassic to Classic transition as a result of Terminal Preclassic droughts. Xcoch, in the Valley of Santa Elena near what would become the Late Classic monumental center of Uxmal, possessed one of the few natural caves in the region that was deep enough to reach the water table. The cave, however, was a limited water source, and Xcoch, too, was abandoned for a spell at the beginning of the Classic Period.[45]

Classic Period Reservoirs

Classic communities learned from the various consequences of Preclassic human-environmental practices and developed new, diverse methods promoting long-term water conservation.[46] Classic water-management systems were frequently tweaked and expanded to accommodate growing populations and shifting climate patterns. The concave microwatershed of the Preclassic gave way to predominantly convex microwatersheds in the Classic, exemplified by Tikal but adopted across the lowlands (Figure 5.2). Civic cores were built atop raised areas or ridges, and plazas were engineered to funnel water into a series of reservoirs that cascaded down the sides of the raised areas.[47] To the west of Tikal, households moved from the concave watershed of the Preclassic site of El Palmar to engineer a convex reservoir-based system at Early Classic El Zotz. This water capture and storage strategy not only provided a hedge against drought-like

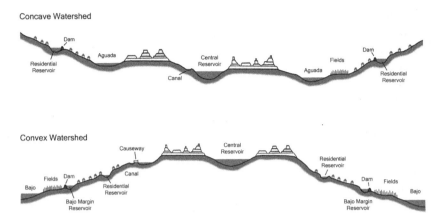

Figure 5.2 While many of the larger Preclassic Period sites took advantage of naturally concave watershed systems and constructed their site centers near where water naturally pooled, many Classic Period communities modified their natural environments to exploit convex watershed systems atop ridges and hills (image courtesy of Vernon Scarborough, color added by author).

conditions but also aided the occupants of the site center in maintaining a more defensible position on the landscape.[48]

Unlike the Preclassic reservoirs, these were to a larger degree *artificial* water storage features formed by excavation and damming. They required more planning and maintenance, but they proved more efficient in promoting long-term stability. They needed to be occasionally dredged, but they were not subject to the same level of sedimentation as the Preclassic concave watersheds. The predominantly artificial reservoir systems required several innovations in civic engineering and long-term planning. Massive amounts of water flooded the Classic Period cities during the rainy season, followed by several months of no rain at all, thus requiring a significant degree of flexibility. The annual variation in rainfall would have made water shortages much more likely than in the river-fed irrigation networks of Mesopotamia or Angkor that could rely on year-round replenishment. At the outset of the Early Classic, engineers gave their systems the best chance to survive and adapt by putting generations of environmental knowledge to work. As Scarborough notes, human inhabitants may have made the ultimate decisions about *how* to construct their reservoirs, but the natural setting narrowed and influenced the choices of *where* to construct them.[49]

When thinking of modern reservoirs, you may be inclined to divide them into two categories: the natural and the artificial. Natural lakes, ponds, and wetlands are on one side, and dammed lakes, metal storage tanks, and large concrete pools are on the other. Classic Period water managers appreciated the importance of natural ecosystems for supporting clean water sources and found a middle ground between these categories. They fashioned their artificial reservoirs to mimic natural features of the landscape and used aquatic plants, fish, bacteria, and algae to help maintain healthy ecosystems. The natural purification systems employed by the Classic Maya sequestered excess nitrogen and phosphorous while maintaining healthy pH balances. Fish and other aquatic animals helped control mosquito and other insect populations attracted to stagnant water, as well as provided additional sources of protein for site residents.[50]

Water lilies, symbols of elite water-management, can only survive in a narrow range of clean water conditions. Their presence not only indicated the well-being of the system, but their large pads also limited evaporation from the reservoirs. In addition to artificial reservoirs, Classic centers continued to take advantage of natural low-lying areas for water capture but augmented their water storage capacities by lining the bottoms with clay or masonry layers of lime plaster and fill stones. Clay linings both prevented seepage of water downward into the limestone and excess calcium leaching upward from the limestone into the water supply.[51]

Maya engineers planned their water systems to address the challenges of annual fluctuations and the longer term challenges of population growth. As communities expanded over the course of the Classic Period, the interconnected series of artificial reservoirs, canals, dikes, and dams were expanded as well. Foresight facilitated flexibility, and even the largest water-management systems were able to grow even larger to keep up with populations that reached 40,000 people or more.[52] Everyday water needs were increasingly met at the household level while new canals, sluice channels, and reservoir tanks expanded the original central systems.

Tikal's Centralized Water System

Vernon Scarborough and colleagues have completed extensive investigations of Tikal's reservoirs, which compose one of the most elaborate Classic Maya water-management systems. What likely began during the Late Preclassic Period as a modest reservoir network fed by natural springs emerging from the Tikal ridge was adapted and modified over the course of the Classic Period to capture as much rainwater as possible. Tikal's Classic system was eventually dominated by six particularly large reservoirs that were interwoven with the massive constructions of the site's elevated central core. A few of these reservoirs were close to the apex of the ridge, while others were downslope, fed by their uphill neighbors via channels and canals (Figure 5.3).[53]

Figure 5.3 A reconstruction of the core of Tikal demonstrating how the central plazas were designed to funnel water into several large reservoirs (image courtesy of Trasancos 3D: Anxo Miján, Alejandro Soriano, Andrés Armesto, Carlos Paz and Diego Blanco).

In addition to the six large and dozens of smaller reservoirs, the Tikal reservoir system also included the huge dams and berms built across natural gullies and spillways that created the central reservoirs. These were connected via channels, sluices, and switching stations engineered to bypass residential areas that also captured plaza runoff and diverted drainage when the reservoirs occasionally needed to be dredged. Large workforces would have been needed to maintain these systems, let alone construct them in the first place.[54] Kenneth Tankersley and colleagues have recently identified an ingenious filtration system within the Corriental reservoir that used sand-sized particles of the minerals zeolite and quartz to absorb contaminants. These minerals were quarried from a source over 18 mi. away. Similar sand- and charcoal-based filtering systems were not used in Western Europe until the 1800s, and the Maya system appears to be unique among tropical civilizations.[55]

The six large reservoirs at the elevated center of the site were the crown jewels of the Tikal water-management system. Scarborough and Gallopin estimate that together they could have captured and stored between 27.7 and 64.4 mi. gal. of water per year based on a lower end estimate of roughly 50 in. of rainfall. The higher end estimate would be the equivalent of over 100 Olympic swimming pools worth of water! Using contemporary ethnographic data from the Maya lowlands that puts daily water consumption at around 17 L. per person per day, Scarborough and colleagues estimate that the six large reservoirs alone could have supported 50,000 people across the year. This did not take into account the myriad other smaller reservoirs across the city. However, soil coring at two of the large reservoirs suggests that they were never filled to the brim, which makes sense if water managers wanted to balance water maintenance with a navigable site center.[56]

The site center was constructed as a large catchment area, with plazas ever so slightly inclined to divert runoff into each of the large reservoirs. Some of the reservoirs were constructed by building large dams across the ravines that had previously served as the natural water filtration channels for the Tikal ridge. The tops of the dams functioned as causeways for crossing the ravines and connecting plaza groups. The largest of these dams, which supported the Palace Reservoir, is approximately 33 ft. high, 260 ft. long, and almost 200 ft. wide at its base to handle the water pressure.[57]

Although it is not yet clear how the uppermost reservoirs would have been periodically emptied and cleaned, Scarborough and colleagues have found tantalizing evidence of a series of possible sluice holes, oriented in vertical columns along the breadth of the dam. They could have been covered and opened via some sort of pulley system to relieve pressure on the dam. They would have allowed for a dispersed pressure release along the length of the dam as water levels slowly dropped and avoided the potential disaster of having one, concentrated egress point. Although such a system has so far only been tentatively identified at Tikal, researchers believe that similar technologies would have been widespread across the lowlands.

Another likely Classic Period innovation was the use of cofferdams at Tikal and a few other sites. Cofferdams allow for the sequestering of water and drying of a principal reservoir so that it can occasionally be dredged and cleaned. At Tikal, Scarborough and Grazioso Sierra hypothesize that the temple reservoir served as a cofferdam for the Palace reservoir, which was dredged at least once during the Classic Period.[58]

As Tikal grew, the city's engineers specifically located their quarries to best facilitate water capture and integration into the larger water-management system. The water from the quarries could be used to support more construction activities, as well as provide residents and workers at the site center with daily rations. As the uppermost reservoirs filled, engineers diverted water via alternative channels and/or opened sluiceways to lower reservoirs. Sluicegates and switching stations helped maximize the diversion of water into the reservoirs ringing the lower levels of the Tikal ridge, as well as their efficient release for agricultural purposes in the surrounding bajo margins and raised fields.[59] The lowest, bajo-margin reservoirs are estimated to have held a combined total of at least 13 million gallons of water. After passing through much of the central part of the city, this water may no longer have been considered fit for human consumption but was still a crucial resource for irrigating crops during the dry season.[60]

Site residents may have first developed their artificial reservoir system in response to the increasingly frequent droughts of the Late Preclassic Period, but they improved and expanded it over the course of the Classic Period to keep up with growing populations.[61] Both the augmentation of containment berms and the diversion of previously used catchment channels indicate that *too much* as opposed to too little rainfall became an issue during some Classic Period rainy seasons.[62]

Water managers at Tikal frequently expanded and adapted their systems for over seven centuries. However, recent research by David Lentz and colleagues suggests that despite occasional dredging and the ingenious filtration systems, even the central reservoirs may have become unpotable by the end of the site's occupation. Sediment analyses from the temple and Palace Reservoirs indicate high levels of phosphates, mercury, and cyanobacteria in the latest layers despite the best efforts of the site's water managers.[63] The development of such infrastructural problems by the Terminal Classic Period indicates that even a highly flexible and adaptive system like Tikal's water storage network might eventually reach its limits. The increasing complexity and interconnectedness of the system likely contributed to the difficulties maintaining its upkeep and also made it increasingly vulnerable to larger scale climatic perturbations. It is unclear whether the contamination of the central reservoirs would have played a critical role in the decline of central authority at Tikal, but the site center and its reservoirs were largely abandoned in the 800s CE.

Caracol: Reservoirs and Terraces Everywhere

Adrian Chase and colleagues recently conducted a large-scale, lidar-based study of water-management practices at the massive site of Caracol in southwestern Belize. They found that differences in topography may have been a key factor influencing the development of a distinct hydrological management strategy from that of Tikal. Caracol dominated the Vaca Plateau, a hilly area on the border with Guatemala with generally steeper terrain than the area around Tikal. The population of the broader Caracol community may have reached upward of 100,000 people by Late Classic, mainly distributed in farmsteads across an area that covered more than 60 sq. mi.[64]

The earliest water-management system at the Caracol monumental site center was similar to that of Tikal. Large reservoirs were built in and around the site core, which was situated on a raised plateau. The initial construction of the central reservoirs dates to the Late Preclassic, when local speleothem data indicate the region was experiencing a series of droughts. The fact that the site center and its reservoirs are located a fair distance from any natural year-round water resources suggests that the initial settlers did indeed have a plan for securing water access at their new home. When larger architectural groups were constructed around the central reservoirs, they were engineered to funnel runoff into the storage facilities. As the site grew, it became increasingly important that these reservoirs were elevated to prevent them from being polluted by garbage and runoff from the thousands of household groups that developed around the site center.[65] As we now know from Tikal, even the uppermost reservoirs of a busy site center might eventually become contaminated. Residents of Caracol recognized that multiple water collection and storage strategies would better serve their long-term well-being.

As farmsteads expanded to cover virtually all the Vaca Plateau during the Classic Period, residents of the broader Caracol community adapted new water-management strategies. Through a combination of lidar digital elevation models and pedestrian survey, members of the Caracol Archaeological Project have identified 1,590 smaller reservoirs distributed relatively evenly across the Plateau. This absolutely dwarfs the seventy-five reservoirs thus far identified at Tikal.[66] The vast majority of Caracol's reservoirs were smaller than 870 sq. ft., but no households would have had to travel more than a tenth of a mile to access a water source. The range of sizes and shapes, as well as the far-flung distribution of these many reservoirs, suggests that centralized or elite control of water access was impossible. Central authorities likely maintained control over the larger reservoirs of the site center and nodes of public architecture to which it was connected via causeway networks, but the majority of water capture and storage was decentralized at Late Classic Caracol.[67]

A critical component of the broader Late Classic Caracol water-management system that *does* appear to have been centralized was the construction of a massive terracing network (Figure 5.4). Lidar imagery has revealed that nearly every inch of the 60-plus sq. mi. of the Vaca Plateau was sculpted into terraces that managed water flow across the landscape. Farmers at Caracol would have faced greater challenges associated with runoff and soil erosion than at Tikal due to the generally steeper terrain. The massive terracing program prevented erosion, slowed runoff, and allowed for groundwater to seep in to saturate the soil. The relative rapidity and uniformity with which the terraces were constructed in the Late Classic suggests centralized planning and implementation, but it is likely

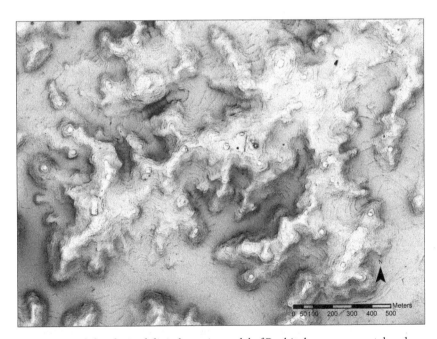

Figure 5.4 A lidar-derived digital terrain model of Puchituk, a monumental node to the northeast of the Caracol site center, created using the Sky View Factor plugin for ArcGIS. The model highlights the ubiquity of terraces at Caracol, which were used for water management and agricultural purposes (image courtesy Adrian S.Z. Chase, Caracol Archaeological Project).

that they were subsequently managed at the household or neighborhood level. The differences between Caracol and Tikal highlight the diverse possibilities for water-management mechanisms and organization strategies in different environmental niches of the Maya lowlands.

Copan: Neighborhood Reservoirs

Located in the highlands of western Honduras, Copan is considered part of the Classic Maya sphere due to its cultural and socio-political connections. Nowhere near the size of Tikal or Caracol, it still functioned as an influential regional hub as well as the gateway to the non-Maya societies of Central America. The Classic polity was strategically located along the Copan River, but the river did not always provide potable water. At times during the rainy season, torrents of water would churn up mud, making it impossible to extract clean water from the river. During the height of the dry season, the river's low levels would likewise lead to contamination by sediment and other pollutants.[68] By the Late Classic Period, growing population centers upriver would have increasingly polluted the waters that reached Copan.

One way that the elite families living near the site center responded to these changing environmental conditions was to construct large semi-artificial reservoirs at the centers of their neighborhoods. In addition to the two central reservoirs built to serve the elite-dominated neighborhoods flanking the site's civic-ceremonial core, a series of springs, streams, and small reservoirs filled out the intricate water-management system in the valley. Tantalizing connections can be made between dispersed water-related population clusters and modern waterhole groups known from ethnographic research.[69]

The civic-ceremonial center of the Copan polity is an acropolis built up over the course of 400 years of centralized rule between the early 400s and early 800s CE. It is flanked by two residential neighborhoods with high percentages of elite structures. Each of these neighborhoods, El Bosque to the west and Las Sepulturas to the East, possess a large lagoon or reservoir at their center. These reservoirs were naturally low-lying areas surrounding artesian springs that were augmented into artificial reservoirs over the course of the Classic Period. They provided fresh water for the surrounding households and served as communal organization features.[70]

The three major catchment areas of the civic-ceremonial center funneled water into the Bosque reservoir through a series of stucco- and stone-lined drains that kept the acropolis plazas from flooding. Similar to Tikal, one of the principal duties of the Copan royals and other elite families may have been water-management. Water lily motifs, including some attached to sculptural headdresses, adorn facades of structures at the site center, as well as in both the Bosque and Sepulturas neighborhoods.[71]

Twentieth-century waterhole groups around the town of Zinacantan in highland Chiapas provide a compelling analogue for Classic Period community organization. Zinacantan's *sna* groups, which bring together members of several different waterhole groups, provide an especially tantalizing model for Copan in particular. Archaeologists working in the Copan River Valley have identified potential water-related boundary markers, a continuation in use of place-names across several centuries, and the iconographic identification of water-hole groups at the *popol nah*, or council house, at the site center. Zinacantan's waterholes serve as physical, literally life-giving, landmarks around which social groups have likely organized for millennia. The belief that watery surfaces represent a veil to the underworld is reflected in community-based ancestral veneration ceremonies conducted around Zinacantan. The waterholes thus serve to both reinforce communal solidarity in the present and tie members to prior generations through shared ideas of a collective ethos.[72]

Barbara Fash postulates that lineage groups similar to Zinacanatan's *snas* or the Chorti *sian otot* combined into large social groups based on control over a shared water source within the Classic Period Copan polity. Maintenance of these jurisdictions included not only constant upkeep and monitoring of the physical conditions of the water source, but also circumambulatory ceremonies and ritual offerings similar to the *composturas* practiced by Lenca groups a little farther to the east of Copan in Honduras. Delegates may have been elected to represent several waterhole groups in a given area of the Copan Valley at meetings of a council in the *popol nah*. The nine toponymic and animal motifs that adorn the façade of the *popol nah* may thus represent waterhole-based social units across the Copan polity represented by these delegates.[73]

The ethnographic analogies provide interesting models for understanding the social aspects of water management as populations boomed during the Late Classic. Water sources served as strong, shared identity markers for communities, especially at sites that did not have one large, centralized water storage system. Controlling water at local neighborhood levels allowed for more adaptability in some cases, as households would have presumably had more of a direct say in how they managed and distributed their local resources.

The Canals of Edzna

Classic communities located in naturally concave water catchment systems continued to employ Preclassic-style water-management systems that required lower energy input. Earlier systems were expanded, and hillsides were not denuded to the same extent. The large Classic site of Edzna, located in the Río Candelaria drainage of eastern Campeche State, Mexico, is perhaps the best known canal center. The Edzna Valley receives an average of 40–50 in. of annual rainfall, almost entirely between June and December. The only natural water sources in the Edzna Valley are a few shallow, seasonally filled *aguadas*, or reservoirs. The water table in this area lies more than 65 ft. below the surface.[74] Unlike residents of many other sites in elevated interior regions, however, Edzna community members did not invest in the construction of many subterranean cisterns, called *chultuns*. Only a dozen or so have been identified in and around the site center, while sites to the north in the Puuc had hundreds.[75]

Edzna's residents relied almost entirely on the large canal network for water, which represents an interesting, localized management plan, perhaps related to sunken-cost considerations. The earliest versions of Edzna's canal network were built during the Late Preclassic Period and were later amplified during the Classic to support growing populations. The canals linked up with one another, creating a network across much of the Edzna Valley that was augmented over time by widening old canals and constructing new ones (Figure 5.5). They were engineered to capture runoff from the slopes surrounding the valley, and some were lined with stone paving. Ray Matheny and colleagues estimate that the system could have captured 88% of the total rain that fell in the 70 sq. mi. catchment area of the valley. The network kept the greater Edzna community supplied with water all the way through the Terminal Classic Period.[76]

The "Great Canal" at the center of the system is at least 7.5 mi. long, averages 160 ft. across, and is roughly 5 ft. deep. It is believed to have once held over 230 million gallons of water on its own. Combined with the other 6-plus mi. worth of canals, the twenty-seven reservoirs, and the artificial moat surrounding part of the site, the total capacity of Edzna's water storage network may have been upward of 590 million gallons![77] This would be roughly the equivalent of 980 Olympic-size swimming pools. Holding and cleaning tanks were also part of the system. Using an ethnographic water consumption analogy from the Edzna Valley today, researchers estimated that the Classic Edzna water-management system at its peak could have supported 432,000 people for six months if necessary.[78] Of course, the actual population of the community was likely much lower than that.

The engineering effort required to create this massive system was extraordinary, rivaling any of the other great construction projects across ancient Mesoamerica. The canal networks were not only oriented to capture runoff from the surrounding hills but also to direct it toward the base of the elevated site center, reinforcing the site's ideological appeal. The canals were arranged somewhat like wheel spokes surrounding the site center and may have reinforced

Figure 5.5 A map of the site center of Edzna, Campeche, highlighting the elaborate water-management system consisting of several large canals (image adapted from Matheny et al. 1983, reproduced and color added by author based on inclusion in Benavides Castillo 2008, Courtesy of the New World Archaeological Foundation).

polity integration not only by diverting water toward the civic-ceremonial center but also as transportation routes for goods and people.[79]

Although Edzna may represent the most prominent archaeological example of Classic Period canal construction, canals were built at many sites across the lowlands. Reservoirs at the site of Ucanal in northeastern Guatemala were fed by diversion canals that captured and funneled runoff from across the site center. Other canals at the site were constructed to drain water from the site center into the nearby Mopan River to prevent flooding during especially heavy rainfall episodes. The canal bottoms were lined with stone pavement in some places and excavated directly into the bedrock in others. They included paths with Z-shaped angles and check dams to slow the velocity of the draining water and thus prevent excessive erosion. At least two of the canals had smaller 20 in. wide mini-canals at their center to efficiently drain water during lighter precipitation events. Walkways bordered by 20 in. raised walls represent another water-management feature at Ucanal that would have allowed these paths to double as drainage corridors. The dating of the water diversion systems at Ucanal to the Terminal Classic Period indicates that they were a late adaptation to the more frequent torrential storms that accompanied an increasingly unpredictable climate.[80]

Smaller Scale Water-Management Features

The great Classic Period reservoir and canal sites have garnered much attention due to their absolute massiveness and the awe that such intricate public works inspire. They were not, however, the only examples of Classic Maya water-management ingenuity or resilience. For every massive reservoir at a regional capital, there existed hundreds of smaller household aguadas and wells. Giant reservoirs at site centers did serve as centralizing forces for many of the Classic Period dynasties, but as mentioned above, this force may have become increasingly ideologically focused over time. Hinterland populations grew rapidly over the Classic Period, and residents of far-flung homesteads would not have been able to make regular journeys to the ceremonial site center just to meet their daily water needs.[81]

Geospatial analyses using lidar digital elevation models make it much easier to identify the thousands of smaller aguadas and wells used by hinterland homesteads. It is likely that most household groups inclined their patios, whether paved with plaster or not, to drain precipitation runoff into the small quarries that they transformed into miniature reservoirs. The quarries were purposely excavated in low-lying areas surrounded by natural catchment zones. Dozens of such small depressions have been identified on the outskirts of Tikal and have been interpreted as localized household-level water storage tanks. At Edzna, these house-mound-based quarry reservoirs would not have been as reliable as the larger centralized networks, but may have added upward of 26 million gallons capacity to the total valley water storage capacity.[82] At sites like Medicinal Trail in Belize and Yaxnohcah in Campeche, even small household reservoirs would have been lined with plaster, clay, or stone pavements, and some even included silting tanks.[83] As mentioned above, nearly 1,600 such smaller reservoirs have been identified in the broader Caracol community.[84]

It would have been difficult, however, for these small tanks to support households through the entire dry season on their own. It is possible that members of the outlying households may have migrated to live closer to the larger centralized reservoirs during extended drought-like conditions. The Zinacantan waterhole groups discussed above provide an alternative mechanism for mitigating risk in the hinterlands. Each household may have had their own small water "tanks" to last through most of the dry season but also may have belonged to broader waterhole groups that shared access to a larger aguada or spring.[85]

The southwestern and eastern edges of the Guatemalan Peten region are uneven landscapes with many faults and troughs that fill with water fed by perennial springs. Rural households used these fault springs as potable water sources. Some households dug their own wells through the soil down to the bedrock, freeing the spring water to flow. They used stone blocks, cobbles, and clay to surround and protect the well mouth from infilling all the way to the surface.[86] Around the small site of Itzan in the southwestern Peten, a series of households took advantage of the natural spring water by digging wells that averaged only 3 ft. deep. In the eastern Peten, where the bedrock is a bit farther down from the surface, residents dug wells to depths as much as 14 to 23 ft. In southern Quintana Roo, residents of the minor site of Margarita Maza created a stone-lined well that was 75 ft. deep! In the Chenes region of eastern Campeche, wells ranging in depth from 8 to 43 ft. did not reach the especially deep water table but collected water that seeped in through the limestone bedrock during the rainy season.[87]

The town of Pich in Campeche used a Late Classic reservoir and well system all the way through the mid-twentieth century. Late Classic Period residents diverted a nearby stream into an artificial reservoir at the center of town. In the dry season, when the stream and reservoir dried up, residents would open wells that extended from the bottom of the reservoir to a perched water table below.[88] Wells were also dug to a shallow water table in the vicinity of the freshwater wetlands of the northeastern Yucatan's Yalahau region. The wetlands themselves would have been used mainly for agriculture. By digging their own wells through the bedrock to the water table, local communities allowed natural filtration of the water that would otherwise have been polluted by the fertilizers and other materials used for agriculture in the wetlands.[89]

Another form of water storage used in the hinterlands was the partial damming of spring mouths and the streams that often emanated from them. Paul Healy identified a 30 ft. long and 10 ft. high Late Classic dam near Blue Hole Camp in the western Maya Mountains of Belize, placed just downhill from a natural spring. This dam was composed of smoothed stones and formed a small pond that could have held close to 80,000 gal. for nearby households. A small hole near the thick base of the dam allowed water to slowly seep out, maintaining the flow of the stream and preventing the pond from overflowing. A smaller, but similarly sustainable type of dam was identified in the Copan Valley.[90]

A nearly 200. ft. long Late Classic dam was built near the site of Tamarindito in the Petexbatun region of Guatemala to trap water from an upland seepage spring. The dam was constructed like a masonry building, with two nearly parallel walls of stone separated by 6.5 ft. of rubble fill, and the whole thing was covered with thick lime plaster to make it watertight. The dam was likely a response to shifting social and environmental challenges and would have prevented erosion of a hillside that featured terraces and residential compounds.[91]

Whether based on small quarry reservoirs, dammed streams, wells dug to the water table, or even jar storage,[92] maintenance and access to water would have been powerful social organizing factors in the hinterlands. At some sites, hinterland household-level water-management systems originated as far back as the Middle Preclassic Period and continued to support group solidarity up through the end of the Classic Period.[93] With growing populations and more people spreading out into the hinterlands between the larger sites, individual households and waterhole groups adapted and developed a wide range of storage systems to survive both the annual dry season and increasingly erratic climatic patterns toward the end of the Classic Period. Investigations around Caracol have demonstrated that smaller groups living in some hinterland areas were able to survive long after elites abandoned local civic-ceremonial centers. A diversification of water storage strategies and more localized administrative mechanisms were likely critical in the longer term survival of these smaller hinterland communities.[94]

Palenque: "Big Water"

Whereas the main water-related challenge facing most lowland Maya sites was storing enough to survive the dry season, Palenque's unique challenge was managing an excess of water. The site's ancient name Lakamha' translates roughly to "Big/Wide Water" and may refer to the largest of a series of streams that course

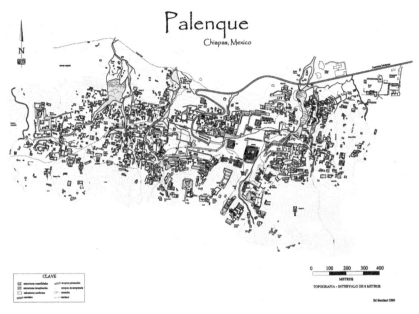

Figure 5.6 A map of Palenque, Chiapas—known as Lakamha' or "Big Water" in Classic Mayan—highlights the numerous streams that cut through the site center from south to north (image courtesy of Ed Barnhart).

through the site center. These streams flowed year-round from natural springs near the northern edge of the highlands of Chiapas, and, when combined with rainy season runoff, they posed several logistical challenges. Palenque's civic engineers managed to divert these natural waterways and augment a series of narrow natural terraces to allow for the construction of one of the great Classic centers.

Nine major waterways course through the site, funneling water from at least fifty-six natural springs and over 40 in. of annual rainfall (Figures 5.6 and 5.7). The net result was a waterlogged plateau with only narrow stretches of flat land on which to build. In order to have enough space to build plazas and temples, let alone residential structures, the engineers of Palenque constructed aqueducts, canals, and dams to manufacture additional building locations. The expert design of this system is evidenced by the fact that most of the ancient waterways are still in use today to make the site viable as a tourist destination.

One of the more distinctive features of Palenque's unique hydrologic situation was the closest thing to a flush toilet in the Maya lowlands, in the sense that rushing water was likely used to carry away human waste. Engineers spun off a small aqueduct from the Otolum stream to run underneath the Classic Period

Figure 5.7 One of the many streams that flows through the site of Palenque, Chiapas. Relatively calm during the dry season, streams like this one can turn into torrents and overflow during the rainy season (photo by author).

palace. This substructural waterway would presumably have allowed royal inhabitants to dispose of their waste directly into the moving water. It is unclear, however, whether the pressure would have built up enough to force water upward into the palace. Water pressures calculated for channel systems elsewhere at the site do suggest that water could indeed have been forced upward, but it is unclear for what purpose this hydraulic technology would have been used.[95]

Palenque's water-management prowess was not limited to the ceremonial site center. Recent research by Keith Prufer and colleagues in the Picota group located in the western expanse of the city has uncovered a series of pools, drains, and aqueducts. At the center of the group is the principal reservoir, a 33 by 13 ft. rectangle excavated 5 ft. deep directly into the bedrock. The bedrock walls were lined with shaped stones averaging 10 in. thick. The Picota group water system, which has three of the six reservoirs yet identified at the site, is fed by three of Palenque's many springs. The main aqueduct of the group is nearly 200 ft. long and runs below structures and plazas. Ethnographic research conducted nearby among highland Chiapas communities like Zinacantan suggests that the pools of

Picota were designed to mimic natural ponds and likely served as focal points for water-related community rituals.[96]

As the site grew over the course of the Late Classic Period, new terraces were cleared, expanded, and dried. Site planners continued to work with the natural environment of the site, recognizing drainage patterns and where new terraces should be constructed to limit erosion. Natural streams and runoff channels were redirected to maintain the structural integrity of the hillside terraces, while at the same time securing controlled access to potable water. The fact that this great Classic center was able to continue expanding for several centuries in such a naturally precarious environment is a testament to both the adaptability and sustainability of the hydrologic engineering projects.

The North

The Northern Plains region of Yucatan is largely devoid of surface water resources save for the Yalahau wetlands of the northeastern corner of the peninsula and approximately sixty small lakes, clustered mainly in the east. However, the idea that the north is impoverished with regard to water resources is a misconception based on Colonial Era and mid-twentieth-century agricultural assessments. In reality, the largest freshwater aquifer in Mexico lies just below the Yucatan. Pre-Colonial residents of the northern lowlands thrived by relying on cenotes (natural sinkholes) and human-made wells to access the subterranean water table for thousands of years (Figure 5.8).[97]

Although the actual number is difficult to assess, there are at least 7,000 known cenotes across the northwest alone.[98] They were so important for supporting populations in the northern Yucatan that towns were named after their local cenotes.[99] Part of the northwestern corner of the peninsula is known as the "cenote zone" due to their prevalence—a remnant of the impact of the Chicxulub meteor 60 million years ago. Recent archaeological work in the region has demonstrated a tremendous density of ancient settlements dating as far back as the Middle Preclassic Period (c. 800 BCE).[100] Cenotes understandably became centers for water-related rituals, especially ceremonies related to the rain god Chahk. They were also occasionally sources of food, as small fish species live in many cenotes.[101]

At the northwestern site of Dzibilchaltun, archaeologists have identified many small wells, less than 3 ft. in diameter that were excavated to access the water table.[102] Similar small wells dotted the site of Chunchucmil, to the southwest of Dzibilchaltun, where the water table was less than 3 ft. below the surface in some places. Groundwater studies by Sheryl Luzzadder-Beach, Tim Beach, and colleagues have demonstrated that despite the proximity of the water table to the

Figure 5.8 Cenotes, or sinkholes, exist all throughout the northern Yucatan providing communities with access to freshwater. Some cenotes remain partly covered by overhangs or cave entrances (top), while others like the Sacred Cenote at Chichen Itza (bottom) are open to the sky (photos courtesy of Ryan Collins).

surface at such northern sites like Chunchucmil, Uci, and Cansahcab, contamination likely remained low. The prevalence of cenotes in the region increases the rate of lateral groundwater flow, dispersing surface contaminants away from the sites.[103] The dilution and dispersal of contaminated groundwater was especially useful at the larger northern sites that likely used higher rates of fertilizers to increase the agricultural potential of the thin soils. Another type of well, called a *buk'te*, was excavated at the bottom of natural aguadas. They were lined with crude stones and served as the final storage locations for the water that filled and eventually evaporated from the rest of the low-lying area.[104]

The great cosmogram city of Chichen Itza is well known as a tourist attraction today and the most visited cenote at the site is popular for its association with sacrifice. The ancient residents of the site, however, would have been more interested in the life-sustaining properties of the many cenotes inside the city's boundaries. Recent investigations of the central pyramid of K'uk'ulkan, known also as the Castillo, suggest that its earliest iterations date back to at least the middle of the Classic Period, indicating that the cenotes made the location appealing from early on. Unsurprisingly, no big surface reservoirs have been identified at this northern capital as the shallow water table and plethora of sinkholes would have rendered them unnecessary. The great plaza surrounding the Castillo was slightly inclined to divert excess rainwater into the nearby cenotes and prevent it from flooding.[105]

At both Chichen Itza and the large site of Coba in the eastern part of the peninsula, centralized water features were gradually supplemented by decentralized household-level water systems. At Chichen Itza, households excavated a series of wells down to the shallow water table. At Coba, households supplemented access to the site's five relatively large lakes by transforming shallow quarries into water collection features.[106] The individual wells and small reservoirs excavated at the household- or neighborhood-level provided a steady source of water that required no centralized mediation. Toward the end of the Classic Period, when populations in the south began to fall and many refugees were likely on the move, any that traveled north would have had to adapt to the unfamiliar water-management landscape. The expansion of populations in the north during the Terminal Classic Period suggests that they most definitely did adapt and survive.

High and Dry in the Hill Country

The Puuc region, or "hill country," is an uplifted area of the northern interior characterized by thousands of low (100–180 ft. high) hills (Figure 5.9). The region experiences roughly 43 in. of rainfall per year, more than 80% of which falls between June and December.[107] Expanses of deep, fertile *kancab* (red earth) soil

Figure 5.9 The landscape of the Puuc ("hill" in Yucatec Mayan) region of the northern Maya lowlands is characterized by thousands of low hills and stretches of flat terrain with deep, fertile soils (photo by author).

made the Puuc an appealing place for agriculture, but the tectonic uplift made the water table nearly inaccessible to Pre-Colonial communities. The challenges of the dry season were thus particularly harsh in the hill country, and the earliest year-round settlements in the region were not founded until around 800 BCE. Preclassic water-management systems focused on larger, communal reservoirs, while later Classic water storage shifted to household-level capture and storage in bell-shaped subterranean cisterns called *chultuns*.

Throughout the Preclassic, larger Puuc sites relied mainly on communal aguadas, or human-modified reservoirs, that took advantage of low areas where water naturally pooled. Some communities created aguadas by plugging natural swallow holes in low-lying areas with clay.[108] Approximately forty large aguadas have been identified across the region thanks in large part to lidar digital elevation models. Lidar-derived imagery is helping to clarify not only the storage capacities of the aguadas but also the extent to which residents built up the edges with large earthen berms and engineered feeder channels. Some of the communal reservoirs in the Puuc were truly massive, holding as much as an estimated 4.7 million gallons of water at the Preclassic site Yaxhom, for example.[109]

Aside from water stored in ceramic vessels, these reservoirs served as the main water resources for the population through the dry season. This risky all-eggs-in-one-basket strategy may have contributed to the depopulation of several sites near the end of the Preclassic Period when lake core and speleothem data indicate the onset of increasingly frequent droughts. Learning from the consequences of the Preclassic strategy, Classic Puuc communities increasingly supplemented their communal aguadas with chultuns that they could manage at the household level. Although the earliest chultuns date to the Preclassic, their numbers appear to have remained relatively low until populations began to expand rapidly in the Classic Period. By the Late and Terminal Classic Periods, Puuc households were excavating the cisterns by the hundreds, if not thousands.[110] This shift in strategy likely represents not only a response to the failures of the Preclassic settlements but also the rapid expansion of Classic populations and changes in socio-political structures.

Chultuns were constructed by digging narrow holes (roughly 2–3 ft. in diameter) down through the hard surface caprock to the softer limestone marl layer (called *sascab*) below. These narrow necks through the hard caprock can range anywhere from 1 to 5 ft. deep. Upon reaching the sascab layer, workers would excavate a wide, bell-shaped tank (Figure 5.10). The interior walls were then coated with thick layers of watertight lime plaster to prevent seepage. Patios and plazas were ever so slightly inclined to drain water into the chultun openings. An average chultun held about 9,000 gal., but some are estimated to have held as much as 25,000 gal.—the equivalent of over thirty-seven Olympic-size swimming pools.[111] Virtually all Late and Terminal Classic Puuc household groups had at least one such subterranean water storage tank, as it became a prerequisite to survive in the region year-round.[112]

Managing water distribution at the household or even nuclear family level would have allowed for more nuanced water rationing through the end of the dry season. Although the bulk of water capture and storage undoubtedly took place during the rainy season, the one or two storms that passed through the region during the dry season may have significantly replenished the chultuns. Changes to central reservoir stores made by these isolated storms would have been minimal by comparison.[113] An additional benefit of the chultun-dominated water-management system included the fact that the narrow openings were easily covered with capstones, preventing both contamination and evaporation of the water. The continued use of central reservoirs at some Terminal Classic Puuc sites in addition to the plethora of household chultuns highlight the importance of diversifying options to support resilience.[114]

Although the site of Xcoch, located in the relatively flat Santa Elena Valley, enjoyed access to one of the few caves in the region that reached the water table, Preclassic residents mainly relied on a reservoir system constructed at the site

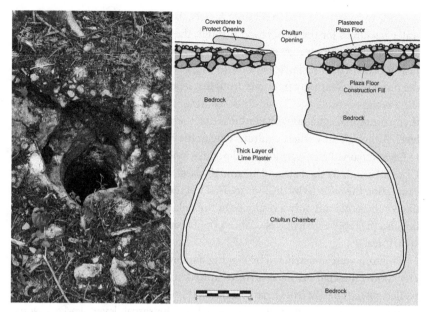

Figure 5.10 Chultuns are human-made subterranean chambers created by Pre-Colonial Maya communities throughout the lowlands. In the Puuc region of the northern lowlands, chultuns were created almost exclusively to serve as water storage tanks with narrow entrances opening into large chambers with watertight lime-plaster coating on the walls (photo and image by author).

center. When droughts became more frequent during the second and third centuries CE, residents responded by expanding the system into an intricate hydrologic network of augmented natural reservoirs, catchment surfaces, and channels to connect them. One of the aguadas is estimated to have held 2.2 million gallons, while the other held over 19.2 million gallons. Terraces around the inside walls of the aguadas allowed residents to continue to access the water as levels dropped during the dry season. Water managers could have also used these terraces to keep track of water levels and plan rations accordingly.[115] Having such an intricate rainfall capture and storage system was only effective so far as there was any rain to catch. Late Preclassic droughts likely became so severe that the site was largely abandoned by the Early Classic Period.

Households began to return to Xcoch around 500 CE and resurrected the old water-management system, expanding it to support growing populations. Excavations of one of the canals that fed one of the site's central aguadas uncovered the use of a mixture of limestone marl (sascab) and clay-rich soils to form a watertight layer.[116] Households also began to construct chultuns on a large scale, especially around the outskirts of the site, which mirrored contemporary trends in water-management elsewhere in the Puuc. The nearby Terminal Classic capital of Uxmal, which dominated the region in the 800s and early 900s CE, possessed both an intricate central reservoir and canal system, and hundreds of household-level chultuns.[117]

The several smaller aguadas that ring the Xcoch site center were built after the site was reoccupied, possibly as late as the Late Classic Period. Their proximity to the surrounding agricultural lands and the presence of channels leading out toward these flatter areas suggest possible irrigation functions for the peripheral aguadas. The fact that the inhabitants of Classic Period Xcoch had both chultuns and aguadas suggests that the chultuns may have been used for residential water needs and the aguadas either represented reserve supplies or irrigation-specific supplies. The aguada as backup source would suggest a level of planning based on a collective memory of the need to abandon the site at the end of the Preclassic due to drought. It is also possible that smaller aguadas on the site's periphery served as neighborhood-centering features and that social groups were organized along similar lines to the waterhole groups of modern Zinacantan and hypothesized for Classic Period Copan.[118]

Summary

A brief overview of Classic Maya water-management systems highlights both the challenges of securing year-round access to water and the variety of solutions engineered by communities across the lowlands to address them. In many regions, communities learned from the shortcomings of their Preclassic forebears and diversified their water capture and storage strategies. The relatively stable climate of the Classic Period contributed to the steady growth of communities for over seven centuries, but the population expansion presented its own challenges. As communities like Tikal and Edzna expanded, they adapted their water-management systems by augmenting the scale of existing reservoir and canal networks and constructing new, smaller reservoirs away from the site center. A massive, centrally planned terrace network transformed the landscape of the Vaca Plateau around Caracol to slow runoff, capture water, and saturate the soil. Palenque's engineers continued to carve new building surfaces out of the site's waterlogged perch on the edge of the highlands by diverting streams and runoff channels into paved conduits. In the Puuc region, Classic residents supplemented existing communal surface reservoirs with individual household cisterns.

Throughout the lowlands, communities modified their natural environments to their advantage. Wherever possible, they excavated wells to a shallow water table, dammed streams, lined natural depressions, and terraced hillsides. They used absorptive minerals to create water filtration systems and developed intricate release mechanisms to control flooding. Settlements from the smallest farmsteads to the largest cities were designed specifically to capture and store water. Even a relatively stable climatic period in the tropics can include significant swings in precipitation from year to year and from subregion to subregion. Classic communities prepared for these uncertainties by diversifying water-management strategies and continuing to adapt their practices.

The various Classic Period adaptive strategies allowed many communities to survive for a century or more through a period of increasingly prolonged droughts, beginning in the 700s CE. In some areas, however, the droughts proved too severe to manage with existing practices, especially amidst an onslaught of additional destabilizing forces. In those cases, populations pursued the last-resort adaptations of social reorganization or migration. A flood of new data from across the lowlands highlights the heterogeneity of responses to the Terminal Classic droughts. I will explore the various responses to the increasingly unstable climatic conditions of the Terminal Classic Period, including their shortcomings, in greater depth in Chapter 7.

6

Stone

Introduction

The Classic Maya culture developed atop a limestone foundation. Literally, the vast majority of the bedrock across the Maya lowlands is composed of the calcium-carbonate sedimentary stone. It is therefore no surprise that Maya communities incorporated limestone into several facets of daily life from architecture to grinding stones to handheld tools. It was also the critical ingredient for making burnt lime—a powdery material with cement-like properties created by heating limestone for an extended period. Burnt lime (hereafter referred to simply as "lime") was both the literal glue that held Maya architecture together and the essential ingredient that allowed maize to become the most important crop. Although limestone itself is a virtually limitless resource in the Maya lowlands, the wood fuel necessary to make lime is not. In the past, researchers have even suggested that the demand for lime may have contributed to excessive Pre-Colonial forest clearance.

Another stone critical to the well-being of Classic Maya communities was salt. Huge natural salt beds exist on the north coast of the Yucatan Peninsula, but salt producers elsewhere in the lowlands needed to boil down brine to make transportable salt cakes. Studies of the fuel consumption necessary for boiling brine to produce enough salt for communities across the lowlands have likewise raised issues about potential deforestation and environmental degradation. More recently, however, in-depth investigations of Maya lime and salt industries have indicated that Classic Period producers developed conservation strategies to protect against the overexploitation of fuel resources. This chapter explores Classic Maya resource-management adaptations related to the processing of limestone into lime and brine into salt.

Limestone and Lime

Lime (calcium hydroxide), also known as slaked lime, hydrated lime, or *cal* in Spanish, is made by heating a calcium-carbonate-rich material to temperatures of at least 750–800°C (1382°–1472°F) for an extended period.[1] It is most often made from limestone but can also be produced from several varieties of animal

The Maya and Climate Change. Kenneth E. Seligson, Oxford University Press. © Oxford University Press 2023.
DOI: 10.1093/oso/9780197652923.003.0006

shells. For example, residents of Palenque and Comalcalco on the western edge of the Maya lowlands likely used snail-shell-derived lime for both dietary and plastering purposes during the Classic Period.[2] Marine shells provided a ready source of calcium carbonate for lime production along the coasts of the Yucatan and Belize.[3]

The extensive heating, a process called calcination, expels carbon dioxide and impurities from the calcium carbonate, leaving behind the caustic compound known as quicklime (calcium oxide).[4] Quicklime usually holds the shape of the parent material, but it can leave chemical burns if it touches bare skin. Thus, the next crucial step is to add water so it collapses into the fine white powder called lime. This can be achieved either by leaving the quicklime to absorb moisture from the air or sprinkling water directly onto it. The chemical reaction that occurs in the conversion from quicklime to lime gives off a lot of heat and thus must be completed carefully. This is one of several reasons why a hands-off method of natural moisture absorption may have been preferred. A batch of pure limestone, if perfectly calcined and hydrated, should leave behind a pile of lime that is roughly 56% of the weight of the original calcium carbonate.[5]

Architectural lime is mixed with water and aggregates to create mortars, plasters, and stuccos. After its application, the lime-based material absorbs carbon dioxide from the air as water evaporates, a process called carbonation. Eventually, the material dries and hardens back into calcium carbonate, but now in the shape and location that suits the builder's needs. The full cycle can be expressed with the following notation:[6]

Calcination:	$CaCO_3$ + heat	$CaO + CO_2$
Hydration:	$CaO + H_2O$	$Ca(OH)_2$ + heat
Carbonation:	$Ca(OH)_2 + CO_2$	$CaCO_3 + H_2O$

Upon a Limestone Foundation

Although the vast majority of the bedrock across the lowlands is composed of limestone, not all grades are equally suitable for making lime. Limestone is a sedimentary rock generally formed by the deposition and compaction of calcium-carbonate-rich skeletal (shell) materials in marine environments. The bedrock of the Maya lowlands formed under ancient shallow seas before slowly emerging over the past 100 million years. Different grades of limestone are the result of variations in (1) the original source material (i.e., which marine flora and fauna contributed to the composition of any given area); (2) how long ago the limestone was formed (affecting the degree of compaction); and (3) how recently it emerged from a marine environment to experience weathering processes.[7]

The limestone bedrock of the Maya lowlands is generally younger and more recently emerged the farther north that you go. Some of the bedrock near the coasts of the northern Yucatan emerged as recently as the Holocene Epoch, which began roughly 12,000 years ago.[8] However, variations in grades of limestone can exist within individual quarries, let alone within subregions. Across much of the lowlands, a hard caprock of varying grades of consolidated limestone covers much of the surface and is generally 2.5 to 4 ft. thick. Below the caprock are pockets of softer, semi-decomposed limestone called *sah kab* or *sascab* meaning "white earth." Although sascab is not viable for making lime, it is used as an aggregate in plasters as well as to make tamped floors.[9] Early lime producers learned which types of limestone were best for producing lime and passed down their knowledge from generation to generation.

Lime in Classic Maya Culture

Architectural Lime

The most prominent use of lime, both in terms of visibility and overall consumption, was for construction. Today, it is difficult to imagine the temple pyramids of Tikal or the thousands of miles of raised causeways gleaming with a fresh coat of white lime plaster when photographs display only gray, weathered stones. We can only try to picture what these grand constructions looked like when the Classic sites were inhabited. The palace at Palenque, impressive as it still looks today, would be that much more awe-inspiring with the fresh coat of plaster that earned it the name Sak Nuk Naah, or "White Skin House,"[10] in the ancient texts (Figure 6.1).

After initial calcination and hydration, architectural lime is left to "mature" for at least two weeks. The longer it sits, the more plastic and workable it becomes, making it more desirable for construction purposes. Sometimes, it sits for as long as three years before use.[11] When deemed ready, masons mix it with aggregates such as sand, very small pieces of limestone, and crushed sascab. In some places, where limestone and sascab were unavailable, they used other materials like volcanic tuff, crushed ceramics, or even charcoal bits. In some cases, there is even evidence that masons ground up and recycled earlier coats of plaster or pieces of lime mortar as aggregates in new layers.[12] In addition to lowering the amount of lime needed (and therefore lowering fuel costs), the use of aggregates prevented the mixture from shrinking and cracking when it dried.[13] The small size of many aggregates makes it difficult to assess ancient lime binder-to-aggregate ratios and

Figure 6.1 A juxtaposition of the Palenque palace as it looks today with a reconstruction of what it may have looked like when coated with a bright layer of lime stucco, which demonstrates the visual significance of architectural lime (photo and reconstruction by author).

therefore estimates from across the lowlands range from as high as 1:1 to even lower than 1:10 (binder-to-aggregate).[14]

All the aggregates mentioned above are non-reactive—that is, they do not chemically react with the calcium hydroxide as it dries. Recent studies have proven that Classic Period lime workers in some regions recognized the benefits of reactive aggregates like silicate-rich clays and volcanic ash. These materials chemically bond with calcium hydroxide to form cements with a greater compressive strength than non-reactive aggregates. Researchers have identified the resulting "hydraulic" or "pozzolanic" cements at several sites including Tikal, Copan, Nakbe, Holmul, Calakmul, Lamanai, Comalcalco, and most recently Río Bec.[15] The volcanic ash used in Río Bec mortars was likely gathered after eruptions in the southern highlands blanketed portions of the lowlands.[16]

Vegetal extracts were a final component added to Classic Period lime plasters in several regions. The most common additives were tree bark extracts that contributed a greater plasticity and eventually durability to the lime mixture when it dried. Preferred tree species for lime additives included *chucum* (*Havardia albicans*, or huisache), *pixoy* (*Guazuma ulmifolia*, or bay cedar), *chacah* (*Bursera simaruba*, or gumbo-limbo), *jolol* (a variety of *Tiliaceae* family species), and *ja'abín* (*Piscidia piscipula*, or dogwood).[17] Honey, which was connected to lime through their shared symbolic associations with fertility and heat, was likely another common additive.[18]

Lime was necessary for the construction of the Maya corbelled vault, which relied on thick walls and massive amounts of mortar and fill in the roof to support the vault stones. Thick masonry walls throughout the lowlands followed a general blueprint that included interior and exterior walls of smooth-sided facing stones glued together and solidified by a mixture of lime mortar and fill stones (Figure 6.2).[19] Although it is sometimes referred to as a "false arch," the fact that hundreds of vaulted structures still stand across the lowlands more than 1,300 years after they were constructed is a testament to the strength of lime mortars.[20] The earliest vaulted structures date to the Middle or Late Preclassic Period in the Peten, eventually becoming widespread across the lowlands during the Classic Period.[21]

Plasters served both to protect buildings from natural elements and to enhance the aesthetics and symbolism of the architecture. Lime-based ceremonial architecture was crucial to the solidification of divine administrations, which used impressive construction programs to reinforce their power.[22] By the start of the Late Preclassic Period, rulers had begun to adorn civic-ceremonial architecture with elaborately carved stucco facades. Early examples of stucco decorations included huge masks of deities that marked structures as arenas for ritual communication between realms.[23] The link between divine power and lime architecture would continue into the Classic Period, exemplified by the explosion of

Figure 6.2 A massive amount of stone fill and lime mortar held Classic Maya stone vaults together. The wedge shape of the vault stones is visible in this image of a partially collapsed residence in the Puuc region of the northern lowlands. Toward the back of the image, one remaining capstone is visible in situ at the top of the arch that would have held the two sides of the arch in place (photo by author).

masonry buildings with stucco sculptural adornments that accompanied the beginning of a new Classic Period dynasty at Copan in the early fifth century CE.[24]

Another key function of architectural lime was to incorporate buildings and floors into a site's water diversion and capture infrastructure. The massive temples became "water mountains" of sustenance, with torrents of rainwater literally flowing off of their terraces. Paved plazas built on ever-so-slight angles funneled the water that cascaded off buildings into channels that carried it into open reservoirs or subterranean cisterns. The floors of some reservoirs were even paved with lime-based plaster. The subterranean cisterns of the Puuc region were made watertight by a thick layer of lime plaster.[25] Despite its water-resistant properties, lime plaster does degrade over time in the tropical humidity. Structure surfaces may have been replastered as often as every five years, with major replastering events every fifty-two years to coincide with larger Mesoamerican cycles of rebirth.[26]

Massive quantities of lime plaster covered plaza, patio, and house floors, as well as the long inter- and intra-site causeways called *sakbeob*, or "white roads." Plastered floors not only *looked* cleaner and were aesthetically pleasing, they also provided healthier foundations upon which to carry out everyday activities. Especially as population densities increased over the course of the Classic Period, lime-plaster coatings of floors and structures provided a more hygienic environment.[27] It is important to recognize, however, that the architectural consumption of lime was not evenly spread across Classic communities. High-status households living in stone-vaulted residences required much higher quantities of architectural lime per capita than lower status households that lived in residences constructed mainly of perishable materials.

Dietary and Other Uses of Lime

The massive lime-based construction projects may never have been possible if not for the incorporation of dietary lime into Mesoamerican food processing. When maize is soaked in lime-infused water, it becomes easier to remove the tougher outer part of the kernels. It also unlocks key nutrients like niacin for easier absorption by the body (Figure 6.3). At the same time, the maize absorbs some calcium, providing a welcome supplement to a diet with few other sources of calcium.[28] Though ancient Mesoamerican food preparers did not know what was happening on a molecular level, over time they realized that individuals who consumed lime-treated maize were healthier than those that did not. Treatment with lime is what allowed maize to go on to become *the* staple crop of Mesoamerica and the backbone of the Classic Maya diet. If maize were consumed as a primary food without lime treatment, populations would suffer pellagra, a niacin deficiency disease.

We do not know when Mesoamericans first developed the *nixtamalization* process– the anglicized version of the Spanish pronunciation of the Nahuatl word *nextamalli*, meaning "lime-treated maize."[29] Recent skeletal isotopic evidence from the Maya Mountains indicates that maize already composed at least 70% of the local diet by approximately 2000 BCE, hinting that lime treatment was already taking place by that point.[30] Although we now know that the Classic Maya diet ranged far beyond just the three sisters, maize still likely contributed the greatest source of calories across the socioeconomic spectrum. Ethnographic research suggests that approximately 11 lbs. of lime were used to process maize per person annually in the Maya lowlands before the onset of the globalized food market.[31] If levels were similar in the Pre-Colonial Era, dietary lime may have composed a significant portion of overall lime production and consumption.

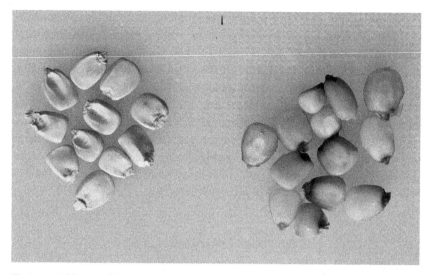

Figure 6.3 Nixtamalization, or the treatment of maize using burnt lime, frees nutrients to be absorbed by the human body and results in a softer kernel that is easier to grind. Pretreated maize (left) versus lime-treated maize (right) (image accessed and used through the public domain under Creative Commons CC0 1.0 Universal Public Domain Dedication).

Lime was also used to preserve food in Classic Maya communities. Ethnohistoric and ethnographic sources refer to lime being used as a desiccant and pest deterrent to preserve harvested maize cobs. Not only the maize itself but also the walls of storerooms were coated with lime to deter rodents, insects, and birds from accessing the food.[32] Lime whitewash was also used as an insect and other pest repellent for agroforestry purposes, painted on the trunks of trees in homegardens, orchards, and even perhaps on especially valuable trees in managed forests. Studies more recently have shown that painting tree trunks white can also protect them from overheating. Lime can also be used to lower the acidity of soils, and you may recognize it as a key ingredient in gardening soil blends today to remedy the same problem. It was also likely sprinkled around milpas to deter intrusions by ants and other insects.[33]

A few additional uses for lime include softening tree bark so it can be more easily mashed into pulp to produce bark paper for codices, the pages of which were then laminated with thin layers of plaster.[34] Lime plaster also coated other small, perishable items like wooden effigies of gods. In some instances, archaeologists have found plaster outlines of the perishable items that they once coated within royal tombs that had been sealed for over 1,000 years.[35] Finally, lime could be used as a fish poison, to help purify water in reservoirs and cisterns, for mixing with chewing tobacco to enhance its stimulant properties, for tanning deerskin and other hides, for medical uses, to lighten dyes derived from plants, and to make soap.[36] With such a wide range of functions, it is clear that lime was a critical material for everyday life in the Classic Maya lowlands.

Pre-Colonial Lime Production

The Earliest Lime

We will likely never know exactly how lime production was first discovered and refined. Incidental occurrences likely characterized many early societies living in the limestone-rich environments and became more frequent as groups became more sedentary. If fires were kindled directly atop limestone bedrock or in limestone caves and kept alive for long enough, they might transform the surface layers to quicklime. Unfortunately, these sporadic, unintentional production events are virtually invisible in the archaeological record. The earliest evidence for the use of architectural lime anywhere in the world comes from the Geometric Kebaran phase in the Levant, dating to approximately 12,500 BCE. The earliest lime kiln yet identified comes from a Natufian culture site in the same region (c. 10,400–10,000 BCE).[37]

The discovery of lime production likely followed a similar pattern in Mesoamerica, albeit a little later. It is possible that cooking methods involving the placement of heated rocks into clay containers to boil water contributed to the discovery.[38] Research in the Oaxaca Valley of Mexico suggests the purposeful production of lime for plastering floors as early as 1400–1150 BCE, but the evidence remains uncertain.[39] The earliest clear evidence for lime production in the Maya lowlands comes from the site of Cuello in northern Belize. There, lime-based plaster floors and wall coatings date to the start of the Middle Preclassic Period, around 1100 BCE.[40] Soon after that, we see lime-based plaster, stucco, and mortar appearing throughout the lowlands, eventually facilitating the development of monumental palaces and temple pyramids by the end of the Middle Preclassic. As mentioned above, however, recent evidence indicates maize became the principal crop in some areas of the lowlands as early as 2000 BCE, and lime treatment would have likely been a prerequisite for this to happen.[41] Thus, although it remains unclear exactly when lime production first became common across the lowlands, by at least the start of the Classic Period, communities in every corner of the Maya area were making and using lime for a range of purposes. The question then becomes, *How did the Classic Maya make lime?*

The "Traditional" Method

Although asking how the Classic Maya made lime may seem like a straightforward question, it is a difficult one to answer and has significant implications for resource-management issues. The ephemeral nature of lime and of many lime-making techniques hinders the detailed analysis of Pre-Colonial production methods. This in turn has led to lime's significance being overlooked or misunderstood. When lime *is* mentioned, especially in public-facing volumes, it is often highlighted as a significant contributor to deforestation.[42]

The connection between lime production and excessive forest clearance is mainly based on ethnographic observations of production techniques in the early 1900s. In 1931, Earl Morris and colleagues documented an aboveground lime production event at Chichen Itza for the Temple of the Warriors consolidation effort.[43] Local workers constructed a massive circular pyre of freshly cut hardwood logs around a central vertical post. They heaped fist-sized limestone cobbles on top of the 6.5 x 18 ft. pyre and then removed the central post to create a "chimney." This style of aboveground "kiln" is called a *calera*.[44] The lime makers waited for the wind to die down and then dropped a starter flame down the chimney. The fire began at the center and slowly burned from the inside-out. The pyre eventually caved in on itself, forming an aboveground oven that surrounded the small pieces of limestone with smoldering wood fuel. Very large caleras like the one at Chichen Itza can burn for twenty-four to thirty hours.

Morris and colleagues' detailed description of the process included the following phrase: "The Yucatecan method of producing lime at the present time is an ancestral heritage that has come down through the centuries with practically no change, except the substitution of steel for stone tools."[45] The aboveground calera technique has been referred to as the "traditional" method ever since (Figure 6.4). With few potential identifications of alternative lime-production features in the archaeological record, researchers have assumed it to be *the* Pre-Colonial method for making lime.[46] Experimental calculations based on the amounts of wood fuel necessary to construct the aboveground pyres have in turn led to dire evaluations of the potential for deforestation wrought by the demand for lime during the Classic Period (Figure 6.5).

In the late 1990s and early 2000s, ethnographic research by Thomas Schreiner identified a wide range of calera forms used across the lowlands.[47] Variations included pyre shape (circular, square, or rectangular), the direction of the wood (horizontal or vertical), and whether the pyre was built directly on flat ground or in a shallow pit.[48] One commonality across all variations was the selection of fuel with high moisture content. This involved selecting tree species with relatively high water contents and using freshly cut "greenwood" instead of dead, dried branches. Fuel efficiencies recorded by Schreiner across twelve regional calera

Figure 6.4 An aboveground calera prepared and ready to be used to produce burnt lime. The wood is carefully stacked in a radial pattern and fist-sized pieces of limestone are placed on top. The pyre will be lit from the center so it will burn slowly from the inside-out and collapse in on itself forming an aboveground oven (image courtesy of Tomás Gallareta Negrón and Rossana May Ciau).

variations ranged from a ratio of 3.8:1 fuel-to-lime to 8.2:1, with an average overall ratio of 5:1.[49] Experiments by other researchers in the northern Yucatan returned fuel efficiencies of 4.4:1 and 7.7:1, falling within that same range.[50]

Preclassic Deforestation

Considering the importance of lime to so many aspects of Classic Maya culture, you can begin to imagine the tremendous quantities that must have been produced annually across the lowlands. Excessive lime production and fuel consumption may have indeed contributed to environmental stress and sociopolitical breakdown within several larger Preclassic communities. The main evidence for an overexploitation of fuel resources during the Late Preclassic Period comes from the Mirador area of northern Guatemala, where there is no denying that the amount of lime consumption would have been massive. El Mirador was one of the largest ever Maya urban centers with some of the most

Figure 6.5 The firing of an experimental pit-kiln modeled on the ancient features demonstrated the increased fuel efficiency provided by the semi-enclosed space (photo by author).

gigantic individual architectural projects, including the Danta and Tigre pyramid complexes.[51]

Even consumption figures modeled for Late Classic Tikal do not come close to those for Late Preclassic El Mirador. Based on Schreiner's average 5:1 fuel-to-lime ratio, David Lentz and colleagues estimated that over 87,000 tons of wood fuel would have been necessary to make enough lime to coat all of the surfaces at Tikal with a one-time layer of 8 cm thick plaster.[52] To coat all of Late Preclassic El Mirador with a layer under 7 cm thick would have required nearly twice as much wood fuel, even without including all the plaza areas between the structures.[53] Richard Hansen and colleagues traced a steady increase in plaster floor thickness at El Mirador from the Middle Preclassic into the Late Preclassic before there was a sharp decrease toward the very end of the site's construction sequence.[54] The sudden drop-off in floor thickness, which was also recorded at the Preclassic site of San Bartolo around the same time, may very well have been due to an exhaustion of fuel supplies.[55]

It is possible that that even the most fuel-efficient lime-production methods may not have been enough to conserve local forests in the Mirador area and that excessive lime production was a factor contributing to the rapid depopulation of the site by 200 CE. Recent lake core evidence suggests that highly efficient lime-production methods were already in use during El Mirador's Late Preclassic peak. The relatively low soot and charcoal concentrations identified in the lake core sediments suggest that Preclassic producers were either already very proficient in constructing efficient aboveground caleras or that they were using non-calera production methods.[56] Schreiner's ethnographic research with lime-production experts in the Peten has demonstrated that well-designed and well-built aboveground pyres produce only limited amounts of smoke early on in the firing episode and burn up all the fuel so hardly any charcoal is left over.

Even if lime production did contribute to environmental degradation, it would not have been the sole factor causing the widespread depopulation of the Mirador area at the end of the Preclassic. Forest clearance for agricultural purposes and climatic stress likely also played key roles.[57] Drought would have been especially destructive, stunting vegetation regrowth at the same time demand was rising for plaster coatings for water-management purposes.[58] Although more work must be done to clarify the full role of lime production in the transformation known as the Late Preclassic Collapse, it is easy to see how production of massive quantities of lime at sites like El Mirador would have negatively affected the local environment. The fact that we see a switch to more sustainable lime-production practices over the course of the Classic Period suggests that communities in several subregions drew on the memories of past mistakes to avoid repeating them.

Classic Period Lime Production

Classic Maya specialists likely developed even more fuel-efficient methods than the "traditional" twentieth-century caleras, which were already quite efficient considering their open-air nature. The local experts who constructed the modern caleras were operating in a cultural and socio-ecological landscape that has changed greatly since the Classic Period. Modern communities do not need lime for quite as many purposes as their Classic forebears, and populations are lower across much of the Maya lowlands today than they were during the Classic Period. Taken together, this means that modern producers do not have to put the same premium on conserving fuel resources as Classic producers would have. Applying the 5:1 average fuel-efficiency ratio to Classic Period production masks the great variation in production techniques and efficiency ratios that likely existed. If, for instance, some Classic Period communities achieved fuel ratios that were 20 or even 40% more efficient, this would drastically change our estimates of lime-related forest clearance.[59]

Given the ephemerality of open-air caleras in the archaeological record and the density of vegetation across much of the lowlands, it is unsurprising that archaeologists have identified relatively few examples of Pre-Colonial above-ground lime-production episodes. The handful of such identifications include seven circular burn features to the west of the Postclassic city of Mayapan that included ash, charcoal, and fist-sized pieces of limestone.[60] The remains of another possible open-air lime-production locale were identified at Placencia Caye in Belize, where archaeologists excavated a small mound that included a mix of calcium carbonate, charcoal, and partially burned shells.[61] The relative paucity of alternative lime-production methods identified in the archaeological record has supported the idea that ephemeral caleras were indeed the primary method of Classic lime production.[62]

More recently, however, archaeologists working in the northern lowlands have identified hundreds of permanent lime pit-kilns that were more fuel-efficient than the "traditional" method. It should come as no surprise that lime production was just as heterogeneous as every other facet of Classic Maya socio-ecology. The recent findings are helping to re-evaluate the premise that lime production disproportionately contributed to environmental mismanagement. Although it is possible that excessive lime production contributed to deforest-ation at Preclassic El Mirador, it would be a gross mischaracterization to say it was a key contributor to environmental breakdown throughout the lowlands during the Classic Period. In fact, the new evidence suggests that Classic Maya communities recognized the potential strains that growing populations would place on fuel resources and took steps to mitigate them. The development of new techniques for producing lime is yet another example of how important socio-ecological flexibility is for long-term survival.[63]

Whether a direct result of the lessons learned from the Preclassic Period or the gradual refinement of production methods through trial and error, communities in the central and northern lowlands adopted sustainable lime-production programs during the Classic Period. Although no cities reached the size of Preclassic El Mirador, the lowlands filled up with many more urban centers, leading to an overall greater population density. Despite the rising populations, even the largest cities were able to sustain lime production and consumption levels into the Late Classic Period. When some communities may have begun to strain their fuel resources toward the end of the Classic, they exhibited the flexibility and adaptability that were hallmarks of Classic Maya socio-ecology.

Up through the early 2000s, archaeologists had only identified a handful of Pre-Colonial lime pit-kilns in the Maya lowlands. Possible examples were un-covered at Copan in Honduras; Cauinal and Dos Pilas in Guatemala; Pulltrouser Swamp in Belize; and in the northern Yucatan at Chan Kom, Sayil, on Cozumel;

and at several smaller sites in the northeast.[64] The only one of these sites where more than five such features were identified was Sayil in the northern Puuc region. There, a large-scale settlement pattern study in the late 1980s led to the identification of over twenty ring-like structures hypothesized to be associated with lime production.[65]

Over the course of the 2010s, archaeologists identified many more ring-like pit-kilns at other sites in the Puuc region,[66] at several sites in the Ichkantijoo region of the northwestern corner of the Yucatan,[67] and around the site of Chactun in eastern Campeche (Figure 6.6) [68] Extensive excavations have confirmed that the ring pit-kilns were used for Pre-Colonial lime production. Unlike the shallow pit-kilns identified at Copan, Cauinal, and Dos Pilas, the ring pit-kilns were excavated into the hard limestone caprock, often breaking through the underlying layer of sascab. On the surface, either one or two concentric double-walls facilitated heat retention and provided additional protection from wind.[69] In 2017, lidar imagery facilitated the identification of over 1,000 ring pit-kilns in a 200 km² zone of the eastern Puuc, confirming that this technology was ubiquitous in the region.[70] These recent findings suggest that similar frequencies of

Figure 6.6 A lime pit-kiln on the outskirts of the site of Kiuic in the northern lowlands. The ring of rough boulders surrounds a central depression where fist-sized pieces of limestone were transformed into quicklime over the course of a twenty-plus hour burning event (photo by author).

permanent fuel-efficient lime-production features may soon be uncovered elsewhere in the central and northern lowlands as lidar flyovers accumulate more spatial data.

In 2015, working with local collaborators from the villages of Kancab and Yaxhachen, I oversaw the construction and firing of a pit-kiln modeled on the ancient ring structures near the Puuc site of Kiuic. Despite the model pit-kiln being on the smaller and shallower side of the ring-structure spectrum, we were able to produce lime with an efficiency of 3.94:1 parts fuel-to-lime.[71] The experiment demonstrated the ancient pit-kilns were likely at least 20% more fuel efficient than the average aboveground calera, which would have saved a significant amount of fuel considering the amount of lime needed by Late Classic populations. It is likely that the larger and deeper pit-kilns excavated in the eastern Puuc could have achieved even greater levels of efficiency through increased protection from the elements and heat insulation.

Radiocarbon, geomagnetic, and ceramic-based dating techniques indicate that while some of the northwestern pit-kilns may have originally been constructed as far back as the Early Classic or Late Preclassic Periods, the majority were constructed during the Late and Terminal Classic Periods.[72] This chronology has significant implications for Classic Maya adaptability with regard to lime production. The earliest permanent settlements in the Puuc date to as early as the Middle Preclassic Period (c. 900 BCE), but populations may have remained relatively low and dispersed through the Early Classic. Near the start of the Late Classic Period (c. 550–600 CE), populations began to grow, and new communities were founded. During the Terminal Classic Period (c. 750–950 CE), the Puuc had one of the densest population concentrations of any subregion in the lowlands. The rapid population growth was accompanied by a relatively high proportion of masonry architecture, which included elaborate multistory structures with iconic Puuc decorated facades (Figure 6.7).[73]

The population and construction boom meant that lime production would have kicked into overdrive during that time. Communities adapted to the demographic boom by adopting the pit-kiln lime-production technology. One of the reasons why expedient aboveground pyres were likely the standard production method before the Late Classic Period was that building pyres close to available fuel sources would have limited labor costs. By constructing and using pit-kilns, lime producers permanently fixed lime-production locales on the landscape and thereby increased the effort needed to transport raw fuel and limestone materials to the firing sites. This suggests that desire to increase fuel efficiency outweighed concerns for increasing labor costs during the Terminal Classic Period.[74]

Several lines of evidence suggest that the widespread adoption of pit-kiln technology in the Puuc represented a proactive adaptation to stave off excessive forest clearance and environmental degradation. First, a large number of pit-kilns were

Figure 6.7 An elaborate stone mosaic façade decorates an elite residence in the Puuc region of the northern lowlands. Such intricate designs graced the front walls of many stone-vaulted structures across the subregion (photo by author).

built at or near the start of the population boom. Second, the Puuc communities continued to expand and use the pit-kilns for approximately two centuries until climatic changes contributed to widespread depopulation of the region. Third, the pit-kilns were ubiquitous across the Terminal Classic Puuc landscape, indicating that it was widely adopted and possibly even became the sole method for producing lime. Finally, estimates of fuel consumption for lime production at Kiuic indicate that the fuel efficiency of the pit-kilns would have prevented the need to deforest the hillslopes.[75]

The adoption of annular structures farther to the north at approximately the same time suggests a parallel concern for conserving resources. Similar patterns of adapting production methods to changing socio-ecological circumstances have also been identified elsewhere in the Maya lowlands. Although archaeologists have not yet specifically dated the pit-kilns of Chactun, the site as whole appears to have peaked during the Late and Terminal Classic Periods, suggesting that this would also have been when the pit-kilns were in use.[76] There are still questions as to the true function of a semi-enclosed kiln identified at Copan, but its dating to the Terminal Classic Period suggests a similar local concern for diminishing fuel supplies and the development of a new method to conserve fuel.[77]

Environmental Knowledge and Sustainability

Producing lime in such large quantities and with such frequency as to sustain steadily growing demands throughout the Classic Period undoubtedly would have led to the honing of production methods. Even if many communities did not adopt pit-kiln technology, they could have minimized fuel costs through their accumulated knowledge of the most efficient pyre arrangements, species compositions, and volumes ratios. Their detailed knowledge of forest species and preference for those with especially high water contents meant that lime producers were not just mowing down entire stretches of forest. Instead, they selected specific species whose primary value would have been as fuel—at least until they adapted to changing circumstances by using more economically valuable trees as indicated by the charcoal record of Naachtun.[78] Fuel specialists may have even cultivated plots of the preferred "water wood" species like *chacah* (gumbo-limbo) that regenerate from cuttings and can grow quickly. Such water wood groves could be harvested every twenty-five years or so to allow for both easier felling with stone axes and the continuous regrowth of the fuel supply.[79]

Detailed knowledge accumulated over centuries of limestone grades and shell types also contributed to the development of more fuel-efficient firing methods. The fact that Yucatecan potters in the 1960s were able to distinguish twenty types of limestone for different uses provides an idea of the intricate knowledge that Classic Era specialists *may* have possessed.[80] Again, ethnographic analogy should not be taken as direct evidence, but it is unlikely that such in-depth knowledge of natural resources is a recent development. Selecting for stones with minimal impurities and higher proportions of calcite, as well as using the optimal amount of stone, would have increased efficiency by limiting the amount of limestone that did not completely calcine during a burn.[81]

Another consideration of sustainable fuel harvesting was its likely integration into the agroforestry and milpa cycles. When agriculturalists were ready to convert fallowed land back into active cropland, they felled nearly all the fallow forest, aside from the most economically valuable trees. The trees cleared from the plot during milpa preparation could be used as fuel, including for lime production.[82] It is even possible that major lime-production events were timed to coincide with milpa clearing episodes so that none of the potential fresh firewood would go to waste and the resulting quicklime could be naturally hydrated when the rains arrived.

Estimates of fuel consumed for lime production are unfortunately very tricky due to the numerous variables involved, many of which are themselves necessarily estimates. However, they can be useful for conceptualizing the potential impact of incorporating more efficient lime-production methods.

Take for example David Lentz and colleagues' estimate that plastering the entirety of Late Classic Tikal would require 49,693 m³ (1.75 million ft.³) of lime plaster. With modern lime plaster weighing an average of 2,000 kg/m³ (125 lb./ft.³), they used Schreiner's estimate of lime composing 16% of the plaster, and his 5:1 fuel ratio to deduce that 79.5 million kg (87,600 tons) of wood needed to be burned to make the necessary lime. If the architecture of the entire site was replastered every fifty years (a conservative estimate based on ethnographic analogies), then the annual plaster consumption rate would be approximately 1.59 million kg (1,750 tons) of wood.[83] However, if the fuel ratio were improved by just 20% to 4:1, that could potentially save 350 tons of wood per year, demonstrating how important slight adjustments to the fuel-efficiency figures could be. If, in addition, lime input was lowered to just 10% of the plaster mix, then annual plaster production would "only" require 795,088 kg (876 tons) of wood.[84] This is almost exactly a 50% reduction in annual fuel requirements for lime production.

Calculations of forest clearance for lime production at the Postclassic site of Mayapan in the northern lowlands suggest that fuel consumption for lime would have been sustainable—that is, fuel sources would be able to grow back in time to be used again. The absence of lime pit-kilns at Mayapan indicate to researchers that lime producers at the site saw no need to increase the efficiency of their production methods.[85] Estimates of Copan's Late Classic plaster needs likewise suggest a negligible effect on forest clearance.[86]

The fact that lime production kept pace with steady population growth throughout the Classic Period clearly indicates that lime production was sustainable. Several communities even took steps to change their consumption patterns *before* it was too late. Pollen evidence suggests that the Copan Valley may have been more forested in the Late Classic than it was during the Early Classic, despite growing populations and an increase in monumental architectural projects. This suggests a change in fuel-consumption patterns toward more sustainable practices. Among other possible adaptations, Late Classic Copanecos appear to have developed a semi-enclosed lime kiln technology, or they repurposed one previously used for ceramic firing, to increase fuel efficiency.[87]

Some researchers point to changes in plaster thickness, binder-to-aggregate ratios, or substitution of clay and sascab for lime-based products over time as evidence for exhausted fuel supplies and environmental degradation.[88] However, it is equally plausible that such examples from Late Classic Palenque, Lamanai, Copan, or El Pilar may represent proactive, preemptive fuel-conservation programs or even changes in labor dynamics.[89] At Lamanai, the switch back to using tamped sascab floors instead of lime-plaster floors is *not* accompanied by evidence for deforestation, suggesting this may have been more closely connected with conservation of both raw materials and labor resources.[90] Taken altogether, these various lines of evidence suggest that Classic Maya communities across large stretches of the lowlands recognized that fuel was not inexhaustible and adjusted their lime-production methods accordingly. After residents of Naachtun and the Terminal Classic Puuc sites changed their fuel-consumption practices, they survived increasingly chaotic circumstances linked with population stress, socio-political transformations, and decreasing climatic stability for 200 years.[91]

The Importance of Salt

Salt is critical not only to improving the taste of food but, more importantly, also as an electrolyte necessary for regulating muscle and nerve functions. A drop in sodium can lead to several severe conditions including impaired cognitive functions, as well as liver and heart failure.[92] The average sedentary person in the United States today requires between 0.5–4 g of salt per day.[93] Ethnographic research in the northern Yucatan in the 1920s[94] and strontium isotope analysis of skeletal materials from Tikal,[95] however, indicate that salt requirements in the Maya lowlands may have been as high as 8–9.2 g per day due to hot and humid climate. Humans can absorb low amounts of salt by consuming meat or certain palm trees, but the majority of Classic Maya households would have met their daily requirements by deliberately adding salt to their food and drink.[96] In addition to its dietary and flavor-enhancing significance, salt was used as a food preservative, for tanning animal hides, fixing colors in dyed textiles, and for ritual purposes.[97]

Although we may think of salt today as ubiquitous, relatively cheap flavor enhancer, it was only locally available in a few areas of the Maya lowlands. The northern coasts of the Yucatan are home to some of the largest natural salt beds in all of Mesoamerica and were important locales for the production of very fine-grade sea salt (Figure 6.8). Merchants carried salt from the northern beds overland to the northern interior sites and paddled it at least partway down the west and east coasts of the Peninsula. However, it is unlikely that northern salt supplied all communities across the lowlands. Instead, two other prominent salt-producing areas likely provided the bulk of the salt needs for southern communities. One was the interior natural salt dome of Salinas de los Nueve Cerros, Guatemala, in the southwestern corner of the lowlands. The other was the southern coast of Belize. Unlike in the northern Yucatan, however, the producers of Nueve Cerros and the Belizean lagoons used the *sal cocida* (cooked salt) method to boil down brine into salt cakes.

Due to its necessity in everyday life, salt was an important trade commodity from early on. Production output unsurprisingly ramped up during the Late

Figure 6.8 The Xtampu salt beds located on the northern coast of Yucatan (photo courtesy of Anthony Andrews).

Classic as growing populations in the interior lowlands demanded more and more imported salt. It was therefore also important as an instrument for socio-economic power and salt. Northern salt may have even been considered a luxury item due its high-quality taste and brilliant white color. Chichen Itza's economic power during the Terminal Classic Period likely stemmed in part from its control over the northern salt beds.[98] The fact that Classic centers like Xcambo were located in the fairly undesirable swampy areas just inland from the coast indicate just how economically important it was to be close the salt beds and the circumpeninsular trade routes.[99]

The value of salt as a trade good is further exemplified by the fine ceramics, ocarinas, jadeite, and other precious materials imported by the salt-producing sites of the southern Belize coast. The decentralized political landscape of Late Classic southern Belize allowed the producing communities a measure of autonomy that benefited them directly in trade negotiations with larger trading partners in the interior.[100] Salt's durability, especially in the form of hardened cakes, facilitated its transportation to markets across the lowlands. The elaborate marketplace murals of the Chi'k Nahb structure at Calakmul include iconographic and textual references to salt distribution including a salt vendor identified as *aj 'atz'aam*—"he of the salt" (Figure 6.9).[101]

Figure 6.9 A scene from the murals adorning the exterior of the Chi'k Nahb structure at Calakmul, specifically from the NE-E1 corner, Structure Sub 1–4, Building 1. A vendor identified as "he of the salt" ladles salt from his basket into a container held by the woman facing him (photo by Rogelio Valencia Rivera, courtesy of the Calakmul Archaeological Project).

Salt Production and Environmental Issues

The Belizean Coast

Solar evaporation of the shallow estuarine lagoons that hug the northern coast leaves behind tons of pure sea salt for local harvesters, precluding the use of any wood fuel in the production process.[102] Farther south, however, at Nueve Cerros and the southern Belizean coastal sites, producers needed to burn wood fuel to boil down brine. Paleobotanical evidence indicates that the southern production communities adapted to several changes in fuel availability, some anthropogenic and some natural, over the course of the Classic Period.

Archaeological evidence of salt production comes in the form of a category of ceramics called "briquetage" that were specifically made to boil and evaporate brine. Briquetage includes large pottery vessels for holding the brine, clay cylinders for supporting the large vessels over the cooking fires, and clay connectors that linked the large vessels (Figure 6.10). Clear ethnographic analogies can be drawn to salt-production methods in the highland Guatemalan town of Sacapulas. There, producers cook the salt down into blackened, concentrated

Figure 6.10 A schematic reconstruction of saltwater-boiling jars excavated by Heather McKillop and colleagues at Stingray Lagoon, Belize. This *sal cocida* (or cooked salt) method was used up and down the Belizean and Yucatecan coasts to create salt cakes that were then transported to the salt-deficient interior sites (image courtesy of Heather McKillop, colorized and adapted by author).

salt cakes that are easier to transport. Standardized salt cakes may have even been used as a form of currency and as an important tribute item during the Late Classic.[103]

Heather McKillop and colleagues have identified over one hundred salt-producing sites in the Punta Ycacos Lagoon system of Paynes Creek National Park in southern Belize that have been submerged since the end of the Classic Period. Although there were no natural salt beds in the area similar to the northern Yucatan, the relatively shallow depth of the lagoons helped concentrate salt levels.[104] The standardized shape and size of briquetage vessels recovered from the Late Classic site of Stingray Lagoon indicates that salt was mass produced at the site, most likely for export to interior communities. As production demand increased over the course of the Classic Period, the coastal producers faced the dual challenges of rising sea levels and the potential exhaustion of nearby mangroves harvested for construction and fuel materials. Workers moved their production locations from sites that are now farther out in the middle of the lagoons during the Early Classic to ones closer to the coastline in the Late Classic, suggesting they were already adapting to rising sea levels.[105]

A comparative analysis of wood usage at the Early Classic site of Chan B'i and the Late Classic site of Atz'aam Na by McKillop and Mark Robinson suggests that producers may have begun to strain local fuel resources by the Late Classic. At Chan B'i, the vast majority of wood used for the construction of platforms and cooking huts came from the local mangrove forests.[106] However, by the Late Classic, producers at Atz'aam Na had switched to using more *Symplocos martinicensis* (Martinique sweetleaf), which grew in the slightly more distant savannahs. The greater effort required to transport fuel from the inland savannahs suggests the depletion of local fuel resources—or perhaps a purposeful attempt to avoid exhausting them. The high frequency of secondary growth species used as fuel during the Late Classic hints at a coherent forest-management strategy designed to promote the growth of the most useful species. In general, the range of exploited taxa increased from the Early to the Late Classic, demonstrating the willingness of salt producers to expand their conceptions of acceptable fuel and construction materials. Maximization of fuel efficiency is further suggested by the use of discarded construction trimmings as fuel for salt production.[107]

Using ethnographic information from Sacapulas as a starting point, McKillop and colleagues estimated that one hundred Late Classic production sites in the Paynes Creek system could have combined to produce approximately 600 tons of salt per four-month dry season. However, they estimate that only twenty-five sites were actually in use in any given year. If an average person consumed 8 g of salt per day, this means that the 125 tons produced by twenty-five sites could have provided the salt needs of close to 90,000 people per year.[108] This number, while impressive, indicates that the Paynes Creek saltworks were definitely not the only source of salt for the large communities of the southern Maya lowlands.

An additional salt-production site identified farther north, near modern Belize City, suggests that similar production locales may have existed all along the Belizean coast and perhaps around the entire Yucatan Peninsula. The nonresidential setting of the briquetage uncovered at the site of Wits Cah Ak'al indicates salt production for export. Similar to other Belizean production sites, the Wits Cah Ak'al saltworks were already up and running in the Early Classic. The site's production peaked during the Late Classic before tapering off in the tenth century CE. Tree pollen analyses from the site indicate consistent levels of each of the main taxa used as wood fuel, indicating that either local output was on the smaller side or that producers carefully conserved their forest resources, or perhaps a combination of both.[109]

Salinas de los Nueve Cerros

A final salt-production center, Salinas de los Nueve Cerros, is the only one yet known to exist in the interior Maya lowlands. Located on the southwestern border with the highlands, its material culture during the Classic Period clearly places it within the lowland sphere. The site centers on a natural salt dome called Cerro Tortugas that covers a little more than 1 sq. mi.[110] A natural stream flows from the dome, providing salt producers with a concentrated brine that they collected and boiled down. During the rainy season, the stream overflows and fans out over an area of roughly 270,000 sq. ft that dries and leaves behind a salt flat from which approximately 4,500–6,000 tons of salt can be harvested annually

(Figure 6.11). Natural and human-made evaporation pools likely supplemented the natural salt flats, as did solar evaporation from wide-rimmed pottery vessels. Salt producers were already taking advantage of the local resource by the Late Preclassic Period, but production increased during the Classic Period.[111]

In addition to using solar evaporation methods, producers at Nueve Cerros boiled brine in a similar fashion to the producers at the Belizean coastal sites. With a virtually inexhaustible supply of salt from Cerro Tortugas, the availability of wood fuel was the main factor limiting annual *sal cocida* production rates. Brent Woodfill and colleagues have recovered rough clay molds from platforms across the site that provide evidence of the standardized sizes and shapes of the salt cakes that would have been traded across the lowlands. Producers conserved fuel by running the briny stream water through salty soil recovered from the flats to concentrate salt levels as much as possible prior to boiling. Another way that they conserved fuel was by covering the façades of their buildings with adobe instead of lime plaster, thus saving the fuel that would have been necessary to produce the lime. Despite efforts to maximize fuel efficiency at Nueve Cerros, by the Late Classic salt producers would almost certainly have needed to import fuel from neighboring areas to avoid completely degrading the local landscape. The site's proximity to the Chixoy River would have facilitated this importation.[112]

Woodfill and colleagues estimate that the Nueve Cerros producers could have exported approximately 32 million lbs. (15,980 tons) of salt every year. Assuming a daily salt intake of around 8 g per day, the annual output from Nueve Cerros would have been able to sustain close to 5 million individuals.[113] Recently revised population estimates suggest the total lowland population was higher than this figure, but we must remember Nueve Cerros would not have been trying to meet the demand alone. Outputs from Nueve Cerros combined with those of a slew of *sal cocida* coastal sites like those of southern Belize would have been sufficient to supply the demand across the lowlands. The northern salt would likely have contributed to sating daily requirements in some areas as well, while also functioning as a higher quality (and thus likely more expensive) alternative traded across the lowlands.

Summary

One thing becoming clearer as more research focuses on ancient Maya stone processing is that techniques and trajectories varied greatly across the Classic lowlands. Communities with larger civic-ceremonial complexes and populations like Tikal and Caracol required that much more lime and salt on an annual basis than smaller polities like Copan or Aguateca. Frequencies of masonry architecture construction likewise varied between communities and subregions.[114] Some

Figure 6.11 The Tortugas Salt Dome (top) is located in west-central Guatemala on the border between the lowlands and highlands. A saltwater stream flowing from the dome evaporates into natural salt beds (bottom). Residents of the Classic Period site of Salinas de los Nueve Cerros harvested the salt and boiled the saltwater down into cakes that could be traded up and down the nearby Chixoy River (photos courtesy of Brent Woodfill).

sites had access to greater quantities of more suitable grades of limestone for making lime than others. There were likely pronounced differences in production and procurement of lime between urban and rural contexts. Communities in some regions developed permanent pit-kiln features to increase fuel efficiency, while others changed which species they used for fuel.[115] Although some sites were able to manage their natural resources better than others, it is clear that communities throughout the lowlands adapted new lime-production practices over the course of the Classic Period to meet the challenges of changing environmental, socio-political, and climatic conditions.[116]

Like lime production, the bulk of the salt production (at least in the southern lowlands) would have required significant amounts of wood fuel. Producers in the interior and along the coasts developed methods to maximize their fuel efficiency and exhibited a capacity to adapt their fuel use when circumstances required it. Despite the possibility of excessive local fuel consumption at Paynes Creek in the Early Classic, the decline of the local salt industry at the end of the Classic Period was unlikely due to anthropogenic environmental changes. Salt producers had been adapting to rising sea levels throughout the Classic Period, and it was only after the sites were abandoned due to a decrease in demand from the interior sites that the saltworks were finally submerged for good. Other coastal sites that were not focused on salt production continued to thrive all the way through the Postclassic Period as exchange networks came to focus more exclusively on coastal trading partners that had access to their own local salt sources.[117] Increasingly detailed investigations of Pre-Colonial lime and salt production are contributing to a more nuanced understanding of Classic Maya communities as proactive and successful natural resource managers.

7

Collapse and Resilience

Asking "Why did the Maya collapse?" is rather like asking "Why did the Maya disappear?" Answers are difficult because the questions are inappropriate. The millions of Maya alive today are the descendants of a civilization that did not collapse at the end of the Classic, although it was transformed to varying degrees, in different places, at different times.

—Aimers 2007:351

Introduction

One of the least remarkable things about Classic Maya civilization is that it did not last forever—no socio-political system does. From the eighth through the eleventh centuries CE, subregions across the lowlands experienced a period breakdown and reorganization commonly referred to as the Classic Maya Collapse. However, applying the term "collapse" to the decline of the Classic Maya socio-political system, while appropriate in many respects and a useful heuristic tool, tends to overshadow the resilience of individual communities and Maya culture in general. This book is far from the first to dissect the term "collapse," but considering that the Classic Maya remain an archetype of civilizational decline in the public imagination, it remains important to reflect on how we frame this era of reorganization. The distinction needs to be reinforced that the breakdown of Classic Maya civilization did not equal the breakdown nor devolution nor disappearance of Maya civilization in general.[1]

The Classic to Postclassic transition was characterized by heterogeneity with regard to timing, scale, and influencing factors across the lowlands. It was an era of migration, shifting trade routes, and, yes, famine and death, but many destabilizing factors had roots in the systems that had worked so well for so many prior centuries.[2] A long-term perspective highlights how the transition to the Postclassic Period was a reorganization phase within the broader lowland Maya adaptive cycle that may have begun even earlier than the eighth century. This chapter provides a brief overview of the main factors that came together to drive the Classic to Postclassic Period transition, with a specific focus on

The Maya and Climate Change. Kenneth E. Seligson, Oxford University Press. © Oxford University Press 2023.
DOI: 10.1093/oso/9780197652923.003.0007

how environmental issues did and did not contribute to the upheaval. In contrast to narratives emphasizing social declines, I will instead highlight the resilience of Maya culture, including examples of community-level socio-ecological adaptations.

In focusing on reorganization and resilience, I do not intend to belie the severity of the societal changes that occurred across the lowlands at the end of the Classic Period. The system of powerful dynasties that inscribed stone monuments and built large funerary temple pyramids did indeed break down. Most of the large Classic Period polities, including Tikal, Calakmul, and Caracol, were essentially abandoned by the start of the Postclassic Period. The southern and central lowlands in particular experienced extreme drops in population densities over the course of the ninth and tenth centuries. Climate change, including lengthy droughts that affected agricultural production, likely played a central role in the transformation of many subregions, but it was not necessarily the sole, nor the most important factor, everywhere. Human-induced environmental stress brought on by growing population densities played an important underlying role in several subregions as well. Socio-political pressures, both internal and external, also contributed to the destabilization of the Classic order. Each of these general categories of factors exacerbated each other's effects, playing out in different combinations and intensities across the lowlands.[3] To piece together what happened, as well as where and how it happened, it is important to integrate data and methods from an array of disciplines, including archaeology, environmental science, history, biology, and chemistry.

Issues with Collapse

Chronology

The first major issue with the term "collapse" is timing. The Classic to Postclassic transition, known to Mayanists as the Terminal Classic Period since the 1960s,[4] is a particularly difficult era to bracket with hard calendar dates. Some favor a shorter (c. 800–900 CE) chronology, while others see the period as extending all the way from 750–1050 CE.[5] It has even been argued that the rise and fall of Mayapan between the eleventh and fourteenth centuries in the northern lowlands should be understood as the true last gasp of the Classic Period tradition, albeit in a heavily modified form.[6] Many researchers that subscribe to the longer timeline prefer not to use the term "collapse" to characterize this era, favoring alternatives like decline, breakdown, transition, release, shift, or transformation. This is because "collapse" carries connotations of suddenness and totality that do not necessarily reflect the circumstances of the transition.[7]

Differential site abandonment chronologies problematize the idea of a clear-cut "collapse" across the entirety of the lowlands. Some polities experienced relatively gradual depopulations over the course of a century or more while others were abandoned rather quickly. Some of the rapid site abandonments, such as the sacking of Aguateca,[8] date to around 800 CE, while others did not happen until a century later. Communities like Ucanal,[9] La Milpa,[10] and Nakum[11] in the south and Chichen Itza[12] in the north were not abandoned until the middle of the tenth or eleventh centuries. In other cases, like that of Copan, the royal dynasty began its decline several decades before there is widespread depopulation of the Copan Valley.[13] At Minanha in Belize, a relatively short-lived royal dynasty was either forced out or deserted the site in the early 800s, long before the community was fully depopulated.[14] A recent reevaluation of the breakdown of centralized rulership at Baking Pot, also in Belize, found that it likely occurred over a protracted timeline of almost one hundred years between the eighth and ninth centuries CE.[15] The populations of some communities and subregions grew tremendously during this same span of time. There were even communities like Lamanai and Santa Rita Corozal in Belize that retained significant populations all the way up through the start of the Colonial Period.[16] In most cases, the longer lived communities in the southern lowlands had access to year-round water sources like rivers or larger lakes.

Pinpointing the start of the Terminal Classic Period depends partly on which cultural or socio-political criteria are given the most weight. An increase in violent conflict has historically been seen as both a symptom and cause of the changes that characterized the transitional era. Several researchers point to the relatively rapid depopulation of the regional capital of Dos Pilas in the Petexbatun after an attack in 761 CE as a good starting point for the Terminal Classic.[17] However, as archaeologists and epigraphers amass more data, it is becoming increasingly difficult to distinguish whether the escalating conflict in eighth-century Petexbatun should be considered the start of a new era of interpolity violence or merely the continuation of a longer term trend. Simon Martin argues that the abandonment of Dos Pilas is better understood in the context of ongoing regional conflicts dating back to the seventh century rather than as a discernible break with earlier practices. He makes a convincing case, based largely on epigraphic and iconographic evidence, that the beginning of the end of the Classic Period should be traced to a socio-political crisis in the southern lowlands around 810 CE.[18] The Petexbatun case highlights the difficulty of distinguishing between the decline of individual centers and subregions, and the broader societal decline implied by the term "collapse."

Regardless of whether one favors a late eighth or early ninth century beginning to the Terminal Classic Period, pinpointing the end of the Terminal Classic Period is perhaps even trickier. In the past, many Mayanists placed the cutoff between the Classic and Postclassic Periods closer to 900 CE, with 909 CE marking the latest known Long Count calendar date in the southern lowlands at the western site of Tonina. Now, many researchers extend the Terminal Classic up to 1000 CE or even later.[19] The re-evaluation is partly due to a proliferation of archaeological and paleoenvironmental research at sites that survived with significant populations into the late and early tenth centuries. It is also due to the reconsideration of the northern site of Chichen Itza as a Late Classic, not an Early Postclassic, capital. It is true that the demographic and architectural peak of the site dated to the Terminal Classic, between the ninth and tenth centuries, but this may have been a culmination of a trajectory that began squarely within the Classic.[20] The difficulties of pinning down the end of ceramic phases and the scarcity of narrow radiocarbon date ranges for this era do not make the situation any easier.

If we take the increasing warfare and destabilization in the southwestern lowlands of the late 700s CE as the starting point for the Terminal Classic and the cessation of monumental construction at Chichen Itza around 1050 CE as a rough ending point, that is a period of over 250 years.[21] In the long arc of human history, two-and-a-half centuries is a relatively short span. It may even be considered a relatively short period within the 4,000-plus year existence of Maya culture. However, considering that the United States of America is not quite 250 years old puts this time scale into perspective. By a conservative estimate, ten generations would have lived through the 250-year transition. Would each individual generation have recognized they were living through a "collapse?"

The breakdown of the southern lowland socio-political order may be narrowed to a roughly century-long span from the early 800s to the early 900s CE,[22] but the transition from Classic to Postclassic Period social orders in the broader Maya lowlands encompassed a much wider period. Individual sites did indeed experience precipitous population declines over the span of a generation or less, but referring to an overarching Classic Maya "collapse" oversimplifies the picture. Zooming out to a much broader temporal scale, we can understand the release and reorganization of the Terminal Classic as part of a longer term series of adaptive cycles of population growth and decline.[23]

Geography

The second issue with the term "collapse" is one of spatial variation. The label "Classic Maya Collapse" might suggest to some that every single lowland site ceased to exist during this period. The idea of a lowlands-wide demise became popular early in the history of Maya archaeology. Many early projects focused on the largest sites of the southern lowlands, where epigraphic evidence suggested a region-wide depopulation in the eighth and ninth centuries.[24] However, the influx of new archaeological data from across the lowlands has exposed the Classic to Postclassic transition to be a patchwork of individual regional trajectories. Several communities survived with relatively significant populations well into the Postclassic Period, and, in some cases, entire subregions thrived during the Terminal Classic while others were declining (Figure 7.1).[25]

Southwestern regions like the Pasión River drainage (including the Petexbatun) were among the first to undergo large-scale depopulations, which began in the late 700s CE.[26] The population of the Río Bec region in the central lowlands may have dropped by as much as 90% by 850 CE, while many sites in the Peten Lakes region and northern Belize, both well-watered areas, largely escaped depopulation until the beginning of the Postclassic Period.[27] However, the great dynastic rivals of Piedras Negras and Yaxchilan, both located along the Usumacinta River, met their demise around the start of the ninth century, several decades before other prominent southern lowlands sites like Tikal were ultimately abandoned. Caracol appears to have survived (and even thrived) until right around 900 CE when an episode of violent conflict likely led to a rapid abandonment of the site center.[28] In southern Belize, depopulation patterns varied at sites that were only separated by a few dozen miles, highlighting the complexity of the processes at play during the Terminal Classic.[29]

While many southern communities were declining or experiencing rapid collapses, other subregions of the lowlands were flourishing. The northern lowlands were home to significant populations since at least as far back as the Middle Preclassic (c. 800 BCE), if not earlier.[30] There were dips in population and construction activities across the north just as there were in other subregions over the course of the Preclassic and Classic Periods. Beginning in the 600s CE, parts of the Puuc region of the northern Yucatan saw a steady demographic expansion that continued into the 900s and may have been supplemented by migration from increasingly unstable regions farther south.[31] The "Puuc Florescence" was characterized by the construction of higher frequencies of stone-vaulted architecture than any other subregion at any point in the Pre-Colonial history of the lowlands.[32] However, while eastern Puuc sites were thriving, many western Puuc sites may have begun to decline by the start of the ninth century.[33] By the mid-tenth century, many eastern Puuc sites were abandoned as well, with some experiencing relatively rapid abandonments.[34] Chichen Itza and a few other Classic Period sites located on the northern plains continued to thrive into the eleventh century.[35] Thus, the rise and fall of northern sites was similarly characterized by a timescale mosaic, but more sites seemed to be on the rise during the Terminal Classic Period than elsewhere in the lowlands.

An additional issue of spatial scale concerns the biases of our research foci. In general, the majority of archaeological research across the lowlands has

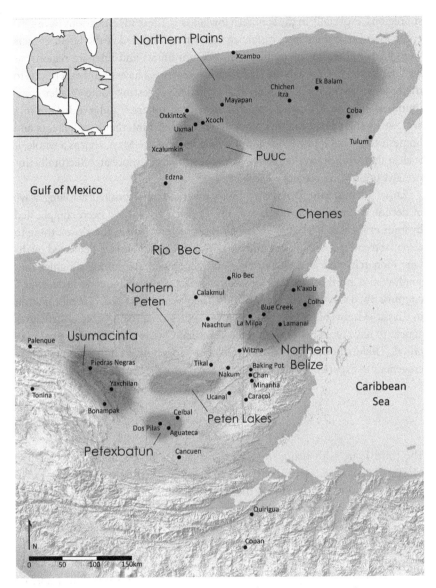

Figure 7.1 Map of the Maya lowlands highlighting the subregions and sites discussed in this chapter (image by author using base map by NASA/JPL).

focused on the largest Classic Period communities and also on bigger domestic compounds. That is not say that there have not been extensive studies of smaller scale communities in some areas. Since the 1950s, archaeologists, geographers, and environmental scientists have completed vast settlement surveys in some subregions, especially in the southern lowlands.[36] These investigations have generally found that the demographic changes first identified at the larger centers were mirrored within many hinterland communities and intersite regions, as well. However, just as with the larger sites, researchers have found exceptions to the broader demographic trends with evidence suggesting some smaller communities were able to persist much longer than others.[37] Lidar-aided surveys are continuing to add to our knowledge of smaller hinterland settlements and homesteads,[38] but if one looks at the archaeology of the Maya area as a whole, it is clear that studies have tended to skew toward larger, more architecturally impressive population centers.

Earlier identifications of spatial-temporal trends that posited a rolling wave of decline from south to north over the Classic Period have been complicated by finds of localized variation in different subregions. Today, the closest thing to a spatial trend is a decline in numbers of inscribed monuments dedicated by divine monarchs and an associated general depopulation running roughly from southwest to northeast across the central Peten. This, again, concentrates on a circumscribed subregion of the lowlands. There was a good deal of local variation in Classic systems of governance and some subregional socio-political structures appear to have fared better during the Terminal Classic period of upheaval than others.[39] Referring to a "Classic Maya Collapse" does not take into account the heterogeneity of experiences across the wide expanse of the broader Maya lowlands.[40]

Scale

The third issue with using the term "collapse" is its connotation of totality. Most archaeologists agree that even the most devastating collapses are rarely complete.[41] So what is it exactly that collapsed? Using the term "Classic Maya Collapse" promotes a sense that everything—the whole system, the people, the material culture—disappeared. By the end of the Terminal Classic Period, the system of divine monarchs, at least those referring to themselves in texts as k'uhul ajaw, or "holy lord," that had characterized Classic Maya civilization was abandoned.[42] Paralleling the demise of the great Classic royal courts was the transformation of the elaborate material culture of their noble supporters. It is also clear that many of the largest Classic Period centers were reduced to a small fraction of their peak populations. These are the most prominent cultural aspects that were transformed or abandoned over the course of the Terminal Classic at sites throughout the lowlands. These also happen to be the cultural markers most visible in the archaeological record.[43]

The precipitous decline in the population of many of the major southern lowland centers over the course of the ninth and early tenth centuries can certainly be understood as a widespread urban demographic collapse. Precise population estimates are notoriously difficult in archaeology, as researchers must take into account issues such as the ambiguity of structure use and contemporaneity, as well as the invisibility of residences constructed of perishable materials, to name a few.[44] That is why archaeological population estimates include such wide margins of error (sometimes to the point of rendering them less than instructive). However, comparing *relative* population levels over time within the same location, while still fraught, is a much safer exercise and the population loss at many of the great Classic centers, as well as in their hinterlands, during the Terminal Classic is quite clear. The severity of the Terminal Classic demographic decline at the larger centers of the southern interior is becoming even more stark as lidar surveys expose the likely magnitude of peak population levels—possibly 7 to 11 million people in the Late Classic central lowlands alone![45]

Despite a marked decline in population at many lowland sites, especially in the southern and central interior, over the course of the Terminal Classic Period, archaeological evidence also suggests that segments of the population lingered on, especially at the peripheries of larger sites.[46] In some cases, people demonstrated their resilience by relocating to new areas with more secure water sources.[47] And although many markers of Classic Period royal and elite culture declined over the course of the Terminal Classic Period, other components of the Classic Maya material record persisted in several areas of the lowlands. Ceramic traditions continued to evolve, and trade networks for imported goods like obsidian shifted predominantly from inland to coastal routes. Continuities can be seen between the Classic and Postclassic in written systems, administrative organizations, language, calendrics, and agricultural practices.[48]

The disappearance of Classic Period–style elite cultural markers in the archaeological record may result partly from a rejection of the prevailing elite culture. It is possible that non-elite populations held on in places like the eastern Puuc beyond the cessation of monumental construction projects. Archaeologists have identified C-shaped civic buildings at sites within the Puuc, on the Northern Plains, and within southern communities like Ceibal and the Peten Lakes zone that date to the ninth through eleventh centuries. Such evidence suggests that the socio-political reorganizations and population declines that have been posited for many regions of the lowlands were much more gradual and perhaps less severe than previously hypothesized.[49]

Causality

A final issue with the term "collapse" centers on causality and the multitude of factors that contributed to the transformations of the Terminal Classic Period.[50]

One of the reasons for the outsized fascination with the end of the Classic Period, beyond those laid out in the introductory chapter, is a desire to isolate a single causative factor for societal decline. Multi-causality does not preclude applying the term "collapse" to aspects of the Classic Maya socio-political system, but it does preclude approaching "the collapse" as a monolithic event.

The decline of the Classic Maya socio-political system is often described as "mysterious" in popular media because the most accurate thing that scholars can say about what happened is that there were a multitude of interwoven factors that contributed to a complex array of processes. Every now and then, newspaper headlines will seize on a new study and exaggerate the claims made therein to say something along the lines of "Severe Droughts Explain the Mysterious Fall of the Maya,"[51] "Did Maya Doom Themselves By Felling Trees?,"[52] or, most recently, "How Do You Know When Society Is About to Fall Apart?"[53] Conversely, a head-line saying "Many Factors Contributed to the Breakdown of the Classic Maya Sociopolitical System: Individual Polities Experienced Their Own Combination of Factors, More Research Needed to the Clarify Picture on Sub-Regional Scale" would not be quite as catchy.

Just as with every other facet of the "collapse," causality is not nearly as straight-forward nor as homogeneous across the board as to fit into a neat explanation. Many of the factors that affected change during this period, such as increasing inter-community competition, were culminations of trends that began well before there were any visible signs of stress in the archaeological record.[54] Others, such as lengthy droughts, were more proximate to the era of transformation. With the explosion of archaeological, paleoenvironmental, iconographic, and epigraphic data recovered over the past few decades, we now have a better understanding of the multivariate social and environmental dynamics at play. The following sections provide an overview of the factors that we now know to have played outsized roles in spurring the Classic to Postclassic transition. The resilience of Classic Maya communities comes into clearer focus when we consider the myriad disruptive forces at play.

Climatic Instability: Water Issues

The varied, intricate, and ever adapting water-management systems of the Classic Period sustained steadily growing populations in the challenging tropical lowland forests for over 700 years in many areas before they met their match in an increasingly unpredictable climate. As outlined in the second chapter, climate change has long been posited as a key contributor to the decline of Classic Period city-states. Since the incorporation of new paleoenvironmental data sets in the 1990s, drought has emerged as a particularly intriguing component of the

Terminal Classic transformation picture.[55] Consensus is building around the identification of more frequent megadroughts afflicting many subregions of the lowlands between 800 and 1000 CE (Figure 7.2). The term "megadrought" in this case refers to the absence or severe diminishment of the usual summer tropical storms for several consecutive years, which would have severely disrupted the potential for agricultural production.[56] However, researchers continue to debate the severity and timing of these decreased rainfall episodes. In many cases, it remains difficult to determine to what degree environmental problems stemmed from natural or anthropogenic causes.[57]

Scientists draw on a range of proxies to understand paleoclimatic changes. A few of these data sets and methods were discussed in greater depth in Chapter 2. Speleothems are cave formations like stalagmites that can be used to identify periods of increased or decreased precipitation through variations in mineral deposition. Lake cores are sediment samples recovered from perennial water sources that frequently include plant waxes, tiny snail shells, and bits of charcoal. Bands of salt and other mineral deposits in the lake cores indicate

Figure 7.2 Extensive droughts affected several subregions of the Maya lowlands between the eighth and eleventh centuries CE and likely played a critical role in the breakdown of the Classic Period socio-political system. An ongoing drought in the Maya lowlands has parched the landscapes around many sites in the northern Yucatan today (photo courtesy of Sarah Taylor).

periods of severe drought when the body of water dried up, and analyses of oxygen isotopes in snail shells can likewise indicate periods of decreased precipitation. Leaf wax analyses involve identifying the ratio of different hydrogen isotopes within the waxy substances produced by plants to protect their leaves against UV light and dehydration. Similar to the oxygen isotope ratio analyses used for snail shells, scientists can identify whether leaf waxes were produced during periods of decreased precipitation when heavier hydrogen isotopes would have predominated within water molecules.[58]

Speleothem records from caves in Belize and northern Yucatan,[59] lake cores and gastropod isotopic analyses from the northern and southern lowlands,[60] and leaf wax analyses from the southern lowlands[61] all point to a downturn in annual precipitation levels during the Terminal Classic. At the same time, slight discrepancies in the severity and specific timing between the different lines of evidence indicate that precipitation patterns were highly localized in their variability.[62] The stalagmite data from Macal Chasm in west-central Belize indicate a first "massive drying event" that peaked around 750 CE. Some researchers see a connection between the drying period leading up to this mid-century peak and demographic instability at several sites in this region in the early 700s.[63] A stalagmite from Yok Balum likewise indicates a drying trend for southern Belize, but this one begins in the middle of the seventh century and culminates in an eighty-year drought in the eleventh century. The drying trend is characterized by a 40% reduction in precipitation from normal levels at its height.[64] Variability in community trajectories, such as the persistence of large populations at Caracol in west-central Belize into the late 800s, indicates that climatic changes in the Maya lowlands can be hyper-localized and/or that precipitation drops were not necessarily a death sentence.

Speleothem analyses by paleoclimatologist Martín Medina-Elizalde and colleagues in the northern Yucatan suggest a series of droughts likewise afflicted subregions in the north. Stalagmites from two caves in northwest Yucatan indicate that a series of three-to-eighteen-year droughts affected the region, leading to an overall 36–56% decrease in precipitation.[65] However, this marked decrease in precipitation may not have begun until after 900 CE, and the Puuc communities may have actually benefited from a switch to predominantly northwesterly winds in the ninth century.[66] The fact that sites like Tzemez Akal, located close to Uxmal in the Santa Elena Valley of the Puuc, were able to persist all the way through the Postclassic Period once again highlights the variability of drought effects. The site was strategically located around five large *aguadas*, but without sufficient rainfall, the aguadas would have been valueless.[67] We must also consider that northern communities were better situated to survive periods of decreased rainfall due to their adaptations to generally dryer conditions than their southern counterparts.[68]

Eventually even the flourishing Puuc sites experienced socio-political reorganizations over the course of the tenth century, though the proximate causes for these local societal transformations remain unclear.[69] The fact that many eastern Puuc sites were depopulated in a relatively rapid manner would suggest that the climatic changes became so challenging during the tenth century that even the local highly adaptable storage systems could no longer persist. Having potable water stored in *chultuns* and aguadas can only help a community survive so long if there is no precipitation to water the agricultural fields. However, it is also possible that socio-political stressors triggered the abandonment of eastern Puuc sites, as they likely did in areas farther south including the Petexbatun.[70]

Analyses of leaf wax thickness from the area of Lake Salpeten in northern Guatemala suggest a decrease in rainfall coinciding with the start of the ninth century. The dry conditions increase in severity through the rest of the Terminal Classic before tapering off in the early 1300s CE.[71] Some researchers also point to the paleoclimatological evidence from a core extracted from the Cariaco Basin off the coast of Venezuela to provide supporting evidence for a general Caribbean-wide series of drying events from the eighth through tenth centuries CE.[72] The fact that each of these independent lines of evidence do not exactly line up with one another in terms of severity or timing reinforces the heterogeneity of the lowland environments.

Communities in the Peten Lakes zone drew on lake resources to survive the climatic challenges better than their neighbors located farther away from year-round water sources. In fact, they may have had to adapt their local status quo to deal with an influx of migrants from the regions that were suffering agricultural failures resulting from a prolonged decrease in rainfall. We see a clustering of Terminal Classic and Early Postclassic communities in the most defensible positions on islands and peninsulas, indicating a concern for protection during this turbulent era.[73] In southern Quintana Roo, communities constructed more irrigation canals during the Terminal Classic Period to capture as much rainwater as possible and presumably support growing numbers of refugees fleeing the worst-hit regions.[74] The localized nature of precipitation variability during this time period is not only exemplified by the Puuc population boom but also by the fact that the residents of Ucanal needed to construct new water dispersion features to deal with bouts of heavy rainfall.[75]

Recent scholarship suggests that the true destructiveness of the droughts in many areas may have been more closely tied to their length and frequency than the severity of year to year precipitation declines. Communities could have survived a severe drop in precipitation for a year or two by consuming mainly root crops with woody stems like manioc or yucca, as well as cactus pads, hearts of palm, and the inner bark of some trees.[76] However, communities would not have been able to survive on famine foods forever. If precipitation did not return to sufficient levels to support milpa crops within five or so years, communities would have faced starvation and/or disbandment.

The Macal Chasm record suggests some uncharacteristically dry periods during the Terminal Classic may have lasted for more than seventy years.[77] It is also likely that the droughts were interrupted by damaging tropical storms and hurricanes that would have been more destructive than rejuvenating (Figure 7.3).[78] Classic Period communities may have grown so large and complex that they limited their capacity to continue adapting. An average 40% reduction in summer rainfall would have pushed many of them over the survival line.[79] Decreased rainfall affected communities in several ways. It parched crops and forests, diminished water available for drinking and for slaking lime, and increased the frequency of wildfires. The occasional crop failure due to poor rainfall was probably quite common and communities could rely on stores of food saved for just those occasions. Multiple consecutive crop failures would have been another story. Prolonged decreases in precipitation cause not only agricultural (and thus food yield) stress but also drinking water stress. These led to lowered levels of health and ability to resist diseases. To compound the problem, community members may have begun to lose faith in a ritual and hierarchical system that could erstwhile be counted upon to guarantee plentiful rain.[80]

Figure 7.3 A tropical storm darkens the sky over the Maya lowlands (photo by author).

The same paleoclimatological records that provide evidence for the Terminal Classic drying periods also indicate periods of drought during the Late Preclassic to Early Classic transition that may have included more severe annual decreases in rainfall.[81] However, the Late Preclassic period of climatic instability was followed by the relatively stable climate of the Early and Middle Classic Periods. This provided the foundation for societal recoveries, followed by population growth and agricultural expansion. When climatic instability arose again during the Classic to Postclassic transition, the unpredictability and general decrease in precipitation lasted on and off for as long as five or six centuries, with several peaks during the Terminal Classic and Early Postclassic Periods. The continuation of unfavorable climatic conditions for such a long time, especially after populations had grown so large and dense during the Classic Period, would have made it very difficult to continue the same socio-ecological practices. Incipient recoveries at some of the larger sites across the lowlands may have been snuffed out by another massive drying event visible in the Early Postclassic portion of the Macal Chasm record.[82] In the north, the last great Pre-Colonial Maya city of Mayapan rose to power precisely during the worst of the Early Postclassic droughts, exemplifying both the resilience of Maya communities and the variability of responses to climatic stressors.[83]

Classic Period communities had experience dealing with occasional hurricanes and consistent, gradual sea-level rise close to the coasts.[84] They had developed adaptive strategies to deal with these known climatic challenges and periodic fluctuations over the course of centuries. However, when these disruptive forces occurred in tandem with additional challenging situations like extensive droughts and social unrest, they would have been that much more destructive. They would have been particularly challenging for coastal communities that were otherwise better situated to survive the precipitation downturns than their counterparts in the interior.[85]

Despite the severe challenges they presented, we should not see droughts as the sole or even necessarily the most important cause of the Terminal Classic transformations. In some areas, like the Petexbatun and the Usumacinta regions, the archaeological record points to localized societal destabilization beginning prior to the onset of the recorded drying episodes.[86] Likewise, Palenque's decline and abandonment in the early 800s CE does not appear related to lack of access to water.[87] In other areas, like the north and closer to the coasts, communities survived periods of massive precipitation drops.[88] It is also important to consider the variable effects that drops in precipitation would have on potable versus agricultural water needs, especially in those communities for which there is no evidence for irrigation infrastructure. In light of these many variations and variables, it would be more accurate to view the Terminal Classic droughts as one of a number of unfavorable conditions that contributed to societal reorganizations.[89]

Perhaps in some areas they served as one of several destabilizing factors, while in others they were experienced as a final crushing blow.

Socio-Politics and Warfare

Civil unrest has been put forth as one of the more prominent issues factoring into the Classic to Postclassic transition.[90] Unrest could take the form of a long-standing dissatisfaction raised to a boil or a rapidly mobilized response to a new challenge. For instance, a change in state policy at Caracol in the ninth century from a more egalitarian, communal ethos to an elite-centric, exclusionary system may have triggered a quick response from a disgruntled citizenry.[91] An increase in the iconographic and epigraphic representation of non-royal elite lineages in several communities during the Late and Terminal Classic Periods indicates the growing influence of the upper ranks of society, perhaps at the expense of the ruling dynasty. Royal families increasingly relied on their elite supporters and complex assemblies of bureaucrats to maintain power over their expanding populace as well as to help them defend their lands against rival polities. These elite families, some enjoying a newly minted noble status, competed with one another for the favor of the court as well as for resources mobilized by the broader community.[92] In doing so, they served a powerful destabilizing force in the uppermost levels of Late Classic Maya society.

Even in those communities that experienced expansions of the nobility during the Late Classic, the bulk of the population was composed of households of lower socioeconomic status. Despite their dramatic underrepresentation in the surviving epigraphic and iconographic records, we should not assume that "commoners" were powerless to effect change within their communities. In some cases, we can imagine individual actors and families "voting with their feet" and leaving their community to join a new one. In others, non-elite families could rebel against local power structures at the behest of or in contradiction to the wishes of their patrons.[93] The eminent twentieth-century Mayanist J. Eric S. Thompson proposed a series of "peasant revolts" as the key factor leading to the decline of Classic Maya civilization.[94] They may have rejected royal decision-makers who sponsored increasing warfare in which non-elite families were most likely to risk lives and livelihoods.[95] In some cases, such as at Cancuen in Guatemala and Colha in northern Belize, the rejection of the existing power structure took the extreme form of violent overthrow, though it is unclear whether the killing of local elites was carried out by the local populace or external groups.[96]

We see an especially drastic series of changes in the southern lowlands over the course of the ninth century, beginning with a possible political crisis around

810 CE. Long-standing ideas about in-migrations from the western periphery of the Maya lowlands disrupting the social order of the lowlands are supported by iconographic and epigraphic evidence. The appearance of new iconographic styles and individuals with non-Mayan names on monuments at many sites in the ninth century, especially in the southern lowlands, hints at the influx of a "new elite" class likely originating from the Gulf Coast region, though the isotopic and archaeological evidence is not conclusive.[97] The past was just as dynamic and complicated as the present, with people constantly moving about the landscape and migrating to new communities for social, political, or economic reasons. Recent isotopic and settlement analyses from the site of Ucanal in the northeastern Peten indicate in-migration from several different subregions of the Maya lowlands and possibly even farther abroad during the Terminal Classic.[98]

As people constantly moved about, they transported new forms of material culture and communicated new ideas. Established elites throughout the Maya lowlands appear to have begun adopting new ideologies into their existing power structures during the Terminal Classic Period. William Ringle and colleagues have identified the spread of a pan-Mesoamerican militaristic political ideology honoring a version of the feathered serpent god Quetzcoatl (K'uk'ulkan in Mayan), first reaching the Maya lowlands during the Early Classic Period but spreading with renewed vigor during the Terminal Classic Period. The adoption of this pan-Mesoamerican politico-religious ideology into Maya communities likewise had a great potential to disrupt existing socio-political arrangements.[99] The breakdown of long-established power structures and influx of outside influences allowed communities to formulate new identities, such as the localized tradition of circular shrine construction in the Sibun Valley of northern Belize.[100]

The decentralized nature of the broader lowland political landscape was a central reason for the lengthy and patchy nature of the political collapse. Given the relatively weak ties that bound many polities to one another, it would probably have been more surprising if communities across the lowlands *had* broken down all at once. However, even if political ties between royal courts were often weak and ceremonial in nature, disruptions in economic ties between communities could have broader consequences for entire regions.[101] For instance, the internal competition and escalating violence within the Petexbatun during the eighth century likely contributed to the breakdown of the trading system along the Pasión and Usumacinta Rivers, destabilizing communities both upriver and downriver.[102] A shift in preferred trade routes could likewise disrupt the economies of communities located along the old ones. Evidence suggests sociocultural changes, perhaps relating to shifting trade and migration patterns, and not drought played a central role in the land-use changes and social reorganization at Lamanai in northern Belize near the end of the Classic Period.[103] The increasing prominence of coastal exchange routes during the Late and Terminal Classic Periods was another factor contributing to the breakdown and reorganization of the Classic socio-political order.[104]

Some researchers point to a rise in the frequency and scale of warfare during the Terminal Classic as both a cause and effect of growing socio-political de-stabilization (Figure 7.4). For instance, violent attacks led to the at least partial abandonments of Dos Pilas in 761 CE, Colha in the late 700s CE, and Aguateca and Cancuen around 800 CE (to name a few).[105] With relatively few examples of site destruction and abandonment prior to this era, some researchers see the Terminal Classic as marking a turning point in Maya warfare away from a largely ceremonial captive-taking exercise to an increasingly desperate competition for dwindling resources and territory.[106] In areas like the Petexbatun, the rivalries of closely packed royal dynasties appear to have triggered the escalating violence in the absence of climatic changes or environmental degradation.[107]

Other researchers point out that while instances of "total warfare" in which communities were sacked and destroyed may have escalated during the Terminal Classic, they were far from new to the Maya lowlands. Maya warfare was, of course, mediated by cultural understandings[108] that included ritual elements, but it was never purely ceremonial. An evaluation of fortifications throughout the upper Usumacinta region around Piedras Negras indicate that site centers were likely attacked and possibly destroyed since as early as the Late Preclassic Period.[109] Recent excavations at the site of Witzna indicate that the community was sacked and burned around 697 CE.[110] We already knew from the hieroglyphic record that two years before Witzna met its end, the Tikal Dynasty

Figure 7.4 A Late Classic Period mural from the small site of Bonampak, Chiapas, depicts a crowded battle scene replete with elaborate armor and costumes, the thrusting of spears, and the taking of captives by the hair (drawing by Linda Schele, copyright David Schele, image courtesy of the Schele Drawing Collection, Los Angeles County Museum of Art).

won such a decisive military victory over their archrivals, the Snake (Kaanu'l) Dynasty, that the latter never fully recovered. It has even been suggested that the breakdown of the Classic system can be traced to this crushing defeat of the Snake kings, who had established the closest thing to a hegemonic empire over the central lowlands in the 600s.[111] Escalating warfare between the Usumacinta River kingdoms of Yaxchilan and Piedras Negras was likely instrumental in the demise of both dynasties soon after the start of the ninth century.[112]

The epigraphic record recounts several instances of site sacking and royal courts being forced to flee, including attacks by the Snake kings on Palenque in 599 and again in 611.[113] It is likely that there were many more similar instances of violent conflict that have yet to be uncovered and that our understanding of Classic Period warfare has been skewed by a research focus on the largest sites.[114] However, even if we focus on the marked increase in particularly violent warfare in the Petexbatun in the latter half of the eighth century as a starting point for the Classic to Postclassic transition, it should not be viewed as a drastic break from earlier traditions. The trend of increasingly violent warfare that would factor into the Classic to Postclassic transition was already building at least as far back as the late 600s, if not earlier.

In the longer arc of Maya civilization, perhaps the Classic Period should not be seen as a relatively stable era bracketed by the turmoil of the Late Preclassic and Terminal Classic Collapses, but instead as a dynamic era of continuous cultural experimentation and evolution. Epigrapher David Stuart has suggested that what some see as the sudden or surprising "undoing" of Classic Maya civilization in the Terminal Classic was actually the culmination of a longer term fraying of the royal socio-political system. The architectural, sculptural, and hieroglyphic traditions that impress us so much today may be obfuscating a socio-political landscape that was constantly churning with intra- and inter-community competition until it finally reached a breaking point.[115]

Environmental Issues

Environmental degradation is another important issue that has factored into discussions of the Classic to Postclassic Period since the early days of Maya archaeology (see Chapter 2). Some authors have seized upon anthropogenic environmental change as the main, or even the sole, cause for the reorganization of Maya society. In doing so, they suggest (either deliberately or unintentionally) that the Maya were the architects of their own demise.[116] Our understandings of ancient Maya human-environment relationships are undoubtedly affected by the visibility of the negative effects of anthropogenic environmental changes in the present (Figure 7.5). We seek parallels to alternatively comfort ourselves and serve as instructional warnings, but in doing so we may prejudice our understanding of the practices of past societies.[117] It is likely that resource exploitation began to exceed sustainable levels within the largest communities by the Terminal Classic Period, but anthropogenic environmental degradation was not necessarily a critical stressor everywhere across the lowlands.

Within some of the largest communities, population growth was certainly an important factor influencing changes in forest-management strategies during the final centuries of the Classic Period. Agroforestry practices were scaled upward and outward as communities expanded but eventually reached the limits of sustainable returns.[118] Pollen and charcoal data from Lamanai indicate that residents had all but used up their local pine resources by the Terminal Classic, leading to changes in ritual practices.[119] At Tikal, the massive construction campaign of the 700s CE challenged resource-management strategies already strained by population growth. The substitution of logwood lumber for sapodilla midway through the eighth-century building spree reflects both the depletion of resources and a proactive conservation measure to allow for the reincorporation of sapodilla wood later.[120] David Lentz and colleagues estimate that at its nadir the forest cover at Tikal may have been anywhere from 40–68% of what it is today, and residents likely had to begin importing fuel and lumber from neighboring regions.[121] The diminishment in forest cover would have decreased the ecosystem's capacity to address a crisis. Likewise, if communities decreased fallow periods and continuously grew multiple annual crops in the same plot, soil nutrient depletion would have made the agricultural lands more susceptible to disease, weed invasion, and changes in climatic conditions.[122]

Reduction in tree cover not only increased soil erosion but also limited the capture and recycling of nutrients such as phosphorous and nitrogen back into the soil.[123] It also depleted the carbon stores of the soil that would not be replaced by secondary forest growth.[124] In some areas, overextended forest clearance contributed to a reduction in lime-plaster production and a decline in the consumption of forest mammals like white-tailed deer.[125] Several climatic models indicate that beyond leaving communities more vulnerable to climatic downturns, rampant forest clearance may have actually contributed to the climatic downturns. The reduction in forest canopy lowered local transpiration rates, removed temperature-stabilizing layers, and diminished soil moisture levels. All these factors may have combined to exacerbate natural decreases in annual precipitation levels by as much as an additional 5–15%.[126] The very intensification schemes that allowed communities to make the most of their natural environments and maintain food supplies for growing populations may have also restricted their abilities to adapt to unstable climatic conditions.[127]

Copan, on the southeastern periphery of the Maya area, presents a complicated case of discrepancies in pollen analysis. In the late 1980s, David Rue and

Figure 7.5 A photograph of a recently cleared stretch of terrain in northern Guatemala (top) and a Google Earth satellite image of the northeastern corner of Guatemala (bottom) show the extent of modern forest clearance and the encroachment of deforestation into the Maya Biosphere of the Peten. The remaining dense tree cover of the Biosphere is visible as a darker green swath in upper part of the image (photo by Omar Alcover Firpi, courtesy of the Proyecto Arqueológico El Zotz; satellite image adapted by author from Google Earth).

colleagues analyzed pollen levels in a core extracted from Petapilla Pond, located on the slopes to the northeast of the site center. Their analysis indicated gradual deforestation culminating in a nearly complete disappearance of pine in the vicinity of the site by the end of the Classic Period.[128] Their analyses helped popularize the idea that Classic Maya communities were steadily overexploiting their natural environments until they reached a breaking point, which was taken by some to indicate that their socio-ecological systems were maladaptive. However, their model for gradual and overwhelming deforestation was based partly on a longer chronology for site habitation that has since been challenged by other researchers.[129]

In 2001, Cameron McNeil and colleagues extracted a new, longer sediment core from the same pond and their re-evaluation of the pollen record using a shorter chronology for the depopulation of the site suggested a different picture of human-environment relationships. They found evidence for significant deforestation by the end of the site's Classic Period occupation, but it appeared to have occurred over a much shorter period. Their deeper core sample was able to demonstrate an early deforestation peak at the start of the first millennium BCE, when agriculturalists first cleared the valley for maize agriculture. Another peak occurred near the start of the fifth century CE, coinciding with the founding of the site's Classic Maya dynasty by K'inich Yax K'uk' Mo' in 426 CE. After that, the pollen record indicated careful management of forest cover, with especially useful species like pine actually *increasing* for much of the Late Classic. It was only toward the very end of the Classic Period that local communities abandoned their sustainable methods and rapidly deforested the landscape.[130] McNeil and colleagues' study is complicated by the fact that they do not address the evidence for significant soil erosion around Copan during the Late Classic Period.[131]

The recent 2,000 km^2 lidar survey in northern Guatemala identified approximately 360 km^2 of modified agricultural lands and 950 km^2 of unmodified uplands that could have been used by swidden farmers.[132] The abundance of unmodified territories, as well as a few survey blocs devoid of residential architecture, suggests that a degree of further agricultural extensification would have been possible if climatic and socio-political conditions allowed. Social obligations, infrastructural sunk costs, and increasingly complex labor relations decreased the capacity of many households and communities to make major changes to their socio-ecological practices. A drop in precipitation levels in the 800s and 900s CE would have exacerbated any environmental challenges, causing many communities to implement short-term survival strategies that may have involved abandoning age-old forest- and land-management policies.[133]

It is unfortunately quite difficult to clarify the relationship between forest-management practices and political crises in communities like Tikal or Copan. Did one beget the other? Were they contemporaneous but relatively independent? It is likewise unknowable whether communities would have continued to successfully adapt their management practices had they not begun to experience erratic climatic conditions in the ninth and tenth centuries.[134] Natural versus anthropogenic environmental degradation is another difficult distinction to make using paleoenvironmental and archaeological evidence.[135] It would also be unwise to try to disentangle Maya environmental practices from all the other factors at play during this period. It is, however, quite clear that the careful forest-management practices that characterized much of the Classic Period were eclipsed by a focus on short-term returns toward the very end at the period within some communities. The rapid depopulation of large site centers is that much more visible in the archaeological record than the forest-management strategies that characterized the many centuries of the Classic Period. The discrepancy in visibility has, unfortunately, contributed to the disproportionate attention on the end of the Classic story at the expense of the long journey that preceded it.

Resilience Amidst Collapse

Returning to a resilience theory framework, the Terminal Classic Period is clearly an archetypal example of the release and reorganization phases of the adaptive cycle.[136] Increasingly complex political and socio-ecological structures may have contributed to the successes of the Classic Period growth phase, but they also likely hastened the demise of many communities by limiting their capacity to adapt to a host of simultaneous stressors during the Terminal Classic. Characterizing the Late Classic Period within the adaptive cycle framework is difficult and differs between regions. In some areas, like the Puuc, it was clearly a continuation of the Early Classic growth phase, but in other areas it may be considered a time of conservation or even release. Destabilizing forces like increasing competition and shifts in trade networks were already escalating during the Late Classic. It is possible that many Classic Maya communities transitioned directly from a growth phase to a release phase. Some releases were more drawn-out, even spanning centuries, while others were more sudden.

By the later centuries of the Classic Period, the socio-ecological systems of some communities began to lose their adaptive flexibility. To a certain extent, decreasing resilience was a result of demographic growth and increasingly complex bureaucratic systems, but it also likely reflected the fact that food-production systems in some areas were approaching the limits of their growth capacities. The dynamic agroforestry systems that had been adapting so well for seven centuries eventually began to reach the limits of their sustainability. Carefully sculpting the landscape to feed ever greater populations would have indeed limited the capacity of communities to switch to alternative production modes when situations became too precarious. Classic Maya socio-political and subsistence systems across the lowlands became increasingly stressed by the end of the Late Classic due to demographic growth, a proliferation of noble families vying for power, and the gradually diminishing returns of food-production systems that were finally approaching their limits. Throw into this mix a downturn in precipitation, and you have a recipe for the breakdown of a system that had existed for seven-plus centuries and was the result of traditions going back several millennia.

However, despite general similarities in socio-ecological practices shared by communities across the Classic Maya lowlands, it is important to remember the heterogeneity of the Maya mosaic. Forest clearance in smaller communities likely never reached levels similar to those of Tikal or Caracol.[137] Even larger communities that were fast approaching the limits of their adaptive capacities still managed to implement a few course corrections in the face of mounting climatic, socio-political, and environment challenges. Many altered their fuel-consumption preferences, limited the culling of certain species, and even shifted exploitation to less densely settled areas. They implemented a mix of agricultural intensification and extensification practices where possible, expanding territory under cultivation through wetland reclamation, forest clearance, or importing fertile soils from other regions. In some cases, adaptation took the form of increased dependence on broader trade networks. For example, some cities in the lowland interior likely began to import food and fuel from neighboring coastal regions.[138] Recent lidar-based analyses in the northern Peten and Río Bec regions support the long-hypothesized idea that larger urban centers were supported in part by the intensification of agricultural practices in neighboring rural areas. The sparser rural populations could produce a surplus of food that was transported to larger towns and cities.[139]

Resilience in this case refers to the capacity and willingness of a society to adapt to changing circumstances. The greater percentages of non-domesticated plants consumed during the Classic to Postclassic transition in several areas does not only reflect the issues that farmers were having with their agricultural yields but also their willingness and ability to diversify their diets as well.[140] Changes in Late Classic Period wood-consumption patterns for construction at Tikal,[141] ceremonial use at Lamanai,[142] and fuel use at Naachtun[143] indicate that residents recognized they were beginning to overexploit their preferred resources. At Palenque, masons began using more clay binders, perhaps in an attempt to conserve the fuel that would have been needed to make lime.[144] By implementing stricter management protocols and shifting fuel consumption to include more fruit-producing species, they were able to prolong the survival of their local socio-ecological systems by more than a century in some cases. The switch to burning more valuable species may have been necessitated by the overexploitation of the usual fuel species, but the dominance of preferred fuel species today indicates that their numbers were never completely exhausted. A noticeable drop in pine pollen and charcoal at Lamanai during the Terminal Classic was followed by a resumption of larger scale pine exploitation in the Early Postclassic, indicating that a shift in exploitation strategies allowed the species to rebound.[145] At Naachtun, socio-ecological adaptations such as changes in fuel-consumption practices that developed during the Late Classic Period helped populations persist through the decline of the local dynastic bureaucracy.[146]

The rapid demographic expansion that began in the Puuc in the 600s CE continued into 900s. New agricultural lands were likely brought under cultivation during this period after prime soil tracts were all claimed by the earlier settlers.[147] The long span of population growth in the region amidst the turmoil engulfing other areas of the lowlands indicates that local communities and socio-organizational structures were able to consistently adapt to the socio-ecological challenges that they faced. For instance, the development and widespread adoption of the lime pit-kiln technology represented a region-wide conservation strategy that likely aided the long-term survival of many communities through the population boom.[148] The identification of new forms of civic architecture, including C-shaped structures with long interior stone benches at sites like Sayil, Uxmal, and Muluchtzekel that date to the tenth and eleventh centuries CE, indicates that the eventual depopulation of the Puuc was a gradual process. Substantial populations may have survived in the high and dry Puuc country, as well as at Classic Period sites on the northern like Ek Balam long after the construction of monumental architecture ceased.[149] Settlement surveys likewise indicate that significant populations of small-scale farmers survived in the central and southern lowlands long after centralized state-level apparatuses had disappeared.[150]

Amidst the endless quest to try to understand why and how the Classic Maya socio-political system broke down, it is important to recognize how many aspects of Maya civilization survived into the Postclassic Period and beyond.[151] Aside from the top-of-the-line elite ceramic complexes such as polychrome codex-style vases, we do not see as complete a break in ceramic traditions as one would expect to accompany an apocalyptic "collapse." Instead, there appears to be more of a gradual transition to new styles, including a hybridization with influences coming from outside the Maya lowlands.[152] Communities continued to import non-local lithic materials like obsidian from sources in the southern Maya highlands and Central Mexico.[153] They continued to tend the same agricultural crops and maintained their ritualistic relationships with the wider animate world, tracking sacred calendrical cycles up through the Colonial Period.[154] Although the practice of inscribing stone monuments trailed off, the Classic script itself continued to evolve through the time of the Spanish invasion.[155] Many rituals, including the Ch'a Chahk ceremony honoring the rain god, continue into the present (Figure 7.6).[156]

Even socio-political complexity, which researchers have largely agreed declined over the course of the transition, may not have declined to the drastic degree previously thought. The central figures in Postclassic communities wielded significant authority and political power over communities, just as in the Classic Period.[157] Prudence Rice and Don Rice see particularly resilient political practices in the Peten Lakes zone, including a continued focus on the god K'awiil as a symbol of political authority and on quadripartite spatial organizations of governance.[158] The absence of large-scale architecture does not automatically in- dicate a decrease in hierarchy, as Postclassic burials have indicated a significant degree of status differentiation.[159] Elaborate socio-political systems continued to evolve from their Classic origins, not necessarily decreasing in the complexity of interrelated components, procedures, and practices, but changing to adapt to a broader transformed landscape. Centralized forms of government continued at sites like Chichen Itza, Mayapan, and Xcalumkin in the north, and within the Peten Lakes zone, albeit incorporating newer elements of shared governance.[160]

Figure 7.6 The continued performance of the Ch'a Chahk ceremony at the start of the rainy season in the northern lowlands, which honors the Maya rain god Chahk, exemplifies the blending of Pre-Colonial and Catholic traditions and the resilience of ancient Maya cultural practices (photo courtesy of Bruce Love).

There was a definite trend away from large, centralized royal court systems toward more decentralized socio-political systems in other areas of the lowlands, but even decentralized governance can still encompass complex maintenance mechanisms.[161]

Chichen Itza exemplifies several of the cultural continuities that link the Late Classic with the Early Postclassic, complicating the notion of a clean break between periods and encouraging a focus on resilience and reorganization. In addition to its possible experimentation with a council style of government, Chichen Itza's resilience strategies included expanding control over circumpeninsular trade routes and possibly embracing the militaristic political ideology associated with Quetzalcoatl. The iconographic record suggests an increased focus on its military prowess, which it exercised against rivals across the northern peninsula. These strategies, along with the hydrological advantages conferred by a plethora of *cenotes*, helped the large northern capital persist through a period of increasingly dire droughts. It is possible that even though the construction of monumental architecture may have ceased at the site by 1000 or 1050 CE, populations continued to thrive at the site and exert influence over a broad area for decades after that.[162] Although the subsequent rise and fall of Mayapan can be squarely placed within the confines of the Postclassic Period, the revival of such Classic Period practices as stelae dedications provides a clear example of cultural resilience.[163]

Many of the changes that would come to exemplify the Postclassic system, such as the increased focus on long-distance and maritime trade, were already developing and growing throughout the Late Classic Period. Changes to the political system during the Terminal Classic both accelerated the expansion of the merchant class and opened them up to greater visibility in the archaeological record as the decentralization of economic networks allowed them to amass more individual wealth.[164] Small-scale farmers continued using Classic Period agricultural and water-management strategies into the Postclassic even in areas of the southern lowlands that saw the depopulation of large centers.[165] The continuation of environmental conservation practices through the present likewise indicate that channels for transmitting socio-ecological knowledge survived, reinforcing the notion that the Terminal Classic "release" phase should focus mainly on the breakdown of the *political* system, not Maya culture as a whole.[166]

The persistence of so many cultural aspects through the turmoil of the Terminal Classic is an amazing example of resilience, but it is important to recognize that the persistence of Classic Period cultural components was just as heterogenous as every other aspect of the Maya world. Diversity of resources to which a society has access is also a key factor in determining resilience.[167] Coastal, riverine, and lacustrine areas had a natural leg up with regard to the resilience of their environmental resource systems in the face of climatic changes.[168] Rivers and lakes provided freshwater for drinking and irrigation, as well as aquatic foodstuffs. Coastal habitats likewise offered a diversity of resource areas to help populations survive through trying times. These factors help explain why regions like the northern Yucatan, the Peten Lakes zone of northern Guatemala, and the river valleys of northern Belize saw the highest retention of population density and greatest cultural continuity into the Postclassic Period.[169]

In contrast, most of the elevated interior portions of the Maya lowlands were generally more susceptible to downturns in precipitation. Additionally, the increasingly complex bureaucratic policymaking systems within the larger Classic Period communities may have stifled their capacities to change.[170] These factors left many interior polities susceptible to more drastic expressions of release while stifling effective reorganization.[171] The drastic drop in the populations of the southern and central lowlands over the course of the Terminal Classic indicates that many households and communities adapted by fleeing the region.[172]

Those refugees that fled north likely had to deal with areas that were already densely populated. There is as of yet no hard archaeological nor skeletal/isotopic data to identify these migrant groups settling in other areas of the lowlands. However, indirect indicators such as the tremendous Terminal Classic population boom in the Puuc suggest at least some northward migration. Local and refugee populations would have had to adapt to the socio-ecological ramifications of the demographic shifts as well as to any cultural differences between the groups. The continuation of the population growth phase in the Puuc into the tenth century (and possibly beyond) indicates any absorption of migrant groups would have been successful. Some refugee populations may have settled on the Northern Plains, which would have required some degree of cultural and subsistence plasticity on the part of southerners accustomed to different topographic, meteorological, and vegetation conditions.[173]

Not all southern populations were forced to resort to the ultimate adaptation of picking up and moving. Some populations that stayed behind in the southern lowlands adapted their socio-political organization to reflect the new normal of living in smaller groups around what few available water sources remained.[174] In general, it appears that rural households were better able to survive the Terminal Classic droughts than their elite counterparts. Evidence from sites like Caracol demonstrates the resilience of small-scale farmers who survived in the region long after the centralized authority structure dissipated. They adapted to changing socio-political circumstances and likely strengthened social ties with other remaining residents living in communities centered on viable water sources.[175]

The story of the Classic to Postclassic transition is thus a complicated one, to say the least. With so many localized trajectories and factors at play, any attempt to develop an overarching framework of causes and effects will necessarily run into trouble. There are plenty of examples of relatively rapid site abandonments, and there are likewise plenty of examples of cultural continuities. If you focus more on demographic shifts and the cessation of royal material culture in the southern lowlands, then the transition starts to look an awful lot like a civilizational collapse. If you focus instead on socio-ecological and ritual practices in the Peten Lakes zone, the coasts of Yucatan, or individual sites like Lamanai, then it looks a lot more like a period of societal stress and reorganization. One thing that is clear if you look at the Maya lowlands as whole, however, is that Maya civilization did not collapse between the eighth and eleventh centuries CE. A strong argument can be made for the Classic Maya socio-political system collapsing and for several other components of Maya culture undergoing transformations, but Maya civilization most certainly survived.

8

Looking Forward

> What needs to be more widely recognized is that the ancient Maya, despite occasional episodes of local mismanagement, have survived and adapted for more than a hundred generations without wide-scale destruction of their forest.
>
> —Fedick 2010:954

Introduction

Maya studies have come a long way since the initial scientific investigations of the early 1900s, integrating data sets and approaches from several complementary disciplines. We now have a much better understanding of how Pre-Colonial Maya communities interacted with their local environments across the lowlands and how their socio-ecological practices changed over time. It is understandable why we in the present remain transfixed by the breakdown of the Classic Maya socio-political system over 1,000 years ago. However, we should not allow this fascination with the end to overshadow our recognition of the longevity of Classic Maya civilization and the resilience of Maya culture up through the present. We should focus at least as much attention on the successful aspects of Maya human-environment relationships as on the shortcomings. The longevity of the Classic socio-political system owes much to the socio-ecological adaptability of individual Maya communities, many of which thrived for over seven centuries.

The managed mosaic model of Maya-environment relationships has been widely accepted in academic circles since at least the early 1990s.[1] At its core is the recognition that communities across the lowlands managed a range of environmental niches. Agroforestry practices influenced local vegetation patterns as much as they were influenced by them. The Classic Maya should neither be seen as destroyers of the pristine forests nor as earth children living amidst, but not disturbing, the trees. From encouraging the regeneration of useful plant species to incorporating natural feedback cycles into their milpa systems, Maya communities carefully sustained a wide range of modified environments across the lowlands. By sculpting the landscape to increase water storage and carefully conserving wood fuel for a wide range of daily needs, Classic Maya communities

The Maya and Climate Change. Kenneth E. Seligson, Oxford University Press. © Oxford University Press 2023.
DOI: 10.1093/oso/9780197652923.003.0008

harnessed the potential of their natural world to support steadily growing populations.

Just as epigraphic developments have provided a more detailed understanding of Classic Maya socio-politics in recent decades, advances in paleoethnobotanical and isotopic methods have allowed for a more detailed understanding of Classic Maya human-environment relationships. Researchers are applying new technologies to the study of both old data sets and a steady stream of new data. Refined lake core, speleothem, and leaf wax analyses provide baselines for understanding climatic changes in subregions of both the southern and northern lowlands. However, more paleoclimatic data still need to be gathered to fill in regional pictures as we know precipitation patterns were highly localized. Phytolith, pollen, starch grain, and isotopic analyses continue to shed light on the diversity of Classic Maya diets and the systems that agroforesters developed to manage such a wide range of domesticated and semi-domesticated crops.

The biggest recent game-changer influencing how we evaluate ancient Maya human-environment relationships is the application of lidar technology to archaeological research. We are still in the early stages of the lidar revolution, but spatial analyses based on lidar-derived data are already uncovering clear evidence of the degrees to which Maya communities modified their natural landscapes in several subregions. Digital terrain models have revealed systems of canals and raised agricultural fields in the *bajos* of the Buenavista Valley west of Tikal[2] and in northern Belize,[3] as well as the degree to which city centers were engineered to capture and store water. They have also demonstrated that nearly every square inch of the Vaca Plateau surrounding Caracol was terraced for agricultural and water retention purposes.[4] It is likely that within the next twenty years more than half of the territory of the Maya lowlands will be scanned with lidar instruments. As flyovers proliferate, we will undoubtedly continue to uncover more and more evidence of the heterogeneity and ingenuity of localized environmental adaptations.

Classic Maya Human-Environment Relationships

The communities that thrived in the lowlands of eastern Mesoamerica between the second and tenth centuries CE benefited from more than two millennia of traditional ecological insights passed down from generation to generation. They also benefited from the social memory of the consequences of rampant environmental exploitation that afflicted several subregions toward the end of the Preclassic Period. The various tropical deciduous forests of the lowlands each provided their own challenges for farmers tasked with feeding populations that ran into the millions by the Late Classic. The sustainable, dynamic approaches that food producers were able to scale upward for many centuries derived in part from the experiences of their forebears. One of the most important lessons learned and deployed was that of socio-ecological flexibility—the ability and willingness to adapt those methods that worked best to address changing conditions.

Forest Exploitation

Ancestral Maya communities began influencing forest growth patterns at least as far back as the Archaic Period; before there is even any evidence for permanent settlements in the Maya lowlands. Forest modification intensified as swidden agricultural groups spread across the lowland interior, denuding hillsides and disrupting hydrological systems. Excessive forest clearance likely contributed to the downfall of several of the larger Preclassic communities and served as a warning to later Classic communities. However, the Preclassic Period also saw the development of several sustainable agroforestry-intensification practices such as raised wetland field cultivation and terracing that would become wide-spread during the Classic Period.

Ethnographic, archaeological, and paleoenvironmental evidence indicate that Classic communities incorporated a diverse range of sustainable forest-management practices for much of the Classic Period, many of which originated in the Preclassic. Agroforesters tended recently fallowed fields to modify succession patterns and produce valuable forest stands while only harvesting individual species at rates that ensured continued reproduction of resources. They gathered tree resources from homegardens, orchards, and young, secondary, and old-growth forests that were woven within mosaics of fields and residential compounds. Natural feedback loops were incorporated into systems that favored the growth of species most valuable to humans, producing food, tools, leisure items, construction materials, and medicines.[5] In some subregions of the lowlands, the management systems allowed for continuous exploitation of forest products for over 700 years! Macro- and micro-botanical evidence from Chan in Belize indicates that residents maintained access to mature forest species all through the end of the Classic Period.[6] Pollen data from Copan demonstrate that tree cover may have been more extensive during the Late Classic population boom than during the Early Classic.[7] When faced with mounting socio-political and climatic stressors during the Terminal Classic Period, some communities were able to adapt their forest exploitation strategies. They shifted fuel and construction wood preferences and developed more fuel-efficient technologies in others that allowed them to persist through centuries of turmoil.

One of the more prominent products harvested from the forests that surrounded and wove through Classic Maya communities was fuel wood. Domestic cooking and heating activities likely represented the majority of fuel consumption in Classic Maya communities, but a significant quantity of wood was also necessary to make the burnt lime as well. Lime was critical for maintaining a healthy maize-based diet, constructing residences, paving plazas, lining reservoirs, protecting food stores, and fertilizing fields. The development and implementation of more fuel-efficient lime-production technologies, at least in some areas of the lowlands, over the course of the Classic Period clearly demonstrate that communities took steps to avoid deforesting their landscapes. In fact, the persistence of communities in several regions of the north through the turmoil of the Terminal Classic Period may have been due in part to the proactive implementation of such fuel-conservation strategies.[8]

Adapting fuel-use strategies to changing climatic and environmental circumstances was also critical for salt-producing communities along the Belizean coast and at the inland Salinas de los Nueve Cerros saltworks. Due in part to the likely overexploitation of mangrove forests for fuel by their predecessors, Late Classic coastal producers began using a wider range of tree species harvested from farther inland. The fact that the mangroves eventually recovered indicates that salt producers adapted their fuel consumption practices and were willing to increase labor costs before they had completely destroyed the coastal forests. At Salinas de los Nueve Cerros, producers incorporated such fuel-conservation measures as limiting the consumption of fuel for non-salt-producing tasks and using the riverine trading route to import fuel from neighboring regions. The fact that salt production was still humming along in the Late Classic and only dropped off when demand fell amidst the turmoil of the Classic to Postclassic transition indicates that the fuel-consumption adaptations were successful.

Agricultural Production

An agricultural system is sustainable if successive generations can continue to harvest comparable returns from their landscape using the same practices as their forebears while conserving the environment.[9] Resilience refers to the capacity of a society to adapt successfully to unfavorable circumstances, ensuring the survival of the population and continuation of cultural practices.[10] Despite the gradual depletion of soil resources in some areas, as well as the eventual breakdown of the Classic Maya socio-political system, Classic Maya agricultural systems were sustainable and resilient in the face of environmental, climatic, and demographic pressures for over seven centuries. The overarching key to this resilience was diversity—of plot sizes and compositions, of crops, of microenvironments, of organizational structures, and of intensification strategies.[11] A variety of agricultural approaches were developed and used across the lowlands, within communities, and even within the same farming households. Through diversification, Classic Maya farmers protected themselves from the risks of individual agricultural sector failures. Collective memory of past failures was undoubtedly a key factor influencing the development of Classic Period resilience, as well.[12]

The willingness and capacity to adapt, was another key attribute that allowed Classic Maya farmers to continue to produce ever greater amounts of food over the centuries. The basic milpa model was adapted to a diverse range of environments and intensification strategies such as terrace construction and raised-field wetland cultivation. Despite the increased labor input necessary to modify the environment, farming communities took the necessary steps to ensure the longer term sustainability of their systems. Not enough can be said about collective knowledge of local landscapes and natural processes that informed these long-term investments in landscape modification. Households worked together over several generations in farming and to build intricate terrace networks that supported sustainable food production throughout the Classic Period. The water-management infrastructure of Classic sites was engineered not only for providing drinking water but also for providing irrigation for crops in homegardens, infields, and outfields in some areas. Organic household refuse was recycled to use in the growing plots.[13] All aspects of the Classic Maya food-production system were embedded within and inseparable from all other aspects of Classic Maya life.

Another key Classic Maya diversification strategy was the mix of community self-sustainability and maintenance of inter-community exchange networks. Local environmental conditions placed some limits on the range of intensification strategies that could be employed within each Classic Period community. Likewise, rainfall patterns are highly localized and can vary from year to year. By maintaining ties across subregions, communities would have been able to provide themselves with some measure of protection should precipitation levels for a given year or decade favor one area over another.[14] Calculations based on pollen analyses and both lidar settlement pattern- and land-use analyses suggest that the largest population centers of the southern lowlands would have needed to import food from neighboring, less populated regions during the Late Classic. This highlights the strong relationships maintained between urban zones and the peri-urban and rural hinterlands that surrounded them, which in turn suggests that there were few sectors of the lowlands that were not integrated into the Classic Period managed mosaic.[15] The fact that many small farming communities continued the same agricultural practices of the Classic Period well beyond the Classic-Postclassic transition and even up through the Colonial Period is a final testament to the sustainability and resilience of these systems.[16]

Water Management

Classic Maya water-management systems were also characterized by heterogeneity and diversification. Central authorities and households across the lowlands maximized their communities' water capture and storage capacities over the course of the Classic Period to survive the stark dry season and the occasional years of diminished precipitation. An early focus on large, centralized reservoirs evolved into systems with multiple components as populations grew and expanded out from site centers. Large and small reservoirs alike incorporated natural and synthetic filtration systems that included plants, animals, and minerals. Households and groups of households converted quarries into small surface reservoirs, constructed large terrace networks, dammed streams, dug wells, excavated subterranean cisterns, and collected rainwater in ceramic vessels in different parts of the lowlands.

Monumental site centers and small residential compounds alike were transformed into water capture mechanisms with inclined plazas and runoff channels. By incorporating several different simultaneous water capture and storage mechanisms into their water-management systems, Classic Maya communities survived for centuries even in areas with few or no perennial bodies of water. The impressive water-management systems only began to fail when droughts began to afflict several subregions simultaneously during the Terminal Classic Period—it did not matter how intricate or ingenious the systems for water capture and storage were if there was no water to capture.[17]

The Classic to Postclassic Transition

The sustainable strategies that Maya communities developed to maintain and exploit their local environments successfully supported booming populations for centuries but eventually met their match in a mix of demographic, political, and climatic stresses that effected the breakdown and reorganization of Classic Maya society. The decline of the Classic Maya socio-political system was a complex and drawn-out process. We see brief recoveries in some places,[18] and we have to imagine that the residents of those communities must have thought that they were weathering the storm and would emerge shortly into a more stable status quo. In other cases, families may have lived from generation to generation over several centuries having no reason to believe that they were living through a period that later historians and archaeologists would refer to as a "collapse" or "gradual demise." They may have noticed a decline in the population of their community or perhaps that they were not able to find certain items at the market anymore, but the situation on the ground need not have been so dire as to cause alarm. In still other cases, families may have recognized that there was an increase in violent conflict in in their region and may have prepared to flee their homes at any given moment.

We may not have the benefit of a chronicler giving us a day-by-day analysis of the breakdown of any Classic Maya communities, but by tying together the lines of evidence that are available to us we can develop a realistic understanding of the many forces at play across the Terminal Classic lowlands. After centuries of population growth managed by ingenious agricultural-intensification strategies, water-management infrastructure, and intricate agroforestry systems, Terminal Classic communities functioned as complex interconnected social networks. Subsistence practices—and human-environmental relationships more generally—were embedded within this complex system of cultural practices. The breakdown or transformation of one aspect of the cultural whole would undoubtedly affect change in other sectors and had the potential to snowball.[19]

Royal dynasties derived some of their power from their connection to divine ancestors and the supernatural world more broadly, but they also relied on the continued support of their elite attendants and non-elite subjects. Competition for power, for wealth, and sometimes for followers, led these royal dynasties to wage war against one another. The incidence of warfare escalated during the Classic to Postclassic transition, and in a few areas the escalation appears to have preceded any environmental or climatic downturns. Unpopular decision-making practices could have led to dissatisfaction among the population and the destabilization of existing power structures, sometimes leading to the overthrow of the royal court and its elite supporters by internal or external forces.[20]

We do not know to what extent individuals believed that their kings and queens were deities on earth who communicated with their divine brethren in the heavens to secure benefits for their people. Blaming socio-political disintegration on dissatisfaction with a ruling structure that was supposed to ensure good harvests every year may be a bit too simplistic. It is quite reasonable to believe, however, that diminishing economic returns made otherwise loyal populations more open to alternative modes of administration.[21] Civil unrest or unease would have been exacerbated and possibly raised to explosive levels by a decrease in rainfall, the severity of which may have been increased by deforestation around the largest Classic communities. A decline in rainfall would have had an outsized effect on crops already made vulnerable to environmental fluctuations by a decrease in soil nutrition and moisture caused by the same forest clearance. Some communities may have intensified their production to levels that would have been difficult to further enhance and may have already been teetering on the edge of sustainability.[22] Several bad harvest years in a row would have served as a final spark to explode a powder keg that had been nearing eruption for some time.

Although individual communities may have had a lot of leeway regarding the internal dynamics of their community structure, as far as we know, no Classic Maya community was a complete socio-political island. Elite lineages were connected across communities by prestige item trade networks, and royal families formed alliances as well as competed with one another. There was enough of a constant flow of ideas between communities that there existed a similar socio-political structure and material culture across a vast area that we can refer to it today as the "Maya" lowlands. The breakdown or abandonment of a power structure within a given community or even a subregion undoubtedly had consequences for neighboring regions as their trade networks were disrupted. They would have also likely had to deal with an influx of migrants fleeing the destabilized region, forcing them to either successfully absorb the migrants into their own communities or succumb to destabilization as well.[23] Many communities, including those in the Puuc region, may have successfully absorbed migrants from other areas. In other cases, the addition of many new mouths to feed may have triggered the demise of local subsistence and socio-political systems already near the breaking point.

In some areas, it is quite clear that socio-political unrest and the increasing frequency of violent conflict predated climatic and environmental downturns. In other regions, a pronounced decline in precipitation predated increases in socio-political unrest. Beyond the three general categories of stressors outlined in Chapter 7—climatic, socio-political, and environmental—factors like pandemics[24] and agricultural pests or diseases[25] may have also contributed to societal destabilizations. Establishing a cause-and-effect relationship is quite difficult in the absence of historical texts. Researchers know that "we cannot be certain" is not a satisfying response to questions about this incredibly important period in Maya history. Unfortunately, presenting an accurate and fact-based picture as possible sometimes involves laying out all the possible or likely scenarios without being able to definitively choose which one is the *most* likely. What we can say for certain is that there were a wide range of deleterious forces at play during this period, some of which represented long-standing trends that were now coming to a head, while others represented new and unforeseen challenges.

Continued Adaptation

Much has changed in the Maya world since the Classic Period, and these changes have only sped up over the past century. Amidst the adoption of new technologies and adaptation to globalizing influences, central aspects of Maya socio-ecological culture persist. Traditional knowledge of sustainable forest exploitation, developed and passed down for millennia, continues to benefit Maya communities in the present. Areas of the Maya lowlands in which forest management is administered by Indigenous communities continue to maintain lower overall levels of deforestation than areas administered by higher level governments or private organizations. Apiarists, now largely adapted to working with nonnative honeybee species, maintain hives in the forests surrounding towns, and agroforesters continue to promote inter-species feedback systems to maintain species diversity.[26] Whenever I am off in the forest mapping archaeological features with my local collaborators, they make sure to take advantage of the natural bounty that surrounds us. They collect fruits, medicine, dyes, flavoring agents, building materials, fuel, and other supplies to make sure they get the most of our sojourn into the semi-wild k'ax.

Since the start of the twentieth century, modern mechanized farming methods have replaced a lot of the day-to-day agricultural practices across the Maya lowlands. Many agriculturalists now share access to gas-powered tractors and use pesticides and fertilizers manufactured in laboratories. They ride out to their milpa outfields on mopeds made abroad. However, despite the unsurprising incorporation of modern farming techniques, the traditional ecological knowledge built up and passed down for generations continues to inform lowland Maya agriculture. Climate change is making it increasingly difficult, but many farmers still draw on their knowledge of weather patterns, humidity levels, and other subtle indicators to decide when to plant their crops near the start of the rainy season. Some even adhere to a prognostication system in which they use the meteorological conditions recorded on each day of January to predict the precipitation patterns for the rest of the year. Maize remains the dominant food crop, complemented by a range of other cultivars that includes all the Pre-Colonial cornucopia plus non-indigenous fruits and vegetables. Milpa fields include a mix of those species that feed and protect one another, ensuring maximum ecological efficiency. Homegardens continue to shelter a range of edible, medicinal, and utilitarian plants, and provide a place to rear an expanded list of domesticated animals.

Water management has perhaps changed the most of any aspect of the Maya socio-ecological system since the Classic Period, though there are certain long-standing practices that continue to promote resilience amidst climatic changes in the present. Communities continue to excavate wells to access the water table and can now do so in areas where it had previously been impossible, like the Puuc, thanks to mechanized equipment. Communities still share access to communal reservoirs, though they are now often located aboveground. Likewise, individual families still maintain their own water storage tanks, though they are now often made of plastic and sit on the surface as opposed to the lime-plastered subterranean *chultuns* of the Classic Period. Most importantly, similar to the Classic Period, many households in the dryer north take care to capture as much rainfall as possible, usually for bathing and homegardening needs. Some courtyards are slightly inclined to funnel rainfall into pooling areas where it can be more easily collected. Pot irrigation and container gardening remain common practices in homegardens.

Final Thoughts

We can trace the consistent evolution of socio-ecological adaptations throughout the Classic Period as communities contended with variations in annual precipitation, interregional socio-political intrigue, and steadily growing populations.[27] The key to the longevity of the Classic Period system lay in their flexibility and planning. Unfortunately, the increasing complexity and interweaving of so many segments of the Classic system steadily diminished this flexibility.[28] Sunk costs likely played an important role in diminishing the ability of communities in some subregions to respond to the accumulated challenges of the Terminal Classic.[29] The Classic Period was not a time of stagnation nor stability; rather, it was similar to all other periods in human history in that human groups were constantly reacting to socio-ecological systems in flux.

The specific, natural resource-management strategies developed by Classic Maya communities do not in and of themselves provide specific blueprints for resilience that we can follow today. Most were so successful because they were tailored to individual microenvironments, species, and rainfall patterns. The critical lessons that we *can* learn from Classic Maya socio-ecological practices regard the importance of planning, diversity, and the capacity to change course. Recommendations by the Intergovernmental Panel on Climate Change set up by the United Nations are pointing us toward the commonsense approaches used by the Maya for centuries, including the diversification of water capture and storage strategies.[30]

We must recognize that all aspects of our global societies are connected, and water conservation cannot be sectioned off from agricultural sustainability or forest management and addressed on its own. Everything is connected. It is obvious that the course we are currently on will not be sustained indefinitely, but we have known this for decades. We know that we cannot just *create* new water resources exponentially. We must focus on the age-old practices of water con-servation and management exemplified by the Classic Maya. One of the main sticking points for us today, which may have also affected Classic Maya communi-ties, is not the capacity to change our forest-management and fuel-consumption strategies, but our *willingness* to do so. Unfortunately, this is proving to be one of the most difficult problems of the climatic crises we now face and will likely re-quire a combination of both top-down and grassroots efforts to address.

Socio-hydrological models of drought indicate that proactive measures that can be taken by societies include slowing population growth and expanding water storage infrastructure.[31] As it seems that our global population growth will not be slowing any time soon, water conservation becomes that much more ur-gent. The vast majority of people today can agree that conservation is a must. It is a concept that carries the benefits of being relatively easily explained and un-derstood, even if implementation is another story. When it comes to implemen-tation of natural resource conservation plans, we run into the other two broad lessons we can learn from the Maya—the importance of diversifying water- and forest-management practices and maintaining flexibility in our systems. Changing our current systems and embracing a multitude of new water storage and consumption norms will undoubtedly be difficult in those areas of the world not yet suffering from dire water shortages, but it is the only solution.[32]

Classic Maya communities were forced to deal with a horrible concatenation of negative forces, all of which afflict modern-day societies in varying combin-ations and varying degrees. As we see today, some communities and regions are better equipped to deal with these challenges than others. It is true that all signs from the archaeological record point to a drastically transformed socio-political landscape in the lowlands by the start of the 1100s CE, but the transformations themselves were not abrupt, total, or spurred by a single cause. Researchers will continue to tease out the intricacies of the many processes at play during those critical centuries of the Terminal Classic on a region-by-region, and even site-by-site, basis. It is unlikely, however, that we will ever completely agree on how to frame the Classic to Postclassic transition, let alone on which factor might be singled out as *the* most important. It depends on subjective definitions and interpretations, as well as the inherent biases of individuals with their own life experiences. It is quite alright if researchers disagree about the broader inter-pretations of the data that we continue to accumulate as long as we are up front about what we do and do not know. It is also our responsibility to engage with broader audiences outside of academia and to push back against misconstrued understandings in the public arena when possible.[33]

Contemporary Maya communities continue to demonstrate the cultural and socio-ecological resilience that has been a key characteristic of Maya culture since the earliest agroforesters began shaping the lowland landscapes. Just as they have at many points in the past, Maya communities face numerous climatic, ecological, and social challenges in the present.[34] Ancient Maya communities weathered the turmoil of the Preclassic to Classic societal reorganizations. They adapted and persevered through socio-political and demographic stress over the course of the Classic Period and into the Terminal Classic Period. Although areas of the lowlands began to suffer waves of extended droughts as early as the late 700s CE, many communities survived for centuries by exercising their adaptive capacities. The breakdown of the Classic Period socio-political system—a release phase in the long-term lowland Maya adaptive cycle—was quickly followed by reorganization as communities adapted to a changing landscape. Ritual, governance, and socio-ecological practices continued relatively unchanged in some subregions and were modified in others depending on localized climatic and demographic conditions in the Early Postclassic Period. In the sixteenth century, communities faced the most difficult challenge to maintaining their cultural and socio-ecological traditions when Spanish conquistadors and missionaries imposed European religious beliefs and lifeways throughout the lowlands. Maya culture proved resilient as communities blended cultural traditions into a new whole.

The main factors that have consistently allowed Maya communities to survive through periods of turmoil and transmit cultural practices to succeeding generations are their capacities, abilities, and willingness to adapt to the changing circumstances. Thus, the main lessons we can learn from the Classic Maya are the importance of knowledge, planning, and structural flexibility. We must put the knowledge that we have of our climates and environments to good use. We must develop plans that do not address only the immediate needs of our growing populations but provide a foundation for future generations to thrive. Knowing that climatic and environmental circumstances are constantly in flux, these plans must include structural flexibility so that they can be shifted or adapted without completely changing the plan. Interconnectedness can be a hindrance to long-term adaptability, but it can also provide an avenue for adaptation in the form of diversifying support systems. It is of the utmost importance that we learn from the experiences and resilience of the Classic Maya to appreciate the long-term impacts of immediate course corrections. The thousands of Maya communities throughout eastern Mesoamerica today are the truest testament to the resilience of cultural traditions and socio-ecological practices that date back more than 4,000 years.

Notes

Chapter 1

1. The recent research conducted by Takeshi Inomata and colleagues (2020, 2021) in the Mexican state of Tabasco, and Marcello Canuto, Francisco Estrada-Belli, Thomas Garrison, and colleagues (2018) in northern Guatemala will be discussed in greater detail in subsequent chapters.
2. Diamond 2005.
3. Yaeger 2020.
4. See Martin 2020 Chapter 11 for an excellent, detailed overview of what Classic Maya inscriptions can tell us about this early ninth-century "crisis" and several new cultural forces at play in the final stages of the Classic Period.
5. Culbert 1973; Demarest et al. 2004; Haldon et al. 2020; Webster 2002; Yaeger 2020.
6. Aimers 2007; Haddon et al. 2020; Hoggarth et al. 2016.
7. Lucero 2018:328; McAnany and Gallareta 2010:145.
8. Haldon et al. 2020; Middleton 2012; Tainter 2014.
9. Houston and Inomata 2009:15–17.
10. Andrews and Robles Castellanos 2018; Kennett et al. 2022; Lohse 2010; Neff et al. 2006; Rosenswig et al. 2014; Sullivan et al. 2018.
11. Inomata et al. 2020, 2021.
12. Saturno et al. 2006; Stuart et al. 2022.
13. Canuto et al. 2018.
14. Stein 2001.
15. Fletcher et al. 2008.
16. Martin 2020:8.
17. Dunning and Houston 2011.
18. Dunning et al. 1998.
19. Fedick 1996.
20. Dunning et al. 1998.

Chapter 2

1. See Tozzer's (1941) translation of Diego de Landa's *Relación de las Cosas de Yucatán*. In the footnotes on pages 7–8 Tozzer explains that the first written record of the term "Maya" comes from a manuscript written by Bartholomew Columbus in 1505 and may have actually referred to an area in modern Honduras. However, Tozzer also suggests the term Maya may have been used to refer to much of the Yucatan

Peninsula in the centuries prior to the Spanish invasion, specifically stemming from the site of Mayapan.

2. Cojtí Cuxil 1994, 2007; Matsumoto 2015; Warren 1998.
3. Joyce 2005.
4. *New York Times*, Mar. 9, 1890.
5. *New York Times*, Oct. 8, 1929.
6. Hagen 1954.
7. Munro 2021.
8. Morello 1959; *New York Times*, Dec. 6, 1964.
9. Rice et al. 2004; Webster 2002.
10. Aimers 2007:351.
11. Rensberger 1980.
12. Anderson 2018; See also Card and Anderson's (2016) edited volume about under- standing the popularity of pseudoarchaeology to read how destructive popular media's fascination with archaeological "mysteries" can be.
13. Child and Golden 2008:87.
14. Del Río et al. 1822.
15. Bancroft 1903; Garcia Saiz 1994:100–101.
16. The basic premise is that so-called *Ancient Aliens* theorists are more inclined to be- lieve in extraterrestrial intervention than the abilities and ingenuity of Indigenous cultures around the world. See Reynolds 2015.
17. Stephens 1848:50–53.
18. Maler 1997.
19. Houston and Inomata 2009.
20. Huntington 1917.
21. Cooke 1931:283–287.
22. Fedick 2003.
23. Morley 1946:71.
24. Thompson 1966.
25. Cooke 1931:287.
26. Morley 1917:145.
27. Huntington 1917:159–160.
28. Culbert 1988:70; Fedick 2003:145–146.
29. Culbert 1988:87.
30. Culbert 1988:89.
31. Culbert 1973, 1988.
32. Rice et al. 2004.
33. Scott Fedick (2003) provides an excellent overview of how scholarly and public trends in socio-ecological thinking tend to reflect predominant contemporary environ- mental themes and concerns.
34. Dunning and Beach 2010:369; Fedick 2003:133; Lentz et al. 2015:152.
35. Santley et al. 1986:125; Turner 2018:62.
36. Fedick 1996.
37. Fedick 2003:152.

38. Fedick 2003:157.
39. Fedick 2003:134–137.
40. Holling 1973.
41. Gardner and Ramsden 2019.
42. Holling 2001:392–394.
43. Redman 2005.
44. Schroder 2020.
45. Masson 2012; Yaeger 2020.
46. Isendahl and Heckbert 2017; Tainter 2006; Tainter and Taylor 2014; Tainter et al. 2018.
47. Culbert 1988:77.
48. See Brenner et al. 2002:145 and Luzzadder-Beach et al. 2016:431 for more details about lake core analysis.
49. Price and Burton 2011:17.
50. Beach et al. 2015a.
51. See Douglas et al. 2016:6–8 and Luzzadder-Beach et al. 2016:432 for more details about speleothem analysis.
52. Beach et al. 2015a; Akers et al. 2019.
53. Santini 2015:38.
54. Rosenswig et al. 2014; Simms 2014:172–173.
55. Rushton et al. 2012:490.
56. Dunning and Beach 2000:88–89.
57. Lentz et al. 2015:165.
58. Fedick 2010:953–954; Ford and Nigh 2009; McNeil 2012:24.
59. Rushton et al. 2012:490.
60. Simms 2014:172.
61. Ford 2008:193.
62. McNeil 2012:28.
63. Lentz et al. 2014a; Sheets et al. 2011; Simms 2014.
64. Lentz and Ramirez-Sosa 2002:40.
65. Lentz et al. 2012.
66. Sheets 2000; Sheets et al. 2011, 2012.
67. Kepecs and Boucher 1996; Lohse and Findlay 2000.
68. Ford and Nigh 2009:226.
69. Fedick 2003; Fedick et al. 2000.
70. Dedrick et al. 2020; Hare et al. 2014.
71. Anselmetti et al. 2007:915.
72. Beach et al. 2011; Burnett et al. 2012:102; Dunning et al. 2019:141; Fernandez et al. 2005; Webb et al. 2004, 2007.
73. Scarborough et al. 2012:12412.
74. Dunning and Beach 2000:89; Ebert et al. 2021; Emery 1997; Rand et al. 2021; Wright and White 1996.
75. Atran 1993; Dahlin et al. 2005:231.
76. Alexander 2006:453; Atran 1993:640, 676.
77. Robin 2006:421.

78. Ortíz Ruiz et al. 2015; Seligson et al. 2017a.
79. Goguichaitvili et al. 2020; Ortiz Ruiz 2019.
80. Al-Bashaireh 2008; Chu et al. 2008; Hale 2003; Hueda-Tanabe et al. 2004; Mathews 2001.
81. See Seligson et al. 2017b for more information of isotopic and SEM analyses; Chu et al. 2008 and Goguichaitvili et al. 2020 about FTIR; and Goguichaitvili et al. 2020 about archaeomagnetometry.
82. Canuto et al. 2018; Chase et al. 2011; Garrison et al. 2019; Houston et al. 2019; Schroder et al. 2020.
83. Fernandez et al. 2014.
84. Gutierrez et al. 2001.
85. Chase et al. 2011, 2012; Weishampel et al. 2011.
86. Awe et al. 2015; Beach et al. 2015a; Brewer 2018; Chase 2016; Chase and Chase 2016; Chase and Weishampel 2016; Chase et al. 2011, 2012; Ebert et al. 2016; Garrison et al. 2019; Hightower et al. 2014; Houston et al. 2019; Hutson et al. 2016; Inomata et al. 2018; Macrae and Iannone 2016; Magnoni et al. 2016; Moyes and Montgomery 2016; Prufer and Thompson 2016; Ringle et al. 2018, 2021; Schroder et al. 2020; Weishampel et al. 2011; Yaeger et al. 2016.
87. Canuto et al. 2018; Garrison et al. 2019; Houston et al. 2019.
88. Garrison et al. 2016; Tokovinine and Estrada Belli 2017.
89. Garrison et al. 2019; Yaeger et al. 2016.
90. Johnson and Ouimet 2018; Prufer et al. 2015.
91. Hutson et al. 2016; Inomata et al. 2018; Magnoni et al. 2016; Prufer and Thompson 2016.
92. Chase et al. 2009.
93. Inomata et al. 2020.

Chapter 3

1. Dennell 2016; Fedick 2003:135–143; Ford and Nigh 2015; Gómez-Pompa and Kaus 1992:273–274.
2. Abrams and Rue 1988:380.
3. Santini 2015:32–33; Thompson et al. 2015:124.
4. Fedick 2003; Ford and Nigh 2009; Lentz et al. 2018.
5. Gómez-Pompa 1987; Campbell et al. 2006:21, 2008:279.
6. Ford and Nigh 2015; Lentz et al. 2015; Robinson and McKillop 2014; Seligson et al. 2017a; Watson et al. 2022; Woodfill et al. 2015:169.
7. Fisher 2020:14; Santini 2015:32.
8. Santini 2015.
9. Atran and Medin 2008.
10. Dunning and Beach 2000:80; McAnany 1998:76.
11. Taube 2003:476–477.
12. Dunning et al. 2012:3656; Hanks 1990.

13. Barrera Vásquez 1980:387.
14. Brown 2004; Hanks 1990; López Austin 2001; Stone 1995; Taube 2003:466–467.
15. Gómez-Pompa and Kaus 1992:272–273.
16. Taube 2003:470, 481–482.
17. Gómez-Pompa and Kaus 1992:271.
18. Lundell 1937.
19. Dunning 1990:44; Thompson et al. 2015:126.
20. Dunning and Beach 2010:373; Dunning et al. 2014:115.
21. Dunning 1990:42–43: Dunning and Beach 2000:83, 2010:371; Dunning et al. 2009:90, 2012:3653; Fedick 2003:141.
22. Dunning et al. 2009:95; Krause et al. 2019:282.
23. Dussol et al. 2017:30, 39.
24. Ford 2008:182; Dussol et al. 2017:30.
25. Thompson et al. 2015:148.
26. Fialko 2001; Lentz et al. 2015, 2016.
27. Alcorn 1984; Atran 1993; Rico-Gray et al. 1991; Thompson et al. 2015.
28. Dunning 1990:44; Terry et al. 2022.
29. Bletter and Daly 2009; Fedick 2020; Lentz et al. 2014b:206; Thompson et al. 2015:143.
30. Ford 2008:180; Gómez-Pompa 1987:2; Lentz et al. 2016:291; Peters 2000:213; Rico-Gray et al. 1991:159; Slotten and Lentz 2021; Thompson et al. 2015:146.
31. Fedick 2003:141.
32. Dussol et al. 2016:53; Lentz et al. 2016; Morell-Hart et al. 2019:14.
33. Dussol et al. 2016:53.
34. Abrams and Rue 1988; Dussol et al. 2016, 2017; Farahani et al. 2017:994; Hansen et al. 2002:288; Lentz et al. 2014b, 2015; Rushton et al. 2012:490; Wernecke 2008.
35. Dussol et al. 2017:30–31, 37.
36. Lentz et al. 2014b:208–209, 2016:290.
37. Watson et al. 2022.
38. Atran 1993; Dussol et al. 2017:30–31.
39. Dine et al. 2019; Gillespie et al. 2004:30; Lentz and Ramirez-Sosa 2002:40.
40. Lentz et al. 2014b:206; Taube 2018:275; Thompson et al. 2015:147.
41. Dussol et al. 2016:66; Lentz 1999:14; Lentz et al. 2016:291; Morehart et al. 2005:256.
42. Breedlove and Laughlin 2000; Lentz et al. 2005:574–575; Morehart et al. 2005; Moyes and Brady 2012; Tedlock 1985:112–113; Watanabe 1992:76.
43. Lentz 1991; Lentz et al. 2014b; McNeil 2012; McNeil 2006 in McNeil 2012:25; Rushton et al. 2012, 2020.
44. Standley and Williams 1961 in Lentz et al. 2014b:208.
45. Lentz et al. 2014b:206.
46. Balick et al. 2000; Breedlove and Laughlin 2000; Lentz et al. 2014b.
47. Lentz et al. 2014b:208.
48. Dussol et al. 2016; Morehart 2011.
49. Emery 2003; Nations and Nigh 1980:20; Rand et al. 2021.
50. Thompson et al. 2015.
51. Bennett et al. 2021.

52. Erlandson et al. 2011.
53. Andrews and Robles Castellanos 2018; Chatters et al. 2014.
54. Andrews and Robles Castellanos 2018:23.
55. Colunga-GarciaMarín and Zizumbo-Villareal 2004; Ford and Nigh 2009:215, 2015; Lentz 2000:90; Neff et al. 2006; Turner and Miksicek 1984.
56. Dunning et al. 1998b:147, 2014:115; Ford and Nigh 2009:215.
57. Andrews and Robles Castellanos 2018; Anselmetti et al. 2007; Dunning and Beach 2010:373; Lohse 2010; Lohse and Awe 2007; McNeil 2012:26; Sullivan et al. 2018.
58. Dunning et al. 1998.
59. Dunning and Beach 2010:373; McAnany 1998:83.
60. Dunning et al. 2014; Wahl et al. 2006, 2007.
61. Anselmetti et al. 2007:916.
62. Dunning et al. 1998:147, 2015:119.
63. McAnany 1998:81.
64. Anselmetti et al. 2007:917; Beach et al. 2008; Dunning and Beach 2010:373; Dunning et al. 1998:142, 2014:118.
65. Cook et al. 2012; Dunning et al. 2014; Hansen et al. 2018.
66. Chase and Chase 1998; Dunning 1996; Dunning et al. 1998:147; Fedick 1996; McNeil 2012; Puleston 1978; Sheets and Woodward 2002; Turner 1978.
67. Leyden 2002; Leyden et al. 1998; McNeil 2012:27.
68. Ford 2008; Ford and Emery 2008; Ford and Nigh 2009:214; Thompson et al. 2015:145–146.
69. Alcorn 1984; Atran 1993:678; Campbell et al. 2006:21; Peters 2000:211.
70. Gómez-Pompa 1987:11; Peters 2000:212–213.
71. Fedick 2010:953; McNeil et al. 2010.
72. Gómez-Pompa 1987:7.
73. Atran 1999; Campbell et al. 2006:30; Nigh 2008:234–235.
74. Ferguson et al. 2003:819; Ford 2008:187; Gómez-Pompa 1987:9; Nations and Nigh 1980:20; Ross and Rangel 2011:146; Santini 2015:32.
75. Levy Tacher et al. 2002; Nigh 2008.
76. Altieri and Nicholls 1999; Ross and Rangel 2011:146.
77. Atran 1993:635; Gómez-Pompa 1987:10; Santini 2015:33.
78. Peters 2000:211.
79. Campbell et al. 2006:31; Ross 2011:82.
80. Gómez-Pompa 1987:7; Peters 2000:212.
81. De Clerck and Negreros-Castillo 2000; Peters 2000:208–209.
82. Emery et al. 2000; Lentz et al. 2014b.
83. Atran et al. 1993; Dine et al. 2019; Dussol et al. 2017:39; Puleston 1968; Roys 1931:272.
84. Dine et al. 2019:517.
85. Peters 2000:211–214; Ross 2011:80–81; Thompson et al. 2015:144.
86. Campbell et al. 2006; Ford 2008:181.
87. Campbell et al. 2006:33; Ford 2008; Ross and Rangel 2011:146.
88. McAnany 1995 in Dunning and Beach 2010:380.
89. McAnany 1995; Vogt 1969, 1976 in McAnany 1998:77; Dussol et al. 2017:37.

90. McNeil 2012:28.
91. Gómez-Pompa 1987:7; Lentz and Hockaday 2009:1350; McNeil et al. 2010; Thompson et al. 2015:146.
92. Dunning et al. 2015; Lentz et al. 2018.
93. Lentz et al. 2018:113.
94. Haviland 1967; Scherer 2007; Thompson et al. 2015; Wright 2005.
95. Abrams and Rue 1988; Lentz et al. 2014a:18514, 2015:166–170; Rico-Gray et al. 1991; Thompson et al. 2015:145.
96. Lentz et al. 2015, 2018:118; Lentz and Hockaday 2009; Scarborough et al. 2012:12413; Thompson et al. 2015.
97. Lentz et al. 2015:178.
98. Haviland 1970; Lentz et al. 2014a.
99. Lentz and Hockaday 2009.
100. Lentz and Hockaday 2009.
101. Lentz et al. 2015:179, 2018:117; McAnany 1995:64–65.
102. Paris et al. 2018; Tozzer 1941; Villanueva-Gutiérrez et al. 2013.
103. Chuchiak 2003:137; Dahlin and Litzinger 1986; Dussol et al. 2016:66; Estrada-Belli 2006; Ocampo Rosales 2013; Paris et al. 2018; Pérez de Heredia et al. 2021; Tozzer 1941:399; Vail and Dedrick 2020.
104. Paris et al. 2018:5.
105. Paris et al. 2018.
106. Chemas and Rico-Gray 1991:17; Ford 2008; Paris et al. 2018:17; Villanueva-Gutiérrez et al. 2013:357.
107. Paris et al. 2018:4.
108. Lentz and Hockaday 2009; Lentz et al. 2015:183.

Chapter 4

1. Beach 1998:761; Canuto et al. 2018:5; Dunning 1996:66–67; Fedick 1996, 2003:145–148, 2020.
2. Dunning et al. 1998:95; Fedick 1996, 2020; Scarborough 2000:203.
3. Beach et al. 2002, 2015a:8; Luzzadder-Beach and Beach 2009; Scarborough 1993.
4. Barthel and Isendahl 2013:227.
5. Canuto et al. 2018:6.
6. Canuto et al. 2018:7; Dunning 1996; Fedick 1996, 2020; McNeil 2012:27; Robin 2003:319.
7. Morell-Hart 2020.
8. See Fedick 2020 for a truly comprehensive list of Maya cultivars.
9. Ebert et al. 2021.
10. Christenson 2003.
11. Fedick 2020.
12. Buckler et al. 1998; Piperno et al. 2009.
13. Doebley et al. 2006; Kwak et al. 2009; Matsuoka et al. 2002; Piperno et al. 2007.

14. Holst et al. 2007.
15. Mora-Aviles 2007.
16. Broughton et al. 2003.
17. Chacon et al. 2005; C. H. Brown 2006.
18. Beebe et al. 2000; Chacon et al. 2005; Kwak et al. 2009.
19. Fedick 2020.
20. Broughton et al. 2003; Mora-Aviles et al. 2007.
21. Fedick 2020.
22. Buckler et al. 1998; Pickersgill 2007; Piperno et al. 2007; Smith 2001.
23. Hart 2004.
24. Pohl et al. 1996:363; Sheets et al. 2012:264.
25. Dine et al. 2019:527; Lentz et al. 1996:256–258, 2014a:18515.
26. Baron 2018; Millon 1955.
27. Henderson and Joyce 2006; Powis et al. 2008.
28. Martin 2006.
29. Baron 2018:212; Garrison et al. 2019:141–43; Gomez-Pompa et al. 1990:251; Lentz et al. 2014a:18515; Millon 1955; Terry et al. 2022.
30. Bronson 1966.
31. Dunning et al. 2019; Meléndez Guadarrama and Hirose López 2018; Sheets et al. 2011.
32. Chen et al. 2022.
33. Dunning et al. 2019:142; Farahani et al. 2017:994.
34. Akpinar-Ferrand et al. 2012; Dunning et al. 2015, 2019.
35. Dunning et al 2015, 2019; Fedick 2020; Lentz et al. 2014a:18515, 2015; Luzzadder-Beach et al. 2017.
36. Fedick 2020.
37. Blanco and Thiagarajan 2017; Castro et al. 2018; Colunga-Garcia Marin and Zizumbo-Villareal 2004.
38. Dahlin et al. 2005:241.
39. Baron 2018:213; Dahlin et al. 2005; Dine et al. 2019:527; Houston et al. 2006:116–22; Tokovinine 2016.
40. Akpinar-Ferrand et al 2012; Brubaker and Wendel 1994.
41. Dunning et al. 2019:142; Lentz and Ramírez-Sosa 2002:37; Lentz et al. 1996:255; Lentz et al. 2014b:209; Simms 2014:78.
42. Ardren and Miller 2020; Schwarcz et al. 2022.
43. Fedick and Santiago 2022.
44. Dine et al. 2019:521,530; Puleston 1968.
45. Martin 2009; Reents-Budet 2009.
46. Dickau et al. 2007; Kennett et al. 2022.
47. Kennett et al. 2022.
48. Morell-Hart 2020:132–134.
49. Dunning et al. 2014; Pohl et al. 1996; Pope et al. 2001.
50. Beach et al. 2015a:8; Dunning et al. 1998:147; Ford and Nigh 2009:227; Pohl et al. 1996.
51. Andrews and Hammond 1990; Hammond 1991; Scarborough 2000:203.

52. Dunning et al. 2014:122, 2015; Hansen et al. 2018; Lentz et al. 2018:116.
53. Beach et al. 2015b:162; Krause et al. 2019:291, 2021; Luzzadder-Beach et al. 2021.
54. Beach et al. 2015a:20; Dunning et al. 2014:122.
55. Wyatt 2012:86.
56. Fedick 1996:128; Hansen et al. 2018:192; Kunen 2001:328; LeCount et al. 2019; McAnany 1995; Thompson and Prufer 2021.
57. Dunning 1992, 1996; Dunning and Beach 2000; Fedick 1996; Ford 1991; Levi 1996; Robin 2003.
58. Kwoka et al. 2021.
59. Fisher 2014:208; McAnany 1998:77,83; Neff 2010; Wyatt 2012:87, 2020.
60. Kunen 2001:326.
61. Thompson and Prufer 2021.
62. Chase and Chase 2014, 2016:6; Chase et al. 2019:2; Murtha 2009.
63. Beach et al. 2002; Canuto et al. 2018:7; Garrison et al. 2019:140.
64. Beach and Dunning 1997:27.
65. Schwarcz et al. 2022.
66. Dine et al. 2019:521; Somerville et al. 2013:1551.
67. Wyatt 2020.
68. Anderson et al. 2012:374; Barthel and Isendahl 2013:227–228; Dine et al. 2019:527; Fedick et al. 2008:296; Lentz et al. 1996.
69. Watson et al. 2022.
70. Calvet-Mir et al. 2016; Castro et al. 2018:1.
71. Anderson 1993; Fedick and Morrison 2004:213; Fisher 2014:197–200; Fletcher and Kintz 1983; Ortega et al. 1993; Simms 2014:298; Wyatt 2020.
72. Kwoka et al. 2021.
73. Dunning 1996:61; Fisher 2014; Isendahl 2010:543; Isendahl and Smith 2013:133–134; Killion 1992.
74. Evans et al. 2021.
75. Anderson et al. 2012:374; Beach 1998:767; Beach et al. 2015a:20; Ford 2019:11; Ford and Nigh 2010; Nigh and Diemont 2013.
76. Boserup 1965:29; Chase and Weishampel 2016:358.
77. Atran 1993:635.
78. Ford and Emery 2008; Gliessman 1983.
79. Lucero 1999; Redfield and Villa Rojas 1934:42–44.
80. Ford 2019:11.
81. Atran 1993:678–681.
82. Lentz et al. 2014a:18515.
83. Ford and Emery 2008:149.
84. Fan et al 2008.
85. Broughton et al 2003; Vera-Nuñez et al 2007.
86. Dawo et al 2009.
87. Dahlin et al. 2005:237.
88. Atran 1993; Barrera 1980; Dahlin et al. 2005; Killion 1992; Nations and Nigh 1980; Stuart 1993; Wiseman 1978.

89. Atran 1993:635; Rice 1991.
90. Beach et al. 2018; Canuto et al. 2018:6; Chase et al. 2011:388; Dunning et al. 2019:140; Šprajc 2008.
91. Beach and Dunning 1995; Beach et al. 2002, 2015a:20, 2019:21474; Dunning and Beach 1994:61–62, 2010:376; Dunning et al. 1997:263; Johnston 2003:139; Kunen 2001:329–331; Macrae and Iannone 2011; Neff 2010; Neff et al. 1995:157; Wyatt 2012:86.
92. Beach et al. 2009; Chase and Chase 1998; Chase and Weishampel 2016; Chase et al. 2011; Dunning and Beach 2010; Dunning et al. 2019:140; Garrison and Dunning 2009; Hansen et al. 2002; Kunen 2001:329.
93. Dunning 1996:62; Dunning and Beach 1994.
94. Johnston 2003:139.
95. Chase and Weishampel 2016:358.
96. Robin 2015:46; Wyatt 2008:249–250.
97. Chase and Chase 2016:6; Chase and Weishampel 2016:365.
98. Beach and Dunning 1997:27.
99. Beach and Dunning 1995; Dunning and Beach 1994; Dunning et al. 1998:141; Fisher 2020:408; Kunen 2001:332; Robin 2015:46; Wyatt 2008, 2012, 2014.
100. Beach et al. 2002; Brewer 2018:203; Dunning and Beach 1994; Dunning et al. 1997; Kunen 2001; Macrae and Iannone 2011.
101. Dunning et al. 2019:142.
102. Keenan et al. 2021.
103. Fisher 2020; Wyatt 2008, 2012, 2014.
104. Chase and Chase 2016:6.
105. Lemonnier and Vanniere 2013:402–403.
106. Kunen 2001:329; Lemonnier and Vanniere 2013:409.
107. Fedick 1994; Kunen 2001; Turner 1983.
108. Chase 2016; Chase et al. 2019:10; Hightower et al. 2014.
109. Chase and Chase 2016:6; Chase and Weishampel 2016:358.
110. Chase and Chase 1998; Kunen 2001.
111. Dunning 2003:56; Dunning et al. 2006:82.
112. Beach et al. 2019:21474; Krause et al. 2019:293, 2021; Luzzadder-Beach et al. 2021; Scarborough 2007:168.
113. Turner and Harrison 1983.
114. Dunning 1996; Luzzadder-Beach et al. 2012; Pohl et al. 1990; Turner and Harrison 1983.
115. Culbert et al. 1991:116; Levi 1996; Luzzadder-Beach and Beach 2008; Luzzadder-Beach et al. 2016.
116. Pohl and Miksicek 1985; Levi 1996.
117. Jacob 1995; Krause et al. 2019:291–293; Pohl et al. 1996:366.
118. Beach et al. 2015b:162, 2019; Krause et al. 2021; Luzzadder-Beach et al. 2012, 2016, 2021.

119. Canuto et al. 2018:5.
120. Fedick et al. 2000; Fedick and Morrison 2004.
121. Tozzer 1941.
122. Fedick 2014.
123. Dedrick et al. 2020; Fedick et al. 2008; Gómez- Pompa et al. 1990; Houck 2006; Munro-Stasiuk et al. 2014.
124. Dedrick et al. 2020; Dine et al. 2019; Gómez-Pompa et al. 1990; Houck 2006; Kepecs and Boucher 1996:77; Munro-Stasiuk et al. 2014:169.
125. Dedrick et al. 2020:6; Kepecs and Boucher 1996:77.
126. Gómez-Pompa 1987; Gómez-Pompa et al. 1990; Peters 2000:213.
127. Beach 1998:762; Fedick et al. 2008:302; Kepecs and Boucher 1996:72.
128. Dunning et al. 2014:119.
129. Beach et al. 2002; Brewer 2018:205; Culbert 2001; Dunning et al. 2006:93, 2015:120, 2019; Dunning and Beach 2010:373; Lentz et al. 2014a:18516–18517; Scarborough 1998:141.
130. Dunning et al. 2015:121; Garrison et al. 2019:139–140; Lentz et al. 2018:117.
131. Beach 1998:786; Dahlin et al. 2005:238; Fedick 2014:78.
132. Akpinar-Ferrand et al. 2012; Dunning et al. 2002; Schwartz and Corzo 2015:81.
133. Scarborough and Valdez 2014.
134. Beach 1998; Dahlin et al. 2005; Nobel 1988.
135. C. T. Brown 2006:173; Fedick 1996:129; Levi 1996:98.
136. Dahlin et al. 2005; Evans et al. 2021; Hansen et al. 2018:187.
137. Chase et al. 2019:5; Keenan et al. 2021.
138. Dahlin et al. 2005:239; Johnston 2003:146; Soane 1998; Thurston 1997.
139. Dahlin et al. 2005:240; Fedick and Morrison 2004:213; Fedick et al. 2000; Morrison and Cozatl-Manzano 2003; Palacios-Mayorga et al. 2003.
140. Beach 1998:783–786.
141. Beach et al. 2015a:20;.Luzzadder-Beach et al. 2017.
142. Dunning and Beach 1994.
143. Farahani et al. 2017:994; Sheets et al. 2012:279.
144. Lentz et al. 1996:255.
145. Farahani et al. 2017:991.
146. Farahani et al. 2017; Lentz et al. 2015:174; Lentz and Ramirez-Sosa 2002; Sheets 2002; Sheets and Woodward 2002; Sheets et al. 2011, 2012.
147. McNeil 2012; Sheets et al. 2011, 2012.
148. Slotten and Lentz 2021.
149. Farahani et al. 2017:985; Lentz et al. 1996:254.
150. Slotten and Lentz 2021.
151. Dine et al. 2019:527; Farahani et al. 2017; Lentz and Ramírez-Sosa 2002; Lentz et al. 1996:255.
152. Ford and Nigh 2009:225.
153. Johnston 2003:137.

Chapter 5

1. UNESCO 2012.
2. Lucero et al. 2011:482.
3. Barthel and Isendahl 2013:231; Scarborough 1998:139.
4. Lucero et al. 2014:36.
5. Halperin et al. 2019:1.
6. Dunning et al. 1998; Lucero et al. 2014.
7. Lucero et al. 2014:31.
8. Gunn et al. 2002a; Lucero 2006.
9. Gunn et al. 1995:12; Isendahl 2011.
10. C. T. Brown 2006:173; Tainter et al. 2018:334.
11. Dunning 2003:56; Dunning et al. 2006:82; Lucero 2006.
12. Dunning et al. 1998:93; Johnston 2004:279.
13. Gunn et al. 2002b:313, 2014:110.
14. Lucero 2006:282.
15. Luzzadder-Beach and Beach 2008:219.
16. Dunning and Houston 2001:58, 63.
17. Based on data accumulated between 1871 and the present.
18. Dunning and Houston 2011:58, 60.
19. Gunn et al. 2002b; Scarborough 1998:138.
20. Canuto et al. 2018.
21. Bacus and Lucero 1999; Lucero et al. 2014.
22. Lucero et al. 2011:482, 2014:31; Normile 2010:807.
23. Healy 2003; Wyatt 2014:454.
24. Abrams 1987; Seligson et al. 2017a.
25. Gunn et al. 2014:108; Lucero 2006:292.
26. Dunning 2003:64; Finamore and Houston 2010; Ford 1996; Lucero 1999; Lucero et al. 2014:32–33; Schultes and Hoffman 1992:67.
27. Lucero 2006:285–286; Lucero et al. 2011:485; Scarborough 1998:136.
28. Chase and Cesaretti 2018.
29. Johnston 2004; Lucero 1999:43.
30. Dunning 2003; Dunning et al. 2014:74.
31. Scarborough 1998:153; Schele and Miller 1986.
32. Freidel et al. 1993.
33. Halperin et al. 2019:10.
34. Demarest et al. 2016; Thornton and Demarest 2019.
35. A colloquialism for city or realm used by kings in the Classic Period was *kabch'een* (earth-sky) (Martin 2020:119).
36. Bassie-Sweet 1996; Scarborough 1998.
37. DiNapoli et al. 2019.
38. Scarborough 2000:149.
39. de Anda et al. 2019.
40. Akpinar Ferrand et al. 2012:99; Gill et al. 2007; Scarborough 2007:172–173.

41. Dunning et al. 2006:89, 92; Lucero et al 2014; Scarborough 1993, 1998:139, 2000:201.
42. Scarborough 2007:169–171.
43. Hodell et al. 2005:1421; Nooren et al. 2018:1261.
44. Dunning 2003:60; Lucero et al. 2011:483, 2014:31; Luzzadder-Beach and Beach 2008:225.
45. Ringle et al. 2018; Smyth and Ortegón Zapata 2008.
46. Akpinar-Ferrand et al. 2012:98; Dunning 2003:62; Lucero et al. 2011:483; Scarborough 1998:139; Tainter et al. 2018:339.
47. Scarborough 2000:201; Tainter et al. 2018:334.
48. Beach et al. 2015d; .Luzzadder-Beach et al. 2017.
49. Scarborough 2000:201–202.
50. Lucero et al. 2011:483–484.
51. Akpinar-Ferrand et al. 2012:98; Gunn et al. 2002b:313; Lucero et al. 2011:483–484.
52. Canuto et al. 2018; Tainter et al. 2018:339.
53. Scarborough 1993, 2003:50–51, 110–111, 2007; Scarborough and Gallopin 1991; Scarborough and Grazioso Sierra 2015:18.
54. Halperin et al. 2019.
55. Scarborough 1993, 2003:50–51, 2007; Scarborough and Gallopin 1991; Scarborough and Grazioso Sierra 2015:19, 30; Tankersley et al. 2020.
56. Gallopin 1990; Lane et al. 2015:57.
57. Scarborough 1998:140; Scarborough and Grazioso Sierra 2015:21–23.
58. Scarborough and Grazioso Sierra 2015.
59. Scarborough 1998:139.
60. Lucero et al. 2014; Scarborough and Gallopin 1991:660–661.
61. Scarborough and Grazioso Sierra 2015:31–32; Scarborough et al. 2012:12408.
62. The greatest augmentations to the system were made between the seventh and ninth centuries CE, most likely at the direction of Yik'in Chan K'awiil, the great twenty-seventh ruler of the city-state, who was in power from 734 to 746 CE. Not long after his reign, however, the socio-political systems that managed the elaborate Classic water-management networks began to fray (Scarborough and Grazioso Sierra 2015).
63. Lentz et al. 2020.
64. Chase 2016; Chase and Cesaretti 2018.
65. Chase and Chase 2014:146, 2017:198, 211; Chase et al. 2019:4; Scarborough and Gallopin 1991:661.
66. Scarborough and Gallopin 1991.
67. Chase 2016; Chase and Cesaretti 2018.
68. Davis-Salazar 2003; Fash 2005; Fash and Davis-Salazar 2006:130; Lucero et al. 2014:33.
69. Davis-Salazar 2003:293–294.
70. Davis-Salazar 2003:285–287.
71. Davis-Salazar 2003:278; Fash 2005:116, 133; Fash and Davis-Salazar 2006:132–136.
72. Davis-Salazar 2003:281; Fash 2005:109–110; Vogt 1969.
73. Davis-Salazar 2003:280; Farriss 1984; Fash 2005; Fash and Davis-Salazar 2006:139–141; Wisdom 1940.

74. Matheny 1978:198.
75. Matheny et al. 1983:67.
76. Benavides 2008; Matheny 1978:199–201; Matheny et al. 1983:67, 73.
77. Matheny et al. 1983:73–74, 80.
78. Matheny 1978:203–205; Matheny et al. 1983:68.
79. Benavides 2008; Gunn et al. 2002b:313; Matheny 1978:201; Matheny et al. 1983:80.
80. Halperin et al. 2019:5–9.
81. Johnston 2004.
82. Matheny et al. 1983:75.
83. Akpinar-Ferrand et al. 2012:98; Brewer 2018:211; Weiss-Krejci and Sabbas 2002:344, 353.
84. Chase 2016; Chase and Cesaretti 2018.
85. Scarborough 1998:142, 147; Vogt 1969.
86. Johnston 2004:268, 279.
87. Harrison 1993:78–81; Johnston 2004:282, 283; Wyatt 2014.
88. Lucero et al. 2011:485.
89. Fedick et al. 2008:295.
90. Healy 1983; Johnston 2004:282; Turner and Johnson 1979; Wyatt 2014.
91. Beach and Dunning 1997:22–28.
92. Weiss-Krejci and Sabbas 2002:353.
93. Brewer 2018:212.
94. Lucero et al. 2011:486.
95. French and Duffy 2010.
96. French et al. 2020.
97. Delgado et al. 2010; Fedick 2014:73–74.
98. Fedick 2014:73.
99. C. T. Brown 2006:173.
100. Anderson et al. 2018.
101. C. T. Brown 2006:180.
102. Johnston 2004:283.
103. Luzzader-Beach 2001; Luzzadder-Beach and Beach 2017.
104. Barrera Rubio and Huchim Herrera 1989; Dunning 1992:22; Isendahl 2011:190; Johnston 2004; Wyatt 2014.
105. Hahn and Braswell 2012:276.
106. Folan 1978:80.
107. Isendahl 2011:187; Isendahl et al. 2014:46.
108. Isendahl 2011:185, 188.
109. Ringle et al. 2018, 2021.
110. Matheny 1978:207.
111. McAnany 1990:268.
112. Isendahl and Smith 2013:135–136; Lucero 2006:288; Lucero et al. 2014:34; Puleston 1971.
113. Matheny 1978:207.
114. Dunning et al. 2014:73–74; Isendahl et al. 2014:50–51; Smyth et al. 2017:506.

115. Dunning et al. 2014; Smyth et al. 2014:45.
116. Smyth et al. 2014:57.
117. Matheny 1978:209.
118. Dunning et al. 2014:73.

Chapter 6

1. Abrams and Freter 1996:426; Chu et al. 2008:905; Rapp 2009:261.
2. Herckis 2015:159; Littmann 1957:138.
3. MacKinnon and May 1990:100.
4. Garcia Solis 2011:194.
5. Rapp 2009:261.
6. Abrams 1996:197; Russell and Dahlin 2007:408–409; Schreiner 2002:12–13; Seligson 2016.
7. Espinosa et al. 1998:410; Ward 1985.
8. Gondwe et al. 2010:2.
9. Hansen 2000:124; Espinosa et al. 1998:411; Littmann 1958:172.
10. Martin and Grube 2008:163.
11. Hansen et al. 2018:173; Morris et al. 1931:223; Rapp 2009:262.
12. Abrams 1984, 1996:198; Garcia Solis 2011:199; Gillot 2014:7; Littmann 1960a; Magaloni 2001; Straulino et al. 2016:24; Villaseñor 2008.
13. Abrams 1996:198; Rapp 2009:264.
14. Abrams et al. 2012:1649; Littmann 1960b:409; Wernecke 2008:203.
15. Gillot 2014; Hansen et al. 1995; Rapp 2009:264; Villaseñor 2010; Villaseñor and Graham 2010:1339.
16. Gillot 2014:6; Villaseñor and Graham 2010:1345.
17. Garcia Solis 2011:194; Littmann 1960a:593–597; Magaloni 2001:161; Meehan Hermanson and Alonso Olvera 2013:222.
18. Hansen 2000; Santiago and Mendonca 1992; Schreiner 2002:111–112, fn. 54.
19. Abrams and Freter 1996:423; Barba Pingarrón 2013:21; Hyman 1970; Staneko 1996:77–78.
20. Arnauld et al. 2013:476.
21. Barba 2013:21.
22. Freidel 2018; Garcia Solis 2011:193; Martin and Grube 2008; Villaseñor 2008:60.
23. Hansen 2000:113; Tokovinine and Estrada-Belli 2017.
24. Sharer et al 1999; Villaseñor 2008:60.
25. Cagnato 2017:89; Dunning et al. 1999:657; Lentz et al. 2014a:18517; Luzzadder-Beach et al. 2016:436; Scarborough et al. 2012.
26. Abrams 1994:75; Lentz et al. 2014a:18514, 2015:169; Tozzer 1941.
27. Barba 2013:19.
28. Biskowski 2000:294; Brumfiel 1991:237–238; Fournier 1998; Rodriguez-Alegria 2012:101–102.

29. Cheetham 2010:346; Rodriguez-Alegria 2012:101–102.

30. Kennett et al. 2020:7.

31. Schreiner 2000: 78.

32. Barba 2013:40; Cagnato 2017:89; Smyth 1990:54.

33. Hansen et al. 2002:285, 2018:187; Straulino 2015:25.

34. Hansen 2000:117.

35. Houk et al. 2010:238; Houston et al. 2006; Taube 1992.

36. Cheetham 2010:346; Hansen 2000:117; Magaloni 1996; Santini 2015:75.

37. Al-Bashaireh 2008:35; Belfer-Cohen 1991; Kingery et al. 1988; Rapp 2009:262.

38. Barba and Córdova 2010; Straulino 2015:26; Villaseñor 2010:53.

39. Barba Pingarrón 2013:29; Marcus and Flannery 1996:83–87.

40. Gerhart and Hammond 1991:99: Hammond et al. 1991:30–32; Schreiner 2002.

41. Kennett et al. 2020.

42. Diamond 2005.

43. Morris et al. 1931:220–222.

44. Hansen 2000:128.

45. Morris et al. 1931:220.

46. Abrams and Freter 1996:425; Garcia Solis 2011:195; Hanson 2008:1494–1495; Wernecke 2008:203.

47. Hansen 2000; Schreiner 2002.

48. Schreiner 2001:357, 2002:31–32.

49. Schreiner 2002:28–29, 62.

50. Hansen 2000:129; Levy Tacher and Hernández Xolocotzi 1995; Russell and Dahlin 2007.

51. Dunning and Beach 2010:375; Dunning et al. 2015:9; Hansen et al 2002; Wahl et al. 2007.

52. Lentz et al. 2014a:18514, 2015:169–170.

53. Schreiner 2002:87–88.

54. Hansen et al. 2018:173.

55. Garrison and Dunning 2009; Hansen 2000; Saturno 2002.

56. Anderson and Wahl 2016:89.

57. Hansen et al. 2002, 2008, 2018:174; Schreiner 2001, 2002; Wahl et al. 2006, 2007.

58. Schreiner 2002:78.

59. Schreiner 2002:62; Wernecke 2008:203–206.

60. Peraza Lope et al. 2006:161; Russell and Dahlin 2007:421.

61. MacKinnon and May 1990.

62. Abrams et al. 2012:1649; Hansen 2000:127.

63. Ortíz Ruiz 2014, 2019; Ortíz Ruiz et al. 2015; Seligson 2016; Seligson et al. 2017a, 2017b, 2017c, 2019.

64. Copan (Viel 1983; Abrams and Freter 1996); Cauinal (Fauvet-Berthelot 1980:5–7); Dos Pilas (Johnston et al. 1989); Chan Kom (Redfield and Villa Rojas 1934); Sayíl (Dunning 1991); Cozumel (Freidel and Sabloff 1984:35); and northeast Yucatan (Barrera Rubio 2013).

65. Dunning 1991:25; Sabloff and Tourtellot 1991.

66. Ringle et al. 2018, 2021; Seligson et al. 2017a, 2017b, 2017c.
67. Ortíz Ruiz et al. 2015; Ortíz Ruiz 2019.
68. Šprajc 2017:13–14, Šprajc et al. 2022.
69. Seligson et al. 2017a, 2017b, 2017c, 2019.
70. Ringle et al. 2018, 2021.
71. Seligson et al. 2017a.
72. Ortíz Ruiz et al. 2015:14; Ortíz Ruíz 2019; Seligson et al. 2017b.
73. Gallareta Negrón et al. 2014; Ringle et al. 2018, 2021.
74. Seligson et al. 2017b, 2017c.
75. Seligson et al. 2017c.
76. Šprajc 2017:7.
77. Abrams 1996:207; Abrams and Freter 1996:426; Abrams and Rue 1988.
78. Dussol et al. 2021; Santini 2015:73–76.
79. Atran 1999; Santini 2015:74; Schreiner 2002:69.
80. Seligson 2016:303; Seligson et al. 2017b.
81. Garcia Solis 2011:255; Schreiner 2002:28–29; Seligson et al. 2017c:290.
82. Abrams 1996:207; Russell and Dahlin 2007:420.
83. Lentz et al. 2015:169–171.
84. ((49,693 m3 x 2,000 kg/m3 x 0.10 x 4)/50) = 795,088 kg.
85. Russell and Dahlin 2007:418–420.
86. Abrams and Rue 1988:390; Schreiner 2002.
87. Abrams 1996; Abrams and Freter 1996; Hansen 2000:130; McNeil et al. 2010; McNeil 2012:25.
88. Garrison 2007:241; Hansen et al. 2018:173; Schreiner 2002:126; Turner and Sabloff 2012:13910; Villaseñor 2008:121–122.
89. Fash and Fash 1996; McNeil 2012:25; Wernecke 2008:205.
90. Villaseñor 2008:153–154.
91. Dussol et al. 2020; Seligson et al. 2017a.
92. Schrier 2010; Woodfill et al. 2015.
93. Andrews 1983:1.
94. Redfield and Rojas 1934.
95. Fenner and Wright 2014.
96. McKillop 1995:216.
97. Andrews 1983:11; McKillop 1995, 2002, 2007; McKillop and Aoyama 2018:2; Williams 2010; Woodfill et al. 2015.
98. Andrews 1990:166; Andrews et al. 1988; Clark 2014; Hoggarth et al. 2016:28; Kepecs 2003, 2007.
99. Sabloff 2007; Sierra Sosa et al. 2014.
100. McKillop 2002, 2009:284, 2010:174; McKillop et al. 2019:514.
101. Carrasco Vargas et al. 2009; Valencia 2020.
102. Andrews 1983:22.
103. McKillop 2021.
104. McKillop 1995:221–225, 2010:175, 2019; McKillop and Aoyama 2018; McKillop et al. 2019.

105. McKillop 1995, 2010:173–174.
106. McKillop 2019; McKillop et al. 2019:504.
107. McKillop 2002; Robinson and McKillop 2013, 2014.
108. McKillop and Aoyama 2018:3.
109. Murata 2011.
110. Dillon 1979, 1987; Woodfill et al. 2011, 2015.
111. Dillon 1988; Woodfill et al. 2015.
112. Dillon et al. 1988; Woodfill et al. 2011, 2015.
113. Woodfill et al. 2015:170.
114. Abrams and Rue 1988; Lentz et al. 2015; Schreiner 2002:84–85; Villaseñor 2008:62.
115. Dussol et al. 2021; Seligson et al. 2019.
116. Arnauld et al. 2017; Dussol et al. 2021:189; Wernecke 2008:206.
117. McKillop 2002, 2005; Robinson and McKillop 2013:3587.

Chapter 7

1. Rice et al. 2004.
2. Culbert 1973; Demarest 2004; Demarest et al. 2004; Halperin et al. 2021; Iannone 2014; Webster 2002; Yaeger 2020.
3. Aimers 2007; Abrams and Rue 1988:392; Culbert 1973; Demarest et al. 2004; Iannone 2005; Masson 2012:18237; Martin 2020; Middleton 2012:275; Rice and Rice 2004; Rice et al. 2004; Tainter 2006:68; Turner 2018:62; Webster 2002; Willey et al. 1967; Yaeger and Hodell 2009.
4. Demarest et al. 2004; Rice et al. 2004.
5. Aimers 2007:330–331; Andrews et al. 2003:151; Culbert 1973; Demarest 2004; Rice and Rice 2004; Webster 2002; Yaeger 2020.
6. Aimers 2007; Proskouriakoff 1955.
7. Haldon et al. 2020.
8. Inomata 2008.
9. Halperin et al. 2019, 2021.
10. Zaro and Houk 2012.
11. Zralka and Hermes 2012.
12. Cobos et al. 2014.
13. Fash 2004 et al 2004; Martin and Grube 2008.
14. Iannone et al. 2014:161–163.
15. Hoggarth et al. 2021.
16. Dunning and Beach 2010:383; Iannone et al. 2014; Pendergast 1985, 1986; Rushton et al. 2020.
17. Demarest 2004; Demarest et al. 2016; Webster 2002.
18. Martin 2020.
19. Aimers 2007; Bey and Gallareta Negrón 2019:138; Braswell et al. 2011; Cobos et al. 2014; Glover et al. 2018.
20. Cobos Palma 2004; Ebert et al. 2014:351; Ringle 2017.

21. Aimers 2007:349–350.

22. Dunning et al. 2012:3652; Halperin et al. 2019; Inomata et al. 2017:1297; Martin 2020; Zaro and Houk 2012:157; Zralka and Hermes 2012.

23. Arnauld et al. 2017:34; Masson 2012.

24. Morley 1946.

25. Zralka and Hermes 2012:182.

26. Demarest 2004:123; Demarest et al. 2016.

27. Aimers 2007:336; Laporte 2004:230; Masson 2000; Rice and Rice 2004.

28. Chase and Chase 2004, 2005.

29. Akers et al. 2016:284; Demarest 2004:120; Ebert et al. 2014:350; Iannone et al. 2014, 2016; Pendergast 1986.

30. Andrews et al. 2018.

31. Carmean et al. 2004; Demarest 2004; Freidel 1981; Smyth et al. 1998; Suhler et al. 2004.

32. Ringle et al. 2020.

33. Benavides 2000; Bey and Gallareta Negrón 2019.

34. Simms et al. 2012.

35. Hoggarth et al. 2016:38, 2017:97.

36. Alcover Firpi and Urquizú 2018; Arroyo et al. 2017; Dunning et al. 2012; Escobedo and Houston 1998; Liendo Stuardo 2002; Lohse and Valdez 2004; Rice 1988, and many others.

37. Clagget 1997; Ebert et al. 2014:349–350; Popson and Clagett 1998; Rice 1986; Rice and Rice 2004; Robin 2015.

38. Garrison et al. 2019.

39. Demarest 2004:123.

40. Demarest 2004:120; Dunning and Beach 2010:383; Ebert et al. 2014:347–348.

41. Cowgill 1988.

42. Demarest 2004:123.

43. Andrews et al. 2003:151; Dunning et al. 2012:3656; Rice and Rice 2004, 2018; Robin 2001.

44. Canuto et al. 2018; Culbert and Rice 1990; Rice and Culbert 1990.

45. Canuto et al. 2018.

46. Aimers 2007; Aimers and Iannone 2014; Akers et al. 2016:284; Ashmore et al. 2004:314; Chase and Chase 2006:169; Dussol et al. 2019, 2020; Ebert et al. 2014:351; Garrison and Dunning 2009:543–544; Guderjan and Hanratty 2016:234; Iannone 2014; Iannone et al. 2016; Lamoureux-St-Hilaire et al. 2015:565–566; Rice 1986, 1988; Rice and Rice 2004, 2018; Rice et al. 2004; Stanton and Magnoni 2008; Webster et al. 2004.

47. Nelson et al. 2014.

48. Rice 2012; Rice and Rice 2004, 2018.

49. Bey et al. 1997:250; Paap 2016, 2017; Rice 1986; Schwarz 2009; Shaw and Johnstone 2006; Tourtellot 1988.

50. Aimers 2007:331–332; Andrews et al. 2003:151; Chase and Chase 2006:168; Culbert 1973, 1988; Demarest et al. 2004; Hoggarth et al. 2017, 2021; Kennett et al. 2012; Webster 2002.

51. Wylie 2016.
52. Honan 1995.
53. Ehrenreich 2020.
54. Demarest 2004; Webster 2002.
55. Dunning et al. 2012:3652; Gill 2000; Hodell et al. 1995.
56. Fedick and Santiago 2022.
57. Aimers 2007:348; Iannone 2014; Lucero et al. 2014:34.
58. Keenan 2020.
59. Beach et al. 2015a; Kennett et al. 2012; Medina-Elizalde et al. 2010; Webster et al. 2007.
60. Beach et al. 2015a; Curtis et al. 1996; Escobar et al. 2010; Hodell et al. 1995, 2005.
61. Beach et al. 2015a; Douglas et al. 2015; Keenan 2020.
62. Medina-Elizalde et al. 2012:956–957.
63. Akers et al. 2016:284.
64. Kennett et al. 2012:791.
65. Dunning et al. 2014:66; Lucero et al. 2011:485; Medina-Elizalde et al. 2010.
66. Gunn et al. 2014:105; Smyth et al. 2017:503.
67. Dunning et al. 2014:67.
68. Dahlin 2002:337.
69. Aimers 2007:338; Carmean et al. 2004; Dunning and Beach 2010:38.
70. Hoggarth et al. 2016, 2017; Simms et al. 2012:285.
71. Douglas et al. 2015:5610–5612.
72. Gill et al. 2007:299.
73. Aimers 2007:337; Demarest 2004; Rice 1986; Rice and Rice 2004, 2018; Rice et al. 2004; Schwarz 2009.
74. Carmean et al. 2004; Lucero et al. 2014:34.
75. Halperin et al. 2019:4.
76. Fedick and Santiago 2022.
77. Akers et al. 2016:284.
78. Smyth et al. 2017:504.
79. Lentz et al. 2014a:18517; Medina-Elizalde et al. 2012:958.
80. Lucero 2002:822.
81. Luzzadder-Beach et al. 2016:437; Medina-Elizalde et al. 2016:101.
82. Akers et al. 2016:284–285; Chase and Chase 2007; Iannone et al. 2014.
83. Hoggarth et al. 2017; Masson et al. 2006; Milbrath and Peraza Lope 2009.
84. Dunning et al. 2012:3655; Luzzadder-Beach and Beach 2009; Luzzadder-Beach et al. 2012; Turner 2018:61; Turner and Harrison 1983.
85. Dunning et al. 2013; Gunn et al. 2014:115.
86. Demarest 2004; Demarest et al. 2016; Halperin et al. 2019:4; Scherer and Golden 2014.
87. Demarest 2004; French and Duffy 2014.
88. Cobos et al. 2014:65; Dunning et al. 2013; Gunn et al. 2014:115; Kennett et al. 2012:791.

89. Aimers and Iannone 2012; Akers et al. 2016; Demarest et al. 2004; Douglas et al. 2015; Dunning et al. 2012:3652; Haddon et al. 2020; Hoggarth et al. 2017:96; Iannone 2014; Iannone et al. 2016; Kennett et al. 2012; McAnany and Gallareta 2010; Turner 2010; Webster 2002.
90. Thompson 1966.
91. Chase and Chase 2007, 2014, 2017; Chase et al. 2020:348.
92. Golden 2003; Houston and Inomata 2009:63; Houston et al. 2003; Iannone et al. 2016; Martin 2020.
93. Houston and Inomata 2009:63; Houston et al. 2003; Iannone et al. 2016.
94. Thompson 1966.
95. Arnauld et al. 2017:34.
96. Barrett and Scherer 2005:113–114; Buttles and Valdez 2016:197; Demarest et al. 2016:181–186.
97. Ek 2016; Martin 2020; Rice 1986; Thompson 1970.
98. Halperin et al. 2021.
99. Ringle et al. 1998.
100. McAnany 2012:130.
101. Martin 2020 Chapter 13.
102. Demarest et al. 2016; Foias 2004: Foias and Bishop 1997; Webster and Houston 2003.
103. Rushton et al. 2020.
104. Golitko et al. 2012:518–520; Turner 2018:62.
105. Barrett and Scherer 2005; Demarest 2004; Demarest et al. 2016; Inomata 2008.
106. Demarest 2004; Webster 2000, 2002.
107. Child and Golden 2008; Demarest 2003, 2004, 2009: Ebert et al. 2014:349; Demarest et al. 2016:176; Houston et al. 2003:228; Tourtellot and Gonzalez 2004.
108. Kim et al. 2021.
109. Golden and Scherer 2006; Scherer et al. 2022.
110. Wahl et al. 2019.
111. Demarest et al. 2016.
112. Golden 2003; Golden and Scherer 2006.
113. Martin 2020; Martin and Grube 2008.
114. Kim et al. 2021.
115. Stuart 1993.
116. Diamond 2005.
117. Rice et al. 2004.
118. Culbert 1988:99–100; Dunning and Beach 2000:84; Dunning et al. 2012:3655; Santley et al. 1986:149; Shaw 2003; Turner and Sabloff 2012; Wahl et al. 2006, 2007; Webster 2002; Wright 1997.
119. Lentz et al. 2016:293.
120. Lentz and Hockaday 2009.
121. Lentz et al. 2014a, 2015:165.
122. Dunning et al. 2012:3654; Perez-Salicrup 2004; Ruyuan et al. 2012; Turner and Sabloff 2012:13910.

123. Dunning et al. 2012:3653–3654.
124. Douglas et al. 2018:4.
125. Emery and Thornton 2008; Turner and Sabloff 2012:13910; Villasenor and Aimers 2008.
126. Cook et al. 2012; Dunning et al. 2012:3653; Oglesby et al. 2010.
127. Culbert 1988; Iannone et al. 2014.
128. Abrams and Rue 1988; Rue 1987.
129. McNeil et al. 2010:1018; Rue 1987.
130. Fedick 2010:954; McNeil 2012; McNeil et al. 2010.
131. Abrams et al. 1996; Webster 2002.
132. Canuto et al. 2018.
133. Isendahl and Heckbert 2017; Tainter et al. 2018; Willey and Shimkin 1973.
134. McNeil 2012:22.
135. Dunning and Beach 2010:386; Dunning et al. 2006; Rosenmeier et al. 2002; Yaeger and Hodell 2009.
136. Dunning et al. 2012; Holling and Gunderson 2002; Lentz et al. 2018:7–8.
137. Robin 2015.
138. Dussol et al. 2021; Ford and Nigh 2009, 2015; Gunn et al. 2002, 2014:116, 2017:11.
139. Canuto et al. 2018; Drennan 1984; Hutson et al. 2021.
140. Dine et al. 2019:4.
141. Lentz and Hockaday 2009.
142. Lentz et al. 2016:293.
143. Dussol et al. 2017:38.
144. Turner and Sabloff 2012; Villaseñor and Aimers 2008.
145. Lentz et al. 2016; Rushton et al. 2020.
146. Dussol et al. 2020:14; Nondédéo et al. 2013.
147. Isendahl et al. 2014:50.
148. Seligson et al. 2017a, 2017b, 2017c.
149. Bey et al. 1997; Paap 2016, 2017; Premm 2006.
150. Beach et al. 2009; Chase and Chase 2014; Chase et al. 2011; Fisher 2020; Ford and Nigh 2015; Kunen 2004; Lentz and Hockaday 2009; Luzzadder-Beach and Beach 2009; Luzzadder- Beach et al. 2012; Rice 1986; Rice and Rice 2004, 2018; Robin et al. 2010.
151. McAnany and Gallareta Negrón 2010.
152. Aimers 2007:335.
153. Aoyama 2001; Braswell et al. 2011.
154. Rice 2012; Rice and Rice 2004.
155. Rice 2012.
156. Flores and Kantún-Balam 1997.
157. McAnany and Gallareta Negrón 2010.
158. Rice 2012; Rice and Rice 2018.
159. Chase and Chase 2006:171.
160. Bequelin et al. 2011; Headrick 2020; Kepecs and Masson 2003; Masson et al. 2006; Rice 2012, 2019; Rice and Rice 2018.

161. Chase and Chase 2006:171; Inomata et al. 2017:1297.
162. Andrews et al. 2003:152; Hoggarth et al. 2016:38; Ringle 2017.
163. Masson et al. 2006; Milbrath and Peraza Lope 2009; Rice and Rice 2004.
164. Glover et al. 2018:16; Sabloff 2007; Sabloff and Rathje 1975.
165. Beach et al. 2015b; Dunning et al. 2006; Garrison and Dunning 2009:543–544; Krause et al. 2019.
166. Barthel and Isendahl 2013:231; Beach et al. 2009; Chase and Chase 2014; Chase et al. 2011; Dunning et al. 2012; Fisher 2020; Ford and Nigh 2015; Isendahl et al. 2014:51; Kunen 2004; Lentz and Hockaday 2009; Luzzadder-Beach and Beach 2009; Luzzadder-Beach et al. 2012.
167. Dahlin 2002:337; Holling 2001; Holling and Gunderson 2002.
168. Buttles and Valdez 2016:201; Hoggarth 2016; McKillop 2005; Pendergast 1986; Rice and Rice 2009; Sabloff 2007; Turner and Sabloff 2012.
169. Masson et al. 2016; McAnany 2012; Milbrath and Peraza Lope 2009; Pendergast 1986; Rice 1986; Rice 2012; Rice and Rice 2004.
170. Douglas et al. 2015:5611.
171. Dunning et al. 2012:3652–3656; Lentz et al. 2018:7–8.
172. Demarest 2004; Nelson et al. 2014; Rice and Rice 2004.
173. Lucero et al. 2014:36.
174. Akpinar-Ferrand et al. 2012; Rice 1986; Rice and Rice 2004, 2018; Tainter et al. 2018:339; Weiss-Krejci and Sabbas 2002.
175. Lucero et al. 2011:486–488.

Chapter 8

1. Fedick 1996.
2. Garrison et al. 2019.
3. Beach et al. 2015b.
4. Chase 2016; Chase and Cesaretti 2018.
5. Santini 2015.
6. Robin et al. 2010.
7. McNeil 2012; McNeil et al. 2010.
8. Ortíz Ruiz 2019; Seligson et al. 2017a, 2019.
9. Fisher 2020:4.
10. Fisher 2020:18; Holling 1973.
11. Barthel and Isendahl 2013:227, 231; Dunning et al. 2019:386; Fedick 2003, 2010; Ford 2008; Ford and Nigh 2009; Lucero et al. 2014.
12. Barthel and Isendahl 2013:225.
13. Chase et al. 2019:3.
14. Dahlin 2002:337; Scarborough and Valdez 2014.
15. Canuto et al. 2018; Garrison et al. 2019; Lentz et al. 2014a, 2015, 2018.
16. Lucero et al. 2014:36.

17. Akpinar Ferrand et al. 2012; Brewer 2018; Chase 2016; Chase and Cesaretti 2018; Halperin et al. 2019; Lucero 2018; Lucero et al. 2011, 2014; Scarborough 2000, 2007.
18. Inomata et al. 2017:1297.
19. Chase and Chase 2017:216–217.
20. Guderjan and Hanratty 2016:241.
21. Iannone et al. 2016:4.
22. Lentz et al. 2014a.
23. Demarest 2004:120–121; Halperin et al. 2021.
24. Hoggarth et al. 2017:98.
25. Brewbaker 1979; Willey and Shimkin 1973.
26. Zequeira-Larios et al. 2021.
27. Masson et al. 2012:18237.
28. Tainter 2014:208; Turner and Sabloff 2012:13911.
29. Isendahl and Heckbert 2017; Tainter and Taylor 2014; Tainter et al. 2018; Turner 2018:62.
30. Lucero et al. 2014:37.
31. Kuil et al. 2019:12.
32. Lucero et al. 2011:488.
33. Card and Anderson 2016.
34. McAnany and Gallareta Negrón 2010; Gunn et al. 2016:14.

References

Abrams, Elliot M. "Economic Specialization and Construction Personnel in Classic Period Copan, Honduras." *American Antiquity* 52, no. 3 (July 1987): 485–99. https://doi.org/10.2307/281595.

Abrams, Elliot M. "The Evolution of Plaster Production and the Growth of the Copan Maya State." In *Arqueologia Mesoamericana: Homenaje a William T. Sanders*, edited by Alba Guadalupe Mastache, Jeffrey Parsons, Robert S. Santley, and Mari C. Serra Puche, 193-208, 2:17. Mexico City: Instituto Nacional de Antropologia e Historia, 1996.

Abrams, Elliot M. *How the Maya Built Their World: Energetics and Ancient Architecture*. Austin: University of Texas Press, 1994.

Abrams, Elliot M. "Systems of Labor Organization in Late Classic Copan, Honduras: The Energetics of Construction." PhD diss., Pennsylvania State University, 1984.

Abrams, Elliot M., and AnnCorinne Freter. "A Late Classic Lime-Plaster Kiln from the Maya Centre of Copan, Honduras." *Antiquity* 70, no. 268 (June 1996): 422–28. https://doi.org/10.1017/S0003598X00083381.

Abrams, Elliot M., AnnCorinne Freter, David J. Rue, and J. Wingard. "The Role of Deforestations in the Collapse of the Late Classic Copan Maya State." In *Tropical Deforestation: The Human Dimension*, edited by Leslie E. Sponsel, Thomas N. Headland, and Robert C. Bailey, 55–75. New York: Columbia University Press, 1996.

Abrams, Elliot M., John Parhamovich, Jared A. Butcher, and Bruce McCord. "Chemical Composition of Architectural Plaster at the Classic Maya Kingdom of Piedras Negras, Guatemala." *Journal of Archaeological Science* 39, no. 5 (May 2012): 1648–54. https://doi.org/10.1016/j.jas.2012.01.002.

Abrams, Elliot M., and David J. Rue. "The Causes and Consequences of Deforestation Among the Prehistoric Maya." *Human Ecology* 16, no. 4 (1988): 377–95. https://doi.org/10.1007/BF00891649.

Aimers, James J. "What Maya Collapse? Terminal Classic Variation in the Maya Lowlands." *Journal of Archaeological Research* 15 (2007): 329–77.

Aimers, James J., and Gyles Iannone. "The Dynamics of Ancient Maya Developmental History." In *The Great Maya Droughts in Cultural Context: Case Studies in Resilience and Vulnerability*, edited by Gyles Iannone, 21–50. Boulder: University Press of Colorado, 2014.

Akers, Pete D., George A. Brook, L. Bruce Railsback, Alex Cherkinksy, Fuyuan Liang, Claire E. Ebert, Julie A. Hoggarth, Jaime J. Awe, Hai Cheng, and R. Lawrence Edwards. "Integrating U-Th, 14C, and 210Pb Methods to Produce a Chronologically Reliable Isotope Record for the Belize River Valley Maya from a Low-Uranium Stalagmite." *The Holocene* 29, no. 7 (2019): 1234–48.

Akpinar Ferrand, Ezgi, Nicholas P Dunning, David L Lentz, and John G Jones. "Use of Aguadas as Water Management Sources in Two Southern Maya Lowland Sites." *Ancient Mesoamerica* 23, no. 1 (2012): 85–101.

Al-Bashaireh, Khaled. "Plaster and Mortar Radiocarbon Dating of Nabatean and Islamic Structures, South Jordan." *Archaeometry* 55, no. 2 (April 2013): 329–54. https://doi.org/10.1111/j.1475-4754.2012.00677.x.

Al-Bashaireh, Khaled Shenwan. "Chronology and Technological Production Styles of Nabatean and Roman Plasters and Mortars at Petra (Jordan)." PhD thesis, University of Arizona, 2008.

Alcorn, Janis B. *Huastec Mayan Ethnobotany*. Austin: University of Texas Press, 1984.

Alcover Firpi, Omar, and Monica Urquizú, eds. *Proyecto Paisaje Piedras Negras Yaxchilan: Informe de La Tercera Temporada de Investigación*. Guatemala City: Report submitted to the Institute of Anthropology and History, 2018.

Alexander, Rani T. "Maya Settlement Shifts and Agrarian Ecology in Yucatán, 1800–2000." *Journal of Anthropological Research* 62, no. 4 (December 2006): 449–70. https://doi.org/10.3998/jar.0521004.0062.401.

Altieri, M. A., and C. I. Nicholls. "Classical Biological Control in Latin America." In *Handbook of Biological Control*, edited by T. S. Bellows and T. W. Fisher, 975–91. San Diego: Academic Press, 1999.

Anderson, David S. "Mysterious Ancient Mysteries and the Problems with Archaeology Made for TV." Forbes.com, December 31, 2018. https://www.forbes.com/sites/davidanderson/2018/12/31/mysterious-ancient-mysteries-and-the-problems-with-archaeology-made-for-tv/?sh=65481313d4e8.

Anderson, David S., Daniel A. Bair, and Richard E. Terry. "Soil Geochemical Analyses at the Preclassic Site of Xtobo, Yucatan, Mexico." *Ancient Mesoamerica* 23, no. 2 (2012): 365–77. https://doi.org/10.1017/S0956536112000247.

Anderson, David S., Fernando Robles Castellanos, and Anthony P Andrews. "The Preclassic Settlement of Northwest Yucatan." In *Pathways to Complexity: A View from the Maya Lowlands*, edited by M. Kathryn Brown and George J. Bey III, 195–222. Gainesville: University Press of Florida, 2018.

Anderson, Eugene N. "Gardens in Tropical America and Tropical Asia." *Biotica, Nueva Epoca* 1 (1993): 81–102.

Anderson, Lysanna, and David Wahl. "Two Holocene Paleofire Records from Peten, Guatemala: Implications for Natural Fire Regime and Prehispanic Maya Land Use." *Global and Planetary Change* 138 (March 2016): 82–92. https://doi.org/10.1016/j.gloplacha.2015.09.012.

Andrews, Anthony P. *Maya Salt Production and Trade*. Tucson: University of Arizona Press, 1983.

Andrews, Anthony P. "The Role of Trading Ports in Maya Civilization." In *Vision and Revision in Maya Studies*, edited by Flora S. Clancy and Peter D. Harrison, 159–68. Albuquerque: University of New Mexico Press, 1990.

Andrews, Anthony P., E. Wyllys Andrews, and Fernando Robles Castellanos. "The Northern Maya Collapse and Its Aftermath." *Ancient Mesoamerica* 14 (2003): 151–56.

Andrews, Anthony P., and Fernando Robles Castellanos. "The Paleo-American and Archaic Periods in Yucatan." In *Pathways to Complexity: A View from the Maya Lowlands*, edited by M. Kathryn Brown and George J. Bey III, 16–34. Gainesville: University Press of Florida, 2018.

Andrews, Anthony P., Tomás Gallareta Negrón, Fernando Robles Castellanos, Rafael Cobos Palma, and Pura Cervera Rivero. "Isla Cerritos: An Itzá Trading Port on the North Coast of Yucatán, Mexico." *National Geographic Research* 4 (1988): 196–207.

Andrews, E. Wyllys, George J. Bey III, and Christopher M. Gunn. "The Earliest Ceramics of the Northern Maya Lowlands." In *Pathways to Complexity: A View from the Maya Lowlands*, edited by M. Kathryn Brown and George J. Bey, 49–86. Gainesville: University Press of Florida, 2018.

Andrews, E. Wyllys, and Norman Hammond. "Redefinition of the Swazey Phase at Cuello, Belize." *American Antiquity* 54 (1990): 570–80.

Anselmetti, Flavio S., David A. Hodell, Daniel Ariztegui, Mark Brenner, and Michael F. Rosenmeier. "Quantification of Soil Erosion Rates Related to Ancient Maya Deforestation." *Geology* 35, no. 10 (2007): 915. https://doi.org/10.1130/G23834A.1.

Aoyama, Kazuo. "Classic Maya State, Urbanism, and Exchange: Chipped Stone Evidence of the Copan Valley and Its Hinterland." *American Anthropologist* 103, no. 2 (2001): 346–60.

Ardren, Traci, and Stephanie Miller. "Household Garden Plant Agency in the Creation of Classic Maya Social Identities." *Journal of Anthropological Archaeology* 60 (December 2020). https://doi.org/10.1016/j.jaa.2020.101212.

Arnauld, M. Charlotte, Eva Lemonnier, Mélanie Forné, Julien Sion, and Erick Ponciano Alvarado. "Early to Late Classic Population Mobility in the Maya Site of La Joyanca and Hinterlands, Northwestern Petén, Guatemala." *Journal of Anthropological Archaeology* 45 (2017): 15–37. https://doi.org/10.1016/j.jaa.2016.10.002.

Arnauld, M. Charlotte, Dominique Michelet, and Philippe Nondédéo. "Living Together in Rio Bec Houses: Coresidence, Rank, and Alliance." *Ancient Mesoamerica* 24, no. 2 (2013): 469–93. https://doi.org/10.1017/S0956536114000029.

Arroyo, Barbara, Luis Méndez Salinas, and Gloria Ajú Álvarez, eds. *XXXI Simposio de Investigaciones Arqueológicas En Guatemala*. Guatemala City: Museo Nacional de Arqueología y Etnología, 2017.

Ashmore, Wendy, Jason Yaeger, and Cynthia Robin. "Commoner Sense: Late and Terminal Classic Social Strategies in the Xunantunich Area." In *The Terminal Classic in the Maya Lowlands: Collapse, Transition, and Transformation*, edited by Arthur A. Demarest, Prudence M. Rice, and Don S. Rice, 302–23. Boulder: University Press of Colorado, 2004.

Atran, Scott. "Classification of Useful Plants by the Northern Peten Maya (Itzaj)." In *Reconstructing Ancient Maya Diet*, edited by Christine D. White, 19–60. Salt Lake City: University of Utah Press, 1999.

Atran, Scott. "Itza Maya Tropical Agro-Forestry." *Current Anthropology* 34, no. 5 (1993): 633–89.

Atran, Scott, and Douglas Medin. *The Native Mind and the Cultural Construction of Nature*. Life and Mind: Philosophical Issues in Biology and Psychology. Cambridge, MA: MIT Press, 2008.

Awe, Jaime J., Claire E. Ebert, and Julie A. Hoggarth. "November 7–9 2014, Calgary, Alberta, Canada." In *Breaking Barriers: Proceedings of the 47th Annual Chacmool Archaeological Conference*, edited by Robyn Crook, Kim Edwards, and Colleen Hughes, 57–75. Calgary: Chacmool Archaeological Association of the University of Calgary, 2015.

Bacus, Elisabeth A., and Lisa J. Lucero. "Introduction: Issues in the Archaeology of Tropical Polities." *Archeological Papers of the American Anthropological Association* 9, no. 1 (1999): 1–11. https://doi.org/10.1525/ap3a.1999.9.1.1.

Balick, Michael, R. Arvigo, G. Shropshire, J. Walker, Campbell, David G, and L. Romero. "The Belize Ethnobotany Project: Safeguarding Medicinal Plants and Traditional

Knowledge in Belize." In *Ethnomedicine and Drug Discovery*, edited by M. Iwu and J. Wootten, 267–81. Advances in Phytomedicine 1. New York: Elsevier, 2002.

Bancroft, Hubert Howe. *The Works of Hubert Howe Bancroft*. San Francisco: ALBancroft, 1903.

Barba Pingarrón, Luis. "El Uso de Cal En El Mundo Prehispanico Mesoamericano." In *La Cal: Historia, Propiedades y Usos*, edited by Luis Barba Pingarrón and Isabel Villaseñor, 19–46. Mexico City: Universidad Nacional Autonoma de Mexico, Instituto de Investigaciones Antropologicas, 2013.

Barba Pingarrón, Luis, and José Luis Córdova Frunz. *Materiales y Energía En La Arquitectura de Teotihuacan*. Mexico City: Universidad Nacional Autonoma de Mexico, Instituto de Investigaciones Antropologicas, 2010.

Baron, Joanne P. "Making Money in Mesoamerica: Currency Production and Procurement in the Classic Maya Financial System: Making Money in Mesoamerica." *Economic Anthropology* 5, no. 2 (June 2018): 210–23. https://doi.org/10.1002/sea2.12118.

Barrera Rubio, Alfredo. "Sobre La Unidad de Habitación Tradicional Campesina y El Manejo de Recursos Bióticos En El Area Maya Yucatánense." *Biótica* 5, no. 3 (1980): 115–29.

Barrera Rubio, Alfredo. "Vestigios de Hornos Prehispánicos En El Nororiente de Yucatán." Campeche, 2013.

Barrera Rubio, Alfredo, and Jose Huchim Herrera. "Exploraciones Recientes En Uxmal (1986–1987)." In *Memorias Del Segundo Coloquio Internacional de Mayistas*, 1:265–86. Mexico City: Universidad Nacional Autonoma de Mexico, 1989.

Barrera Vazquez, Alfredo, ed. *Diccionario Maya Cordemex (SIBE)*. Merida, Mexico: Ediciones Cordemex, 1980. http://bibliotecasibe.ecosur.mx/sibe/book/000016541.

Barrett, Jason W., and Andrew K. Scherer. "Stones, Bones, and Crowded Plazas: Evidence for Terminal Classic Maya Warfare at Colha, Belize." *Ancient Mesoamerica* 16, no. 1 (2005): 101–18. https://doi.org/10.1017/S0956536105050091.

Barthel, Stephan, and Christian Isendahl. "Urban Gardens, Agriculture, and Water Management: Sources of Resilience for Long-Term Food Security in Cities." *Ecological Economics* 86 (February 2013): 224–34. https://doi.org/10.1016/j.ecolecon.2012.06.018.

Bassie-Sweet, Karen. *The Edge of the World: Caves and Late Classic Maya World View*. Norman: University of Oklahoma Press, 1996.

Beach, Tim, Sheryl Luzzadder-Beach, Duncan Cook, Nicholas Dunning, Douglas J. Kennett, Samantha Krause, Richard Terry, Debora Trein, and Fred Valdez. "Ancient Maya Impacts on the Earth's Surface: An Early Anthropocene Analog?" *Quaternary Science Reviews* 124 (2015a): 1–30. https://doi.org/10.1016/j.quascirev.2015.05.028.

Beach, Tim, Sheryl Luzzadder-Beach, Thomas Guderjan, and Samantha Krause. "The Floating Gardens of Chan Cahal: Soils, Water, and Human Interactions." *CATENA* 132 (2015b): 151–64. https://doi.org/10.1016/j.catena.2014.12.017.

Beach, Tim, Sheryl Luzzadder-Beach, Samantha Krause, Stanley Walling, Nicholas Dunning, Jonathan Flood, Thomas Guderjan, and Fred Valdez. "'Mayacene' Floodplain and Wetland Formation in the Rio Bravo Watershed of Northwestern Belize." *The Holocene*, no. Special Issue: The Anthropocene in the Long Duree (2015c): 1612–26.

Beach, Timothy. "Soil Constraints on Northwest Yucatán, Mexico: Pedoarchaeology and Maya Subsistence at Chunchucmil." *Geoarchaeology: An International Journal* 13, no. 8 (1998): 759–91.

Beach, Timothy, and Nicholas Dunning. "An Ancient Maya Reservoir and Dam at Tamarindito, El Peten, Guatemala." *Latin American Antiquity* 8, no. 1 (March 1997): 20–29. https://doi.org/10.2307/971590.

Beach, Timothy, and Nicholas P. Dunning. "Ancient Maya Terracing and Modern Conservation in the Peten Rainforest of Guatemala." *Soil and Water Conservation* 50 (1995): 138–45.

Beach, Timothy, Sheryl Luzzader-Beach, Duncan Cook, Samantha Krause, Colin Doyle, Sara Eshleman, Greta Wells, et al. "Stability and Instability on Maya Lowlands Tropical Hillslope Soils." *Geomorphology* 305 (2018): 185–208.

Beach, Timothy P., Sheryl Luzzadder-Beach, Nicholas P. Dunning, and Duncan Cook. "Human and Natural Impacts on Fluvial and Karst Systems in the Maya Lowlands." *Geomorphology* 101 (2008): 301–31.

Beach, Timothy, Sheryl Luzzadder-Beach, Nicholas Dunning, Jon Hageman, and Jon Lohse. "Upland Agriculture in the Maya Lowlands: Ancient Maya Soil Conservation in Northwestern Belize." *Geographical Review* 92, no. 3 (2002): 372–97.

Beach, Timothy, Sheryl Luzzadder-Beach, Nicholas P. Dunning, John G. Jones, Thomas H. Guderjan, Steven R. Bozarth, S. Millspaugh, and T. Bhattacharya. "A Review of Human and Natural Changes in Maya Lowlands Wetlands over the Holocene." *Quaternary Science Reviews* 28 (2009): 1710–24.

Beach, Timothy, Sheryl Luzzadder-Beach, Jonathan Flood, Stephen D. Houston, Thomas G. Garrison, Edwin Roman, Steven R. Bozarth, and James Doyle. "A Neighborly View: Water and Environmental History of the El Zotz Region." In *Tikal: Paleoecology of an Ancient Maya City*, edited by David L. Lentz, Nicholas P. Dunning, and Vernon L. Scarborough, 258–79. Cambridge: Cambridge University Press, 2015d.

Beach, Timothy, Sheryl Luzzadder-Beach, Samantha Krause, Tom Guderjan, Fred Valdez, Juan Carlos Fernandez-Diaz, Sara Eshleman, and Colin Doyle. "Ancient Maya Wetland Fields Revealed Under Tropical Forest Canopy from Laser Scanning and Multiproxy Evidence." *Proceedings of the National Academy of Sciences* 116, no. 43 (October 22, 2019): 21469–77. https://doi.org/10.1073/pnas.1910553116.

Beach, Timothy, Sheryl Luzzadder-Beach, Richard Terry, Nicholas Dunning, Stephen Houston, and Thomas Garrison. "Carbon Isotopic Ratios of Wetland and Terrace Soil Sequences in the Maya Lowlands of Belize and Guatemala." *Catena (Giessen)* 85, no. 2 (2011): 109–18. https://doi.org/10.1016/j.catena.2010.08.014.

Becquelin, Pierre, Dominique Michelet, and Antonio Benavides Castillo. "¿Una organización dualista en Xcalumkín antes del inicio del estilo Puuc Temprano?" *Mexicon* 33, no. 2 (2011): 38–46.

Beebe, Stephen, Paul Skroch, Joe Tohme, Myriam Duque, Fabio Pedraza, and James Nienhuis. "Structure of Genetic Diversity Among Common Bean Landraces of Middle American Origin Based on Correspondence Analysis of RAPD." *Crop Science* 40, no. 1 (2000): 264–73. https://doi.org/10.2135/cropsci2000.401264x.

Belfer-Cohen, Anna. "The Natufian in the Levant." *Annual Review of Anthropology* 20 (1991): 167–86.

Benavides Castillo, Antonio. "Edzna: A Lived Place Through Time." In *Ruins of the Past: The Use and Perception of Abandoned Structures in the Maya Lowlands*, edited by Travis W. Stanton, Aline Magnoni, Wendy Ashmore, and Denise Brown, 223–55. Boulder: University Press of Colorado, 2008.

Benavides Castillo, Antonio. "Ichmac, un sitio Puuc de Campeche." *Mexicon* 22, no. 6 (2000): 134–39.

Bennett, Matthew R., David Bustos, Jeffrey S. Pigati, Kathleen B. Springer, Thomas M. Urban, Vance T. Holliday, Sally C. Reynolds, Marcin Budka, Jeffrey S. Honke, and others. "Evidence of humans in North America during the Last Glacial Maximum." *Science* 373, no. 6562 (2021): 1528–31.

Bey, George J., III, and Tomás Gallareta Negrón. "Reexamining the Role of Conflict in the Development of Puuc Maya Society." In *Seeking Conflict in Mesoamerica: Operational, Cognitive, and Experiential Approaches*, edited by Meaghan Peuramaki-Brown, 122–41. Boulder: University Press of Colorado, 2019.

Bey, George J., III, Craig A. Hanson, and William M. Ringle. "Classic to Postclassic at Ek Balam, Yucatan: Architectural and Ceramic Evidence for Defining the Transition." *Latin American Antiquity* 8, no. 3 (1997): 237–54. https://doi.org/10.2307/971654.

Biskowski, Martin. "Maize Preparation and the Aztec Subsistence Economy." *Ancient Mesoamerica* 11 (2000): 293–306.

Blanco, L., and T. Thiagarajan. "Ethno-Botanical Study of Medicinal Plants Used by the Yucatec Maya in the Northern District of Belize." *International Journal of Herbal Medicine* 5 (2017): 33–42.

Bletter, Nathaniel, Cameron, and Douglas C. Daly. "Cacao and Its Relatives in South America: An Overview of Taxonomy, Ecology, Biogeography, Chemistry, and Ethnobotany." In *Chocolate in Mesoamerica*, edited by Cameron L. McNeil, 31–68. Gainesville: University Press of Florida, 2009. https://doi.org/10.5744/florida/9780813029535.001.0001.

Boserup, Ester. *The Conditions of Agricultural Growth*. New Brunswick, NJ: Aldine Transaction, 1965.

Braswell, Geoffrey E., Iken Paap, and Michael D. Glascock. "The Obsidian and Ceramics of the Puuc Region: Chronology, Lithic Procurement, and Production at Xkipche, Yucatan, Mexico." *Ancient Mesoamerica* 22 (2011): 135–54.

Breedlove, D. E., and R. M. Laughlin. *The Flowering of Man: A Tzotzil Botany of Zinacantan.* (abridged ed.). Washington, DC: Smithsonian Institution Press, 2000.

Brenner, Mark, Michael Rosenmeier, David Hodell, and Jason Curtis. "Paleolimnology of the Maya Lowlands: Long-Term Perspectives on Interactions Among Climate, Environment, and Humans." *Ancient Mesoamerica* 13 (2002): 141–57. https://doi.org/10.1017/S0956536102131063.

Brewbaker, James L. "Diseases of Maize in the Wet Lowland Tropics and the Collapse of the Classic Maya Civilization." *Economic Botany* 33, no. 2 (1979): 101–18.

Brewer, Jeffrey L. "Householders as Water Managers: A Comparison of Domestic-Scale Water Management Practices from Two Central Maya Lowland Sites." *Ancient Mesoamerica* 29, no. 1 (2018): 197–217. https://doi.org/10.1017/S0956536117000244.

Bronson, Bennet. "Roots and Subsistence of the Ancient Maya." *Southwestern Journal of Anthropology* 22 (1966): 251–79.

Broughton, William, Georgina Hernández, Matthew Blair, Stephen Beebe, Paul Gepts, and Jos Vanderleyden. "Beans (Phaseolus Spp.)—Model Food Legumes." *Plant and Soil* 252, no. 1 (2003): 55–128. https://doi.org/10.1023/A:1024146710611.

Brown, Cecil H. "Prehistoric Chronology of the Common Bean in the New World: The Linguistic Evidence." *American Anthropologist* 108, no. 3 (2006): 507–16.

Brown, Clifford T. "Water Sources at Mayapán, Yucatán, Mexico." In *Water Management: Ideology, Ritual, and Power*, edited by Lisa J. Lucero and Barbara W. Fash, 171–85. Tucson: University of Arizona Press, 2006.

Brown, Linda A. "Dangerous Places and Wild Spaces: Creating Meaning with Materials and Space at Contemporary Maya Shrines on El Duende Mountain." *Journal of Archaeological Method and Theory* 11, no. 1 (2004): 31–58. https://doi.org/10.1023/B:JARM.0000014347.47185.f9.

Brubaker, Curt L., and Jonathan F. Wendel. "Reevaluating the Origin of Domesticated Cotton (Gossypium Hirsutum; Malvaceae) Using Nuclear Restriction Fragment Length Polymorphisms (RFLPs)." *American Journal of Botany* 81, no. 10 (1994): 1309–26.

Brumfiel, Elizabeth. "Weaving and Cooking: Women's Production in Aztec Mexico." In *Engendering Archaeology: Women and Prehistory*, edited by Joan A. Gero and Margaret W. Conkey, 224–51. Oxford: Basil Blackwell, 1991.

Bryant, Douglas D., and Thomas A. Lee, Jr. "North Group Elite Domestic Mounds, Civic-Ceremonial Mounds, and Plaza Excavations." In *Postclassic and Colonial Sites of the Upper Grijalva River Basin in Chiapas Mexico: Los Encuentros, Coapa, and Coneta*, edited by Douglas Donne Bryant and Thomas A Lee, Jr., 132–40. Salt Lake City: Papers of the New World Archaeological Foundation, no. 86, 2020.

Buckler, Edward S., Deborah M. Pearsall, and Timothy P. Holtsford. "Climate, Plant Ecology, and Central Mexican Archaic Subsistence." *Current Anthropology* 39, no. 1 (1998): 152–64.

Burnett, Richard L., Richard E. Terry, Marco Alvarez, Christopher Balzotti, Timothy Murtha, David Webster, and Jay Silverstein. "The Ancient Agricultural Landscape of the Satellite Settlement of Ramonal near Tikal, Guatemala." *Quaternary International* 265 (2012): 101–15. https://doi.org/10.1016/j.quaint.2011.03.002.

Buttles, Palma, and Fred Valdez. "Social-Political Manifestations of the Terminal Classic: Colha, Northern Belize, as a Case Study." In *Ritual, Violence, and the Fall of the Classic Maya Kings*, edited by Gyles Iannone, Brett A. Houk, and Sonja A. Schwake, 187–202. Gainesville: University Press of Florida, 2016.

Cagnato, Clarissa. "Underground Pits (Chultunes) in the Southern Maya Lowlands: Excavation Results from Classic Period Maya Sites in Northwestern Peten." *Ancient Mesoamerica* 28, no. 1 (2017): 75–94. https://doi.org/10.1017/S0956536116000377.

Calvet-Mir, Laura, Carles Riu-Bosoms, Marc Gonzalez-Puente, Isabel Ruiz-Mallen, Victoria Reyes-Garcia, and José Luis Molina. "The Transmission of Home Garden Knowledge: Safeguarding Biocultural Diversity and Enhancing Social–Ecological Resilience." *Society & Natural Resources* 29 (2016): 556–71.

Campbell, David G., Anabel Ford, Karen S. Lowell, Jay Walker, Jeffrey K. Lake, Constanza Ocampo, Andrew Townesmith, and Michael Balick. "The Feral Forests of the Eastern Peten." In *Time and Complexity in Historical Ecology: Studies in the Neotropical Lowlands*, edited by William L. Balée and Clark L. Erickson, 21–55. Historical Ecology. New York: Columbia University Press, 2006.

Campbell, David G., John Guittar, and Karen S. Lowell. "Are Colonial Pastures the Ancestors of the Contemporary Maya Forest?" *Journal of Ethnobiology* 28, no. 2 (2008): 278–89. https://doi.org/10.2993/0278-0771-28.2.278.

Canuto, Marcello A., Francisco Estrada-Belli, Thomas G. Garrison, Stephen D. Houston, Mary Jane Acuña, Milan Kováč, Damien Marken, et al. "Ancient Lowland Maya Complexity as Revealed by Airborne Laser Scanning of Northern Guatemala." *Science* 361, no. 6409 (2018). https://doi.org/10.1126/science.aau0137.

Card, Jeb J., and David S. Anderson, eds. *Lost City, Found Pyramid: Understanding Alternative Archaeologies and Pseudoscientific Practices*. Tuscaloosa: University of

Alabama Press, 2016. http://www.uapress.ua.edu/product/Lost-City-Found-Pyra mid,6360.aspx.

Carmean, Kelli, Nicholas P. Dunning, and Jeffrey K. Kowalski. "High Times in the Hill Country: A Perspective from the Terminal Classic Puuc Region." In *The Terminal Classic in the Maya Lowlands: Collapse, Transition, and Transformation*, edited by Arthur A. Demarest, Prudence M. Rice, and Don S. Rice, 424–49. Boulder: University Press of Colorado, 2004.

Carrasco Vargas, Ramon, Veronica A. Vazquez Lopez, and Simon Martin. "Daily Life of the Ancient Maya Recorded on Murals at Calakmul, Mexico." *Proceedings of the National Academy of Sciences* 106, no. 46 (2009): 19245–49. https://doi.org/10.1073/pnas.0904374106.

Castro, Andy, Maite Lascurain-Rangel, Jorge Antonio Gómez-Díaz, and Victoria Sosa. "Mayan Homegardens in Decline: The Case of the Pitahaya (Hylocereus Undatus), a Vine Cactus with Edible Fruit." *Tropical Conservation Science* 11 (2018): 1–10. https://doi.org/10.1177/1940082918808730.

Chacón S, Mari I., Barbara Pickersgill, and Daniel G. Debouck. "Domestication Patterns in Common Bean (Phaseolus Vulgaris L.) and the Origin of the Mesoamerican and Andean Cultivated Races." *Theoretical and Applied Genetics* 110, no. 3 (2005): 432–44. https://doi.org/10.1007/s00122-004-1842-2.

Chase, Adrian S. Z. "Beyond Elite Control: Residential Reservoirs at Caracol, Belize." *WIRES Water* 3, no. 6 (2016): 885–97.

Chase, Adrian S. Z., and Rudolf Cesaretti. "Diversity in Ancient Maya Water Management Strategies and Landscapes at Caracol, Belize, and Tikal, Guatemala." *Wiley Interdisciplinary Reviews: Water* 6, no. 2 (March 2019): e1332. https://doi.org/10.1002/wat2.1332.

Chase, Adrian S. Z., Diane Chase, and Arlen Chase. "Ethics, New Colonialism, and Lidar Data: A Decade of Lidar in Maya Archaeology." *Journal of Computer Applications in Archaeology* 3, no. 1 (2020): 51–62. https://doi.org/10.5334/jcaa.43.

Chase, Adrian S. Z., and John Weishampel. "Using Lidar and GIS to Investigate Water and Soil Management in the Agricultural Terracing at Caracol, Belize." *Advances in Archaeological Practice* 4, no. 3 (2016): 357–70. https://doi.org/10.7183/2326-3768.4.3.357.

Chase, Arlen F., and Diane Z. Chase. "The Ancient Maya City: Anthropogenic Landscapes, Settlement Archaeology, and Caracol, Belize." *Research Reports in Belizean Archaeology* 13 (2016): 3–14.

Chase, Arlen F., and Diane Z. Chase. "Contextualizing the Collapse: Hegemony and Terminal Classic Ceramics from Caracol Belize." In *Geographies of Power: Understanding the Nature of Terminal Classic Pottery in the Maya Lowlands*, edited by S. L. Lopez Varela and Antonia E. Foias, 73–92. BAR International Series 1447. Oxford: British Archaeological Reports, 2005.

Chase, Arlen F., and Diane Z. Chase. "Scale and Intensity in Classic Maya Agriculture: Terracing and Agriculture in the 'Garden City' of Caracol, Belize." *Culture and Agriculture* 20 (1998): 60–77.

Chase, Arlen F., and Diane Z. Chase. "Terminal Classic Status-Linked Ceramics and the Maya 'Collapse': De Facto Refuse at Caracol, Belize." In *The Terminal Classic in the Maya Lowlands: Collapse, Transition, and Transformation*, edited by Arthur A. Demarest, Prudence M. Rice, and Don S. Rice, 342–66. Boulder: University Press of Colorado, 2004.

Chase, Arlen F., and Diane Z. Chase. "This Is the End: Archaeological Transitions and the Terminal Classic Period at Caracol, Belize." *Research Reports in Belizean Archaeology* 4 (2007): 13–27.

Chase, Arlen F., Diane Z. Chase, and Adrian S. Z. Chase. "Markets and the Socio-Economic Integration of Caracol, Belize:" Belize: Belize Institute of Archaeology and Alphawood Foundation, 2019.

Chase, Arlen F., Diane Z. Chase, Christopher T. Fisher, Stephen J. Leisz, and John F. Weishampel. "Geospatial Revolution and Remote Sensing LiDAR in Mesoamerican Archaeology." *Proceedings of the National Academy of Sciences* 109, no. 32 (2012): 12916–21. https://doi.org/10.1073/pnas.1205198109.

Chase, Arlen F., Diane Z. Chase, John F. Weishampel, Jason B. Drake, Ramesh L. Shrestha, K. Clint Slatton, Jaime J. Awe, and William E. Carter. "Airborne LiDAR, Archaeology, and the Ancient Maya Landscape at Caracol, Belize." *Journal of Archaeological Science* 38, no. 2 (2011): 387–98. https://doi.org/10.1016/j.jas.2010.09.018.

Chase, Diane Z., and Arlen F. Chase. "Ancient Maya Markets and the Economic Integration of Caracol, Belize." *Ancient Mesoamerica* 25, no. 1 (2014): 239–50. https://doi.org/10.1017/S0956536114000145.

Chase, Diane Z., and Arlen F. Chase. "Caracol, Belize, and Changing Perceptions of Ancient Maya Society." *Journal of Archaeological Research* 25, no. 3 (2017): 185–249. https://doi.org/10.1007/s10814-016-9101-z.

Chase, Diane Z., and Arlen F. Chase. "Framing the Maya Collapse: Continuity, Discontinuity, Method, and Practice in the Classic to Postclassic Southern Maya Lowlands." In *After Collapse: The Regeneration of Complex Societies*, edited by Glenn M. Schwartz and John J. Nichols, 168–87. Tucson: University of Arizona Press, 2006.

Chase, Diane Z., and Arlen F. Chase. "Path Dependency in the Rise and Denouement of a Classic Maya City: The Case of Caracol, Belize: The Case of Caracol, Belize." *Archeological Papers of the American Anthropological Association* 24, no. 1 (2014): 142–54. https://doi.org/10.1111/apaa.12034.

Chatters, J. C., Douglas J. Kenneth, Y. Asmerom, B. M. Kemp, V. Polyak, A. N. Blank, P. A. Beddows, et al. "Late Pleistocene Human Skeleton and MtDNA Link Paleoamericans and Modern Native Americans." *Science* 344, no. 6185 (2014): 750–54.

Cheetham, David. "Corn, Colanders, and Cooking: Early Maize Processing in the Maya Lowlands and Its Implications." In *Pre-Columbian Foodways*, edited by John Staller and Michael Carrasco, 345–68. New York: Springer, 2010. https://doi.org/10.1007/978-1-4419-0471-3_14.

Chemas, A., and V. Rico-Gray. "Apiculture and Management of Associated Vegetation by the Maya of Tixcacaltuyub, Yucatan, Mexico." *Agroforestry Systems* 13 (1991): 13–25.

Chen, Ran, Yahui He, Xinwei Li, Jorge Ramos, Moran Li, and Li Liu. "Fermented Maize Beverages as Ritual Offerings: Investigating Elite Drinking During Classic Maya Period at Copan, Honduras." *Journal of Anthropological Archaeology* 65 (2022): 101373. https://doi.org/10.1016/j.jaa.2021.101373.

Child, Mark B., and Charles W. Golden. "The Transformation of Abandoned Architecture at Piedras Negras." In *Ruins of the Past: The Use and Perception of Abandoned Structures in the Maya Lowlands*, edited by Travis W. Stanton, Aline Magnoni, Wendy Ashmore, and Denise Brown, 65–89. Boulder: University Press of Colorado, 2008.

Christenson, A. J. *Popol Vuh*. London: Allen Bell, 2003.

Chu, Vikki, Lior Regev, Steve Weiner, and Elisabetta Boaretto. "Differentiating Between Anthropogenic Calcite in Plaster, Ash and Natural Calcite Using Infrared

Spectroscopy: Implications in Archaeology." *Journal of Archaeological Science* 35, no. 4 (2008): 905–11. https://doi.org/10.1016/j.jas.2007.06.024.

Chuchiak, John F., IV. "'It Is Their Drinking That Hinders Them': Balché and the Use of Ritual Intoxicants Among the Colonial Yucatec Maya, 1550–1780." *Estudios de Cultura Maya* 24 (2003): 137–71.

Clagett, Heather. "Household Archaeology at Chan Cahal: A Step Beyond Functionalism." In *The Blue Creek Project, Working Papers from the 1996 Field Season*, edited by W. David Driver, Heather Clagett, and Helen Haines, 61–70. San Antonio: Maya Research Program, St. Mary's University, 1997.

Clark, Dylan J. "The Residential Spaces, Social Organization and Dynamics of Isla Cerritos, an Ancient Maya Port Community." PhD diss., Harvard University, 2014.

Cobos Palma, Rafael. "Chichén Itzá: Settlement and Hegemony During the Terminal Classic Period." In *The Terminal Classic in the Maya Lowlands: Collapse, Transition, and Transformation*, edited by Arthur A. Demarest, Prudence M. Rice, and Don S. Rice, 517–44. Boulder: University Press of Colorado, 2004.

Cobos Palma, Rafael, Guillermo de Anda Alanis, and Roberto Garcia Moll. "Ancient Climate and Archaeology: Uxmal, Chichen Itza, and Their Collapse at the End of the Terminal Classic Period." *Archeological Papers of the American Anthropological Association* 24 (2014): 56–71.

Cojtí Cuxil, Demetrio. "Indigenous Nations in Guatemalan Democracy and the State: A Tentative Assessment." *Social Analysis* 51, no. 2 (2007). https://doi.org/10.3167/sa.2007.510207.

Cojtí Cuxil, Demetrio. *Políticas para la reivindicación de los Mayas de hoy: Fundamento de los derechos específicos de pueblo Maya*. 1st ed. Guatemala: Editorial Cholsamaj: SPEM, 1994.

Colunga-GarcíaMarín, Patricia, and Daniel Zizumbo-Villarreal. "Domestication of Plants in Maya Lowlands." *Economic Botany* 58, no. sp1 (2004): S101–10. https://doi.org/10.1663/0013-0001(2004)58[S101:DOPIML]2.0.CO;2.

Cook, B. I., K. J. Anchukaitis, J. O. Kaplan, M. J. Puma, M. Kelley, and D. Gueyffier. "Pre-Columbian Deforestation as an Amplifier of Drought in Mesoamerica." *Geophysical Research Letters* 39 (2012): L16706.

Cooke, C. Wythe. "Why the Mayan Cities of the Peten District, Guatemala, Were Abandoned." *Journal of the Washington Academy of Sciences* 21, no. 13 (1931): 283–87.

Cowgill, George L. "Onward and Upward with Collapse." In *The Collapse of Ancient States and Civilizations*, edited by Norman Yoffee and George L. Cowgill, 244–76. Tucson: University of Arizona Press, 1988.

Culbert, T. Patrick. "Ancient Maya Wetland Agriculture." *FAMSI*, 2001. http://www.famsi.org/reports/94033/.

Culbert, T. Patrick. *The Classic Maya Collapse*. 1st ed. School of American Research Advanced Seminar Series. Albuquerque: University of New Mexico Press, 1973.

Culbert, T. Patrick. "The Collapse of Classic Maya Civilization." In *The Collapse of Ancient States and Civilizations*, by Norman Yoffee and George L. Cowgill, 69–99. Tucson: University of Arizona Press, 1988.

Culbert, T. Patrick, Laura Levi, and Luis Cruz. "Lowland Maya Wetland Agriculture: The Rio Azul Agranomy Program." In *Vision and Revision in Maya Studies*, edited by F. Clancy and Peter D. Harrison, 115–24. Albuquerque: University of New Mexico Press, 1991.

Culbert, T. Patrick, and Don S. Rice, eds. *Precolumbian Population History in the Maya Lowlands*. Albuquerque: University of New Mexico Press, 1990.

Curtis, Jason H., David A. Hodell, and Mark Brenner. "Climate Variability on the Yucatan Peninsula (Mexico) During the Past 3500 Years, and Implications for Maya Cultural Evolution." *Quaternary Research* 46 (1996): 37–47.

Dahlin, Bruce H. "Climate Change and the End of the Classic Period in Yucatan: Resolving a Paradox." *Ancient Mesoamerica* 13, no. 2 (2002): 327–40. https://doi.org/10.1017/S0956536102132135.

Dahlin, Bruce H., Timothy Beach, Sheryl Luzzadder-Beach, David Hixson, Scott Hutson, Aline Magnoni, Eugenia Mansell, and Daniel E. Mazeau. "Reconstructing Agricultural Self-Sufficiency at Chunchucmil, Yucatan, Mexico." *Ancient Mesoamerica* 16, no. 2 (2005): 229–47. https://doi.org/10.1017/S0956536105050212.

Dahlin, Bruce H., and William J. Litzinger. "Old Bottle, New Wine: The Function of Chultuns in the Maya Lowlands." *American Antiquity* 51, no. 4 (1986): 721–36.

Davis-Salazar, Karla L. "Late Classic Maya Water Management and Community Organization at Copan, Honduras." *Latin American Antiquity* 14, no. 3 (2003): 275–99. https://doi.org/10.2307/3557561.

Dawo, Mohamed I., J. Michael Wilkinson, and David J. Pilbeam. "Interactions Between Plants in Intercropped Maize and Common Bean." *Journal of the Science of Food and Agriculture* 89, no. 1 (2009): 41–48.

De Anda, Guillermo, Karla Ortega, and James Brady. "Chichén Itzá y El Gran Acuífero Maya." *Arqueología Mexicana* 156 (2019): 34–41.

De Clerck, F. A., and P. Negreros-Castillo. "Plant Species of Traditional Mayan Homegardens of Mexico as Analogs for Multistrata Agroforests." *Agroforestry Systems* 48 (2000): 303–17.

Dedrick, Maia, Elizabeth A. Webb, Patricia A. McAnany, José Miguel Kanxoc Kumul, John G. Jones, Adolfo Iván Batún Alpuche, Carly Pope, and Morgan Russell. "Influential Landscapes: Temporal Trends in the Agricultural Use of Rejolladas at Tahcabo, Yucatán, Mexico." *Journal of Anthropological Archaeology* 59 (2020). https://doi.org/10.1016/j.jaa.2020.101175.

Delgado, Ma. Carmen, Julia Pacheco, A. Cabrera, Eduardo Batllori, Roger Orellana, and Francisco Bautista. "Quality of Groundwater for Irrigation in Tropical Kart Environment: The Case of Yucatan, Mexico." *Agricultural Water Management* 7 (2010): 1423–1433.

Demarest, Arthur A. "After the Maelstrom: Collapse of the Classic Maya Kingdoms and the Terminal Classic in Western Peten." In *The Terminal Classic in the Maya Lowlands: Collapse, Transition, and Transformation*, edited by Arthur A. Demarest, Prudence M. Rice, and Don S. Rice, 102–24. Boulder: University Press of Colorado, 2004.

Demarest, Arthur A. "Maya Archaeology for the Twenty-First Century: The Progress, the Perils, and the Promise." *Ancient Mesoamerica* 20, no. 2 (2009): 253–63. https://doi.org/10.1017/S0956536109990150.

Demarest, Arthur A. "Nuevos Datos e Interpretaciones de Los Reinos Occidentales Del Clasico Tardio: Hacia Una Vision Sintetica de La Historia Pasion/Usumacinta." In *XVI Simposio de Investigaciones Arqueologicas En Guatemala 2002*, edited by Juan Pedro Laporte, Hector L. Escobedo, and Barbara Arroyo, 159–74. Guatemala City: Museo Nacional de Arqueología y Etnología, Guatemala, 2003.

Demarest, Arthur A., Claudia Quintanilla, and Jose Samuel Suasnavar. "The Collapses in the West and the Violent Ritual Termination of the Classic Maya Capital Center of Cancuen." In *Ritual, Violence, and the Fall of the Classic Maya Kings*, edited by Gyles Iannone, Brett A. Houk, and Sonja A. Schwake, 159–86. Gainesville: University Press of Florida, 2016.

Demarest, Arthur A., Prudence M. Rice, and Don S. Rice, eds. *The Terminal Classic in the Maya Lowlands: Collapse, Transition, and Transformation.* Boulder: University Press of Colorado, 2004.

Dennell, Robin. "Tropical Rainforests as Long- Established Cultural Landscapes." In *Tropical Forest Conservation: Long-Term Processes of Human Evolution, Cultural Adaptations and Consumption Patterns*, edited by Rachel Christina Lewis, Jose Pulido Mata, and Connaughton, Chantal, 14–27. Mexico: United Nations Educational, Scientific and Cultural Organization, 2016.

Diamond, Jared M. *Collapse: How Societies Choose to Fail or Succeed.* New York: Penguin Books, 2005.

Dickau, Ruth, Anthony J. Ranere, and Richard G. Cooke. "Starch Grain Evidence for the Preceramic Dispersals of Maize and Root Crops into Tropical Dry and Humid Forests of Panama." *Proceedings of the National Academy of Sciences* 104, no. 9 (2007): 3651–56.

Dillon, Brian Dervin. "Meatless Maya? Ethnoarchaeological Implications for Ancient Subsistence." *Journal of New World Archaeology* 7, no. 2/3 (1988): 59–70.

Dillon, Brian Dervin. "The Archaeological Ceramics of Salinas de Los Nueve Cerros, Alta Verapaz, Guatemala." PhD diss., University of California, 1979.

Dillon, Brian Dervin. "The Highland-Lowland Maya Frontier: Archaeological Evidence from Alta Verapaz, Guatemala." In *The Periphery of the Southeastern Classic Maya Realm*, edited by Gary Pahl, 135–43. Latin American Studies 61. Los Angeles: University of California, 1987.

Dillon, Brian Dervin, Kevin O. Pope, and Michael Love. "An Ancient Extractive Industry: Maya Saltmaking at Salinas de Los Nueve Cerros, Guatemala." *Journal of New World Archaeology* 7, no. 2/3 (1988): 37–58.

DiNapoli, Robert J., Carl P. Lipo, Tanya Brosnan, Terry L. Hunt, Sean Hixon, Alex E. Morrison, and Matthew Becker. "Rapa Nui (Easter Island) Monument (Ahu) Locations Explained by Freshwater Sources." Edited by John P. Hart. *PLOS ONE* 14, no. 1 (2019): e0210409. https://doi.org/10.1371/journal.pone.0210409.

Dine, Harper, Traci Ardren, Grace Bascopé, and Celso Gutiérrez Báez. "Famine Foods and Food Security in the Northern Maya Lowlands: Modern Lessons for Ancient Reconstructions." *Ancient Mesoamerica* 30, no. 3 (2019): 517–34. https://doi.org/10.1017/S0956536118000408.

Doebley, John F., Brandon S. Gaut, and Bruce D. Smith. "The Molecular Genetics of Crop Domestication." *Cell* 127, no. 7 (2006): 1309–21. https://doi.org/10.1016/j.cell.2006.12.006.

Douglas, Peter M. J., Mark Brenner, and Jason H. Curtis. "Methods and Future Directions for Paleoclimatology in the Maya Lowlands." *Global and Planetary Change*, Climate Change and Archaeology in Mesoamerica: A Mirror for the Anthropocene, 138 (2016): 3–24. https://doi.org/10.1016/j.gloplacha.2015.07.008.

Douglas, Peter M. J., Mark Pagani, Marcello A. Canuto, Mark Brenner, David A. Hodell, Timothy I. Eglinton, and Jason H. Curtis. "Drought, Agricultural Adaptation, and Sociopolitical Collapse in the Maya Lowlands." *Proceedings of the National Academy of Sciences* 112, no. 18 (2015): 5607–12. https://doi.org/10.1073/pnas.1419133112.

Douglas, Peter M. J., Mark Pagani, Timothy I. Eglinton, Mark Brenner, Jason H. Curtis, Andy Breckenridge, and Kevin Johnston. "A Long-Term Decrease in the Persistence of Soil Carbon Caused by Ancient Maya Land Use." *Nature Geoscience* 11, no. 9 (2018): 645–49. https://doi.org/10.1038/s41561-018-0192-7.

Drennan, Robert D. "Long-Distance Movement of Goods in the Mesoamerican Formative and Classic." *American Antiquity* 49, no. 1 (1984): 27–43.

Dunning, Nicholas. "Birth and Death of Waters: Environmental Change, Adaptation and Symbolism in the Southern Maya Lowlands." In *Espacios Mayas: Representaciones, Usos, Creencias*, edited by A. Breton, A. Monod-Becquelin, and M. H. Ruz, 49–76. Mexico City: UNAM, 2003. https://doi.org/10.13140/2.1.3643.0722.

Dunning, Nicholas, Timothy Beach, Pat Farrell, and Sheryl Luzzadder-Beach. "Prehispanic Agrosystems and Adaptive Regions in the Maya Lowlands." *Culture & Agriculture* 20, no. 2–3 (1998): 87–101. https://doi.org/10.1525/cag.1998.20.2-3.87.

Dunning, Nicholas, and Stephen D. Houston. "Chan Ik': Hurricanes as a Destabilizing Force in the Pre-Hispanic Maya Lowlands." In *Ecology, Power, and Religion in Maya Landscapes*, edited by Christian Isendahl and Bodil Liljefors Persson, 57–67. Markt Schwaben: Verlag Anton Saurwein, 2011. https://www.academia.edu/36850371/Chan_Ik_Hurricanes_as_a_Destabilizing_Force_in_the_Pre_Hispanic_Maya_Lowlands.

Dunning, Nicholas, David J. Rue, Timothy Beach, Alan Covich, and Alfred Traverse. "Human-Environment Interactions in a Tropical Watershed: The Paleoecology of Laguna Tamarindito, El Petén, Guatemala." *Journal of Field Archaeology* 25, no. 2 (1998): 139–51. https://doi.org/10.1179/009346998792005487.

Dunning, Nicholas, Vernon Scarborough, Fred Valdez, Sheryl Luzzadder-Beach, Timothy Beach, and John G. Jones. "Temple Mountains, Sacred Lakes, and Fertile Fields: Ancient Maya Landscapes in Northwestern Belize." *Antiquity* 73, no. 281 (1999): 650–60. https://doi.org/10.1017/S0003598X0006525X.

Dunning, Nicholas P. "Appendix 1: Soils and Settlement in the Sayil Valley: A Preliminary Assessment." In *The Ancient Maya City of Sayil: The Mapping of a Puuc Region Center*, edited by Jeremy A. Sabloff and Gair Tourtellot, 20–27. New Orleans: Middle American Research Institute, Tulane University, 1991.

Dunning, Nicholas P. *Lords of the Hills: Ancient Maya Settlement in the Puuc Region, Yucatan, Mexico*. Monographs in World Archaeology 15. Madison, WI: Prehistory Press, 1992.

Dunning, Nicholas P. "Prehispanic Settlement Patterns of the Puuc Region, Yucatan, Mexico." PhD diss., University of Minnesota, 1990.

Dunning, Nicholas P. "A Reexamination of Regional Variability in the Pre-Hispanic Agricultural Landscape." In *The Managed Mosaic: Ancient Maya Agriculture and Resource Use*, edited by Scott L. Fedick, 53–68. Salt Lake City: University of Utah Press, 1996.

Dunning, Nicholas P., and Timothy Beach. "Farms and Forests: Spatial and Temporal Perspectives on Ancient Maya Landscapes." In *Landscapes and Societies*, edited by I. Peter Martini and Ward Chesworth, 369–89. Dordrecht: Springer Netherlands, 2010. https://doi.org/10.1007/978-90-481-9413-1_23.

Dunning, Nicholas P., and Timothy Beach. "Soil Erosion, Slope Management, and Ancient Terracing in the Maya Lowlands." *Latin American Antiquity* 5 (1994): 51–69.

Dunning, Nicholas P, and Timothy Beach. "Stability and Instability in Prehispanic Maya Landscapes." In *Imperfect Balance: Landscape Transformations in the Pre-Columbian*

Americas, edited by David Lentz, 179–202. New York: Columbia University Press, 2000. https://doi.org/10.7312/lent11156-010.

Dunning, Nicholas P, Timothy Beach, Liwy Grazioso Sierra, John G Jones, David L Lentz, Sheryl Luzzadder-Beach, Vernon L. Scarborough, and Michael P. Smyth. "A Tale of Two Collapses: Environmental Variability and Cultural Disruption in the Maya Lowlands." *Dialogo Andino* 41 (2013): 171–83.

Dunning, Nicholas P., Timothy Beach, and Sheryl Luzzadder-Beach. "Environmental Variability Among Bajos in the Southern Maya Lowlands and Its Implication for Ancient Maya Civilization and Archaeology." In *Precolumbian Water Management*, by Lisa J. Lucero and Barbara W. Fash, 81–99. Tucson: University of Arizona Press, 2006.

Dunning, Nicholas P, Timothy P. Beach, and Sheryl Luzzader-Beach. "Kax and Kol: Collapse and Resilience in Lowland Maya Civilization." *Proceedings of the National Academy of Sciences* 109, no. 10 (2012): 3652–57. https://doi.org/10.1073/pnas.111 4838109.

Dunning, Nicholas P, Timothy Beach, and David Rue. "The Paleoecology and Ancient Settlement of the Petexbatun Region." *Ancient Mesoamerica*, no. 8 (1997): 255–66.

Dunning, Nicholas P., Robert Griffin, John G. Jones, Richard E. Terry, Z. Larsen, and Christopher Carr. "Life on the Edge: Tikal in a Bajo Landscape." In *Tikal: Paleoecology of an Ancient Maya City*, edited by David L. Lentz, Nicholas P. Dunning, and Vernon Scarborough, 95–123. Cambridge: Cambridge University Press, 2015.

Dunning, Nicholas P., Armando Anaya Hernández, Timothy Beach, Christopher Carr, Robert Griffin, John G. Jones, David L. Lentz, Sheryl Luzzadder-Beach, Kathryn Reese-Taylor, and Ivan Šprajc. "Margin for Error: Anthropogenic Geomorphology of Bajo Edges in the Maya Lowlands." *Geomorphology* 331 (2019): 127–45. https://doi.org/10.1016/j.geomorph.2018.09.002.

Dunning, Nicholas P., David Wahl, Timothy Beach, John G. Jones, Sheryl Luzzadder-Beach, and Carmen McCane. "The End of the Beginning: Drought, Environmental Change, and the Preclassic to Classic Transition in the East-Central Yucatan Peninsula." In *The Great Maya Droughts in Cultural Context: Case Studies in Resilience and Vulnerability*, edited by Gyles Iannone, 107–29. Boulder: University Press of Colorado, 2014.

Dussol, Lydie, Michelle Elliott, Dominique Michelet, and Philippe Nondédéo. "Ancient Maya Sylviculture of Breadnut (Brosimum Alicastrum Sw.) and Sapodilla (Manilkara Zapota (L.) P. Royen) at Naachtun (Guatemala): A Reconstruction Based on Charcoal Analysis." *Quaternary International* 457 (2017): 29–42. https://doi.org/10.1016/j.qua int.2016.10.014.

Dussol, Lydie, Michelle Elliott, Grégory Pereira, and Dominique Michelet. "The Use of Firewood in Ancient Maya Funerary Rituals: A Case Study from Rio Bec (Campeche, Mexico)." *Latin American Antiquity* 27, no. 1 (2016): 51–73. https://doi.org/10.7183/ 1045-6635.27.1.51.

Dussol, Lydie, Julien Sion, and Philippe Nondédéo. "Late Fire Ceremonies and Abandonment Behaviors at the Classic Maya City of Naachtun, Guatemala." *Journal of Anthropological Archaeology* 56 (2019). https://doi.org/10.1016/j.jaa.2019.101099.

Dussol, Lydie, Michelle Elliott, Dominique Michelet, and Philippe Nondédéo. "Fuel Economy, Woodland Management and Adaptation Strategies in a Classic Maya City: Applying Anthracology to Urban Settings in High Biodiversity Tropical Forests." *Vegetation History and Archaeobotany* 30 (2021): 175–92.

Ebert, Claire E., Julie A. Hoggarth, and Jaime J. Awe. "Integrating Quantitative Lidar Analysis and Settlement Survey in the Belize River Valley." *Advances in Archaeological Practice* 4, no. 3 (2016): 284–300. https://doi.org/10.7183/2326-3768.4.3.284.

Ebert, Claire E., Keith M. Prufer, Martha J. Macri, Bruce Winterhalder, and Douglas J. Kennett. "Terminal Long Count Dates and the Disintegration of Classic Period Maya Polities." *Ancient Mesoamerica* 25, no. 2 (2014): 337–56. https://doi.org/10.1017/S0956536114000248.

Ebert, Claire E., Asta J. Rand, Kirsten Green-Mink, Julie A. Hoggarth, Carolyn Freiwald, Jaime J. Awe, Willa R. Trask, et al. "Sulfur Isotopes as a Proxy for Human Diet and Mobility from the Preclassic Through Colonial Periods in the Eastern Maya Lowlands." Edited by Dorothée Drucker. *PLOS ONE* 16, no. 8 (2021): e0254992. https://doi.org/10.1371/journal.pone.0254992.

Ehrenreich, Ben. "How Do You Know When Society Is About to Fall Apart?" *New York Times*, November 4, 2020, sec. Magazine. https://www.nytimes.com/2020/11/04/magazine/societal-collapse.html.

Ek, Jerald D. "Pottery and Politics: Contextualizing the Classic to Postclassic Transition in Champoton, Campeche." *Latin American Antiquity* 27, no. 4 (2016): 527–48.

Emery, Kitty. "The Noble Beast: Status and Differential Access to Animals in the Maya World." *World Archaeology* 34, no. 3 (2003): 498–515. https://doi.org/10.1080/0043824021000026477.

Emery, Kitty F. "The Maya Collapse: A Zooarchaeological Perspective." PhD diss., Cornell University, 1997.

Emery, Kitty F., and Erin Kennedy Thornton. "Zooarchaeological Habitat Analysis of Ancient Maya Landscape Changes." *Journal of Ethnobiology* 28 (2008): 154–78.

Emery, Kitty F., Lori E. Wright, and Henry P. Schwarcz. "Isotopic Analysis of Ancient Deer Bone: Biotic Stability in Collapse Period Maya Land-Use." *Journal of Archaeological Science* 27 (2000): 537–50.

Erlandson, J. M., T. C. Rick, T. J. Braje, M. Casperson, B. Culleton, B. Fulfrost, T. Garcia, et al. "Paleoindian Seafaring, Maritime Technologies, and Coastal Foraging on California's Channel Islands." *Science* 331, no. 6021 (2011): 1181–85. https://doi.org/10.1126/science.1201477.

Escobar, J., Jason H. Curtis, Mark Brenner, David A. Hodell, and J. Holmes. "Isotope Measurement of Ostracod and Gastropod Shells for Climate Reconstruction: Evaluation of Within-Sample Variability and Determination of Optimum Sample Size." *Journal of Paleolimnology* 43, no. 4 (2010): 921–38.

Escobedo, Hector L., and Stephen D. Houston, eds. *Proyecto Arqueológico Piedras Negras: Informe Preliminar No. 1, Primera Temporada 1997*. Guatemala City: Report submitted to the Instituto de Antropología e Historia de Guatemala, 1998.

Espinosa, L., M. Cerón, and Y. A. Sulub. "Limestone Rocks of the Yucatan Peninsula. Description of the Lithology and Physical Properties Based on the Results of Exploration, Investigation and Laboratory Tests." *International Journal of Rock Mechanics and Mining Sciences* 35, no. 4–5 (1998): 410–11. https://doi.org/10.1016/S0148-9062(98)00147-8.

Evans, Daniel L., Benjamin N. Vis, Nicholas P. Dunning, Elizabeth Graham, and Christian Isendahl. "Buried Solutions: How Maya Urban Life Substantiates Soil Connectivity." *Geoderma* 387 (2021). https://doi.org/10.1016/j.geoderma.2020.114925.

Fan, Fenliang, Fusuo Zhang, Zhi Qu, and Yahai Lu. "Plant Carbon Partitioning Below Ground in the Presence of Different Neighboring Species." *Soil Biology and Biochemistry* 40, no. 9 (2008): 2266–72. https://doi.org/10.1016/j.soilbio.2008.05.003.

Farahani, Alan, Katherine L. Chiou, Anna Harkey, Christine A. Hastorf, David L. Lentz, and Payson Sheets. "Identifying 'Plantscapes' at the Classic Maya Village of Joya de Cerén, El Salvador." *Antiquity* 91, no. 358 (2017): 980–97. https://doi.org/10.15184/aqy.2017.119.

Farriss, Nancy M. *Maya Society Under Colonial Rule: The Collective Enterprise of Survival.* Princeton: Princeton University Press, 1984.

Fash, Barbara W. "Iconographic Evidence for Water Management and Social Organization at Copan." In *Copan: The History of an Ancient Maya Kingdom*, edited by E. Wyllys Andrews and William L. Fash, 38. Santa Fe: School of American Research, 2005.

Fash, Barbara W., and Karla L. Davis-Salazar. "Copan Water Ritual and Management: Imagery and Sacred Place." In *Precolumbian Water Management: Ideology, Ritual, and Power*, edited by Lisa J. Lucero and Barbara W. Fash, 129–43. Tucson: University of Arizona Press, 2006.

Fash, William L., E. Wyllys Andrews, and T. Kam Manahan. "Political Decentralization, Dynastic Collapse, and the Early Postclassic in the Urban Center of Copan, Honduras." In *The Terminal Classic in the Maya Lowlands: Collapse, Transition, and Transformation*, edited by Arthur A. Demarest, Prudence M. Rice, and Don S. Rice, 260–87. Boulder: University Press of Colorado, 2004.

Fash, William L., and Barbara W. Fash. "Building a World-View: Visual Communication in Classic Maya Architecture." *RES: Anthropology and Aesthetics* 29–30 (1996): 127–47.

Fauvet-Berthelot, Marie-France. "Taille de l'Obsidienne et Fabrication de La Chaux: Deux Exemples d'Activite Specialisee a Cauinal." In *Cahiers de La R.C.P. 500 2. Rabinal et La Vallée Moyenne Du Rio Chixoy, Baja Verapaz—Guatemala*, edited by M.F. Fauvet-Berthelot, A. Ichon, N. Percheron, and A. Breton, 5–37. Paris: Centre National de la Recherche Scientifique. Institut d'Ethnologie, 1980.

Fedick, Scott. "In Search of the Maya Forest." In *In Search of the Rain Forest*, edited by Candace Slater, 133–64. Raleigh: Duke University Press, 2003.

Fedick, Scott L. "Ancient Maya Agricultural Terracing in the Upper Belize River Area: Computer-Aided Modeling and the Results of Initial Field Investigations." *Ancient Mesoamerica* 5 (1994): 107–27.

Fedick, Scott L., ed. *The Managed Mosaic: Ancient Maya Agriculture and Resource Use.* Salt Lake City: University of Utah Press, 1996.

Fedick, Scott L. "Maya Cornucopia: Indigenous Food Plants of the Maya Lowlands." In *The Real Business of Ancient Maya Economies: From Farmers' Fields to Rulers' Realms*, edited by Marilyn A. Masson, David Freidel, and Arthur A. Demarest, 224–37. Gainesville: University Press of Florida, 2020.

Fedick, Scott L. "The Maya Forest: Destroyed or Cultivated by the Ancient Maya?" *Proceedings of the National Academy of Sciences* 107, no. 3 (2010): 953–54. https://doi.org/10.1073/pnas.0913578107.

Fedick, Scott L. "A Reassessment of Water and Soil Resources in the Flatlands of the Northern Maya Lowlands: A Reassessment of Water and Soil." *Archeological Papers of the American Anthropological Association* 24, no. 1 (2014): 72–83. https://doi.org/10.1111/apaa.12030.

Fedick, Scott L., Maria De Lourdes Flores Delgadillo, Sergey Sedov, Elizabeth Solleiro Rebolledo, and Sergio Palacios Mayorga. "Adaptation of Maya Homegardens by

'Container Gardening' in Limestone Bedrock Cavities." *Journal of Ethnobiology* 28, no. 2 (2008): 290–304. https://doi.org/10.2993/0278-0771-28.2.290.

Fedick, Scott L., and Bethany A. Morrison. "Ancient Use and Manipulation of Landscape in the Yalahau Region of the Northern Maya Lowlands." *Agriculture and Human Values* 21, no. 2/3 (2004): 207–19. https://doi.org/10.1023/B:AHUM.0000029401.39131.ad.

Fedick, Scott L, Bethany A. Morrison, Bente J. Anderson, Sylviane Boucher, Jorge Ceja Acosta, and Jennifer P. Mathews. "Wetland Manipulation in the Yalahau Region of the Northern Maya Lowlands." *Journal of Field Archaeology* 27, no. 2 (2000): 131–52.

Fedick, Scott L., and Louis S. Santiago. "Large Variation in Availability of Maya Food Plant Sources During Ancient Droughts." *Proceedings of the National Academy of Sciences* 119, no. 1 (January 5, 2022): e2115657118. https://doi.org/10.1073/pnas.2115657118.

Fenner, Jack N., and Lori E. Wright. "Revisiting the Strontium Contribution of Sea Salt in the Human Diet." *Journal of Archaeological Science* 44 (2014): 99–103. https://doi.org/10.1016/j.jas.2014.01.020.

Ferguson, Bruce G., John Vandermeer, Helda Morales, and Daniel M. Griffith. "Post-Agricultural Succession in El Peten, Guatemala." *Conservation Biology* 17, no. 3 (2003): 818–28. https://doi.org/10.1046/j.1523-1739.2003.01265.x.

Fernandez, Fabian G., Kristofer D. Johnson, Richard E. Terry, Sheldon Nelson, and David Webster. "Soil Resources of the Ancient Maya at Piedras Negras, Guatemala." *Soil Science Society of America Journal* 69 (2005): 2020–32.

Fernandez-Diaz, Juan, William Carter, Ramesh Shrestha, and Craig Glennie. "Now You See It . . . Now You Don't: Understanding Airborne Mapping LiDAR Collection and Data Product Generation for Archaeological Research in Mesoamerica." *Remote Sensing* 6, no. 10 (2014): 9951–10001. https://doi.org/10.3390/rs6109951.

Fialko, Vilma. *Investigaciones Arqueológicas En El Bajo de Santa Fe y La Cuenca Del Río Holmul, Petén*. Guatemala City: Programa Nacional Tikal-Triangulo, 2001.

Finamore, Daniel, and Stephen D. Houston. *Fiery Pool: The Maya and the Mythic Sea*. New Haven, CT: Yale University Press, 2010. https://scholar.google.com/scholar_lookup?title=Fiery%20Pool%3A%20the%20Maya%20and%20the%20Mythic%20Sea&author=D.%20Finamore&publication_year=2010.

Fisher, Chelsea. "Archaeology for Sustainable Agriculture." *Journal of Archaeological Research* 28, no. 3 (2020): 393–441. https://doi.org/10.1007/s10814-019-09138-5.

Fisher, Chelsea. "The Role of Infield Agriculture in Maya Cities." *Journal of Anthropological Archaeology* 36 (2014): 196–210.

Fletcher, L., and E. R. Kintz. "Solares, Kitchen Gardens, and Social Status at Coba." In *Coba: A Classic Maya Metropolis*, edited by William J. Folan, E. R. Kintz, and L. Fletcher, 103–19. New York: Academic Press, 1983.

Fletcher, Roland, Dan Penny, Damian Evans, Christophe Pottier, Mike Barbetti, Matti Kummu, Terry Lustig, and Authority for the Protection and Management of Angkor and the Region of Siem Reap (APSARA) Department of Monuments and Archaeology Team. "The Water Management Network of Angkor, Cambodia." *Antiquity* 82 (2008): 658–70.

Flores, José Salvador, and Juan G. Kantún-Balam. "Importance of Plants in the Ch'a Chaak Maya Ritual in the Peninsula Yucatan." *Journal of Ethnobiology* 17 (1997): 97–108.

Foias, Antonia E. *Ceramics, Trade, and Exchange System of the Petexbatun: The Economic Parameters of the Classic Maya Collapse*. Nashville: Vanderbilt University Press, 2004.

Foias, Antonia E., and Ronald L. Bishop. "Changing Ceramic Production and Exchange in the Petexbatun Region, Guatemala: Reconsidering the Classic Maya Collapse." *Ancient Mesoamerica* 8 (1997): 275–91.

Folan, William J. "Coba, Quintana Roo, Mexico: An Analysis of a Prehispanic and Contemporary Source of *Sascab*." *American Antiquity* 43, no. 1 (1978): 79–85. https://doi.org/10.2307/279634.

Ford, Anabel. "Archaeology Under the Canopy: Exploring the Culture and Nature of El Pilar and the Maya Forest." In *Forward Together: A Culture-Nature Journey Towards More Effective Conservation in a Changing World,* Papers presented at the 2018 US/ICOMOS Symposium, edited by Nora Mitchell, Archer St. Clair, Jessica Brown, Brenda Barrett, and Anabelle Rodríguez. San Francisco: US/ICOMOS, 2019.

Ford, Anabel. "Critical Resource Control and the Rise of the Classic Period Maya." In *The Managed Mosaic: Ancient Maya Agriculture and Resource Use,* edited by Scott L. Fedick, 297–303. Salt Lake City: University of Utah Press, 1996.

Ford, Anabel. "Dominant Plants of the Maya Forest and Gardens of El Pilar: Implications for Paleoenvironmental Reconstructions." *Journal of Ethnobiology* 28, no. 2 (2008): 179–99. https://doi.org/10.2993/0278-0771-28.2.179.

Ford, Anabel. "Economic Variation of Ancient Maya Residential Settlement in the Upper Belize River Area." *Ancient Mesoamerica* 2 (1991): 35–46.

Ford, Anabel, and Kitty F. Emery. "Exploring the Legacy of the Maya Forest." *Journal of Ethnobiology* 28, no. 2 (2008): 147–53. https://doi.org/10.2993/0278-0771-28.2.147.

Ford, Anabel, and Ronald Nigh. "Origins of the Maya Forest Garden: Maya Resource Management." *Journal of Ethnobiology* 29, no. 2 (2009): 213–36. https://doi.org/10.2993/0278-0771-29.2.213.

Ford, Anabel, and Ronald B. Nigh. *The Maya Forest Garden: Eight Millennia of Sustainable Cultivation of the Tropical Woodlands.* New York: Routledge, 2015.

Ford, Anabel, and Ronald B. Nigh. "The Milpa Cycle and the Making of the Maya Forest Garden." *Research Reports in Belizean Archaeology* 7 (2010): 183–90.

Fournier, Patricia. "El Complejo Nixtamal/Comal/Tortilla En Mesoamerica." *Boletin de Antropologia Americana* 32 (1998): 13–40.

Freidel, David. "Children of the First Father's Skull: Terminal Classic Warfare in the Northern Maya Lowlands and the Transformation of Kingship and Elite Hierarchies." In *Mesoamerican Elites: An Archaeological Assessment,* edited by Diane Z. Chase and Arlen F. Chase, 99–117. Norman: University of Oklahoma Press, 1993.

Freidel, David. "Continuity and Disjunction: Late Postclassic Settlement Patterns in Northern Yucatan." In *Lowland Maya Settlement Patterns,* edited by Wendy Ashmore, 311–32. Albuquerque: University of New Mexico Press, 1981.

Freidel, David. "Maya and the Idea of Empire." In *Pathways to Complexity: A View from the Maya Lowlands,* edited by M. Kathryn Brown and George J. Bey, 363–86. Gainesville: University Press of Florida, 2018.

Freidel, David, and Jeremy A. Sabloff. *Cozumel: Late Classic Settlement Patterns.* Orlando: Academic Press, 1984.

French, Kirk D., and Christopher J. Duffy. "Prehispanic Water Pressure: A New World First." *Journal of Archaeological Science* 37, no. 5 (2010): 1027–32. https://doi.org/10.1016/j.jas.2009.12.003.

French, Kirk D., and Christopher J. Duffy. "Understanding Ancient Maya Water Resources and the Implications for a More Sustainable Future: Understanding Ancient

Maya Water Resources." *Wiley Interdisciplinary Reviews: Water* 1, no. 3 (2014): 305–13. https://doi.org/10.1002/wat2.1024.

French, Kirk D., Kirk D. Straight, and Elijah J. Hermitt. "Building the Environment at Palenque: The Sacred Pools of the Picota Group." *Ancient Mesoamerica* 31, no. 3 (2020): 409–30. https://doi.org/10.1017/S0956536119000130.

Gallareta Negrón, Tomás, George J. Bey III, and William M. Ringle. *Investigaciones Arqueológicas En Las Ruinas de Kiuic y La Zona Labná Kiuic, Distrito de Bolonchén, Yucatán, México, Temporada 2013*. Merida: Manuscript on file, Consejo de Arqueología de Instituto Nacional de Antropología e Historia, 2014.

Gallopin, Gary G. "Water Storage Technology at Tikal, Guatemala." MA thesis, University of Cincinnati, 1990.

García Sáiz, Concepción. "Antonio del Rio y Guillermo Dupaix: El Reconocimiento de una Deuda Historica." *Anales del Museo de America* 2 (1994): 99–119.

Garcia Solis, Claudia Araceli. "La Tecnologia de La Escultura Arquitectonica Modelada En Estuco de La Sub II C-1: Implicaciones Sociales Para El Preclasico En Calakmul." MA thesis, Universidad Autonoma de Yucatan, 2011.

Garrison, Thomas G. "Ancient Maya Territories, Adaptive Regions, and Alliances: Contextualizing the San Bartolo-Xultun Intersite Survey." PhD diss., Harvard University, 2007.

Garrison, Thomas G., and Nicholas P. Dunning. "Settlement, Environment, and Politics in the San Bartolo-Xultun Territory, El Peten, Guatemala." *Latin American Antiquity* 20, no. 4 (2009): 525–52.

Garrison, Thomas G., Stephen Houston, and Omar Alcover Firpi. "Recentering the Rural: Lidar and Articulated Landscapes Among the Maya." *Journal of Anthropological Archaeology* 53 (2019): 133–46. https://doi.org/10.1016/j.jaa.2018.11.005.

Garrison, Thomas G., Dustin Richmond, Perry Naughton, Eric Lo, Sabrina Trinh, Zachary Barnes, Albert Lin, Curt Schurgers, Ryan Kastner, and Sarah E. Newman. "Tunnel Vision: Documenting Excavations in Three Dimensions with Lidar Technology." *Advances in Archaeological Practice* 4, no. 2 (2016): 192–204. https://doi.org/10.7183/2326-3768.4.2.192.

Gerhart, Juliette C., and Norman Hammond. "The Community of Cuello: The Ceremonial Core." In *Cuello: An Early Maya Community in Belize*, edited by Norman Hammond, 98–117. Cambridge: Cambridge University Press, 1991.

Gill, Richardson. *The Great Maya Droughts: Water, Life, and Death*. Albuquerque: University of New Mexico Press, 2000.

Gill, Richardson B., Paul A. Mayewski, Johan Nyberg, Gerald H. Haug, and Larry C. Peterson. "Drought and the Maya Collapse." *Ancient Mesoamerica* 18, no. 2 (2007): 283–302. https://doi.org/10.1017/S0956536107000193.

Gillespie, A. R., D. M. Bocanegra-Ferguson, and J. J. Jimenez. "The Propagation of Ramon (Brosimum Alicastrum Sw.; Moraceae) in Mayan Homegardens of the Yucatan Peninsula of Mexico." *New Forests* 27 (2004): 25–38.

Gillot, Céline. "The Use of Pozzolanic Materials in Maya Mortars: New Evidence from Río Bec (Campeche, Mexico)." *Journal of Archaeological Science* 47 (2014): 1–9. https://doi.org/10.1016/j.jas.2014.03.037.

Gliessman, Stephen R. "Allelopathic Interactions in Crop-Weed Mixtures: Applications for Weed Management." *Journal of Chemical Ecology* 9, no. 8 (1983): 991–99. https://doi.org/10.1007/BF00982206.

Glover, Jeffrey B., Zachary X. Hruby, Dominique Rissolo, Joseph W. Ball, Michael D. Glascock, and M. Steven Shackley. "Interregional Interaction in Terminal Classic Yucatan: Recent Obsidian and Ceramic Data from Vista Alegre, Quintana Roo, Mexico." *Latin American Antiquity* 29, no. 3 (2018): 475–94.

Goguitchaichvili, Avto, Soledad Ortiz-Ruiz, Juan Morales, Vadim A. Kravchinsky, Oscar de Lucio, Rubén Cejudo, Rafael Garcia, Eunice Uc González, José Luis Ruvalcaba, and Luis Barba Pingarrón. "Pyrotechnological Knowledge in the Pre-Hispanic Maya Society: Magnetic and Infrared Spectrometry Surveys of Limekilns in the Western Yucatan Peninsula (Mexico)." *Journal of Archaeological Science: Reports* 33 (2020). https://doi.org/10.1016/j.jasrep.2020.102457.

Golden, Charles, and Andrew Scherer. "Border Problems: Recent Archaeological Research along the Usumacinta River." *The PARI Journal* 7, no. 2 (2006): 1–16.

Golden, Charles W. "The Politics of Warfare in the Usumacinta Basin: La Pasadita and the Realm of Bird Jaguar." In *Ancient Mesoamerican Warfare*, edited by M. Kathryn Brown and Travis W. Stanton, 31–48. Walnut Creek: AltaMira Press, 2003.

Golitko, Mark, James Meierhoff, Gary M. Feinman, and Patrick Ryan Williams. "Complexities of Collapse: The Evidence of Maya Obsidian as Revealed by Social Network Graphical Analysis." *Antiquity* 86, no. 332 (2012): 507–23. https://doi.org/10.1017/S0003598X00062906.

Gómez-Pompa, Arturo. "On Maya Silviculture." *Mexican Studies/Estudios Mexicanos* 3, no. 1 (1987): 1–17.

Gómez-Pompa, Arturo, José Salvador Flores, and Mario Aliphat Fernández. "The Sacred Cacao Groves of the Maya." *Latin American Antiquity* 1, no. 3 (1990): 247–57. https://doi.org/10.2307/972163.

Gómez-Pompa, Arturo, and Andrea Kaus. "Taming the Wilderness Myth: Environmental Policy and Education Are Currently Based on Western Beliefs About Nature Rather Than on Reality." *BioScience* 42, no. 4 (1992): 271–79. https://doi.org/10.2307/1311675.

Gondwe, Bibi R. N., Sara Lerer, Simon Stisen, Luis Marín, Mario Rebolledo-Vieyra, Gonzalo Merediz-Alonso, and Peter Bauer-Gottwein. "Hydrogeology of the South-Eastern Yucatan Peninsula: New Insights from Water Level Measurements, Geochemistry, Geophysics and Remote Sensing." *Journal of Hydrology* 389, no. 1–2 (2010): 1–17. https://doi.org/10.1016/j.jhydrol.2010.04.044.

Guderjan, Thomas H., and C. Colleen Hanratty. "Events and Processes Leading to the Abandonment of the Maya City of Blue Creek, Belize." In *Ritual, Violence, and the Fall of the Classic Maya Kings*, edited by Gyles Iannone, Brett A. Houk, and Sonja A. Schwake, 223–42. Gainesville: University Press of Florida, 2016.

Gunn, Joel D., William J. Folan, Christian Isendahl, María del Rosario Domínguez Carrasco, Betty B. Faust, and Beniamino Volta. "Calakmul: Agent Risk and Sustainability in the Western Maya Lowlands." *Archaeological Papers of the American Anthropological Association* 24, no. 1 (2014): 101–23. https://doi.org/10.1111/apaa.12032.

Gunn, Joel D., William J. Folan, and Hubert R. Robichaux. "A Landscape Analysis of the Candelaria Watershed in Mexico: Insights into Paleoclimates Affecting Upland Horticulture in the Southern Yucatan Peninsula Semi-Karst." *Geoarchaeology* 10, no. 1 (1995): 3–42. https://doi.org/10.1002/gea.3340100103.

Gunn, Joel D., John E. Foss, William J. Folan, Maria del Rosario Domínguez Carrasco, and Betty B. Faust. "Bajo Sediments and the Hydraulic System of Calakmul, Campeche,

Mexico." *Ancient Mesoamerica* 13, no. 2 (2002b): 297–315. https://doi.org/10.1017/S0956536102132184.

Gunn, Joel D., Ray T. Matheny, and William J. Folan. "Climate-Change Studies in the Maya Area: A Diachronic Analysis." *Ancient Mesoamerica* 13, no. 1 (2002a): 79–84. https://doi.org/10.1017/S0956536102131105.

Gunn, Joel D., Vernon L. Scarborough, William J. Folan, Christian Isendahl, Arlen F. Chase, Jeremy A. Sabloff, and Beniamino Volta. "A Distribution Analysis of the Central Maya Lowlands Ecoinformation Network: Its Rises, Falls, and Changes." *Ecology and Society* 22, no. 1 (2016): 1–19. https://doi.org/10.5751/ES-08931-220120.

Gutierrez, Roberto, James C Gibeaut, Rebecca C Smyth, Tiffany L Hepner, and John R Andrews. "Precise Airborne LiDAR Surveying for Coastal Research and Geohazards Applications." *International Archives of Photogrammetry and Remote Sensing* 34 (2001): 185–92.

Hagen, Victor W. von. "The Maya Enigma: The Rise and Fall of Maya Civilization. By J. Eric S. Thompson. Illustrated. 287 Pp. Norman: University of Oklahoma Press. $5. (Published 1954)." *New York Times*, October 3, 1954, sec. Archives. https://www.nytimes.com/1954/10/03/archives/the-maya-enigma-the-rise-and-fall-of-maya-civilization-by-j-eric-s.html.

Hahn, Lauren D., and Geoffrey E. Braswell. "Interpreting Site Perimeter Walls in the Northern Maya Lowlands and Beyond." In *The Ancient Maya of Mexico: Reinterpreting the Past of the Northern Maya Lowlands*, edited by Geoffrey E. Braswell, 264–81. Approaches to Anthropological Archaeology. New York: Routledge, 2012.

Haldon, John, Arlen F. Chase, Warren Eastwood, Martin Medina-Elizalde, Adam Izdebski, Francis Ludlow, Guy Middleton, Lee Mordechai, Jason Nesbitt, and B. L. Turner. "Demystifying Collapse: Climate, Environment, and Social Agency in Pre-Modern Societies." *Millennium* 17, no. 1 (2020): 1–33. https://doi.org/10.1515/mill-2020-0002.

Hale, John, Jan Heinemeier, Alf Lindroos, Lynne Lancaster, and Åsa Ringbom. "Dating Ancient Mortar." *American Scientist* 91, no. 2 (2003): 130. https://doi.org/10.1511/2003.2.130.

Halperin, Christina, Jean-Baptiste Le Moine, and Enrique Pérez Zambrano. "Infrastructures of Moving Water at the Maya Site of Ucanal, Petén, Guatemala." *Journal of Anthropological Archaeology* 56 (2019): 101102, 1–15.

Halperin, Christina T., Yasmine Flynn-Arajdal, Katherine A. Miller Wolf, and Carolyn Freiwald. "Terminal Classic Residential Histories, Migration, and Foreigners at the Maya Site of Ucanal, Petén, Guatemala." *Journal of Anthropological Archaeology* 64 (December 2021). https://doi.org/10.1016/j.jaa.2021.101337.

Hammond, Normand. *Cuello: An Early Maya Community in Belize*. Cambridge: Cambridge University Press, 1991.

Hammond, Norman, and Juliette C. Gerhart. "Stratigraphy and Chronology in the Reconstruction of Preclassic Developments at Cuello." In *Cuello: An Early Maya Community in Belize*, edited by Norman Hammond, 23–60. Cambridge: Cambridge University Press, 1991.

Hanks, William F. *Referential Practice: Language and Lived Space Among the Maya*. Chicago: University of Chicago Press, 1990.

Hansen, Eric Floyd. "Ancient Maya Burnt-Lime Technology: Cultural Implications of Technological Styles." PhD diss., University of California, Los Angeles, 2000.

Hansen, Eric Floyd, Richard D Hansen, and M. R. Derrick. "Los Análisis de Los Estucos y Pinturas Arquitectónicas de Nakbe: Resultados Preliminares de Los Estudios de Los Métodos y Materiales de Producción." In *VIII Simposio de Investigaciones Arqueológicas En Guatemala, 1994*, edited by Juan Pedro Laporte and Hector L. Escobedo, 456–70. Guatemala City: Museo Nacional de Arqueología y Etnología, Guatemala, 1995.

Hansen, Richard D., Steven Bozarth, Jacob J. Wahl, and Thomas P Schreiner. "Climatic and Environmental Variability in the Rise of Maya Civilization." *Ancient Mesoamerica* 13, no. 2 (2002): 273–95.

Hansen, Richard D., Donald W. Forsyth, James C. Woods, Thomas P. Schreiner, and Gene L. Titmus. "Developmental Dynamics, Energetics, and Complex Economic Interactions of the Early Maya of the Mirador-Calakmul Basin, Guatemala, and Campeche, Mexico." In *Pathways to Complexity: A View from the Maya Lowlands*, edited by M. Kathryn Brown and George J. Bey, 147–94. Gainesville: University Press of Florida, 2018.

Hansen, Richard D., Wayne K. Howell, and Stanley P. Guenter. "Forgotten Structures, Haunted Houses, and Occupied Hearts." In *Ruins of the Past: The Use and Perception of Abandoned Structures in the Maya Lowlands*, edited by Travis W. Stanton, Aline Magnoni, Wendy Ashmore, and Denise Brown, 25–64. Boulder: University Press of Colorado, 2008.

Hanson, Craig A. "The Late Mesoamerican Village." PhD diss., Tulane University, 2008.

Hare, Timothy S., Marilyn A. Masson, and Carlos Peraza Lope. "The Urban Cityscape." In *Kukulkan's Realm: Urban Life at Ancient Mayapán*, edited by Marilyn A. Masson and Carlos Peraza Lope, 149–92. Boulder: University Press of Colorado, 2014. https://upc olorado.com/university-press-of-colorado/item/2025-kukulcan-s-realm.

Harrison, Peter D. "Aspects of Water Management in the Southern Maya Lowlands." *Research in Economic. Anthropology* Supplement 7 (1993): 71–119.

Hart, John P. "Can Cucurbita Pepo Gourd Seeds Be Made Edible?" *Journal of Archaeological Science* 31, no. 11 (2004): 1631–33. https://doi.org/10.1016/j.jas.2004.04.004.

Haviland, William A. "Stature at Tikal, Guatemala: Implications for Ancient Maya Demography and Social Organization." *American Antiquity* 32, no. 3 (1967): 316–25.

Haviland, William A. "Tikal, Guatemala and Mesoamerican Urbanism." *World Archaeology* 2, no. 2 (1970): 186–98.

Headrick, Annabeth. "Empire at Chichén Itzá Revisited." In *A Forest of History: The Maya After the Emergence of Divine Kingship*, edited by Travis W. Stanton and M. Kathryn Brown, 187–203. Boulder: University Press of Colorado, 2020. https://doi.org/10.5876/ 9781646420469.c011.

Healy, Paul F. "An Ancient Maya Dam in the Cayo District, Belize." *Journal of Field Archaeology* 102, no. 2 (1983): 9147–54.

Henderson, John S., and Rosemary A. Joyce. "Brewing Distinction: The Development of Cacao Beverages in Formative Mesoamerica." In *Chocolate in Mesoamerica: A Cultural History of Cacao*, edited by Cameron L. McNeil, 140–53. Gainesville: University Press of Florida, 2006.

Herckis, Lauren R. "Cultural Variation in the Maya City of Palenque." PhD diss., University of Michigan, 2015.

Hightower, Jessica N., A. Christine Butterfield, and John F. Weishampel. "Quantifying Ancient Maya Land Use Legacy Effects on Contemporary Rainforest Canopy Structure." *Remote Sensing* 6 (2014): 10716–32.

Hodell, David A., Mark Brenner, and Jason H. Curtis. "Terminal Classic Drought in the Northern Maya Lowlands Inferred from Multiple Sediment Cores in Lake Chichancanab (Mexico)." *Quaternary Science Reviews* 24 (2005): 1413–27.

Hodell, David A., Jason H. Curtis, and Mark Brenner. "Possible Role of Climate in the Collapse of Classic Maya Civilization." *Nature* 375, no. 1 (1995): 391–94.

Hoggarth, Julie A., Sebastian F. M. Breitenbach, Brendan J. Culleton, Claire E. Ebert, Marilyn A. Masson, and Douglas J. Kennett. "The Political Collapse of Chichén Itzá in Climatic and Cultural Context." *Global and Planetary Change* 138 (2016): 25–42. https://doi.org/10.1016/j.gloplacha.2015.12.007.

Hoggarth, Julie A, Brendan J. Culleton, Jaime J. Awe, Christophe Helmke, Sydney Lonaker, J. Britt Davis, and Douglas J. Kennett. "Building High-Precision AMS C14 Bayesian Models for the Formation of Peri-Abandonment Deposits at Baking Pot, Belize." *Radiocarbon* 63, no. 3 (2021): 977–1002. https://doi.org/10.1017/RDC.2021.30.

Hoggarth, Julie A., Matthew Restall, James W. Wood, and Douglas J. Kennett. "Drought and Its Demographic Effects in the Maya Lowlands." *Current Anthropology* 58, no. 1 (2017): 82–113. https://doi.org/10.1086/690046.

Holling, C. S. "Resilience and Stability of Ecological Systems." *Annual Review of Ecology and Systematics* 4, no. 1 (1973): 1–23. https://doi.org/10.1146/annurev.es.04.110 173.000245.

Holling, C. S. "Understanding the Complexity of Economic, Ecological, and Social Systems." *Ecosystems* 4, no. 5 (2001): 390–405. https://doi.org/10.1007/s10021-001-0101-5.

Holling, Crawford S., and Lance H. Gunderson. "Resilience and Adaptive Cycles." In *Panarchy: Understanding Transformations in Human and Natural Systems*, edited by Lance H. Gunderson and Crawford S. Holling, 25–62. Washington, DC: Island Press, 2002.

Holst, I., J. E. Moreno, and D. R. Piperno. "Identification of Teosinte, Maize, and Tripsacum in Mesoamerica by Using Pollen, Starch Grains, and Phytoliths." *Proceedings of the National Academy of Sciences* 104, no. 45 (2007): 17608–13. https://doi.org/10.1073/pnas.0708736104.

Honan, William H. "Did Maya Doom Themselves by Felling Trees?" *New York Times*, April 11, 1995, Section C, page 12. https://www.nytimes.com/1995/04/11/science/did-maya-doom-themselves-by-felling-trees.html?searchResultPosition=3.

Houck, Charles W., Jr. "Cenotes, Wetlands, and Hinterland Settlement." In *Lifeways in the Northern Maya Lowlands: New Approaches to Archaeology in the Yucatán Peninsula*, edited by Jennifer P. Mathews and Bethany A. Morrison, 56–76. Tucson: University of Arizona Press, 2006.

Houk, Brett A., Hubert R. Robichaux, and Fred Valdez. "An Early Royal Maya Tomb from Chan Chich, Belize." *Ancient Mesoamerica* 21, no. 2 (2010): 229–48. https://doi.org/10.1017/S0956536110000301.

Houston, Stephen D., Hector L. Escobedo, Mark B. Child, Charles W. Golden, and René Muñoz. "The Moral Community: Maya Settlement Transformation at Piedras Negras, Guatemala." In *The Social Construction of Ancient Cities*, edited by Monica L. Smith, 212–53. Washington, DC: Smithsonian Books, 2003.

Houston, Stephen D., Thomas G. Garrison, and Omar Alcover. "Citadels and Surveillance: Conflictive Regions and Defensive Design in the Buenavista Citadels of Guatemala." *Contributions in New World Archaeology* 13 (2019): 9–36.

Houston, Stephen D., and Takeshi Inomata. *The Classic Maya.* Cambridge World Archaeology. New York: Cambridge University Press, 2009.

Houston, Stephen D., Sarah E. Newman, Edwin Roman, and Thomas G. Garrison. *Temple of the Night Sun: A Royal Tomb at El Diablo, Guatemala*. San Francisco: Precolumbia Mesoweb Press, 2015.

Houston, Stephen D., David S. Stuart, and Karl Taube. *The Memory of Bones: Body, Being and Experience Among the Classic Maya*. Austin: University of Texas Press, 2006.

Hueda-Tanabe, Y., A. M. Soler-Arechalde, J. Urrutia-Fucugauchi, L. Barba, L. Manzanilla, M. Rebolledo-Vieyra, and A. Goguitchaichvili. "Archaeomagnetic Studies in Central Mexico—Dating of Mesoamerican Lime-Plasters." *Physics of the Earth and Planetary Interiors* 147, no. 2–3 (2004): 269–83. https://doi.org/10.1016/j.pepi.2004.06.006.

Huntington, Ellsworth. "Maya Civilization and Climatic Changes." In *Proceedings of the Nineteenth Congress of Americanists*, edited by F. W. Hodge, 150–64. Washington, DC: Congress of Americanists, 1917.

Hutson, Scott R., Nicholas P. Dunning, Bruce Cook, Thomas Ruhl, Nicolas C. Barth, and Daniel Conley. "Ancient Maya Rural Settlement Patterns, Household Cooperation, and Regional Subsistence Interdependency in the Río Bec Area: Contributions from G-LiHT." *Journal of Anthropological Research* 77, no. 4 (2021): 550–79. https://doi.org/10.1086/716750.

Hutson, Scott R., Barry Kidder, Céline Lamb, Daniel Vallejo-Cáliz, and Jacob Welch. "Small Buildings and Small Budgets: Making Lidar Work in Northern Yucatan, Mexico." *Advances in Archaeological Practice* 4, no. 3 (2016): 268–83. https://doi.org/10.7183/2326-3768.4.3.268.

Hyman, David S. *Precolumbian Cements: A Study of the Calcareous Cements in Prehispanic Mesoamerican Building Construction*. Baltimore: Johns Hopkins University Press, 1970.

Iannone, Gyles. *The Great Maya Droughts in Cultural Context: Case Studies in Resilience and Vulnerability*. Boulder: University Press of Colorado, 2014.

Iannone, Gyles. "The Rise and Fall of a Maya Petty Royal Court." *Latin American Antiquity* 16 (2005): 26–44.

Iannone, Gyles, Brett A. Houk, and Sonja A. Schwake. *Ritual, Violence, and the Fall of the Classic Maya Kings*. Gainesville: University Press of Florida, 2016.

Iannone, Gyles, Keith Prufer, and Diane Z. Chase. "Resilience and Vulnerability in the Maya Hinterlands." *Archeological Papers of the American Anthropological Association* 24, no. 1 (2014): 155–70. https://doi.org/10.1111/apaa.12035.

Independent researcher, Yucatán, México, Eduardo Pérez de Heredia, Péter Bíró, and Sylviane Boucher. "Maíz y balché. Una revisión de la iconografía de los murales de Tulum." *Estudios de Cultura Maya* 57 (2021): 117–49. https://doi.org/10.19130/iifl.ecm.57.2021.18655.

Inomata, Takeshi. "The Last Day of a Fortified Classic Maya Center: Archaeological Investigations at Aguateca, Guatemala." *Ancient Mesoamerica* 8 (1997): 337–51.

Inomata, Takeshi. *Warfare and the Fall of a Fortified Center: Archaeological Investigations at Aguateca*. Vol. 3. Vanderbilt Institute of Mesoamerican Archaeology. Nashville: Vanderbilt University Press, 2008.

Inomata, Takeshi, Erick Ponciano, Oswaldo Chinchilla, Otto Roman, Veronique Breuil-Martinez, and Oscar Santos. "An Unfinished Temple at the Classic Maya Centre of Aguateca, Guatemala." *Antiquity* 78, no. 302 (2004): 798–811.

Inomata, Takeshi, Daniela Triadan, and Kazuo Aoyama. "After 40 Years: Revisiting Ceibal to Investigate the Origins of Lowland Maya Civilization." *Ancient Mesoamerica* 28, no. 1 (2017): 187–201. https://doi.org/10.1017/S0956536117000037.

Inomata, Takeshi, Daniela Triadan, Verónica A. Vázquez López, Juan Carlos Fernandez-Diaz, Takayuki Omori, María Belén Méndez Bauer, Melina García Hernández, et al. "Monumental Architecture at Aguada Fénix and the Rise of Maya Civilization." *Nature* 582, no. 7813 (2020): 530–33. https://doi.org/10.1038/s41586-020-2343-4.

Inomata, Takeshi, Juan Carlos Fernandez-Diaz, Daniela Triadan, Miguel García Mollinedo, Flory Pinzón, Melina García Hernández, Atasta Flores, Ashley Sharpe, Timothy Beach, et al. "Origins and Spread of Formal Ceremonial Complexes in the Olmec and Maya Regions Revealed by Airborne Lidar." *Nature Human Behaviour* 5 (2021): 1487–501.

Isendahl, Christian. "Greening the Ancient City: The Agro-Urban Landscapes of the Pre-Hispanic Maya." *Studies in Global Archaeology* 15 (2010): 527–52.

Isendahl, Christian. "The Weight of Water: A New Look at Pre-Hispanic Puuc Maya Water Reservoirs." *Ancient Mesoamerica* 22, no. 1 (2011): 185–97. https://doi.org/10.1017/S0956536111000149.

Isendahl, Christian, Nicholas P. Dunning, and Jeremy A. Sabloff. "Growth and Decline in Classic Maya Puuc Political Economies: Growth and Decline in Classic Maya Puuc Political Economies." *Archeological Papers of the American Anthropological Association* 24, no. 1 (2014): 43–55. https://doi.org/10.1111/apaa.12028.

Isendahl, Christian, and Scott Heckbert. "Tradeoffs in Pre-Columbian Maya Water Management Systems: Complexity, Sustainability, and Cost." In *The Give and Take of Sustainability*, edited by Michelle Hegmon, 125–47. Cambridge: Cambridge University Press, 2017. https://doi.org/10.1017/9781139939720.007.

Isendahl, Christian, and Michael E. Smith. "Sustainable Agrarian Urbanism: The Low-Density Cities of the Mayas and Aztecs." *Cities* 31 (2013): 132–43.

Jacob, John S. "Ancient Maya Wetland Agricultural Fields in Cobweb Swamp, Belize: Construction, Chronology, and Function." *Journal of Field Archaeology* 22, no. 2 (1995): 175–90.

Johnson, Katharine M., and William B. Ouimet. "An Observational and Theoretical Framework for Interpreting the Landscape Palimpsest Through Airborne LiDAR." *Applied Geography* 91 (2018): 32–44. https://doi.org/10.1016/j.apgeog.2017.12.018.

Johnston, Kevin J. "Lowland Maya Water Management Practices: The Household Exploitation of Rural Wells." *Geoarchaeology: An International Journal* 19, no. 3 (2004): 265–92.

Johnston, Kevin J. "The Intensification of Pre-Industrial Cereal Agriculture in the Tropics: Boserup, Cultivation Lengthening, and the Classic Maya." *Journal of Anthropological Archaeology* 22, no. 2 (2003): 126–61. https://doi.org/10.1016/S0278-4165(03)00013-8.

Johnston, Kevin J., Takeshi Inomata, and Joel Palka. "Excavaciones de Operación 1." In *El Proyecto Archaeological Regional Petexbatun: Informe No. 1*, edited by Arthur A. Demarest and Stephen D. Houston, 29–52. Guatemala City: Report submitted to the Institute of Anthropology and History, 1989.

Joyce, Rosemary A. "Archaeology of the Body." *Annual Review of Anthropology* 34, no. 1 (2005): 139–58. https://doi.org/10.1146/annurev.anthro.33.070203.143729.

Keenan, Benjamin. "Late Classic Climate Change and Societal Response in the Maya Lowlands." *Journal of the Council for Research on Religion* 2, no. 1 (December 30, 2020): 17–40. https://doi.org/10.26443/jcreor.v2i1.36.

Keenan, Benjamin, Anic Imfeld, Kevin Johnston, Andy Breckenridge, Yves Gélinas, and Peter M. J. Douglas. "Molecular Evidence for Human Population Change Associated with Climate Events in the Maya Lowlands." *Quaternary Science Reviews* 258 (2021): 106904. https://doi.org/10.1016/j.quascirev.2021.106904.

Kennett, D. J., S. F. M. Breitenbach, V. V. Aquino, Y. Asmerom, J. Awe, J. U. L. Baldini, P. Bartlein, et al. "Development and Disintegration of Maya Political Systems in Response to Climate Change." *Science* 338, no. 6108 (2012): 788–91. https://doi.org/10.1126/scie nce.1226299.

Kennett, Douglas J., Mark Lipson, Keith M. Prufer, David Mora-Marín, Richard J. George, Nadin Rohland, Mark Robinson, et al. "South-to-North Migration Preceded the Advent of Intensive Farming in the Maya Region." *Nature Communications* 13, no. 1 (December 2022): 1530. https://doi.org/10.1038/s41467-022-29158-y.

Kennett, Douglas J., Keith M. Prufer, Brendan J. Culleton, Richard J. George, Mark Robinson, Willa R. Trask, Gina M. Buckley, et al. "Early Isotopic Evidence for Maize as a Staple Grain in the Americas." *Science Advances* 6, no. 23 (2020): eaba3245. https://doi.org/10.1126/sciadv.aba3245.

Kepecs, Susan. "Chichen Itza, Tula, and the Epiclassic/Early Postclassic Mesoamerican World System." In *Twin Tollans: Chichén Itzá, Tula, and the Epiclassic to Early Postclassic Mesoamerican World*, edited by Jeffrey K. Kowalski and C. Kristan-Graham, 129–50. Washington, DC: Dumbarton Oaks, 2007.

Kepecs, Susan. "Chikinchel." In *The Postclassic Mesoamerican World*, edited by Michael E Smith and Frances F. Berdan, 259–68. Salt Lake City: University of Utah Press, 2003.

Kepecs, Susan, and Boucher, S. "The Pre-Hispanic Cultivation of Rejolladas and Stone-Lands: New Evidence from Northeast Yucatan." In *The Managed Mosaic: Ancient Maya Agriculture and Resource Use*, edited by Scott L. Fedick, 69–91. Salt Lake City: University of Utah Press, 1996.

Kepecs, Susan, and Marilyn A. Masson. "Political Organization in Yucatán and Belize." In *The Postclassic Mesoamerican World*, edited by Michael E. Smith and Frances F. Berdan, 40–44. Salt Lake City: University of Utah Press, 2003.

Killion, Thomas W. "The Archaeology of Settlement Agriculture." In *Gardens of Prehistory: The Archaeology of Settlement Agriculture in Greater Mesoamerica*, edited by Thomas W. Killion, 1–13. Tuscaloosa: University of Alabama Press, 1992.

Kim, Nam C., Christopher Hernandez, Justin Bracken, and Kenneth Seligson. "Cultural Dimensions of Warfare in the Maya World." *Ancient Mesoamerica*, Forthcoming.

Kingery, W. David, Pamela B. Vandiver, and Martha Prickett. "The Beginnings of Pyrotechnology, Part II: Production and Use of Lime and Gypsum Plaster in the Pre-Pottery Neolithic near East." *Journal of Field Archaeology* 15, no. 2 (1988): 219–44.

Krause, Samantha, Timothy Beach, Sheryl Luzzadder-Beach, Thomas H. Guderjan, Fred Valdez, Sara Eshleman, Colin Doyle, and Steven R. Bozarth. "Ancient Maya Wetland Management in Two Watersheds in Belize: Soils, Water, and Paleoenvironmental Change." *Quaternary International* 502 (2019): 280–95. https://doi.org/10.1016/j.qua int.2018.10.029.

Krause, Samantha, Timothy P. Beach, Sheryl Luzzadder-Beach, Duncan Cook, Steven R. Bozarth, Fred Valdez, and Thomas H. Guderjan. "Tropical Wetland Persistence Through the Anthropocene: Multiproxy Reconstruction of Environmental Change in a Maya Agroecosystem." *Anthropocene* 34 (2021): 100284. https://doi.org/10.1016/j.anc ene.2021.100284.

Kuil, Linda, Gemma Carr, Alexia Prskawetz, José Luis Salinas, Alberto Viglione, and Günter Blöschl. "Learning from the Ancient Maya: Exploring the Impact of Drought on Population Dynamics." *Ecological Economics* 157 (March 1, 2019): 1–16. https://doi. org/10.1016/j.ecolecon.2018.10.018.

Kunen, Julie L. "Ancient Maya Agricultural Installations and the Development of Intensive Agriculture in NW Belize." *Journal of Field Archaeology* 28, no. 3–4 (2001): 21.

Kunen, Julie L. *Ancient Maya Life in the Far West Bajo: Social and Environmental Change in the Wetlands of Belize.* Tucson: University of Arizona Press, 2004.

Kwak, Myounghai, James A. Kami, and Paul Gepts. "The Putative Mesoamerican Domestication Center of Phaseolus Vulgaris Is Located in the Lerma-Santiago Basin of Mexico." *Crop Science* 49, no. 2 (2009): 554–63. https://doi.org/10.2135/cropsci2 008.07.0421.

Kwoka, Joshua J., Thomas H. Guderjan, Sara Eshleman, Thomas Ruhl, Justin Telepak, Timothy Beach, Sheryl Luzzadder-Beach, Will McClatchey, and Grace Bascopé. "A Multimethod Approach to the Study of Classic Maya Houselots and Land Tenure: Preliminary Results from the Three Rivers Region, Belize." *Journal of Archaeological Science: Reports* 38 (2021). https://doi.org/10.1016/j.jasrep.2021.103049.

Lamoureux-St-Hilaire, Maxime, Scott Macrae, Carmen A. McCane, Evan A. Parker, and Gyles Iannone. "The Last Groups Standing: Living Abandonment at the Ancient Maya Center of Minanha, Belize." *Latin American Antiquity* 26, no. 4 (2015): 550–69. https:// doi.org/10.7183/1045-6635.26.4.550.

Lane, Brian, Vernon L. Scarborough, and Nicholas P. Dunning. "At the Core of Tikal: Terrestrial Sediment Sampling and Water Management." In *Tikal: Paleoecology of an Ancient Maya City*, edited by David L. Lentz, Nicholas P. Dunning, and Vernon L. Scarborough, 46–58. Cambridge: Cambridge University Press, 2015.

LeCount, Lisa J., Chester P. Walker, John H. Blitz, and Ted C. Nelson. "Land Tenure Systems at the Ancient Maya Site of Actuncan, Belize." *Latin American Antiquity* 30, no. 2 (2019): 245–65. https://doi.org/10.1017/laq.2019.16.

Lemonnier, Eva, and Boris Vannière. "Agrarian Features, Farmsteads, and Homesteads in the Rio Bec Nuclear Zone, Mexico." *Ancient Mesoamerica* 24, no. 2 (2013): 397–413. https://doi.org/10.1017/S0956536113000242.

Lentz, David L. "Anthropocentric Foodwebs in the Precolumbian Americas." In *Imperfect Balance: Landscape Transformations in the Pre-Columbian Americas*, edited by David Lentz, 89–120. New York: Columbia University Press, 2000. https://doi.org/10.7312/ lent11156-011.

Lentz, David, L. "Maya Diets of the Rich and Poor: Paleoethnobotanical Evidence from Copán." *Latin American Antiquity* 2 (1991): 269–87.

Lentz, David L. "Plant Resources of the Ancient Maya: The Paleoethnobotanical Evidence." In *Reconstructing Ancient Maya Diet*, edited by Christine D. White, 3–18. Salt Lake City: University of Utah Press, 1999.

Lentz, David L., Marilyn P. Beaudry-Corbett, Maria Luisa Reyna de Aguilar, and Lawrence Kaplan. "Foodstuffs, Forests, Fields, and Shelter: A Paleoethnobotanical Analysis of Vessel Contents from the Ceren Site, El Salvador." *Latin American Antiquity* 7, no. 3 (1996): 247–62. https://doi.org/10.2307/971577.

Lentz, David L., Nicholas P. Dunning, Vernon L. Scarborough, and Liwy Grazioso. "Imperial Resource Management at the Ancient Maya City of Tikal: A Resilience Model of Sustainability and Collapse." *Journal of Anthropological Archaeology* 52 (2018): 113– 22. https://doi.org/10.1016/j.jaa.2018.08.005.

Lentz, David L., Nicholas P. Dunning, Vernon L. Scarborough, Kevin S. Magee, Kim M. Thompson, Eric Weaver, Christopher Carr, et al. "Forests, Fields, and the Edge of

Sustainability at the Ancient Maya City of Tikal." *Proceedings of the National Academy of Sciences* 111, no. 52 (2014a): 18513–18. https://doi.org/10.1073/pnas.1408631111.

Lentz, David L., Elizabeth Graham, Xochitl Vinaja, Venicia Slotten, and Rupal Jain. "Agroforestry and Ritual at the Ancient Maya Center of Lamanai." *Journal of Archaeological Science: Reports* 8 (2016): 284–94. https://doi.org/10.1016/j.jas rep.2016.06.030.

Lentz, David L., Trinity L. Hamilton, Nicholas P. Dunning, Vernon L. Scarborough, Todd P. Luxton, Anne Vonderheide, Eric J. Tepe, et al. "Molecular Genetic and Geochemical Assays Reveal Severe Contamination of Drinking Water Reservoirs at the Ancient Maya City of Tikal." *Scientific Reports* 10, no. 1 (2020): 10316. https://doi.org/10.1038/s41598-020-67044-z.

Lentz, David L., and Brian Hockaday. "Tikal Timbers and Temples: Ancient Maya Agroforestry and the End of Time." *Journal of Archaeological Science* 36, no. 7 (2009): 1342–53. https://doi.org/10.1016/j.jas.2009.01.020.

Lentz, David L., Brian Lane, and Kim Thompson. "Food, Farming, and Forest Management at Aguateca." In *Life and Politics at the Royal Court of Aguateca: Artifacts, Analytical Data, and Synthesis*, edited by Takeshi Inomata and Daniela Triadan, 201–15. Salt Lake City: University of Utah Press, 2014b.

Lentz, David L., Kevin Magee, Eric Weaver, Angela Hood, Carmen E Ramos Hernandez, and Nicholas P Dunning. "Agroforestry and Agricultural Practices of the Ancient Maya at Tikal." In *Tikal, Paleoecology of an Ancient Maya City*, edited by David L. Lentz, Nicholas P. Dunning, and Vernon L. Scarborough, 35, 152–85. Cambridge: Cambridge University Press, 2015.

Lentz, David L., and Carlos R. Ramírez-Sosa. "Cerén Plant Resources: Abundance and Diversity." In *Before the Volcano Erupted: The Ancient Ceren Village in Central America*, edited by Payson Sheets, 33–42. Austin: University of Texas Press, 2002.

Lentz, David L., Jason Yaeger, Cynthia Robin, and Wendy Ashmore. "Pine, Prestige and Politics of the Late Classic Maya at Xunantunich, Belize." *Antiquity* 79 (2005): 573–85.

Lentz, David, L. Woods, A. Hood, and M. Murph. "Agroforestry and Agricultural Production of the Ancient Maya at Chan." In *Chan: An Ancient Maya Farming Community*, edited by Cynthia Robin, 89–109. Gainesville: University Press of Florida, 2012.

Levi, Laura J. "Sustainable Production and Residential Variation: A Historical Perspective on Pre-Hispanic Domestic Economies in the Maya Lowlands." In *The Managed Mosaic: Ancient Maya Agriculture and Resource Management*, edited by Scott L. Fedick, 92–106. Salt Lake City: University of Utah Press, 1996.

Levy Tacher, Samuel, J. R. Aguirre Rivera, M. M. Martinez Romero, and A. Duran Fernandez. "Caracterizacion Del Uso Tradicional de La Flora Espontanea En La Comunidad Lacandona de Lacanha, Chiapas, Mexico." *Interciencia* 27 (2002): 512–20.

Levy Tacher, Samuel, and Efrain Hernandez Xolocotzi. "Aprovechamiento Forestal Tradicional de Los Hubches En Yucatán." In *La Milpa En Yucatán: Un Sistema de Producción Agrícola Tradicional*, edited by Efrain Hernandez Xolocotzi, E. Bello Baltazar, and Samuel Levy Tacher, 1:247–70. Mexico City: Colegio de Postgraduados, 1995.

Leyden, B. "Pollen Evidence for Climatic Variability and Cultural Disturbance in the Maya Lowlands." *Ancient Mesoamerica* 13 (2002): 85–101.

Leyden, B., Mark Brenner, and Bruce H. Dahlin. "Cultural and Climatic History of Cobá, a Lowland Maya City in Quintana Roo, Mexico." *Quaternary Research* 49 (1998): 111–22.

Liendo Stuardo, Rodrigo. "An Archaeological Study of Settlement Distribution in the Palenque Area, Chiapas, Mexico." *Anthropological Notebooks* 11 (2005): 31–44.

Littmann, Edwin R. "Ancient Mesoamerican Mortars, Plasters, and Stuccos: Comalcalco, Part I." *American Antiquity* 23, no. 2Part1 (1957): 135–40. https://doi.org/10.2307/276436.

Littmann, Edwin R. "Ancient Mesoamerican Mortars, Plasters, and Stuccos: The Composition and Origin of Sascab." *American Antiquity* 24, no. 2 (1958): 172–76. https://doi.org/10.2307/277478.

Littmann, Edwin R. "Ancient Mesoamerican Mortars, Plasters, and Stuccos: The Puuc Area." *American Antiquity* 25, no. 3 (1960b): 407–12. https://doi.org/10.2307/277528.

Littmann, Edwin R. "Ancient Mesoamerican Mortars, Plasters, and Stuccos: The Use of Bark Extracts in Lime Plasters." *American Antiquity* 25, no. 4 (1960a): 593–97. https://doi.org/10.2307/276642.

Lohse, Jon C. "Archaic Origins of the Lowland Maya." *Latin American Antiquity* 21, no. 3 (2010): 312–52.

Lohse, Jon C., and Jaime J. Awe. "In Search of the First Belizeans: The Paleo-Indian and Archaic Hunter-Gatherers of Belize." *Belizean Studies* 29 (2007): 29–49.

Lohse, Jon C., and Patrick N. Findlay. "A Classic Maya House-Lot Drainage System in Northwestern Belize." *Latin American Antiquity* 11 (2000): 175–85.

Lohse, Jon C., and Fred Valdez, Jr., eds. *Ancient Maya Commoners*. Austin: University of Texas Press, 2004.

Lopez Austin, Alfredo. "Cosmovision." In *The Oxford Encyclopedia of Mesoamerican Cultures: The Civilizations of Mexico and Central America*, edited by David Carrasco, 268–74. Oxford: Oxford University Press, 2001.

Lucero, Lisa J. "The Collapse of the Classic Maya: A Case for the Role of Water Control. *American Anthropologist* 104, no. 3 (2002): 814-26.

Lucero, Lisa J. "Agricultural Intensification, Water, and Political Power in the Southern Maya Lowlands." In *Agricultural Strategies*, edited by Joyce Marcus and Charles Stanish, 281–305. Los Angeles: The Cotsen Institute of Archaeology. UCLA, Los Angeles, 2006.

Lucero, Lisa J. "A Cosmology of Conservation in the Ancient Maya World." *Journal of Anthropological Research* 74, no. 3 (2018): 327–59. https://doi.org/10.1086/698698.

Lucero, Lisa J. "Water Control and Maya Politics in the Southern Maya Lowlands." *Archeological Papers of the American Anthropological Association* 9, no. 1 (1999): 35–49. https://doi.org/10.1525/ap3a.1999.9.1.35.

Lucero, Lisa J., Scott L. Fedick, Nicholas P. Dunning, David L. Lentz, and Vernon L. Scarborough. "3 Water and Landscape: Ancient Maya Settlement Decisions." *Archeological Papers of the American Anthropological Association* 24, no. 1 (2014): 30–42.

Lucero, Lisa J., Joel D. Gunn, and Vernon L. Scarborough. "Climate Change and Classic Maya Water Management." *Water* 3 (2011): 479–94.

Lundell, Cyrus. *The Vegetation of Petén: With an Appendix: Studies of Mexican and Central American Plants*. Vol. 1. Washington, DC: Carnegie Institution of Washington, 1937.

Luzzadder-Beach, Sheryl. "Water Resources of the Chunchucmil Maya." *The Geographical Review* 90 (2001): 493–510.

Luzzadder-Beach, Sheryl, and Timothy Beach. "Arising from the Wetlands, Mechanisms and Chronology of Landscape Aggradation in the Northern Coastal Plain of Belize." *Annals of the American Association of Geographers* 99, no. 1 (2009): 1–26.

Luzzadder-Beach, Sheryl, and Timothy Beach. "Hydrology on the Edge of the Chicxulub Crater: Chunchucmil and Ucí-Cansahcab Groundwater Resources." In *Ancient Maya Commerce: Multidisciplinary Research at Chunchucmil*, edited by Scott R. Hutson, 157–67. Boulder: University Press of Colorado, 2017. https://doi.org/10.5876/9781607325 550.c007.

Luzzadder-Beach, Sheryl, and Timothy Beach. "Water Chemistry Constraints and Possibilities for Ancient and Contemporary Maya Wetlands." *Journal of Ethnobiology* 28, no. 2 (2008): 211–30. https://doi.org/10.2993/0278-0771-28.2.211.

Luzzadder-Beach, Sheryl, Timothy Beach, Thomas Garrison, Stephen Houston, James Doyle, Edwin Román, Steven Bozarth, Richard Terry, Samantha Krause, and Jonathan Flood. "Paleoecology and Geoarchaeology at El Palmar and the El Zotz Region, Guatemala." *Geoarchaeology* 32, no. 1 (2017): 90–106. https://doi.org/10.1002/gea.21587.

Luzzadder-Beach, Sheryl, Timothy Beach, Scott Hutson, and Samantha Krause. "Sky-Earth, Lake-Sea: Climate and Water in Maya History and Landscape." *Antiquity* 90, no. 350 (2016): 426–42. https://doi.org/10.15184/aqy.2016.38.

Luzzadder-Beach, Sheryl, Timothy P. Beach, and Nicholas P. Dunning. "Wetland Farming and the Early Anthropocene: Globally Upscaling from the Maya Lowlands with LiDAR and Multiproxy Verification." *Annals of the American Association of Geographers* 111, no. 3 (2021): 795–807. https://doi.org/10.1080/24694452.2020.1820310.

Luzzadder-Beach, Sheryl, Timothy P. Beach, and Nicholas P. Dunning. "Wetland Fields as Mirrors of Drought and the Maya Abandonment." *Proceedings of the National Academy of Sciences* 109, no. 10 (2012): 3646–51. https://doi.org/10.1073/pnas.1114919109.

MacKinnon, J. Jefferson, and Emily M. May. "Small-Scale Maya Lime Making in Belize: Ancient and Modern." *Ancient Mesoamerica* 1, no. 2 (1990): 197–203. https://doi.org/10.1017/S0956536100000213.

Macrae, Scott, and Gyles Iannone. "Investigations of the Agricultural Terracing Surrounding the Ancient Maya Centre of Minanha, Belize." *Research Reports in Belizean Archaeology* 8 (2011): 183–97.

Macrae, Scott, and Gyles Iannone. "Understanding Ancient Maya Agricultural Terrace Systems Through Lidar and Hydrological Mapping." *Advances in Archaeological Practice* 4, no. 3 (2016): 371–92. https://doi.org/10.7183/2326-3768.4.3.371.

Magaloni, Diana. "El Espacio Pictórico Teotihuacano: Tradición y Técnica." In *La Pintura Mural Prehispánica En México: Teotihuacán*, edited by B. de la Fuente, 187–225. Mexico City: Universidad Nacional Autonoma de Mexico, Instituto de Investigaciones Estéticas, 1996.

Magaloni, Diana. "La Técnica Pictórica en el área maya." In *La Pintura Mural Prehispánica En México II: Area Maya Book III Estudios*, edited by B. de la Fuente, 155-98. Mexico City: Instituto de Investigaciones Estéticas, Universidad Nacional Autonoma de Mexico, 2001.

Magnoni, Aline, Travis W. Stanton, Nicolas Barth, Juan Carlos Fernandez-Diaz, José Francisco Osorio León, Francisco Pérez Ruíz, and Jessica A. Wheeler. "Detection Thresholds of Archaeological Features in Airborne Lidar Data from Central Yucatán." *Advances in Archaeological Practice* 4, no. 3 (2016): 232–48. https://doi.org/10.7183/2326-3768.4.3.232.

Maler, Teobert. *Peninsula Yucatan*. Edited by Hans J. Prem. 3 vols. Berlin: Ibero-Amerikanisches Institut, 1997.

Marcus, Joyce, and Kent Flannery. *Zapotec Civilization: How Urban Society Evolved in Mexico's Oaxaca Valley.* London: Thames and Hudson, 1996.

Martin, Simon. *Ancient Maya Politics: A Political Anthropology of the Classic Period 150– 900 CE.* New York: Cambridge University Press, 2020.

Martin, Simon. "Cacao in Ancient Maya Religion: First Fruit from the Maize Tree and Other Tales from the Underworld." In *Chocolate in Mesoamerica: A Cultural History of Cacao,* edited by Cameron L. McNeil, 154–83. Gainesville: University Press of Florida, 2006.

Martin, Simon, and Nikolai Grube. *Chronicle of the Maya Kings and Queens: Deciphering the Dynasties of the Ancient Maya.* Second edition. London: Thames and Hudson, 2008.

Masson, Marilyn A. *In the Realm of Nachan Kan: Postclassic Maya Archaeology at Laguna de On, Belize.* Boulder: University Press of Colorado, 2000.

Masson, Marilyn A. "Maya Collapse Cycles." *Proceedings of the National Academy of Sciences* 109, no. 45 (2012): 18237–38. https://doi.org/10.1073/pnas.1213638109.

Masson, Marilyn A., Timothy S. Hare, and Carlos Peraza Lope. "Postclassic Maya Society Regenerated at Mayapan." In *After Collapse: The Regeneration of Complex Societies,* edited by Glenn M. Schwartz and John J. Nichols, 189–207. Tucson: University of Arizona Press, 2006.

Masson, Marilyn A., Timothy S. Hare, Carlos Peraza Lope, Barbara Escamilla Ojeda, Elizabeth H. Paris, Betsy Kohut, Bradley Russell, and Wilberth Cruz Alvarado. "Household Craft Production in the Prehispanic Urban Setting of Mayapan, Yucatan, Mexico." *Journal of Archaeological Research* 24, no. 3 (2016): 229–74.

Matheny, Ray T. "Northern Maya Lowland Water Control Systems." In *Pre-Hispanic Maya Agriculture,* edited by P. D. Harrison and Billie L. Turner, 185–210. Albuquerque: University of New Mexico Press, 1978.

Matheny, Ray T., Deanne L. Gurr, Donald W. Forsyth, and F. Richard Hauck. *Investigations at Edzna, Campeche, Mexico.* Vol. 1. Papers of the New World Archaeological Foundation. Provo, UT: New World Archaeological Foundation, Brigham Young University, 1983.

Mathews, Jennifer P. "Radiocarbon Dating of Architectural Mortar: A Case Study in the Maya Region, Quintana Roo, Mexico." *Journal of Field Archaeology* 28, no. 3–4 (2001): 395–400. https://doi.org/10.1179/jfa.2001.28.3-4.395.

Matsumoto, Mallory E. "La estela de Iximche' en el contexto de la revitalización lingüística y la recuperación jeroglífica en las comunidades mayas de guatemala." *Estudios de Cultura Maya* 45, no. 45 (2015): 225–58. https://doi.org/10.1016/S0185-2574 (15)30008-3.

Matsuoka, Yoshihiro, Yves Vigouroux, and Major M Goodman. "A Single Domestication for Maize Shown by Multilocus Microsatellite Genotyping." *Proceedings of the National Academy of Sciences* 99, no. 9 (2002): 6080–84.

McAnany, Patricia A. *Living with the Ancestors: Kinship and Kingship in Ancient Maya Society.* Austin: University of Texas Press, 1995.

McAnany, Patricia A. "Obscured by the Forest: Property and Ancestors in Lowland Maya Society." In *Property in Economic Context,* edited by R. C. Hunt and A. Gilman, 73–87. Lanham, MD: University Press of America, 1998.

McAnany, Patricia A. "Water Storage in the Puuc Region of the Northern Maya Lowlands: A Key to Population Estimates and Architectural Variability." In *Precolumbian Population History in the Maya Lowlands,* edited by T. Patrick Culbert and Don S. Rice, 263–99. Albuquerque: University of New Mexico Press, 1990.

McAnany, Patricia A., and Tomás Gallareta Negrón. "Bellicose Rulers and Climatological Peril? Retrofitting Twenty-First Century Woes on Eighth-Century Maya Society." In *Questioning Collapse: Human Resilience, Ecological Vulnerability, and the Aftermath of Empire*, edited by Patricia A. McAnany and Norman Yoffee, 142–75. Cambridge: Cambridge University Press, 2010.

McAnany, Patricia A. "Terminal Classic Maya Heterodoxy and Shrine Vernacularism in the Sibun Valley, Belize." *Cambridge Archaeological Journal* 22, no. 1 (2012): 115–34.

McKillop, Heather. "Ancient Mariners on the Belize Coast: Salt, Stingrays, and Seafood." *Belizean Studies* 29 (2007): 15–28.

McKillop, Heather. "Ancient Maya Canoe Navigation and Its Implications for Classic to Postclassic Maya Economy and Sea Trade: A View from the South Coast of Belize." *Journal of Caribbean Archaeology: Special Publication* 3 (2010): 93–105.

McKillop, Heather. "Finds in Belize Document Late Classic Maya Salt Making and Canoe Transport." *Proceedings of the National Academy of Sciences* 102 (2005): 5630–34.

McKillop, Heather. "Mapping Ancient Maya Wooden Architecture on the Sea Floor, Belize." *ACUA Underwater Archaeology Proceedings 2009* (2009): 277–86.

McKillop, Heather. *Maya Salt Works.* Gainesville: University Press of Florida, 2019.

McKillop, Heather. "Salt as a Commodity or Money in the Classic Maya Economy." *Journal of Anthropological Archaeology* 62 (2021): 101277. https://doi.org/10.1016/j.jaa.2021.101277.

McKillop, Heather. *Salt: White Gold of the Ancient Maya.* Gainesville: University Press of Florida, 2002.

McKillop, Heather. "Underwater Archaeology, Salt Production, and Coastal Maya Trade at Stingray Lagoon, Belize." *Latin American Antiquity* 6, no. 3 (1995): 214–28. https://doi.org/10.2307/971673.

McKillop, Heather, and Kazuo Aoyama. "Salt and Marine Products in the Classic Maya Economy from Use-Wear Study of Stone Tools." *Proceedings of the National Academy of Sciences* 115, no. 43 (2018): 10948–52. https://doi.org/10.1073/pnas.1803639115.

McNeil, C. L., D. A. Burney, and L. P. Burney. "Evidence Disputing Deforestation as the Cause for the Collapse of the Ancient Maya Polity of Copan, Honduras." *Proceedings of the National Academy of Sciences* 107, no. 3 (2010): 1017–22. https://doi.org/10.1073/pnas.0904760107.

McNeil, Cameron L. "Deforestation, Agroforestry, and Sustainable Land Management Practices Among the Classic Period Maya." *Quaternary International* 249 (2012): 19–30. https://doi.org/10.1016/j.quaint.2011.06.055.

Medina-Elizalde, M., and E. J. Rohling. "Collapse of Classic Maya Civilization Related to Modest Reduction in Precipitation." *Science* 335, no. 6071 (2012): 956–59. https://doi.org/10.1126/science.1216629.

Medina-Elizalde, Martín, Stephen J. Burns, David W. Lea, Yemane Asmerom, Lucien von Gunten, Victor Polyak, Mathias Vuille, and Ambarish Karmalkar. "High Resolution Stalagmite Climate Record from the Yucatán Peninsula Spanning the Maya Terminal Classic Period." *Earth and Planetary Science Letters* 298, no. 1–2 (2010): 255–62. https://doi.org/10.1016/j.epsl.2010.08.016.

Medina-Elizalde, Martin, Stephen J. Burns, Josue M. Polanco-Martinez, Timothy P. Beach, Fernanda Lases-Hernandez, Chuan-Chou Shen, and Hao-Cheng Wang. "High-Resolution Speleothem Record of Precipitation from the Yucatan Peninsula Spanning the Maya Preclassic Period." *Global and Planetary Change* 138 (2016): 93–102.

Meehan Hermanson, Patricia, and Alejandra Alonso Olvera. "Los Recubrimientos de Proteccion y Sacrificio Como Alternativa de Conservación in Situ Para Monumentos Históricos y Arqueológicos." In *La Cal: Historia, Propiedades y Usos*, edited by Luis Barba Pingarrón and Isabel Villaseñor, 203–32. Mexico City: Universidad Nacional Autonoma de Mexico, Instituto de Investigaciones Antropologicas, 2013.

Meléndez Guadarrama, L., and J. Hirose López. "Patrones Culinarios Asociados al Camote (Ipomaoea Batatas) y La Yucca (Manihot Esculenta) Entre Los Maya Yucatecos, Ch'oles y Huastecos." *Estudios de Cultura Maya* 52 (2018): 193–226.

Middleton, Guy D. "Nothing Lasts Forever: Environmental Discourses on the Collapse of Past Societies." *Journal of Archaeological Research* 20, no. 3 (2012): 257–307. https://doi.org/10.1007/s10814-011-9054-1.

Milbrath, Susan, and Carlos Peraza Lope. "Survival and Revival of Terminal Classic Traditions at Postclassic Mayapán." *Latin American Antiquity* 20, no. 4 (2009): 581–606. https://doi.org/10.1017/S1045663500002881.

Millon, Rene F. "When Money Grew on Trees: A Study of Cacao in Ancient Mesoamerica." PhD diss., Columbia University, 1955.

Mora-Aviles, Alejandra, Bibiana Lemus-Flores, Rita Miranda-Lopez, David Hernandez-Lopez, Jose L. Pons-Hernandez, Jorge A. Acosta-Gallegos, and Salvador H. Guzman-Maldonado. "Effects of Common Bean Enrichment on Nutritional Quality of Tortillas Produced from Nixtamalized Regular and Quality Protein Maize Flours." *Journal of the Science of Food and Agriculture* 87 (2007): 880-86.

Morehart, Christopher. *Food, Fire and Fragrance. Paleoethnobotanical Perspectives on Classic Maya Cave Rituals*. BAR International Series 2186. Oxford: Archaeopress, 2011.

Morell-Hart, Shanti. "Plant Foodstuffs of the Ancient Maya: Agents and Matter, Medium and Message." In *Her Cup for Sweet Cacao: Food in Ancient Maya Society*, edited by Traci Ardren, 124–60. Austin: University of Texas Press, 2020.

Morell-Hart, Shanti, Rosemary A. Joyce, John S. Henderson, and Rachel Cane. "Ethnoecology in Pre-Hispanic Central America: Foodways and Human-Plant Interfaces." *Ancient Mesoamerica* 30, no. 3 (2019): 535–53. https://doi.org/10.1017/S0956536119000014.

Morello, Ted. "Metropolis of the Great Maya Civilizationn." *New York Times*, February 1, 1959, sec. Archives. https://www.nytimes.com/1959/02/01/archives/metropolis-of-the-great-maya-civilization.html.

Morley, Sylvanus Griswold. *The Ancient Maya*. Redwood City, CA: Stanford University Press, 1946.

Morley, Sylvanus Griswold. "The Rise and Fall of the Maya Civilization in the Light of the Monuments and the Native Chronicles." In *Proceedings of the Nineteenth Congress of Americanists*, edited by F.W. Hodge, 138–49. Congress of Americanists: Washington, DC, 1917.

Morris, Earl H., Jean Charlot, and Ann A. Morris. *The Temple of the Warriors*. New York: Charles Scribner's Sons, 1931.

Morrison, Bethany A., and Roberto Cozatl-Manzano. "Initial Evidence for Use of Periphyton as an Agricultural Fertilizer by the Ancient Maya Associated with the El Eden Wetland, Northern Quintana Roo, Mexico." In *The Lowland Maya Area: Three Millennia at the Human–Wildland Interface*, edited by Arturo Gomez-Pompa, Scott L. Fedick, and Juan J. Jiménez-Osornio, 401–14. New York: Food Products Press, 2003.

Moyes, Holley, and James Brady. "Caves as Sacred Space in Mesoamerica." In *Sacred Darkness: A Global Perspective on the Ritual Use of Caves*, edited by Holley Moyes, 151–70. Boulder: University Press of Colorado, 2012.

Moyes, Holley, and Shane Montgomery. "Mapping Ritual Landscapes Using Lidar: Cave Detection Through Local Relief Modeling." *Advances in Archaeological Practice* 4, no. 3 (2016): 249–67. https://doi.org/10.7183/2326-3768.4.3.249.

Munro, Lisa. "Crafting the Secrets of the Ancient Maya: Media Representations of Archaeological Exploration and the Cultural Politics of US Informal Empire in 1920s Yucatan." *Bulletin of the History of Archaeology* 31, no. 1 (May 10, 2021): 3. https://doi.org/10.5334/bha-652.

Munro-Stasiuk, Mandy J., T. Kam Manahan, Trent Stockton, and Traci Ardren. "Spatial and Physical Characteristics of Rejolladas in Northern Yucatán, Mexico: Implications for Ancient Maya Agriculture and Settlement Patterns." *Geoarchaeology* 29, no. 2 (2014): 156–72. https://doi.org/10.1002/gea.21468.

Murata, Satoru. "Maya Salters, Maya Potters: The Archaeology of Multicrafting on Non-Residential Mounds at Wits Cah Ak'al, Belize." PhD diss., Boston University, 2011.

Murtha, Timothy. *Land and Labor: Maya Terraced Agriculture: An Investigation of the Settlement Economy and Intensive Agricultural Landscape of Caracol, Belize.* Saarbrücken: DM Verlag Dr. Müller, 2009.

Nations, James D., and Ronald Nigh. "The Evolutionary Potential of Lacandon Maya Sustained-Yield Tropical Forest Agriculture." *Journal of Anthropological Research* 36, no. 1 (1980): 1–30. https://doi.org/10.1086/jar.36.1.3629550.

Neff, Hector, Deborah M. Pearsall, John G. Jones, Barbara Arroyo, Shawn K. Collins, and Dorothy Freidel. "Early Maya Adaptive Patterns: Mid-Late Holocene Paleoenvironmental Evidence from Pacific Guatemala." *Latin American Antiquity* 17, no. 3 (2006): 287–315.

Neff, L. Theodore. "Population, Intensive Agriculture, Labor Value, and Elite-Commoner Political Power in the Xunantunich Hinterlands." In *Classic Maya Provincial Politics: Xunantunich and Its Hinterlands*, edited by Lisa J. LeCount and Jason Yaeger, 250–71. Tucson: University of Arizona Press, 2010.

Neff, L. Theodore, Cynthia Robin, Kevin Schwarz, and Mary K. Morrison. "The Xunantunich Settlement Survey." In *Report of the Xunantunich Archaeological Project 1995 Field Season*, edited by Richard Leventhal, 139–63. Los Angeles: University of California, 1995.

Nelson, Ben A., Adrian S. Z. Chase, and Michelle Hegmon. "Transformative Relocation in the U.S. Southwest and Mesoamerica: Transformative Relocation." *Archeological Papers of the American Anthropological Association* 24, no. 1 (2014): 171–82. https://doi.org/10.1111/apaa.12036.

New York Times. "MAYA CIVILIZATION." October 8, 1929, sec. Archives. https://www.nytimes.com/1929/10/08/archives/maya-civilization.html.

New York Times. "TEMPLES OF ANCIENT MAYA; RUINS OF UXMAL, CAPITAL OF A GREAT RACE. WHERE MAYA MAIDENS DWELT IN CLOISTER AND HUMAN LIVES WERE SACRIFICED TO GODS OF STONE." March 9, 1890, sec. Archives. https://www.nytimes.com/1890/03/09/archives/temples-of-ancient-maya-ruins-of-uxmal-capital-of-a-great-race.html.

New York Times. "TWO TOMBS SHED LIGHT ON MAYANS; Discoveries at Tikal Hold Skeletons of 5 Indians." December 6, 1964, sec. Archives. https://www.nytimes.com/

1964/12/06/archives/two-tombs-shed-light-on-mayans-discoveries-at-tikal-hold-skeletons.html.

Nigh, Ronald B., and S. A. W. Diemont. "The Maya Milpa: Fire and the Legacy of Living Soil." *Frontiers in Ecology and the Environment* 11, no. s1 (2013): e45–54.

Nobel, P. S. *Environmental Biology of Agaves and Cacti.* New York: Cambridge University Press, 1988.

Nondédéo, P., A. Patiño, and J. Sion. "Crisis Múltiples En Naachtun: Aprovechadas, Superadas e Irreversibles." In *Millenary Maya Societies: Past Crises and Resilience,* Papers from the International Colloquium, edited by M. Charlotte Arnauld and A. Breton, 120–47. MesoWeb, 2013.

Nooren, Kees, Wim Z. Hoek, Brian J. Dermody, Didier Galop, Sarah Metcalfe, Gerald Islebe, and Hans Middelkoop. "Climate Impact on the Development of Pre-Classic Maya Civilisation." *Climate of the Past* 14, no. 8 (2018): 1253–73. https://doi.org/10.5194/cp-14-1253-2018.

Normile, D. "SNP Study Supports Southern Migration Route to Asia." *Science* 326, no. 5959 (2009): 1470–1470. https://doi.org/10.1126/science.326.5959.1470.

Ocampo Rosales, Genova R. "Medicinal Uses of Melipona Beechii Honey, by the Ancient Maya." In *Pot-Honey: A Legacy of Stingless Bees,* edited by Patricia Vit, Silvia R. M. Pedro, and David W. Roubik, 229–39. New York: Springer, 2013.

Oglesby, R. J., T. L. Sever, W. Saturno, D. J. Erickson, and J. Srikishen III. "Collapse of the Maya: Could Deforestation Have Contributed?" *Journal of Geophysical Research* 115, no. D12106 (2010): 1–10.

Ortega, L. M., S. Avendano, Arturo Gomez-Pompa, and E. Ucan Ek. "Los Solares de Chunchucmil, Yucatan, Mexico." *Biotica, Nueva Epoca* 1 (1993): 37–51.

Ortiz Ruiz, Soledad. "Caracterización de Las Estructuras Anulares de La Región Del Occidente de Las Tierras Bajas Mayas." MA diss., El Colegio de Michoacan A.C., Centro de Estudios Arqueologicos, n.d.

Ortiz Ruiz, Soledad. "El Conocimiento Pirotecnologico de La Sociedad Maya Prehispanica: Estudio de Los Hornos Para Cal En Las Tierras Bajas Mayas Del Norte." PhD diss, Universidad Nacional Autonoma de Mexico, 2019.

Ortiz Ruiz, Soledad, Avto Goguitchaichvili, and Juan Morales. "Sobre la edad de los hornos de cal en el área maya." *Arqueologia Iberoamericana* 28 (2015): 9–15.

Paap, Iken. "Archaeological Fieldwork in the Transitional Zone Between Puuc and Chenes (Campeche, Mexico)." In *Recent Investigations in the Puuc Region of Yucatan,* edited by Meghan Rubenstein, 87–98. Archaeopress Pre-Columbian Archaeology 8. Oxford: Archaeopress, 2017.

Paap, Iken. "Arquitectura post-monumental en el Puuc y la zona transitoria Puuc-Chenes." *Tambo. Boletín de Arqueología* 3 (2016): 145–72.

Palacios-Mayorga, Ana Luisa Anaya, Eleazar Gonzalez-Velazquez, Lazaro Huerta-Arcos, and Arturo Gomez-Pompa. "Periphyton as a Potential Biofertilizer in Intensive Agriculture of the Ancient Maya." In *The Lowland Maya Area: Three Millennia at the Human–Wildland Interface,* edited by Arturo Gomez-Pompa, Scott L. Fedick, and Juan J. Jiménez-Osornio, 389–400. New York: Food Products Press, 2003.

Paris, Elizabeth H., Carlos Peraza Lope, Marilyn A. Masson, Pedro C. Delgado Kú, and Bárbara C. Escamilla Ojeda. "The Organization of Stingless Beekeeping (Meliponiculture) at Mayapán, Yucatan, Mexico." *Journal of Anthropological Archaeology* 52 (2018): 1–22. https://doi.org/10.1016/j.jaa.2018.07.004.

Pendergast, David M. "Stability Through Change: Lamanai, Belize, from the Ninth to the Seventeenth Century." In *Late Lowland Maya Civilization: Classic to Postclassic*, edited by Jeremy A. Sabloff and E. Wyllys Andrews, 223–49. Albuquerque: University of New Mexico Press, 1985.

Pendergast, David M. "Under Spanish Rule: The Final Chapters in Lamanai's Maya History." *Belcast Journal of Belizean Affairs* 3 (1986): 1–7.

Peraza Lope, Carlos, Marilyn A. Masson, Timothy S. Hare, and Pedro Candelario Delgado Ku. "The Chronology of Mayapan: New Radiocarbon Evidence." *Ancient Mesoamerica* 17 (2006): 153–75.

Pérez-Salicrup, D. "Forest Types and Their Implications." In *Integrated Land-Change Science and Tropical Deforestation in the Southern Yucatan*, edited by Billie L. Turner, J. Geoghagen, and D. R. Foster, 63–80. New York: Oxford University Press, 2004.

Peters, Charles M. "Precolumbian Silviculture and Indigenous Management of Neotropical Forests." In *Imperfect Balance: Landscape Transformations in the Pre-Columbian Americas*, edited by David Lentz, 203–24. New York: Columbia University Press, 2000. https://doi.org/10.7312/lent11156-011.

Pickersgill, Barbara. "Domestication of Plants in the Americas: Insights from Mendelian and Molecular Genetics." *Annals of Botany* 100, no. 5 (2007): 925–40. https://doi.org/10.1093/aob/mcm193.

Piperno, D. R., J. E. Moreno, J. Iriarte, I. Holst, M. Lachniet, J. G. Jones, A. J. Ranere, and R. Castanzo. "Late Pleistocene and Holocene Environmental History of the Iguala Valley, Central Balsas Watershed of Mexico." *Proceedings of the National Academy of Sciences* 104, no. 29 (2007): 11874–81. https://doi.org/10.1073/pnas.0703442104.

Piperno, D. R., A. J. Ranere, I. Holst, J. Iriarte, and R. Dickau. "Starch Grain and Phytolith Evidence for Early Ninth Millennium B.P. Maize from the Central Balsas River Valley, Mexico." *Proceedings of the National Academy of Sciences* 106, no. 13 (2009): 5019–24. https://doi.org/10.1073/pnas.0812525106.

Pohl, Mary D., Paul R. Bloom, and Kevin O. Pope. "Interpretation of Wetland Farming in Northern Belize: Excavations at San Antonio, Rio Hondo." In *Ancient Maya Wetland Agriculture: Excavations on Albion Island, Northern Belize*, edited by Mary D. Pohl, 187–254. Boulder: Westview Press, 1990.

Pohl, Mary D., John G. Jones, John S. Jacob, Dolores R. Piperno, Susan D. deFrance, David L. Lentz, John A. Gifford, Marie E. Danforth, and J. Kathryn Josserand. "Early Agriculture in the Maya Lowlands." *Latin American Antiquity* 7, no. 4 (1996): 355–72.

Pohl, Mary D., and Charles H. Miksicek. "The Development and Impact of Ancient Maya Agriculture: Section A: Cultivation Techniques and Crops." In *Prehistoric Lowland Maya Environment and Subsistence Economy*, edited by Mary D. Pohl, 10–20. Cambridge, MA: Harvard University Press, 1985.

Pope, Kevin O., Mary D. Pohl, John G. Jones, David L. Lentz, Christopher von Nagy, Francisco J. Vega, and Irvy R. Quitmyer. "Origin and Environmental Setting of Ancient Agriculture in the Lowlands of Mesoamerica." *Science* 292 (2001): 1370–73.

Popson, Colleen, and Heather Clagett. "Excavations at Chan Cahal, Blue Creek, the 1997 Field Season." In *The Blue Creek Project, Working Papers from the 1997 Field Season*, edited by W. David Driver, Thomas H. Guderjan, and Helen Haines. San Antonio: Maya Research Program, St. Mary's University, 1998.

Powis, Terry G., W. Jeffrey Hurst, Maria del Carmen Rodriguez, C. Ponciano Ortiz, Michael Blake, David Cheetham, Michael Coe, and John Hodgson. "The Origins of Cacao Use in Mesoamerica." *Mexicon* 30, no. 2 (2008): 35–38.

Prem, Hans J. "A Donde Se Habran Ido Todas Las Piedras? La Profanacion de Edificios Del Clasico Terminal." In *Mayas de Ayer y Hoy: Memorias Del Primer Congreso Internacional de Cultura Maya*, edited by Alfredo Barrera Rubio and Ruth Gubler, 250–74. Merida: INAH, 2006.

Price, T. Douglas, and James H. Burton. *An Introduction to Archaeological Chemistry*. New York: Springer New York, 2011. https://doi.org/10.1007/978-1-4419-6376-5.

Proskouriakoff, Tatiana. "The Death of a Civilization." *Scientific American* 192 (1955): 82–88.

Prufer, Keith, and Amy E. Thompson. "Lidar-Based Analyses of Anthropogenic Landscape Alterations as a Component of the Built Environment." *Advances in Archaeological Practice* 4, no. 3 (2016): 393–409.

Prufer, Keith M., Amy E. Thompson, and Douglas J. Kennett. "Evaluating Airborne LiDAR for Detecting Settlements and Modified Landscapes in Disturbed Tropical Environments at Uxbenka, Belize." *Journal of Archaeological Science* 57 (2015): 1–13.

Puleston, Dennis E. "An Experimental Approach to the Function of Maya Chultuns." *American Antiquity* 36 (1971): 322–35.

Puleston, Dennis E. "Brosimum Alicastrum as a Subsistence Alternative for the Classic Maya of the Central Southern Lowlands." MA thesis, University of Pennsylvania, 1968.

Puleston, Dennis E. "Terracing, Raised Fields, and Tree Cropping in the Maya Lowland: A New Perspective on the Geography of Power." In *Pre-Hispanic Maya Agriculture*, edited by Peter D. Harrison and Billie L. Turner, 225–46. Albuquerque: University of New Mexico Press, 1978.

Rand, Asta J., Carolyn Freiwald, and Vaughan Grimes. "A Multi-Isotopic ($\Delta 13C$, $\Delta 15N$, and $\Delta 34S$) Faunal Baseline for Maya Subsistence and Migration Studies." *Journal of Archaeological Science: Reports* 37 (2021): 102977.

Rapp, George. *Archaeomineralogy*. Natural Science in Archaeology. Berlin, Heidelberg: Springer Berlin Heidelberg, 2009. https://doi.org/10.1007/978-3-540-78594-1.

Redfield, R., and A. Villa Rojas. *Chan Kom: A Maya Village*. Chicago: University of Chicago Press, 1934.

Redman, Charles L. "Resilience Theory in Archaeology." *American Anthropologist* 107, no. 1 (2005): 70–77.

Reents-Budet, Dorie. "The Social Context of Kakaw Drinking Among the Ancient Maya." In *Chocolate in Mesoamerica: A Cultural History of Cacao*, edited by Cameron L. McNeil, 202–23. Jacksonville: University Press of Florida, 2009.

Rensberger, Boyce. "Knowledge of Mayas Greatly Extended; Findings Extend Knowledge of Mayas Five Stages May Be Represented No Pottery Found at Sites." *New York Times*, May 13, 1980, sec. Archives. https://www.nytimes.com/1980/05/13/archives/knowledge-of-mayas-greatly-extended-findings-extend-knowledge-of.html.

Reynolds, Cerisa R. "Fighting Ancient Aliens in the Classroom: Restoring Credit to Peoples of the Past in Introduction to Archaeology Courses." *Teaching Anthropology: Proceedings of the 2015 AAA Meeting* 21, no. 1 (2015): 8.

Rice, Don S. "Classic to Postclassic Maya Household Transitions in the Central Peten, Guatemala." In *Household and Community in the Mesoamerican Past*, edited by Richard R. Wilk and Wendy Ashmore, 227–47. Albuquerque: University of New Mexico Press, 1988.

Rice, Don S. "The Peten Postclassic: A Settlement Perspective." In *Late Lowland Maya Civilization: Classic to Postclassic*, edited by Jeremy A. Sabloff and E. Wyllys Andrews, 301–44. Albuquerque: University of New Mexico Press, 1986.

Rice, Don S. "Roots: Resourceful Maya Farmers Enabled a Mounting Population to Survive in a Fragile Tropical Forest Habitat." *Natural History* 2 (1991): 10–14.

Rice, Don S., and T. Patrick Culbert. "Historical Contexts for Population Reconstruction in the Maya Lowlands." In *Precolumbian Population History in the Maya Lowlands*, edited by T. Patrick Culbert and Don S. Rice, 1–36. Albuquerque: University of New Mexico Press, 1990.

Rice, Prudence M. "Continuities in Maya Political Rhetoric: K'awiils, K'atuns, and Kennings." *Ancient Mesoamerica* 23, no. 1 (2012): 103–14. https://doi.org/10.1017/S0956536112000077.

Rice, Prudence M. "Late Maya Factionalism and Alliances: The Case of Contact-Period Central Petén, Guatemala." *Journal of Anthropological Archaeology* 56 (2019). https://doi.org/10.1016/j.jaa.2019.101083.

Rice, Prudence M., Arthur A. Demarest, and Don S. Rice. "The Terminal Classic and the 'Classic Maya Collapse' in Perspective." In *The Terminal Classic in the Maya Lowlands: Collapse, Transition, and Transformation*, edited by Arthur A. Demarest, Prudence M. Rice, and Don S. Rice, 1–11. Boulder: University Press of Colorado, 2004.

Rice, Prudence M., and Don S. Rice. "Classic-to-Contact-Period Continuities in Maya Governance in Central Petén, Guatemala." *Ethnohistory* 65, no. 1 (2018): 25–50.

Rice, Prudence M., and Don S. Rice. "Late Classic to Postclassic Transformations in the Peten Lakes Region, Guatemala." In *The Terminal Classic in the Maya Lowlands: Collapse, Transition, and Transformation*, edited by Arthur A. Demarest, Prudence M. Rice, and Don S. Rice, 125–39. Boulder: University Press of Colorado, 2004.

Rico-Gray, V., A. Chemás, and S. Mandujano. "Uses of Tropical Deciduous Forest Species by the Yucatecan Maya." *Agroforestry Systems* 14, no. 2 (1991): 149–61. https://doi.org/10.1007/BF00045730.

Ringle, William M. "Debating Chichen Itza." *Ancient Mesoamerica* 28, no. 1 (2017): 119–36. https://doi.org/10.1017/S0956536116000481.

Ringle, William M., Tomás Gallareta Negrón, and George J. Bey III. "Stone for My House: The Economics of Stoneworking and Elite Housing in the Puuc Hills of Yucatán." In *The Real Business of Ancient Maya Economies: From Farmers' Fields to Rulers' Realms*, edited by Marilyn A. Masson, David Freidel, and Arthur A. Demarest, 98–116. Gainesville: University Press of Florida, 2020.

Ringle, William M., Tomás Gallareta Negrón, Rossana May Ciau, Kenneth E. Seligson, Juan C. Fernandez-Diaz, and David Ortegón Zapata. "Lidar Survey of Ancient Maya Settlement in the Puuc Region of Yucatan, Mexico." Edited by Andrea Zerboni. *PLOS ONE* 16, no. 4 (2021): e0249314. https://doi.org/10.1371/journal.pone.0249314.

Ringle, William M., Tomás Gallareta Negrón, Kenneth E. Seligson, and David Vlcek. "Hidden in the Hills No Longer: LiDAR Imaging in the Puuc Region, Yucatan, Mexico." Washington, DC: N.p., 2018.

Ringle, William M., Tomás Gallareta Negrón, and George J. Bey. "The Return of Quetzalcoatl: Evidence for the Spread of a World Religion During the Epiclassic Period." *Ancient Mesoamerica* 9, no. 2 (1998): 183–232. https://doi.org/10.1017/S0956536100001954.

Río, Antonio del, Paul Felix Teatro critico Cabrera, Frédéric de Waldeck, and H. (Henry) Berthoud. *Description of the Ruins of an Ancient City, Discovered Near Palenque, in the Kingdom of Guatemala, in Spanish America:* London: Published by Henry Berthoud, no. 65, Regent's Quadrant, Piccadilly; and Suttaby, Evance and Fox, Stationer's Court, 1822. http://archive.org/details/descriptionofrui00roan_0.

Robin, Cynthia. "Gender, Farming, and Long-Term Change: Maya Historical and Archaeological Perspectives." *Current Anthropology* 47, no. 3 (2006): 409–33. https://doi.org/10.1086/503060.

Robin, Cynthia. "New Directions in Classic Maya Household Archaeology." *Journal of Archaeological Research* 11, no. 4 (2003): 307–56.

Robin, Cynthia. "Of Earth and Stone: The Materiality of Maya Farmers' Everyday Lives at Chan, Belize: The Materiality of Maya Farmers' Everyday Lives at Chan, Belize." *Archeological Papers of the American Anthropological Association* 26, no. 1 (2015): 40–52. https://doi.org/10.1111/apaa.12066.

Robin, Cynthia. "Peopling the Past: New Perspectives on the Ancient Maya." *Proceedings of the National Academy of Sciences* 98 (2001): 18–21.

Robin, Cynthia, Jason Yaeger, and Wendy Ashmore. "Living in the Hinterlands of a Provincial Polity." In *Classic Maya Provincial Politics*, edited by Lisa J. LeCount and Jason Yaeger, 315–33. Tucson: University of Arizona Press, 2010.

Robinson, Mark, and Heather McKillop. "Ancient Maya Wood Selection and Forest Exploitation: A View from the Paynes Creek Salt Works, Belize." *Journal of Archaeological Science* 40 (2013): 3584–95.

Robinson, Mark, and Heather McKillop. "Fuelling the Ancient Maya Salt Industry." *Economic Botany* 68, no. 1 (2014): 96–108. https://doi.org/10.1007/s12231-014-9263-x.

Rodriguez-Alegria, Enrique. "From Grinding Corn to Dishing Out Money: A Long-Term History of Cooking in Xaltocan, Mexico." In *The Menial Art of Cooking: Archaeoogical Studies of Cooking and Food Preparation*, edited by Sarah R. Graff and Enrique Rodriguez-Alegria, 99–117. Boulder: University Press of Colorado, 2012.

Rosenmeier, Michael F., David A. Hodell, Mark Brenner, and Jason H. Curtis. "A 4000-Year Lacustrine Record of Environmental Change in the Southern Maya Lowlands, Peten, Guatemala." *Quaternary Research* 57 (2002): 183–90.

Rosenswig, Robert M., Deborah M. Pearsall, Marilyn A. Masson, Brendan J. Culleton, and Douglas J. Kenneth. "Archaic Period Settlement and Subsistence in the Maya Lowlands: New Starch Grain and Lithic Data from Freshwater Creek, Belize." *Journal of Archaeological Science* 41 (2014): 308–21.

Ross, Nanci J. "Modern Tree Species Composition Reflects Ancient Maya 'Forest Gardens' in Northwest Belize." *Ecological Applications* 21, no. 1 (2011): 75–84. https://doi.org/10.1890/09-0662.1.

Ross, Nanci J., and Thiago F. Rangel. "Ancient Maya Agroforestry Echoing Through Spatial Relationships in the Extant Forest of NW Belize: Ancient Agroforestry Impacting Spatial Patterns." *Biotropica* 43, no. 2 (2011): 141–48. https://doi.org/10.1111/j.1744-7429.2010.00666.x.

Roys, Ralph. *The Ethno-Botany of the Maya.* Chicago: University of Chicago Press, 1931.

Rue, David J. "Early Agriculture and Early Postclassic Occupation in Western Honduras." *Nature* 326, no. 6110 (1987): 285–86.

Runyan, Christiane W., Paulo D'Odorico, and Deborah Lawrence. "Physical and biological feedbacks of deforestation." *Reviews of Geophysics* 50, no. 4 (2012): 1–32.

Rushton, Elizabeth A. C., Bronwen S. Whitney, and Sarah E. Metcalfe. "A Tale of Maize, Palm, and Pine: Changing Socio-Ecological Interactions from Pre-Classic Maya to the Present Day in Belize." *Quaternary* 3, no. 4 (October 17, 2020): 30. https://doi.org/10.3390/quat3040030.

Rushton, Elizabeth A. C., Sarah E. Metcalfe, and Bronwen S. Whitney. "A Late-Holocene Vegetation History from the Maya Lowlands, Lamanai, Northern Belize." *The Holocene* 23, no. 4 (2012): 485–93. https://doi.org/10.1177/0959683612465449.

Russell, Bradley, and Bruce H. Dahlin. "Traditional Burnt-Lime Production at Mayapán, Mexico." *Journal of Field Archaeology* 32, no. 4 (2007): 407–23.

Sabloff, Jeremy A. "It Depends on How We Look at Things: New Perspectives on the Postclassic Period in the Northern Maya Lowlands." *Proceedings of the American Philosophical Society* 151, no. 1 (2007): 11–26.

Sabloff, Jeremy A., and William L. Rathje. "The Rise of a Maya Merchant Class." *Scientific American* 233, no. 4 (1975): 72–82. https://doi.org/10.1038/scientificamerican1075-72.

Sabloff, Jeremy A., and Gair Tourtellot, eds. *The Ancient Maya City of Sayil: The Mapping of a Puuc Region Center*. New Orleans: Middle American Research Institute, Tulane University, 1991.

Santiago, Cybele Celestino, and Mario Mendonca. "Organic Additives in Brazilian Lime Mortars." In *Lime and Other Alternative Cements*, edited by N. Hill, S. Holmes, and D. Mather, 203–10. London: Intermediate Technology, 1992.

Santini, Lauren Mee. "The Fabricated Forest." PhD diss., Harvard University, 2015.

Santley, Robert S., Thomas W. Killion, and Mark T. Lycett. "On the Maya Collapse." *Journal of Anthropological Research* 42, no. 2 (1986): 123–59.

Saturno, W. A. "Early Maya Writing at San Bartolo, Guatemala." *Science* 311, no. 5765 (March 3, 2006): 1281–83. https://doi.org/10.1126/science.1121745.

Scarborough, V. L., and G. G. Gallopin. "A Water Storage Adaptation in the Maya Lowlands." *Science* 251, no. 4994 (1991): 658–62. https://doi.org/10.1126/science.251.4994.658.

Scarborough, Vernon L. "Colonizing a Landscape: Water and Wetlands in Ancient Mesoamerica." In *The Political Economy of Ancient Mesoamerica: Transformations During the Formative and Classic Periods*, edited by Vernon L. Scarborough and John Clark, 163–74. Albuquerque: University of New Mexico Press, 2007.

Scarborough, Vernon L. "Ecology and Ritual: Water Management and the Maya." *Latin American Antiquity* 9, no. 2 (1998): 135–59. https://doi.org/10.2307/971991.

Scarborough, Vernon L. "Resilience, Resource Use, and Socioeconomic Organization: A Mesoamerican Pathway." In *Environmental Disaster and the Archaeology of Human Response*, edited by Garth Bawden and Richard Martin Reycraft, 195–212. Albuquerque: University of New Mexico Press, 2000.

Scarborough, Vernon L. "Water Management in the Southern Maya Lowlands: An Accretive Model for the Engineered Landscape." In *Economic Aspects of Water Management in the Prehispanic New World*, edited by Vernon L. Scarborough and B. L. Isaac, Supplement 7:17–69. Research in Economic Anthropology. Greenwich: JAI Press, 1993.

Scarborough, Vernon L., Nicholas P. Dunning, Kenneth B. Tankersley, Christopher Carr, Eric Weaver, Liwy Grazioso, Brian Lane, et al. "Water and Sustainable Land Use at the Ancient Tropical City of Tikal, Guatemala." *Proceedings of the National Academy of Sciences* 109, no. 31 (2012): 12408–13. https://doi.org/10.1073/pnas.1202881109.

Scarborough, Vernon L., and Liwy Grazioso Sierra. "The Evolution of an Ancient Waterworks System at Tikal." In *Tikal: Paleoecology of an Ancient Maya City*, edited by David L. Lentz, Nicholas P. Dunning, and Vernon L. Scarborough, 16–45. Cambridge: Cambridge University Press, 2015.

Scarborough, Vernon L., and Fred Valdez. "The Alternative Economy: Resilience in the Face of Complexity from the Eastern Lowlands: The Alternative Economy." *Archeological Papers of the American Anthropological Association* 24, no. 1 (2014): 124–41. https://doi.org/10.1111/apaa.12033.

Schele, Linda, and Mary E. Miller. *Blood of Kings: Dynasty and Ritual in Maya Art.* New York, Fort Worth: George Braziller/Kimball Art Museum, 1986.

Scherer, Andrew, and Charles W. Golden. "War in the West: History, Landscape, and Classic Maya Conflict." In *Embattled Places, Embattled Bodies: War in Pre-Columbian Mesoamerica and the Andes,* edited by Andrew Scherer and John W. Verano, 57-87. Washington, DC: Dumbarton Oaks Research Library and Collection, 2014.

Scherer, Andrew K. "Population Structure of the Classic Period Maya." *American Journal of Physical Anthropology* 132 (2007): 367–80.

Scherer, Andrew K., Charles Golden, Stephen Houston, Mallory E. Matsumoto, Omar A. Alcover Firpi, Whittaker Schroder, Alejandra Roche Recinos, et al. "Chronology and the Evidence for War in the Ancient Maya Kingdom of Piedras Negras." *Journal of Anthropological Archaeology* 66 (2022). https://doi.org/10.1016/j.jaa.2022.101408.

Schreiner, Thomas P. "Fabricación de Cal En Mesoamérica: Implicaciones Para Los Mayas Del Preclásico En Nakbe, Petén." In *XIV Simposio de Investigaciones Arqueológicas En Guatemala, 2000,* edited by Juan Pedro Laporte, A. C. Suasnavar, and Barbara Arroyo, 356-68. Guatemala City: Museo Nacional de Arqueología y Etnología, Guatemala, 2001.

Schreiner, Thomas P. "Traditional Maya Lime Production: Environmental and Cultural Implications of a Native American Technology." PhD diss., University of California, 2002.

Schrier, Robert. "Does 'Asymptomatic Hiponatremia' Exist?" *Nature Reviews Nephrology* 6 (n.d.): 185.

Schroder, Whittaker, Timothy Murtha, Charles Golden, Armando Anaya Hernández, Andrew Scherer, Shanti Morell-Hart, Angelica Almeyda Zambrano, Eben Broadbent, and Madeline Brown. "The Lowland Maya Settlement Landscape: Environmental LiDAR and Ecology." *Journal of Archaeological Science: Reports* 33 (2020): 102543.

Schultes, R. E., and A. Hoffman. *Plants of the Gods: Their Sacred, Healing and Hallucinogenic Powers.* Rochester, VT: Healing Arts Press, 1992.

Schwarcz, Henry P., Anabel Ford, Martin Knyf, and Anil Kumar. "The Green Deer: Chaya as a Potential Source of Protein for the Ancient Maya." *Latin American Antiquity* 33, no. 1 (March 2022): 175–86. https://doi.org/10.1017/laq.2021.71.

Schwartz, Norman B., and Amilcar Rolando Corzo M. "Swidden Counts: A Petén, Guatemala, Milpa System: Production, Carrying Capacity, and Sustainability in the Southern Maya Lowlands." *Journal of Anthropological Research* 71, no. 1 (2015): 69–93. https://doi.org/10.3998/jar.0521004.0071.104.

Schwarz, Kevin R. "Eckixil: Understanding the Classic to Postclassic Survival and Transformation of a Peten Maya Village." *Latin American Antiquity* 20, no. 3 (2009): 413–41.

Seligson, Kenneth E. "The Prehispanic Maya Burnt Lime Industry: Socio-Economy and Environmental Resource Management in the Terminal Classic Period Northern Lowlands (650–950 AD)." PhD diss., University of Wisconsin, 2016.

Seligson, Kenneth, Tomás Gallareta Negrón, Rossana May Ciau, and George J. Bey. "Burnt Lime Production and the Pre-Columbian Maya Socio-Economy: A Case Study from the Northern Yucatán." *Journal of Anthropological Archaeology* 48 (2017c): 281–94. https://doi.org/10.1016/j.jaa.2017.09.003.

Seligson, Kenneth, Tomás Gallareta Negrón, Rossana May Ciau, and George J. Bey. "Lime Powder Production in the Maya Puuc Region (A.D. 600–950): An Experimental Pit-Kiln." *Journal of Field Archaeology* 42, no. 2 (2017a): 129–41. https://doi.org/10.1080/00934690.2017.1286722.

Seligson, Kenneth E., Tomás Gallareta Negrón, Rossana May Ciau, and George J. Bey. "Using Multiple Lines of Evidence to Identify Prehispanic Maya Burnt-Lime Kilns in the Northern Yucatan Peninsula." *Latin American Antiquity* 28, no. 4 (2017b): 558–76. https://doi.org/10.1017/laq.2017.37.

Seligson, Kenneth E., Soledad Ortiz Ruiz, and Luis Barba Pingarrón. "Prehispanic Maya Burnt Lime Industries: Previous Studies and Future Directions." *Ancient Mesoamerica* 30, no. 2 (2019): 199–219. https://doi.org/10.1017/S0956536117000347.

Sharer, Robert J., Loa P. Traxler, David W. Sedat, Ellen E. Bell, Marcello A. Canuto, and Christopher Powell. "Early Classic Architecture Beneath the Copan Acropolis: A Research Update." *Ancient Mesoamerica* 10 (1999): 3–23.

Shaw, Justine M. "Climate Change and Deforestation: Implications for the Maya Collapse." *Ancient Mesoamerica* 14 (2003): 157–67.

Shaw, Justine M., and Dave Johnstone. "El Papel de La Arquitectura Postmonumental En El Norte de Yucatan." *Los Investigadores de La Cultura Maya* 14, no. 1 (2006): 267–78.

Sheets, Payson. *Before the Volcano Erupted: The Ancient Cerén Village in Central America.* Austin: University of Texas Press, 2002.

Sheets, Payson. "Provisioning the Ceren Household: The Vertical Economy, Village Economy, and Household Economy in the Southeastern Maya Periphery." *Ancient Mesoamerica* 11, no. 2 (2000): 217–30. https://doi.org/10.1017/S0956536100112039.

Sheets, Payson, Christine Dixon, Monica Guerra, and Adam Blanford. "Manioc Cultivation at Ceren, El Salvador: Occasional Kitchen Garden Plant or Staple Crop." *Ancient Mesoamerica* 22, no. 1 (2011): 1–11.

Sheets, Payson, David Lentz, Dolores Piperno, John Jones, Christine Dixon, George Maloof, and Angela Hood. "Ancient Manioc Agriculture South of the Ceren Village, El Salvador." *Latin American Antiquity* 23, no. 3 (2012): 259–81. https://doi.org/10.7183/1045-6635.23.3.259.

Sheets, Payson, and M. Woodward. "Cultivating Biodiversity: Milpas, Gardens, and the Classic Period Landscape." In *Before the Volcano Erupted: The Ancient Cerén Village in Central America*, edited by Payson Sheets, 184–91. Austin: University of Texas Press, 2002.

Simms, Stephanie R. "Prehispanic Maya Foodways: Archaeological and Microbotanical Evidence from Escalera al Cielo, Yucatan, Mexico." PhD diss., Boston University, 2014.

Simms, Stephanie R., Evan Parker, George J. Bey, and Tomás Gallareta Negrón. "Evidence from Escalera al Cielo: Abandonment of a Terminal Classic Puuc Maya Hill Complex in Yucatán, Mexico." *Journal of Field Archaeology* 37, no. 4 (2012): 270–88. https://doi.org/10.1179/0093469012Z.00000000025.

Slotten, Venicia, and David L. Lentz. "Trees, Shrubs, and Forests at Joya de Ceren, a Late Classic Mesoamerican Village." *Quaternary International* 593-594 (2021): 270-83.

Smith, B. D. "Documenting Plant Domestication: The Consilience of Biological and Archaeological Approaches." *Proceedings of the National Academy of Sciences* 98, no. 4 (2001): 1324–26. https://doi.org/10.1073/pnas.98.4.1324.

Smyth, Michael P. "Maize Storage Among the Puuc Maya: The Development of an Archaeological Method." *Ancient Mesoamerica* 1, no. 1 (1990): 51–69. https://doi.org/10.1017/S0956536100000079.

Smyth, Michael P., Nicholas P. Dunning, Eric M. Weaver, Philip van Beynen, and David Ortegón Zapata. "The Perfect Storm: Climate Change and Ancient Maya Response in the Puuc Hills Region of Yucatán." *Antiquity* 91, no. 356 (2017): 490–509. https://doi.org/10.15184/aqy.2016.266.

Smyth, Michael P., and David Ortegón Zapata. "A Preclassic Center in the Puuc Region: A Report on Xcoch, Yucatan, Mexico." *Mexicon* 30, no. 3 (2008): 63–68.

Smyth, Michael P., David Ortegón Zapata, Nicholas P. Dunning, and Eric M. Weaver. "Settlement Dynamics, Climate Change, and Human Response at Xcoch in the Puuc Region of Yucatán, Mexico." In *The Archaeology of Yucatán: New Directions and Data*, edited by Travis W. Stanton, 45–64. Archaeopress Pre-Columbian Archaeology. Oxford: Archaeopress, 2014.

Smyth, Michael P., José Ligorred Perramon, David Ortegón Zapata, and Pat Farrell. "An Early Classic Center in the Puuc Region: New Data from Chac II, Yucatan, Mexico." *Ancient Mesoamerica* 9, no. 2 (1998): 233–57. https://doi.org/10.1017/S095653610 0001966.

Soane, B. D. "Land Clearing, Drainage, Tillage, and Weed Control." In *Agriculture in the Tropics*, edited by C. C. Webster and P. N. Wilson, 113–43. Oxford: Blackwell Science, 1998.

Somerville, Andrew D., Mikael Fauvelle, and Andrew W. Froehle. "Applying New Approaches to Modeling Diet and Status: Isotopic Evidence for Commoner Resiliency and Elite Variability in the Classic Maya Lowlands." *Journal of Archaeological Science* 40 (2013): 1539–53.

Sosa, Thelma Sierra, Andrea Cucina, T. Douglas Price, James H. Burton, and Vera Tiesler. "Maya Coastal Production, Exchange, Life Style, and Population Mobility: A View from the Port of Xcambo, Yucatan, Mexico." *Ancient Mesoamerica* 25, no. 1 (2014): 221–38. https://doi.org/10.1017/S0956536114000133.

Šprajc, Ivan. *Paisaje arqueológico y dinámica cultural en el área de Chactún, Campeche (2016–2018): Informe de la temporada 2017.* Ljubljana: Centro de Investigaciones de la Academia Eslovena de Ciencias y Artes, 2017.

Šprajc, Ivan, ed. *Reconocimiento Arqueológico En El Sureste Del Estado de Campeche: 1996– 2005.* Paris Monographs in American Archaeology 19. BAR International Series 1742. Oxford: Archaeopress, 2008.

Šprajc, Ivan, Aleš Marsetič, Jasmina Štajdohar, Sara Dzul Góngora, Joseph W. Ball, Octavio Esparza Olguín, and Žiga Kokalj. "Archaeological Landscape, Settlement Dynamics, and Sociopolitical Organization in the Chactún Area of the Central Maya Lowlands." Edited by John P. Hart. *PLOS ONE* 17, no. 1 (2022): e0262921. https://doi.org/10.1371/journal.pone.0262921.

Standley, P. C., and L. O. Williams. *Flora of Guatemala. Fieldiana: Botany Vol. 24, Part VII.* Chicago: Field Museum of Natural History Press, 1961.

Staneko, Justine C. "Peeking at the Puuc: New Views on the Design, Engineering, and Construction of Ancient Maya Architecture from Yucatan and Northern Campeche, Mexico." PhD diss., University of California, 1996.

Stanton, Travis W., and Aline Magnoni. *Ruins of the Past: The Use and Perception of Abandoned Structures in the Maya Lowlands.* Boulder: University Press of Colorado, 2008.

Stein, Gil J. "Understanding Ancient States in the Old World." In *Archaeology at the Millennium: A Sourcebook*, edited by Gary M. Feinman and T. Douglas Price, 353–79. New York: Kluwer Academic/Plenum, 2001.

Stephens, John L. *Incidents of Travel in Yucatan*. Vol. 1. Project Gutenberg, 1848. http://www.gutenberg.org/ebooks/33129.

Stone, Andrea. *Images from the Underworld: Naj Tunich and the Tradition of Maya Cave Painting*. Austin: University of Texas Press, 1995.

Straulino Mainou, Luisa. "Hacer Mezclas de Cal En Dzibanche Durante El Clasico Temprano: La Temporalidad y La Funcion Arquitectonica Como Determinantes." MA thesis, Universidad Nacional Autonoma de Mexico, 2015.

Straulino Mainou, Luisa, Sergey Sedov, Ana Soler Arechalde, Teresa Pi Puig, Gerardo Villa, Sandra Balanzario Granados, María-Teresa Doménech-Carbó, Laura Osete-Cortina, and Daniel Leonard. "Maya Lime Mortars—Relationship Between Archaeomagnetic Dating, Manufacturing Technique, and Architectural Function—The Dzibanché Case." *Geosciences* 6, no. 4 (2016): 49. https://doi.org/10.3390/geosciences6040049.

Stuart, David. "Historical Inscriptions and the Maya Collapse." In *Lowland Maya Civilization in the Eighth Century AD*, edited by Jeremy A. Sabloff and John S. Henderson, 321–54. Washington, DC: Dumbarton Oaks, 1993.

Stuart, David, Heather Hurst, Boris Beltrán, and William Saturno. "An Early Maya Calendar Record from San Bartolo, Guatemala." *Science Advances* 8 (2022): eabl9290.

Stuart, James W. "Contribution of Dooryard Gardens to Contemporary Yucatecan Maya Subsistence." *Biótica, Nueva Epoca* 1 (1993): 53–61.

Suhler, C. K., Traci Ardren, David Freidel, and David Johnstone. "The Rise and Fall of Terminal Classic Yaxuna, Yucatan, Mexico." In *The Terminal Classic in the Maya Lowlands: Collapse, Transition, and Transformation*, edited by Arthur A. Demarest, Prudence M. Rice, and Don S. Rice, 450–84. Boulder: University Press of Colorado, 2004.

Sullivan, Lauren A., Jaime J. Awe, and M. Kathryn Brown. "The Cunil Complex: Early Villages in Belize." In *Pathways to Complexity: A View from the Maya Lowlands*, edited by M. Kathryn Brown and George J. Bey, 35–48. Gainesville: University Press of Florida, 2018.

Tainter, Joseph A. "Archaeology of Overshoot and Collapse." *Annual Review of Anthropology* 3 (2006): 59–74.

Tainter, Joseph A. "Collapse and Sustainability: Rome, the Maya, and the Modern World." *Archeological Papers of the American Anthropological Association* 24, no. 1 (2014): 201–14. https://doi.org/10.1111/apaa.12038.

Tainter, Joseph A., Vernon L. Scarborough, and Timothy F. H. Allen, "Resource Gain and Complexity: Water Past and Future." In *Water and Society from Ancient Times to the Present: Resilience, Decline, and Revival*, edited by Federica Sulas and Innocent Pikirayi, 328–47. Routledge, 2018.

Tainter, Joseph A., and Temis G. Taylor. "Complexity, Problem-Solving, Sustainability and Resilience." *Building Research & Information* 42 (2014): 168–81.

Tankersley, Kenneth Barnett. "Zeolite Water Purification at Tikal, an Ancient Maya City in Guatemala." *Scientific Reports* 10, no. 18021 (2020). 10.1038/s41598-020-75023-7.

Taube, Karl. "Ancient and. Contemporary Maya Conceptions About Field and Forest." In *The Lowland Maya Area: Three Millennia at the Human-Wildland Interface*, edited by Arturo Gomez-Pompa, Michael F. Allen, Scott L. Fedick, and Juan J. Jiménez-Osornio, 461–92. New York: Food Products Press, 2003.

Taube, Karl. "The Ballgame, Boxing and Ritual Blood Sport in Ancient Mesoamerica." In *Ritual, Play and Belief, in Evolution and Early Human Societies*, edited by Colin Renfrew, Iain Morley, and Michael Boyd, 264–301. Cambridge: Cambridge University Press, 2017. https://doi.org/10.1017/9781316534663.017.

Taube, Karl Andreas. *The Major Gods of Ancient Yucatan*. Studies in Pre-Columbian Art and Archaeology. Washington, DC: Dumbarton Oaks Research Library and Collection, 1992.

Tedlock, Dennis. *The Popol Vuh: The Mayan Book of the Dawn of Life*. New York: Simon and Schuster, 1985.

Terry, Richard E., Bryce M. Brown, Travis W. Stanton, Traci Ardren, Tanya Cariño Anaya, Justin Lowry, José Francisco Osorio León, et al. "Soil Biomarkers of Cacao Tree Cultivation in the Sacred Cacao Groves of the Northern Maya Lowlands." *Journal of Archaeological Science: Reports* 41 (February 2022). https://doi.org/10.1016/j.jas rep.2021.103331.

Thompson, Amy E., and Keith M. Prufer. "Household Inequality, Community Formation, and Land Tenure in Classic Period Lowland Maya Society." *Journal of Archaeological Method and Theory* 28 (2021): 1276–313. https://doi.org/10.1007/s10816-020-09505-3.

Thompson, J. Eric S. *Maya History and Religion*. Norman: University of Oklahoma Press, 1970.

Thompson, J. Eric S. (John Eric Sidney). *The Rise and Fall of Maya Civilization*. 2nd ed. enlarged. Civilization of the American Indian Series; v. 39. Norman: University of Oklahoma Press, 1966.

Thompson, Kim M., Angela Hood, Dana Cavallaro, and David L. Lentz. "Connecting Contemporary Ecology and Ethnobotany to Ancient Plant Use Practices of the Maya at Tikal." In *Tikal, Paleoecology of an Ancient Maya City*, edited by David L. Lentz, Nicholas P. Dunning, and Vernon L. Scarborough, 124–51. Cambridge: Cambridge University Press, 2015.

Thornton, Erin Kennedy, and Arthur A. Demarest. "At Water's Edge: Ritual Maya Animal Use in Aquatic Contexts at Cancuen, Guatemala." *Ancient Mesoamerica* 30, no. 3 (2019): 473–91. https://doi.org/10.1017/S0956536118000251.

Thurston, H. D. *Slash/Mulch Systems: Sustainable Methods for Tropical Agriculture*. Boulder: Westview Press, 1997.

Tokovinine, Alexandre. "'It Is His Image with Pulque': Drinks, Gifts, and Political Networking in Classic Maya Texts and Images." *Ancient Mesoamerica* 27, no. 1 (2016): 13–29.

Tokovinine, Alexandre, and Francisco Estrada Belli. "From Stucco to Digital: Topometric Documentation of Classic Maya Facades at Holmul." *Digital Applications in Archaeology and Cultural Heritage* 6 (2017): 18–28. https://doi.org/10.1016/j.daach.2017.04.004.

Tourtellot, Gair, John A. Graham, Mary Pohl, and Gordon R. Willey. Vol. 16. *Excavations at Seibal, Department of Peten, Guatemala: Peripheral Survey and Excavation; Settlement and Community Patterns*. Memoirs of the Peabody Museum of Archaeology and Ethnology. Cambridge, MA: Harvard University Press, 1988.

Tourtellot, Gair, and J. Gonzalez. "The Last Hurrah: Continuity and Transformation at Seibal." In *The Terminal Classic in the Maya Lowlands: Collapse, Transition, and Transformation*, edited by Arthur A. Demarest, Prudence M. Rice, and Don S. Rice, 60–82. Boulder: University Press of Colorado, 2004.

Tozzer, Alfred Marston. *Landa's Relacion De Las Cosas De Yucatan*. Vol. 2. Memoirs of the Peabody Museum of American Archaeology and Ethnology. Cambridge, MA: Harvard University, 1941.

Turner, B. L., and J. A. Sabloff. "Classic Period Collapse of the Central Maya Lowlands: Insights About Human-Environment Relationships for Sustainability." *Proceedings of the National Academy of Sciences* 109, no. 35 (2012): 13908–14. https://doi.org/10.1073/pnas.1210106109.

Turner, Billie L. "Ancient Agricultural Land Use in the Central Maya Lowlands." In *Pre-Hispanic Maya Agriculture*, edited by Peter D. Harrison and Billie L. Turner, 163–84. Albuquerque: University of New Mexico Press, 1978.

Turner, Billie L. "The Ancient Maya: Sustainability and Collapse?" In *Routledge Handbook of the History of Sustainability*, edited by Jeremy L. Cardona, 57–68. London: Routledge, 2018.

Turner, Billie L. *Once Beneath the Forest: Prehistoric Terracing in the Rio Bec Region of the Maya Lowlands*. Boulder: Westview Press, 1983.

Turner, Billie L. "Unlocking the Ancient Maya and Their Environment: Paleo-Evidence and Dating Resolution." *Geology* 38 (2010): 575–76.

Turner, Billie L., and Peter D. Harrison, eds. *Pulltrouser Swamp: Ancient Maya Habitat, Agriculture, and Settlement in Northern Belize*. Austin: University of Texas Press, 1983.

Turner, Billie L., and W. C. Johnson. "An Ancient Maya Check-Dam in the Copan Valley." *American Antiquity* 44 (1979): 299–305.

Turner, Billie L., and C. H. Miksicek. "Economic Plant Species Associated with Prehistoric Agriculture in the Maya Lowlands." *Economic Botany* 38 (1984): 179–93.

UNESCO. *Managing Water Under Uncertainty and Risk*. Vol. 3: *Facing the Challenges*. United Nations World Water Development Report. Paris: UNESCO, 2012.

Vail, Gabrielle, and Maia Dedrick. "Human-Deity Relationships Conveyed Through Balche' Rituals and Resource Procurement." In *Her Cup for Sweet Cacao: Food in Ancient Maya Society*, edited by Traci Arden, 334–65. Austin: University of Texas Press, 2020.

Valencia Rivera, Rogelio. "Aj atz'aam, 'los de la sal.' El uso de la sal en la ciudad maya de Calakmul." *Estudios de Cultura Maya* 55 (January 9, 2020): 11–40. https://doi.org/10.19130/iifl.ecm.2020.55.0001.

Vera-Núñez, J. A., J. P. Infante-Santiago, V. Velasco-Velasco, S. Salgado-García, D. J. Palma-López, O. A. Grageda-Cabrera, R. Cárdenas, and J. J. Peña-Cabriales. "Influence of P Fertilization on Biological Nitrogen Fixation in Herbaceous Legumes Grown in Acid Savannah Soils from the Tabasco State, Mexico." *Journal of Sustainable Agriculture* 31 (2007): 25–42.

Viel, Rene. "Evolución de La Ceramica En Copán: Resultados Preliminarios." In *Introducción a La Arqueología de Copán, Honduras*, edited by C. Bandery, 1:471–550. Tegucigalpa: Secretaria De Estado en Despacho de Turismo y Cultura, 1983.

Villanueva-Gutiérrez, Rogel, David W. Roubik, Wilberto Colli-Ucán, Francisco J. Güemez-Ricalde, and Stephen L. Buchmann. "A Critical View of Colony Losses in Managed Mayan Honey-Making Bees (Apidae: Meliponini) in the Heart of Zona Maya." *Journal of the Kansas Entomological Society* 86, no. 4 (2013): 352–62.

Villaseñor, Isabel. *Building Materials of the Ancient Maya: A Study of Archaeological Plasters*. Saarbrücken: Lambert Academic, 2010.

Villaseñor, Isabel. "Lowland Maya Lime Plaster Technology: A Diachronic Approach." PhD diss., University College London, 2008.

Villaseñor, Isabel, and James J. Aimers. "Una de Cal Por Las Que Can de Arena: Un Estudio Diacrónico de Los Estucos de Calakmul y Palenque." *Estudios de Cultura Maya* 33 (2008): 25–50.

Villaseñor, Isabel, and Elizabeth Graham. "The Use of Volcanic Materials for the Manufacture of Pozzolanic Plasters in the Maya Lowlands: A Preliminary Report." *Journal of Archaeological Science* 37, no. 6 (2010): 1339–47. https://doi.org/10.1016/j.jas.2009.12.038.

Vogt, Evon Z. *Zinacantan: A Maya Community in the Highlands of Chiapas.* Cambridge, MA: Harvard University Press, 1969.

Wahl, David, Lysanna Anderson, Francisco Estrada-Belli, and Alexandre Tokovinine. "Palaeoenvironmental, Epigraphic and Archaeological Evidence of Total Warfare Among the Classic Maya." *Nature Human Behaviour* 3 (2019): 1049–54.

Wahl, David, Roger Byrne, Thomas P. Schreiner, and Richard D. Hansen. "Holocene Vegetation Change in the Northern Peten and Its Implications for Maya Prehistory." *Quaternary Research* 65 (2006): 680–89.

Wahl, David, Thomas P. Schreiner, Roger Byrne, and Richard D. Hansen. "A Paleoecological Record from a Maya Reservoir in the North Peten." *American Antiquity* 18 (2007): 212–22.

Ward, William C. "Quaternary Geology of Northeastern Yucatan Peninsula, Part 2." In *Geology and Hydrogeology of the Yucatan and Quaternary Geology of Northeastern Yucatan Peninsula*, edited by William C. Ward, Alfred E. Weidie, and William Back, 23–53. New Orleans: New Orleans Geological Society, University of New Orleans, 1985.

Warren, Kay B. *Indigenous Movements and Their Critics: Pan-Maya Activism in Guatemala.* Princeton: Princeton University Press, 1998.

Watanabe, John M. *Maya Saints and Souls in a Changing World.* Austin: University of Texas Press, 1992.

Watson, Sarah E., Joshua T. Schnell, Shanti Morell-Hart, Andrew K. Scherer, and Lydie Dussol. "Healthcare in the Marketplace: Exploring Maya Medicinal Plants and Practices at Piedras Negras, Guatemala." *Ancient Mesoamerica* (published online 2022). doi:10.1017/S0956536122000037.

Webb, Elizabeth A., Henry P. Schwarcz, and Paul F. Healy. "Detection of Ancient Maize in Lowland Maya Soils Using Stable Carbon Isotopes: Evidence from Caracol, Belize." *Journal of Archaeological Science* 31, no. 8 (2004): 1039–52. https://doi.org/10.1016/j.jas.2004.01.001.

Webb, Elizabeth A., Henry P. Schwarcz, Christopher T. Jensen, Richard E. Terry, Matthew D. Moriarty, and Kitty F. Emery. "Stable Carbon Isotope Signature of Ancient Maize Agriculture in the Soils of Motul de San José, Guatemala." *Geoarchaeology* 22, no. 3 (2007): 291–312. https://doi.org/10.1002/gea.20154.

Webster, David. *The Fall of the Ancient Maya.* London: Thames and Hudson, 2002.

Webster, David. "The Not So Peaceful Civilization: A Review of Maya War." *Journal of World Prehistory* 14, no. 1 (2000): 65–119.

Webster, David, AnnCorinne Freter, and Rebecca Storey. "Dating Copan Culture-History: Implications for the Terminal Classic and the Collapse." In *The Terminal Classic in the Maya Lowlands: Collapse, Transition, and Transformation*, edited by Arthur A. Demarest, Prudence M. Rice, and Don S. Rice, 231–59. Boulder: University Press of Colorado, 2004.

Webster, David, and Stephen D. Houston. "Piedras Negras: The Growth and Decline of a Classic Maya Court Center." In *El Urbanismo En Mesoamerica: Urbanism in Mesoamerica*, edited by William T. Sanders, Alba Guadalupe Mastache, and Robert H. Cobean, 427–50. Mexico City: Instituto Nacional de Antropologia e Historia, 2003.

Webster, J. W., G. A. Brook, L. Bruce Railsback, H. Cheng, R. Lawrence, C. Alexander, and P. Reeder. "Stalagmite Evidence from Belize Indicating Significant Droughts at the Time of Preclassic Abandonment, the Maya Hiatus, and the Classic Maya Collapse." *Paleogeography, Paleoclimatology, Paleoecology* 250 (2007): 1–17.

Weishampel, John, Jessica Hightower, Arlen Chase, Diane Chase, and Ryan Patrick. "Detection and Morphologic Analysis of Potential Below-Canopy Cave Openings in the Karst Landscape Around the Maya Polity of Caracol Using Airborne Lidar." *Journal of Cave and Karst Studies* 73, no. 3 (2011): 187–96. https://doi.org/10.4311/2010E X0179R1.

Weiss-Krejci, Estella, and Thomas Sabbas. "The Potential Role of Small Depressions as Water Storage Features in the Central Maya Lowlands." *Latin American Antiquity* 13, no. 3 (2002): 343–57. https://doi.org/10.2307/972115.

Wernecke, D. Clark. "A Burning Question: Maya Lime Technology And The Maya Forest." *Journal of Ethnobiology* 28, no. 2 (2008): 200–10. https://doi.org/10.2993/ 0278-0771-28.2.200.

Willey, Gordon, T. Patrick Culbert, and Robert Adams. "Maya Lowland Ceramics: A Report from the 1965 Guatemala City Conference." *American Antiquity* 32, no. 3 (1967): 289–315.

Willey, Gordon R., and Demitri B. Shimkin. "The Maya Collapse: A Summary View." In *The Classic Maya Collapse*, edited by T. Patrick Culbert, 457–502. Santa Fe: School of American Research, 1973.

Williams, Eduardo. "Salt Production and Trade in Ancient Mesoamerica." In *Precolumbian Foodways: Interdisciplinary Approaches to Food, Culture, and Markets in Ancient Mesoamerica*, edited by John Staller and Michael Carrasco, 175–90. Berlin: Springer, 2010.

Wisdom, Charles. *The Chorti Indians of Guatemala*. Chicago: University of Chicago Press, 1940.

Wiseman, Frederick M. "Agricultural and Historical Ecology of the Maya Lowlands." In *Pre-Hispanic Maya Agriculture*, edited by Peter D. Harrison and Billie L. Turner, 23–34. Albuquerque: University of New Mexico Press, 1978.

Woodfill, Brent K. S., Brian Dervin Dillon, Marc Wolf, Carlos Avendaño, and Ronald Canter. "Salinas De Los Nueve Cerros, Guatemala: A Major Economic Center in the Southern Maya Lowlands." *Latin American Antiquity* 26, no. 2 (2015): 162–79. https:// doi.org/10.7183/1045-6635.26.2.162.

Woodfill, Brent K. S., Mirza Monterroso, Erin Sears, Donaldo Castillo, and Jose Luis Garrido Lopez. "Proyecto Salinas de Los Nueve Cerros: Resultados de Ia Primera Temporada de Campo, 2010." In *XXIV Simposio de Lnvestigaciones Arqueologicos En Guatemala*, edited by Barbara Arroyo, Lorena Paiz Aragon, Adriana Linares Palma, and Ana Lucia Arroyave, 135–48. Guatemala City: Ministerio de Cultura y Deportes, 2011.

Wright, Lori E. "Biological Perspectives on the Collapse of the Pasíon Maya." *Ancient Mesoamerica* 8 (1997): 267–73.

Wright, Lori E. "Identifying Immigrants to Tikal, Guatemala: Defining Local Variability in Strontium Isotope Ratios of Human Tooth Enamel." *Journal of Archaeological Science* 32 (2005): 555–66.

Wright, Lori E., and Christine D. White. "Human Biology in the Classic Maya Collapse: Evidence from Paleopathology and Paleodiet." *Journal of World Prehistory* 10, no. 2 (June 1996): 147–98. https://doi.org/10.1007/BF02221075.

Wyatt, Andrew R. "Agricultural Practices at Chan: Farming and Political Economy in an Ancient Maya Community." In *Chan: An Ancient Maya Farming Community*, edited by Cynthia Robin, 71–88. Gainesville: University Press of Florida, 2012. https://doi.org/10.5744/florida/9780813039831.003.0004.

Wyatt, Andrew R. "Gardens of the Maya." In *The Real Business of Ancient Maya Economies: From Farmers' Fields to Rulers' Realms*, edited by Marilyn A. Masson, David Freidel, and Arthur A. Demarest, 187–209. Jacksonsville: University Press of Florida, 2020.

Wyatt, Andrew R. "Pine as an Element of Household Refuse in the Fertilization of Ancient Maya Agricultural Fields." *Journal of Ethnobiology* 28, no. 2 (2008): 244–58.

Wyatt, Andrew R. "The Scale and Organization of Ancient Maya Water Management: Maya Water Management." *Wiley Interdisciplinary Reviews: Water* 1, no. 5 (2014): 449–67. https://doi.org/10.1002/wat2.1042.

Wylie, Robin. "Severe Droughts Explain the Mysterious Fall of the Maya." BBC.Com, February 22, 2016. http://www.bbc.com/earth/story/20160222-severe-droughts-explain-the-mysterious-fall-of-the-maya.

Yaeger, Jason. "Collapse, Transformation, Reorganization: The Terminal Classic Transition in the Maya World." In *The Maya World*, edited by Scott R. Hutson and Traci Ardren, 777–93. London: Routledge, 2020.

Yaeger, Jason, M. Kathryn Brown, and Bernadette Cap. "Locating and Dating Sites Using Lidar Survey in a Mosaic Landscape in Western Belize." *Advances in Archaeological Practice* 4, no. 3 (2016): 339–56. https://doi.org/10.7183/2326-3768.4.3.339.

Yaeger, Jason, and David A. Hodell. "The Collapse of Maya Civilization: Assessing the Interaction of Culture, Climate, and Environment." In *El Niño, Catastrophism, and Culture Change in Ancient America*, edited by Daniel H. Sandweiss and Jeffrey Quilter, 187–242. Cambridge, MA: Harvard University Press, 2009.

Zaro, Gregory, and Brett A. Houk. "The Growth and Decline of the Ancient Maya City of La Milpa, Belize: New Data and New Perspectives from the Southern Plazas." *Ancient Mesoamerica* 23, no. 1 (2012): 143–59.

Zequeira-Larios, Carolina, Diego Santiago-Alarcon, Ian MacGregor-Fors, and Ofelia Castillo-Acosta. "Tree Diversity and Composition in Mexican Traditional Smallholder Cocoa Agroforestry Systems." *Agroforestry Systems* 95 (2021): 1589–602. https://doi.org/10.1007/s10457-021-00673-z.

Żrałka, Jaroslaw, and Bernard Hermes. "Great Development in Troubled Times: The Terminal Classic at the Maya Site of Nakum, Peten, Guatemala." *Ancient Mesoamerica* 23, no. 1 (2012): 161–87.

Index